Understanding Theology

Volume 2

Understanding Theology

Volume 2

R. T. Kendall

CHRISTIAN
FOCUS

to those who enrolled
in the School of Theology
at Westminster Chapel
1992-2000

ISBN 978-1-85792-767-2

First published in 2000
and reprinted in 2002 and 2017
by
Christian Focus Publications,
Geanies House, Fearn, Ross-shire,
IV20 1TW, Scotland
www.christianfocus.com

Cover design by Owen Daily

Printed and bound in Great Britain by the CPI Group (UK Ltd), Croydon

Contents

PREFACE

I want to express my heartfelt thanks once more to Malcolm Maclean, Editor, and the people of Christian Focus for their continued confidence in publishing the edited notes that form the basis for my lectures in our School of Theology,

I have dedicated the book to those dear people who have enrolled at one time or another in our School of Theology over the years 1992-2000. This volume is affectionately dedicated to them

R.T. Kendall
Westminster Chapel, London
Spring, 2000

INTRODUCTION

No one was more surprised than I that my notes for our School of Theology on Friday nights would ever be published in the first place. To be perfectly candid, I thought the Publisher had made a great mistake! I had no idea that those notes would ever make a book and I was quite surprised indeed when Christian Focus came to me to have them published.

And now, I find it almost overwhelming, Volume 2 now has been published. It only goes to show that people do want to learn theology and that, if given a chance, will take advantage of the opportunity. My intention from the beginning was to make theology simple. 'Theology put simply' was our motto, and I think I have succeeded to some extent, although sometimes people feel it is a bit heavy. But perhaps not too often.

Sincere thanks go to William Mackenzie and Malcolm Maclean for determining which lessons would be included in this volume. This is entirely their choice, and I stand in amazement at the choice they made, and I thank them with all my heart.

I sincerely pray that this volume will bless many people, whether those in the pew or those in the pulpit – in church leadership or wherever found throughout the world. I want these notes to bring great honour and glory to God, and nothing thrills me more than to think that this might turn out to be the case.

1

HOW TO UNDERSTAND
THE OLD TESTAMENT

INTRODUCTION

A. The Bible is in two parts; 66 books with some 40 writers.
   1. Old Testament (39 books).
   2. New Testament (27 books).

B. Both the Old Testament and New Testament are equally inspired.
   1. *Jesus and Paul refer to the Old Testament as Scripture.*
      a. John 7:38.
      b. 2 Timothy 3:16.
   2. *Peter tells us about the men and their method of writing (2 Pet. 1:20-21).*
      a. They didn't 'think it up'.
      b. They spoke 'from God as they were carried along by the Holy Spirit'.
      c. All Scripture is at bottom: prophecy – it is God's Word.
         (1) This does not mean it is all prophecy as the word is commonly understood.
         (2) It means the Spirit of prophecy lay behind its formation (Heb. 1:1).

C. There is nothing more exciting than the Old Testament. Why study it?
   1. *The same Spirit who wrote it is in us!*
      a. He will make it come alive to us.
      b. We therefore need to be on good terms with the Holy Spirit.
         (1) To be suspicious of the Old Testament is to grieve the Holy Spirit.
         (2) To honour the Old Testament is to honour the Holy Spirit.

2. *The Old Testament is the only Scripture the early church had.*
  a. Peter did not preach from the New Testament on the Day of Pentecost.
    (1) He was a part of the New Testament in the making!
    (2) He quoted from Joel and the Psalms (see Acts 2).
  b. The church continued for years and years after Pentecost without anything but the Old Testament and the Holy Spirit.
    (1) At best it had the 'oral tradition' of Jesus' sayings alongside apostolic teaching.
    (2) Eventually some very fortunate congregations had perhaps one book or epistle.
  c. What did the church do during all those years?
    (1) Christians searched the Old Testament for proof of Jesus as Messiah.
    (2) The had to 'dig out' their faith for themselves.
  d. Note: Wouldn't it be wonderful if we were filled with the Spirit as they were?
    (1) We would see for ourselves what they saw.
    (2) We might see things in the Old Testament not specifically recorded by the early church (1 Cor. 2:9).
3. *The devil hates the Old Testament.*
  a. It points to his demise, his ultimate defeat – Genesis 3:15.
  b. It glorifies his arch-enemy, the Lord Jesus Christ.
  c. It shows how he is defeated today, namely, the way Israel defeated its enemies.
  d. It shows how God honoured blood sacrifices and why we today should honour Christ's blood – which Satan hates.
  e. The devil will direct you from the Old Testament; to keep you from reading it, understanding it or finding it interesting.
4. *Liberal theologians want to discredit the Old Testament.*
  a. They want God to look awful, not awesome.
  b. They deny the miraculous as 'myths'.
  c. They deny that Moses wrote the Pentateuch (first five books).

I. How Jesus understood the Old Testament

A. He never apologised for the God of the Old Testament.
  1. The God of the Old Testament was Jesus' Father (John 5:16-18).
  2. What Jesus affirmed we too should affirm.

B. He regarded the Old Testament with absolute authority: 'It is written'.
1. Matthew 4:4,7.
2. John 6:45.

C. He affirmed Mosaic authority of the Pentateuch (John 5:46).

D. He regarded the people referred to as literal persons.
1. Jonah – Matthew 12:40.
2. Abel – Luke 11:51.
3. Abraham – John 8:58.

II. How Paul understood the Old Testament

A. Adam was a literal person.
1. Sin began with one man (Rom. 5:12ff).
2. Death came from one man to all born since (1 Cor. 15:22).

B. Justification by faith began in the Old Testament.
1. Abraham (Gen. 15:6; Rom. 4:3ff).
2. David (Ps. 32:1,2; Rom. 4:7-8).

C. Predestination was unfolded in the Old Testament.
1. Jacob (Gen. 25:23; Mal. 1:2-3; Rom. 9:11-13).
2. Moses (Ex. 33:19; Rom. 9:15).

D. The gospel was unveiled in the Old Testament (Gal. 3:8).
1. The Law came in after the gospel (Rom. 5:20).
2. The Law is a 1300 year parenthesis (Gal. 3:19).

III. How Jesus generally divided the Old Testament (Luke 24:44).

A. The Law of Moses – understood two ways.
1. *The first five books of the Old Testament* (Pentateuch). See John 5:46; John 1:17.
2. *The Law given to Moses at Sinai in 1300 BC.*
   a. The Moral Law – the Ten Commandments (Ex. 20:1-17).
   b. The Ceremonial Law – largely the Book of Leviticus.
   c. The Civil Law – how the people of Israel should govern themselves – e.g. Exodus 21–23.

3. *Note: The first five books of Moses included history.*
  a. Jesus thus affirmed the history contained in these books.
    (1) Genesis
      Creation and Fall
      Pre-patriarchal period (Abel, Enoch, Noah, the Tower of Babel)
      Patriarchs (Abraham, Isaac, Jacob)
    (2) Exodus
      Moses
      Plagues of Egypt
      Passover and crossing of the Red Sea
      The giving of the Law at Sinai
    (3) Leviticus (details of the Mosaic Law)
    (4) Numbers (statistics and description of Israel's wandering in the desert)
    (5) Deuteronomy (rehearsal of the Law)
  b. We may safely assume he affirmed the history of the 'historical' books as well. Luke 4:25-27, draws on I and II Kings.

B. Prophets

  1. *This could include some historical books.*
    a. Joshua, who functioned as a prophet.
      (1) Moses' successor.
      (2) Arrival of Israel in Canaan.
    b. Judges, which shows prophetic people like Deborah.
      (1) Dearth of greatness.
      (2) Few leaders – like Gideon.
    c. 1 and 2 Samuel, 1 and 2 Kings, 1 and 2 Chronicles.
      (1) Rise of kingship.
      (2) Rise of prophetic ministry.

  2. *The 'major' and 'minor' prophets.*
  Note: This refers to the size of books, not their authority or significance.

  3. *The dates below are only approximate and the themes given are general. A specific study of each book is called for. What follows are guidelines:*

a. Major prophets:

    (1) Isaiah (c. 720 – 700 BC)

        Theme: The glory of Christ (see John 12:41).

        Setting: The Southern Kingdom, Judah, at the time the Northern Kingdom, Israel, was destroyed by the Assyrians.

Contemporary Kings of Judah:

Uzziah	787-735 BC,	a good king
Jotham	747-734 BC,	a good king
Ahaz	741-726 BC,	a wicked king
Hezekiah	726-697 BC,	a good king
Manasseh	697-642 BC,	a wicked king

    (2) Jeremiah (c. 600 BC)

        Theme: Impending Babylonian captivity.

        Setting: Judah

Contemporary Kings of Judah:

Manasseh	697-642 BC,	a wicked king
Amon	641-640 BC,	reigned only two years
Josiah	639-608 BC,	a good king
Jehoahaz	608 BC,	reigned three months
Jehoiakim	609-597 BC,	a wicked king
Jehoiachin	597 BC,	reigned three months
Zedekiah	597-586 BC,	a weak king

Contemporary prophets:
Ezekiel, Daniel, Habakkuk, Nahum, Obadiah

    (3) Ezekiel (c. 580 BC)

        Theme: The restoration of Israel.

        Setting: Babylon. Ezekiel preached among the exiles the same things Jeremiah preached in Jerusalem.

    (4) Daniel (c. 580 toward the end of the Captivity in 516 BC)

        Theme: The sovereignty of God.

        Setting: Babylon.

        Note: The Book of Daniel is sometimes called 'the little Book of Revelation', especially chapters 7–12.

b. Lamentations (c. 586 BC)

Note: This may not technically be called a 'minor' prophet since the authorship is not given, but it is thought to be the work of Jeremiah.

Theme: Lament over Jerusalem's destruction.

c. Minor prophets:

(1) Hosea (c. 750 BC)

Theme: The apostasy and restoration of Israel.

Setting: Largely the Northern Kingdom, Israel.

Contemporary Kings of Israel:

Jeroboam II 790-749 BC, a wicked king.

Other kings reigned briefly: Zechariah, Shallum, Manahem, Pekahiah, Pekah and Hoshea.

(2) Joel (date is largely speculative; possibly 830 BC–750 BC or even after the Babylonian captivity which ended in 516 BC).

Theme: The Day of the Lord.

Setting: Judah, following an unprecedented plague of locusts.

(3) Amos (c. 750 BC)

Theme: The doom and future glory of Israel.

Setting: Though a prophet of Judah, his message was largely to Israel, the Northern Kingdom.

Contemporary King of Israel:

Jeroboam II 790-749 BC

(4) Obadiah (c. 586 BC)

Theme: The doom of Edom (the Edomites, descendants of Esau, were Israel's enemies).

Setting: Judah.

(5) Jonah (c. 785 BC)

Theme: The God of the 'second look'; revival in Nineveh.

Setting: Israel and Nineveh.

(6) Micah (c. 750 BC)
Theme: The impending fall and restoration of Israel and Judah.
Setting: Judah.

(7) Nahum (c. 630 BC)
Theme: The doom of Nineveh.

(8) Habakkuk (c. 607 BC)
Theme: Praising God in adverse circumstances.
Setting: Judah.

(9) Zephaniah (c. 610 BC)
Theme: The day of doom is at hand.
Setting: Judah.

Contemporary King:
Josiah

(10) Haggai (c. 516 BC)
Theme: The rebuilding of the Temple.
Setting: Judah, near the end of the Babylonian captivity.

(11) Zechariah (c. 516 BC)
Theme: Rebuilding the Temple and the coming Messiah.
Setting: Judah, near the end of the Babylonian captivity.

(12) Malachi (c. 400 BC)
Theme: The coming of the Day of the Lord.
Setting: Judah.

C. Psalms – the hymnody of Israel. Poetry set to music.
  1. 73 of the psalms are ascribed to David (before or after he was king).
  2. Many of the psalms were prophetic, e.g., Psalms 16, 110, pointing to Christ.
  3. They were sung and used in worship. We have the names of some of the tunes, e.g. 'Do not destroy'; Psalms 57, 59.

D. Note: Jesus' division of the Old Testament was general. The other books could be categorised:

1. *Historical books (referred to above) including also:*
  a. Ruth: the story of the great-grandmother of David.
  b. Ezra: the return from captivity, the Temple rebuilt.
  c. Nehemiah: rebuilding Jerusalem's walls.
  d. Esther: the extraordinary providence of God.
2. *Wisdom literature.*
  a. Job: the problem of suffering.
  b. Proverbs: wise sayings learned by experience.
  c. Ecclesiastes: the vanity of pinning your hopes on this world.
  d. Song of Songs: undying love.

IV. How the Epistle to the Hebrews understands the Old Testament

A. It gives prominence to the ministry of angels (Heb. 1:5-14).
  1. Angels are sometimes called cherubim (Gen. 3:24).
  2. Angels are sometimes called seraphim (Isa. 6:2).
  3. Angels are sometimes named (Dan. 9:21).
  4. Angels are sometimes simply called angels (Pss. 34:7; 91:11).

B. It shows the people of Israel were responsible before God.
  1. Every sin was subject to punishment (Heb. 2:1-3; 3:7-19).
  2. The high priest of the Old Testament pointed to Jesus (Heb. 3:1; 4:14; 7:1-28).
  3. The old covenant was temporary and pointed to Christ (Heb. 8:7-13).
  4. The tabernacle pointed to Christ (Heb. 9:1-28).
  5. Old Testament men of God did what they did by faith (Heb. 11:1-40).
  6. Creation is embraced by faith (Heb. 11:3).
    a. We should not take our cue from science when it comes to Genesis 1 and 2.
    b. There is no room for evolution, according to Hebrews 11:3.

V. Some Old Testament themes

A. Sin – rebellion
  1. Unbelief (Gen. 3:1-2).
  2. Pride (Gen. 3:5).
  3. Shame (Gen. 3:7).

B. Covenant – a promise based upon a condition
   1. The Hebrew word is *berith*.
   2. A contract between two parties based upon a mutually agreed condition.

C. Election – God's choice of a people
   1. Israel was God's chosen people.
   2. That choice was made by God's grace, not man's works.

D. Promise – God's declaration of what he will do
   1. Sometimes the promise was like a covenant, based upon man's obedience.
   2. Sometimes the promise was an oath, which was irrevocable.

E. Salvation/redemption
   1. Salvation means deliverance; redemption means buying back.
   2. God instituted the saving of his people, beginning with Genesis 3:15.

F. Priests (from the tribe of Levi) were appointed teachers. They were a hereditary class, often wicked but remained teachers.
   1. They were responsible for worship liturgy, e.g., the offering of sacrifices, the care of the tabernacle and (later on) the Temple. They were supported by the tithes of the people.
   2. The High Priest alone went into the Holy of Holies once a year (on the Day of Atonement) to sprinkle blood on the Mercy Seat (a slab of gold on the top of the chest called the Ark of the Covenant).

G. Prophets (from any tribe) were not a hereditary class although sometimes prophets came in families that were apparently 'prophetic'. Jeremiah and Ezekiel were prophets but also priests. Each got his call directly from God.
   1. There were canonical prophets whose prophecies were written up in a book after their name. These are either 'major' or 'minor' prophets.
   2. Some prophets functioned with great power but did not have a book associated with their names, e.g., Elijah and Elisha.

VI. SOME IMPORTANT DATES (approximate)

A. Abraham – 1700 BC

B. Moses – 1300 BC

C. David – 1050 BC

D. Solomon – 1000 BC

E. Division of the kingdom – 930 BC
1. Ten of the tribes (Northern Israel) were cut off from the Southern Kingdom.

2. Only Judah and Benjamin (Southern Kingdom) and some Levites remained.

F. The Fall of Jerusalem – 586 BC; the beginning of the Babylonian Captivity.

G. The return of the exiles from Babylon – 516 BC.

VII. INTERPRETING THE OLD TESTAMENT

A. There are generally two ways to interpret the Old Testament:
1. *Literal, e.g.:*
   a. The Garden of Eden was a place on the map, the committing of the first sin a date in history.
   b. Jonah was actually swallowed by a great fish.

2. *Allegorical – when an event symbolises a deeper meaning, e.g.:*
   a. The Song of Songs can be seen as Christ's love for his church.
   b. The nation of Israel can sometimes be seen as a type of the church.

B. Remember that all persons from the Fall of Adam and Eve – from Abel to Malachi – were like us.
1. We could have been living then.

2. Learn to identify with every person you read about.

CONCLUSION

The Old Testament is as much the Word of God as the New. It was the Bible that Jesus had and he regarded it as having absolute authority. It was also the Bible of the early church. Our study of the Bible should cover both Testaments, not favouring one or the other. The Old Testament is fulfilled in the New, and the New Testament can only be understood in the light of the Old.

The best way to understand the Old Testament is to see it through the eyes of the New Testament, beginning with Jesus and Paul. Do not attempt to understand the Old Testament without the help of the Holy Spirit. Remember that the God of the Old Testament is your God and Father and that the Holy Spirit who wrote it lives in you.

We must avoid seeing the Old Testament only as history and the New Testament only as theology. If we seek the guidance of the Holy Spirit in our study of the Old Testament we will find it to be all of a piece with the New, all the inspired and inerrant Word of God.

2

HOW TO UNDERSTAND
THE NEW TESTAMENT

INTRODUCTION

A. The New Testament is made up of 27 books, virtually half of which were written by the Apostle Paul.
   1. The Old Testament is the New Testament concealed.
   2. The New Testament is the Old Testament revealed.

B. This study may well do two things:
   1. Show that you know more than you had realised.
   2. Show that you know less than you had realised.

C. The question is: where do we begin?
   1. *Do we begin with the Synoptic Gospels (Matthew, Mark, Luke)?*
      a. Synoptic comes from a Greek word *synopsis* which means 'seeing together'.
      b. This word is used because of the high degree of similarity found in Matthew, Mark and Luke in their presentation of the ministry of Jesus.
         (1)Over 97 per cent of Mark's Gospel has a parallel in Matthew.
         (2)Over 88 per cent of Mark's Gospel has a parallel in Luke.
   2. *Do we begin with the Gospel of John?*
      a. John, the son of Zebedee, was perhaps closest to Jesus.
      b. John's Gospel has the most to say about the Holy Spirit.
      c. John gives us a 'high' Christology (definition: the doctrine of Christ).
         (1) The Synoptics begin from 'below' (Matt. 1:18ff; Mark 1:1).
         (2) John begins from 'above' (John 1:1-14).
   3. *Do we begin with Acts?*
      a. Acts presents us with the way the Apostles understood Jesus after the coming of the Holy Spirit.
      b. It is the first account of Church history.

   4. *Do we begin with the Apostle Paul?*
   a. Paul's teaching eventually 'upstaged' the writings of the other Apostles.
   b. Though appearing on the scene later he was sovereignly chosen to be the leading light among the New Testament writers.
   c. If we begin with Paul, which letter?

D. What are the arguments for each letter as a starter for understanding the New Testament? (They are all equally inspired and God can and has used any part of the New Testament to bring a person to Christ.)
   1. *The Synoptics: beginning with Jesus' earthly ministry.*
   a. Matthew – placed first in the canon (definition: the collection of sacred writings that are infallible).
      (1) Since it is placed first it seems reasonable to start there.
      (2) It stresses the continuity between the Old and New Testaments.
   b. Mark – the shortest and (perhaps) simplest of the Gospels.
   c. Luke – originally written to describe the life of Jesus to one who may have been an outsider.
   2. John – stresses the Deity (God or Godhood) of Jesus, often printed by itself to give to a non-Christian.
   3. Acts – written by Luke, describing what actually happened after Jesus ascended and how the Apostles finally came to understand Jesus' ministry.
   4. Paul – who most clearly defined the gospel.

E. There is something to be said for beginning with any of the above as an introduction to the New Testament.
   1. *But this course is in* theology.
   a. Were this merely a School of the Bible we may well begin with the Synoptics.
   b. But we want to have an overall theological grasp of the New Testament.
   2. *If we begin with a sound theological grasp of Paul's thinking we can have a 'head start' with the teachings of Jesus.*
   a. We could read the Synoptics and never understand Paul.
      (1) Some say 'Jesus, yes' but 'Paul, no'.
      (2) Some hate Paul for changing the face of Christianity.

    b. But if we understand Paul we can better grasp the teachings of Jesus as he himself understood them.

      (1) Not as they were necessarily understood at the time by his hearers or followers.

      (2) But as he consciously understood what he taught.

  3. *Jesus himself implicitly directs us to what the Holy Spirit would later reveal* – John 16:12: 'I have much more to say to you, more than you can now bear.'

    a. John 16:12 is perhaps the best reason for beginning with Paul.

    b. What Paul later taught, the disciples could not handle at the time. The question is, can *we* handle Paul?

F. We shall begin with Paul, and I recommend that the rest of the New Testament be read, as it were, through Pauline eyes. Why?

  1. John 16:12. What Jesus didn't say then, he later said to Paul.

  2. Paul's central concern was the gospel in the light of Christ's death and resurrection. It should be ours too.

  3. *Paul got his teachings from none other than Jesus himself* (Gal. 1:12).

    a. Paul's Gospel is Jesus' gospel.

    b. The teaching of Paul, then, is Jesus' own teaching.

      (1) Never see Paul's theology as his own.

      (2) When you understand Paul you understand Jesus – both as he was meant to be understood and as he knew Paul would later explain what Jesus could not unveil to his disciples.

  4. This will make you good theologians.

I. THE CONTRIBUTION OF THE APOSTLE PAUL

A. We therefore begin with Paul, generally; the book of Romans particularly.

  1. *Paul in a sense had two careers.*

    a. Initial ministry, immediately after his conversion (Acts 9:20).

      (1) We don't know exactly how long this lasted, probably not long.

      (2) His original message summed up: Jesus is the Christ (Acts 9:22).

b. God recruited Paul for a wider ministry – Galatians 1:15.

    (1) He was taken out of the mainstream – Galatians 1:16-24.

    (2) He was unheard of for fourteen years – Galatians 2:1.

2. *Now prepared and ready Paul became Apostle to the Gentiles – Galatians 2:9.*

    a. Paul made every effort however to reach Jews first – Romans 1:16.

        (1) Philippi – Acts 16:13ff.

        (2) Thessalonica – Acts 17:1ff.

        (3) Corinth – Acts 18:1-8.

    b. Paul's epistles were largely addressed to churches he founded.

        (1) He answered questions they asked.

        (2) There was generally no need to explain in his letters *all* he had already preached to them (it was assumed).

3. *The Epistle to the Romans was different.*

    a. Paul had not met the Christians of Rome, but hoped to (Rom. 1:10).

        (1) It is not known for sure how the church at Rome was founded.

        (2) It may have begun because of some Roman Jews converted on the Day of Pentecost (Acts 2:10) who took their new faith home.

    b. As far as we know no Apostle founded the church at Rome.

        (1) They therefore lacked theological leadership.

        (2) Paul would not therefore be moving in where another Apostle had been.

    c. The Book of Romans, therefore, contained the whole of Paul's *soteriological* thinking.

        (1) He wanted them to know what he believed before he arrived there.

        (2) As a result, we have an outline of 'the purest gospel', as Martin Luther described the Book of Romans.

    d. Romans is the best place to begin.

        (1) It is not always easy to understand.

        (2) But God has used that book powerfully in church history, arguably more than he has used any other New Testament book.

C. Date and place of writing of Romans.
1. Date: c. 57 A.D., near the end of Paul's third missionary journey.
2. Place: from Corinth, as Paul was preparing to go to Jerusalem, with Rome as his next destination.

D. Outline of the Gospel, speaking generally.
1. *The righteousness of God by faith* (Rom. 1:17)
   a. Romans 1:17 is explained by 3:22.
      (1) The faith of Christ refers to his perfect faith as a man and his obedience unto death (Rom. 5:10).
      (2) All he did for us is of no value until we believe (Rom. 3:26).
   b. In a word: we are declared righteous before God by faith alone (Rom. 4:1-12).
2. *The wrath of God* (Rom. 1:18)
   a. Paul puts this at the beginning that we might know it was an assumption in his thinking from then on.
      (1) Jesus had said virtually all we need to know about hell.
      (2) Paul thus assumes this (Rom. 5:9).
   b. By 'wrath', then, Paul means:
      (1) God's justice in punishing sin (Rom. 1:18–2:29).
      (2) What must be satisfied in order that we do not suffer God's judgement (Rom. 3:19-31).
3. *Sin of man without excuse*
   a. What is punished with justice (Rom. 1:18ff).
   b. What is true, whether Jew or Gentile (Rom. 2).
      (1) All have sinned (Rom. 3:23ff).
      (2) All the world is guilty (Rom. 3:19).
4. *Atonement for sin by Jesus Christ*
   a. His faith and life (Rom. 3:23; 5:10).
      (1) He kept the Law for us.
      (2) Justification by his resurrection (Rom. 4:25).
5. *Assurance of salvation*
   a. Objective assurance (Rom. 5:1).
      (1) Christ died for all who believe (Rom. 3:22).
      (2) We are justified by grace (Rom. 3:24).
   b. Subjective assurance (Rom. 5:2).
      (1) Faith assures us (Rom. 3:26).
      (2) The Holy Spirit witnesses to this (Rom. 5:5).

    6. *Holiness of life*
        a. Repudiation of antinomianism (Rom. 6:1).
            (1) Paul was accused of this (Rom. 3:8).
            (2) It is not possible (Rom. 6:2).
        b. Conversion brings new life (Rom. 6:4).
            (1) How we are to see ourselves (Rom. 6:11).
            (2) How we are to live (Rom. 6:12-22).
    7. *The place of the Law*
        a. Must be fulfilled (Rom. 2:12).
            (1) Fulfilment of it brings eternal life (Rom. 2:7).
            (2) Must be fulfilled by a substitute (Rom. 2:26).
        b. The Christian is set free from the Law (Rom. 7:6).
            (1) Living by the Law brings frustration (Rom. 7:14ff).
            (2) No condemnation to those in Christ (Rom. 8:1-4).
        c. Note: Romans 8 is largely an explanation of two things:
            (1) How the new life is to be lived (Rom. 8:5-13).
            (2) Our status as children of God (Rom. 8:14-39).
    8. *Election and predestination*
        a. God's choice was before we were born (Rom. 9:11).
        b. Those predestined will be glorified (Rom. 8:30).
    9. *The place of Israel*
        a. Their advantage (Rom. 3:1).
        b. Israel seen two ways:
            (1) Natural Israel (Rom. 9:6).
            (2) Spiritual Israel (Rom. 9:8).
        c. Eschatological Israel (Rom. 11).
    10. *The place of evangelism*
        a. Passion for the lost (Rom. 10:1).
        b. Only believers will be saved (Rom. 10:9).
        c. Hearing the gospel is essential to salvation (Rom. 10:14).
        d. Preaching the gospel is our responsibility (Rom. 10:15).

D. Romans 12–15 is the application of doctrine.
    1. Call for sacrificial service (Rom. 12:1).
    2. Gifts in the Body of Christ (Rom. 12:3-8).
    3. Love of one another (Rom. 12:9-21).
    4. Submission to governing authorities (Rom. 13).
    5. Bearing with weaker Christians (Rom. 14, 15).

E. Paul's other letters

1. *Letters to Corinth*

   a. 1 Corinthians

   (1) Date: between 52 and 55 A.D.

   (2) Place: from Ephesus.

   (3) Theme: a reply to their letter to him, beginning with his concern for them.

   (a) Chapters 1–6 addressing their problem of disunity.

   (b) Chapters 7–16 answering their questions.

   b. 2 Corinthians

   (1) Date: between 56 and 57 A.D.

   (2) Place: from somewhere in Macedonia.

   (3) Theme: Paul rejoices over their reaction to his first letter and gives them other pastoral exhortations and warnings.

2. *Galatians*

   a. Whether this was to north or south Galatia is a matter of scholarly debate, but I think the latter is more likely.

   b. Date: 48 A.D.

   c. Place: uncertain.

   d. Theme: Paul's horror that they had been influenced by 'Judaizers' (as they are commonly called) in superimposing the Law on their faith.

3. *Ephesians*

   a. Date: early 60s.

   b. Place: from prison in Rome.

   c. Theme: our blessings in Christ, arguably the most sublime (and profound) of Paul's letters.

4. *Philippians*

   a. Date: early 60s.

   b. Place: probably from prison in Rome.

   c. Theme: encouragement to Christians to be like Jesus; note the great Christological passage in 2:5-11.

5. *Colossians*

   a. Date: early 60s.

   b. Place: probably from prison in Rome.

   c. Theme: the person of Jesus Christ and warnings against false teaching.

6. *Letters to Thessalonica*
   a. 1 Thessalonians
      (1) Date: 51 A.D.
      (2) Place: written from Corinth.
      (3) Theme: strong pastoral affirmation of them along with valuable eschatological insights.
   b. 2 Thessalonians
      (1) Date: 51 or 52 A.D.
      (2) Place: written from Corinth.
      (3) Theme: eschatology.

7. *Letters to Timothy, Paul's convert and now a superintendent of churches.*
   a. 1 Timothy
      (1) Date: early 60s.
      (2) Place: unknown, possibly from somewhere in Macedonia.
      (3) Theme: very personal letter together with advice concerning direction of churches.
   b. 2 Timothy
      (1) Date: middle 60s, possibly Paul's last letter before his martyrdom in 67 A.D.
      (2) Place: from prison in Rome.
      (3) Theme: solemn but triumphant personal letter.

8. *Letter to Titus, bishop of Crete*
   a. Date: 57 A.D.
   b. Place: possibly from Corinth.
   c. Theme: a pastoral letter with instructions for a church leader on handling people.

9. *Philemon, an old friend of Paul*
   a. Date: early 60s.
   b. Place: Probably from prison in Rome.
   c. Theme: that Onesimus, a slave who deserted Philemon, should be accepted back; a brilliant example of diplomacy.

II. OTHER NEW TESTAMENT EPISTLES

A. Hebrews
1. It is not known for sure who wrote Hebrews. It could have been written by Paul; most scholars however think otherwise.
2. Date: 60s, certainly before 70 A.D. because references are made to the Temple that was still standing.
3. Possibly written to Christian Jews in Rome who were small in number.
4. Place of writing: unknown.
5. Theme: a long exhortation to discouraged Christians not to repeat history (the children of Israel in the wilderness) in the light of so great salvation, together with the only New Testament depiction of Christ as our High Priest.

B. James
1. Author: the Lord's (half) brother.
2. Date: early or middle 40s (the first New Testament book to be written).
3. Written to Jewish Christians, possibly in Jerusalem, from unknown origin.
4. Theme: dignifying the trial, showing faith by works, the need to guard the tongue; this Epistle shows a primitive Christianity but one which coheres perfectly with Pauline theology.

C. Letters of Peter
1. *1 Peter*
   a. Date: some time in the 60s.
   b. Place: written from Rome.
   c. Theme: rejoicing in sufferings.
2. *2 Peter*
   a. Date: late 60s.
   b. Place: written from Rome.
   c. Theme: make our calling and election sure.

D. Jude
1. Author: the Lord's (half) brother (cf. Mark 6:3).
2. Date: late 60s.
3. Place: origin unknown.
4. Theme: earnestly contending for the faith delivered to the saints together with a warning against emerging Gnosticism (though not called by that name).

III. THE SYNOPTIC GOSPELS

A. Matthew

1. Author: Matthew, one of the Twelve (also called Levi).
2. Date: 60s.
3. Place: probably written in Syria or Antioch.
4. Theme: Christ has fulfilled Old Testament prophecies.
5. *Contributions:*
   a. Large blocks of Jesus' teaching, including the Sermon on the Mount.
      (1) Kingdom of Heaven.
      (2) Parables.
   b. Virgin birth cast in Joseph's perspective.
   c. Use of the Old Testament.

B. Mark

1. Author: John Mark (cf. Acts 12:12), traditionally thought to have got his information from Peter.
2. Date: c.60 A.D, this being the first of the Synoptic Gospels to be written.
3. Place: Probably written from Rome.
4. Theme: the ministry of Jesus, 'a passion narrative with an extended introduction'.
5. *Contributions:*
   a. 'Creator of the Gospel in its literary form', both Matthew and Luke probably followed his order of events.
      (1) Miracles.
      (2) Exorcisms.
      (3) Parables.
   b. Jesus as the suffering Son of God.
   c. Importance of discipleship.

C. Luke

1. Author: Luke, a Gentile physician (cf. Col. 4:14).
2. Date: early 60s.
3. Place: unknown but possibly written from Achaia.
4. Theme: life and ministry of Jesus.
5. *Contributions:*
   a. The birth of John the Baptist.
   b. Most of what we know about the birth and boyhood of Jesus.
   c. Emphasis upon the sinner and the poor.

IV. THE JOHANNINE WRITINGS

A. The Gospel of John
1. Author: John son of Zebedee.
2. Date: 60s.
3. Place: probably written in Ephesus.
4. Theme: the eternal Deity of Christ.
5. *Contributions:*
    a. The pre-existence of the Word before he became flesh.
    b. The rivalry between John the Baptist's disciples and those of Jesus.
    c. The relationship between the Father and the Son.
    d. Emphasis upon the Holy Spirit.
6. *Not found in John's Gospel:*
    a. Parables.
    b. Exorcisms.
    c. The Transfiguration.
    d. Record of the Institution of the Lord's Supper.
7. *Relation to the Synoptics:*
    a. Christology
        (1) Synoptics begin from below; birth, baptism, ministry.
        (2) John begins in Eternity.
    b. The person and ministry of Jesus
        (1) Synoptics give the 'perfect photograph'.
        (2) John gives the perfect portrait, 'but the great portrait painter may give a representation which no photographer can emulate' (William Temple).
    c. The words of Jesus
        (1) The Synoptics tell us what Jesus said, like the front page of a newspaper.
        (2) John tells us what Jesus meant, like an editorial.

B. The epistles of John
1. *1 John*
    a. Date: early 90s.
    b. Place: written from Ephesus.
    c. Theme: continuing the theme of the fourth Gospel, John's burden is probably to warn against Gnosticism.

2. *2 John*
   a. Date: early 90s.
   b. Place: written from Ephesus.
   c. Theme: warning against dangers inherent in being travelling preachers.

3. *3 John*
   a. Date: early 90s.
   b. Place: written from Ephesus.
   c. Theme: warning Gaius of Diotrophes.

C. The Book of Revelation
   1. Author: John son of Zebedee.
   2. Date: 95 or 96 A.D.
   3. Place: written from Patmos, an island 40 miles south-west of Ephesus.
   4. Theme: unveiling of things to come.

V. THE BOOK OF ACTS

A. Author: Luke.

B. Date: middle 60s.

C. Place: unknown, possibly Achaia.

D. Theme: history of the earliest church after Jesus ascended to Heaven and the Holy Spirit fell on the Day of Pentecost; 'a whirlwind tour of three decades of church history.'

E. Contributions:
   1. Peter's sermon on the Day of Pentecost.
   2. Conversion of Saul of Tarsus.
   3. Jerusalem Council.
   4. Paul's missionary journeys.

CONCLUSION

A study of the life, teaching, death and resurrection of Christ could begin with any of the four Gospels. A study of theology could start there, but more helpfully could begin with the writings of Paul, particularly the Epistle to the Romans. God did not stop speaking with the last words of Christ on earth. Jesus said, 'I have much more to say to you, more than you can now bear' (John 16:12). That includes the Acts of the Apostles, the New Testament letters and the Revelation to John on Patmos.

3

THE INCLUSIVE BIBLE

INTRODUCTION

A. In recent years a number of publishing houses have produced a translation of the Bible known for its 'inclusive language'.
  1. *The purpose of this translation is to provide 'a sensitive and balanced gender-inclusive text'.*
  2. *It is stated that where terms used in the original languages 'refer to both men and women' the new translation 'has been revised to reflect the original' as opposed to using a word that is 'exclusively masculine' (as in, say, the Authorised Version or even the New International Version).*
     a. Among these new translations is the New International Version Inclusive Language Edition (NIVI), quoted above, published by Hodder & Stoughton.
     b. In the Preface it is stated that it was 'often appropriate to mute the patriarchalism of the culture of the biblical writers through gender-inclusive language when this could be done without compromising the message of the Spirit.'
        (1) Gender-inclusive language (def.): including men and women simultaneously (not just men).
        (2) Mute (def.): to deaden or muffle.
        (3) Patriarchalism (def.): male headship.
     c. The assumption is therefore twofold:
        (1) The Bible was written by men whose culture was male dominated.
        (2) Had the Bible been written in today's culture the writers would use gender-inclusive language.
     d. The translators of the NIVI believe they have not compromised the message of the Spirit.
     e. The translators have promised to reflect the original languages (Hebrew and Greek) but admit to muting the patriarchal language.

B. The purpose of this study is to examine the NIVI and draw some conclusions. We will ask these questions:
1. Is this version of the Bible necessary for today's culture?
2. Is the translation consistently accurate?
3. Is the original Hebrew and Greek often found to reflect both men and women?
4. Is muting references to the word 'men' ever valid?
5. Is the message of the Spirit ever compromised when references to men in the original are translated 'men and women', 'they', 'brothers and sisters' or 'you'?

C. Why is this lesson important?
1. *The plenary (def.: 'all' or 'full') inspiration of the scriptures is at stake.*
    a. Was the Holy Spirit bound by culture in the formation of the Bible?
    b. Did the writers merely follow their culture?
    c. Are references to men accidental?
    d. Is every word of Scripture inspired?
2. *Do we take into account a rising generation of people who are increasingly being taught with gender-inclusive language?*
    a. Many textbooks are written by people who avoid 'he' and refer to 'they' or 'one' or 'you'.
    b. Should the Bible in the hands of a new generation reflect this as well?
    c. Magazines and newspapers, not to mention radio and television, are increasingly sensitive to references to men when 'they' or 'he and she' can be used.
    d. It is argued that women under 30 have great difficulty coping with language that is essentially masculine only.
3. *Is Paul's principle 'I have become all things to all men so that by all possible means I might save some' (1 Cor. 9:22) to be applied to the extent that his words should read, 'I have become all things to all people so that by all possible means I might save some'?*
    a. If this would mean reaching people who are offended by the original NIV, is it not worth it to make it gender-inclusive?
    b. Or should we expect people to adjust to the references – of which the above is one example – to men?

4. *Is there a danger of serious theological issues being compromised?*
   a. Are the references to men theologically necessary in some cases?
   b. Or are references to men ever capable of referring to both sexes without any theological implications?
5. *Should the day come that versions such as the NIVI replace all other translations – in the home and in the pew?*
   a. Would you hope that versions such as the NIVI would become standard?
   b. Would there be any great loss to the reader or the believer were this to happen?

I. EXAMPLES OF THE NIV AND NIVI

Negative criticisms of the NIVI

A. From the references to creation.

1. *Genesis 1:27 says, God created man in his own image.*
   a. This account assumes the creation of woman, in Genesis 2:21ff.
      (1) God intended the creation of Adam to be distinct from the creation of woman.
      (2) For man (Heb. Adam) no suitable helper was found.
   b. 'So the LORD God caused the man to fall into a deep sleep; and while he was sleeping, he took one of the man's ribs and closed up the place with flesh. Then the LORD God made a woman from the rib he had taken out of the man, and he brought her to the man. The man said, "This is now bone of my bones and flesh of my flesh; she shall be called 'woman,' for she was taken out of man"' (Gen. 2:21-23).
      (1) The NIVI says 'God created human beings in his own image. . '
      (2) This translation therefore usurps the intention of the writer to show how man, Adam (Heb.), could refer to both sexes by the use of the first man, Adam.

2. *Genesis 5:1-2 says, 'When God created man, he made him in the likeness of God. He created them male and female ... he blessed them and called them man (adam).'*
   a. The name *man* is placed on both male and female, as together they constitute the human race.

    b. The Hebrew word 'adam' is used to mean man but also Adam in particular.

       (1) It is sometimes used to refer to man in distinction from woman: 'The man and his wife were both naked, and they felt no shame' (Gen. 2:25).

       (2) The English word 'man' most accurately translates 'adam', because it is the only word that we have that has these same two meanings (the human race or a male human being).

3. *One can conclude that, from this usage of 'adam', it is not wrong, insensitive or discriminatory to use the same word to refer to male human beings in particular and to name the human race.*

    a. God himself does this in his Word.

    b. But in the NIVI the name 'man' has disappeared in the aforementioned passages.

       (1) 'Human beings' are not names that refer to man in distinction from woman.

       (2) Clearly this is a less accurate translation of 'adam' than the word 'man', the male overtones of the Hebrew word are lost.

4. *The word 'man' for the whole human race suggests some male headship in the race.*

    a. God did not name the race with a Hebrew term that corresponds to our word 'woman'.

    b. God did not choose or devise a gender-neutral term without male overtones.

    c. God named the race with a Hebrew term that most closely corresponds to the English word 'man'.

B. References to Jesus Christ

1. *Psalm 34:20 is a messianic prophecy: 'He protects all his bones, not one of them will be broken.'*

    a. John's Gospel refers to this: 'These things happened so that the scripture would be fulfilled: "Not one of his bones will be broken"' (John 19:36).

    b. But the NIVI apparently does not want such a prediction about an individual man, so the prediction is plural: 'He protects all their bones, not one of them will be broken.'

    c. The individuality of the messianic tradition, so wonderfully fulfilled in Jesus' death, is lost; the Hebrew is singular: 'his bones'.

    d. This change was made because the NIVI translators wanted to mute the patriarchalism of the culture of the biblical writers.

2. *Psalm 8:4 says, 'What is man that you are mindful of him, the son of man that you care for him?'*

    a. This is quoted in Hebrews 2:6 where the writer is clearly putting this in a messianic context.

    b. The NIVI instead refers to 'mere mortals' instead of man and 'human beings' instead of son of man.

3. *1 Timothy 2:5 says, 'For there is one God and one mediator between God and men, the man Christ Jesus.'*

    a. This clearly refers to Christ's mediatorship, emphasising that Jesus Christ is male.

    b. The NIVI says, 'For there is one God and one mediator between God and human beings, Christ Jesus, himself human.'

    c. The latter's undertranslation diminishes the impact Paul intended.

4. *Hebrews 5:1 says, 'Every high priest is selected from among men and is appointed to represent them in matters related to God, to offer gifts and sacrifices for sins.'*

    a. Clearly this translation must be accurate, for no woman could be a high priest in the Old Testament.

    b. The NIVI changes 'from among men' to 'from among mortals'.

    c. Whatever could be the translators' purpose in changing this?

5. *1 Corinthians 15:21 says, 'For since death came through a man, the resurrection of the dead comes also through a man.'*

    a. The NIVI seems not to want to call a man a man.

    b. The NIVI says that death came 'through a human being' and so too the resurrection of the dead 'comes also through a human being'.

    c. This is theologically important.

        (1) The representative headship of Adam and Christ as men is omitted.

        (2) What would be the purpose of the NIVI here? Surely this verse has nothing whatever to do with a patriarchal culture.

C. General references to men

1. Acts 15:22 says that Judas Barsabbas and Silas were leading 'men' sent from Jerusalem, but the NIVI simply says they were 'leaders'.
2. We know that there were only men who were elders at Ephesus, so Paul warned that 'men' would arise and distort that truth; but the NIVI changes this to 'some' (Acts 20:30).
3. Clearly these references should not offend women today; the actual historical situations could only have meant men. Why the need to translate them in gender-neutral ways?

D. The move away from the individual believers

1. *The NIVI finds the little word 'he' troubling.*
   a. 'Jesus replied, "If anyone loves me, he will obey my teaching. My Father will love him, and we will come to him and make our home with him' (John 14:23).
   b. The NIVI says, 'Jesus replied, "Those who love me will obey my teaching. My Father will love them, and we will come to them and make our home with them.'
2. *The problem is, Jesus did not speak with plural pronouns here; he used singulars to specify the individual believer. The individual application of familiar verses is lost.*
   a. 'Here I am! I stand at the door and knock. If anyone hears my voice and opens the door, I will come in and eat with him, and he with me' (Rev. 3:20).
   b. 'Here I am! I stand at the door and knock. If anyone hears my voice and opens the door, I will come in and eat with them, and they with me' (Rev. 3:20 NIVI).

II. In defence of the NIVI

A. The issue (it is said) is not a gender issue but a matter of translation theory.

1. *The question is: Whether formal equivalence (literal translation) or functional equivalence (thought-for-thought) as Bible translation theories produces the best translation for our day.*
   a. Formal equivalence (def.): literal translation, that the original wording, grammar and syntax should be retained so long as the resulting translation is understandable. The AV and NIV are examples.

   b. Functional equivalence (def.): dynamic translation, that the
      text should have the same impact on the modern reader as
      the original had on the ancient reader.
      (1) It is not the original terms but the meaning of the whole
         that is important.
      (2) What matters: a 'thought-for-thought' translation versus
         a 'word-for-word' translation. The Good News Bible
         and the Living Bible are examples of the former.
   2. *The use of inclusive pronouns in translation falls within the
      realm of dynamic translation theory.*
      a. In the ancient world it was common to say 'man' or 'he'
         when speaking of all people.
      b. Within the last twenty years this has been practised less and
         less, and those who have not grown up in church can
         misunderstand such male-orientated language.
   3. A basic principle of all translation theory is to express the ancient
      text in the thoughts and idioms of the people of today.

B. Even Paul took liberties when he quoted the Old Testament.
   1. 'Blessed is he whose transgressions are forgiven, whose sins
      are covered' (Ps. 32:1).
   2. 'Blessed are they whose transgressions are forgiven, whose
      sins are covered' (Rom. 4:7).
   3. Surely Paul was not capitulating to a feminist agenda.

C. In the discipleship sayings of Jesus he addresses the crowds.
   1. In the ancient setting most of them were males.
   2. In the modern setting both men and women are assumed to be
      among those called to be disciples. Hence, 'And those who do
      not carry their cross and follow me cannot be my disciples'
      (Luke 14:27 NIVI).

**D. As for the Hebrew 'adam' in the creation account, it can mean
   mankind as well as man when referring to the human race as
   a whole.**
   1. Adam can be called 'them' in Genesis 1:27 and 5:2.
   2. It is perfectly valid to render it 'people'.

E. As for Acts 20:30, referring to Ephesus, 'some' would have included women since the leader of the cult movement in Thyatira (a church planted from Ephesus) was a woman – Jezebel (Rev. 2:20).

F. In 1 Corinthians 13:11 Paul says, 'When I became a man, I put childish ways behind me.'
   1. The contrast lies with 'a child', so the NIVI translates, 'When I became an adult'.
   2. This captures the contrast with clarity.

G. Ephesians 4:13 says 'mature man' in Greek but even the NIV translates *aner* as 'mature'. It refers to the whole church and not just to men.

H. The New Testament itself often translates the Old Testament in a dynamic fashion.
   1. Compare Ephesians 4:8 and Psalm 68:18.
   2. Compare Hebrews 1:7 and Psalm 104:4.
   3. These are examples of how the New Testament writers translated the Old Testament.

I. Changing 'he' to 'you' or 'they' does not distort the meaning of the text.
   1. 'Then he called the crowd to him along with his disciples and said: "Those who would come after me must deny themselves and take up their cross and follow me' (Mark 8:34 NIVI).
   2. 'No one can come to me unless the Father who sent me draws them, and I will raise them up at the last day' (John 6:44 NIVI).
   3. 'Jesus replied, "Those who love me will obey my teaching. My Father will love them, and we will come to them and make our home with them"' (John 14:23 NIVI).

J. Inclusive language has long been used in Bible translations.
   1. William Tyndale translated Matthew 5:9, 'Blessed are the peacemakers, for they shall be called children (Gr. 'sons') of God.'
   2. The AV translates 'sons of Israel' 644 times as 'children of Israel'.

K. Some unbelievers are offended by the generic 'he'.
    1. Gender-specific translations would be counter-productive in secular universities.
    2. Translations for the general public should not erect unnecessary barriers to the gospel.

CONCLUSION

A. When the Preface of the NIVI referred to the 'patriarchalism' of the culture of the biblical writers, it was sadly a dead give-away of deep theological biases.
    1. *In this sweeping statement there was an implicit assumption that:*
        a. Patriarchalism is inherently evil.
        b. Patriarchalism is not what God intended.
        c. Patriarchalism is a cultural phenomenon that just happened to emerge before people became enlightened.
    2. *If however the Genesis account of creation and the Fall is an accurate description of what happened, it follows that:*
        a. The Garden of Eden was a place on the map.
            (1) God made man first, then woman.
            (2) 'For man did not come from woman, but woman from man; neither was man created for woman, but woman for man' (1 Cor. 11:8-9).
        b. The patriarchal situation was God's idea from the beginning.
            (1) Like it or not, this is the way it was – by God's design.
            (2) This continued through the formation of the New Testament.
    3. *This renders the theory of evolution out of the question.*
        a. If evolution is the way it happened, then the patriarchalism of ancient times was by accident or a sad development of male domination.
        b. The reference to patriarchalism in the Preface of the NIVI smacks of a belief that evolution somehow went before God's involvement in his creation – and that he has been working in modern times to correct what went wrong (and which he had nothing to do with).
    4. *If the Fall of man is a date in history, then part of the punishment of the Fall was what some want to call patriarchalism.*
        a. God said to the woman, 'Your desire will be for your husband, and he will rule over you' (Gen. 3:16).

    b. Paul makes a big point of this. A woman was not to have
authority over a man because of two things:

      (1) Adam was formed first, then Eve (1 Tim. 2:13).

      (2) 'And Adam was not the one deceived; it was the woman
who was deceived and became a sinner' (1 Tim. 2:14).

  5. The bottom line: Patriarchalism, like it or not, was God's idea;
to object to it betrays a most unfortunate bias.

  6. *I sincerely sympathise with thoughtful women today, who have
been genuinely alarmed at abuses of patriarchalism.*

    a. They may have also been hurt by an insensitive and brutal
chauvinism that is unbiblical.

    b. Gently but honestly taught, many women want to embrace
what the Bible teaches.

**B. Nobody seriously questions that the biblical writers lived in a
patriarchal society.**

  1. But it was God the Creator who made man 'male and female'
(Gen. 1:27).

  2. The apostle Paul said, 'Now I want you to realise that the head
of every man is Christ, and the head of the woman is man, and
the head of Christ is God' (1 Cor. 11:3).

  3. Peter referred to the wife as the 'weaker partner' (1 Pet. 3:7).

  4. As Wayne Grudem put it, 'What if those very same "patriarchal"
elements in Scripture are part of what the Holy Spirit intended
to be there?' *Christianity Today*, October 27 1997. Note: I am
deeply indebted to this issue of *Christianity Today* for much
of the present study.

  5. If we hold to the absolute divine authority of Scripture, then we
should not seek to mute any content that the Holy Spirit caused
to be there.

**C. There are times when the Hebrew or Greek may indeed refer
to all people when it says 'he' or 'man'.**

  1. *Anthropoi* (Gr.) refers to people in general and can be translated
'people' rather than 'men'.

  2. Indefinite pronouns as *tis* (Gr.) can be translated 'anyone' rather
than 'any man'; *oudeis* (Gr.) can be translated 'no one' rather
than 'no man'; *pas* (Gr.) can be translated 'all people' or
'everyone'.

D. Every word of the original is exactly what God wanted it to be, because 'all Scripture is God-breathed' (2 Tim. 3:16). The NIVI admits (Preface) that it was 'often appropriate' to 'mute the patriarchalism of the culture of the biblical writers through gender-inclusive language.' I fear they went too far.

4

OPENNESS TO GOD'S WORD

A. In a future chapter called 'Openness to the Holy Spirit' we will deal more fully with point 1.

    1. *Every generation has a stigma by which the believer's faith is tested.*

        a. Yesterday's stigma is easily accepted today.

        b. The Pharisees felt righteous because they affirmed yesterday's prophets.

            (1) 'Woe to you, teachers of the law and Pharisees, you hypocrites! You build tombs for the prophets and decorate the graves of the righteous. And you say, "If we had lived in the days of our forefathers, we would not have taken part with them in shedding the blood of the prophets"' (Matt. 23:29-30).

            (2) But Jesus exposed their hypocrisy by adding: 'So you testify against yourselves that you are the descendants of those who murdered the prophets. Fill up, then, the measure of the sin of your forefathers!' (Matt. 23:31-32).

In other words, they showed their phoniness by rejecting the stigma of their own day, namely, Jesus the promised Messiah who was right before their eyes!

    2. *Jonathan Edwards taught that the task of every generation is to discern in which direction the Sovereign Redeemer is moving, then to move in that direction.*

        a. This comes by being open to the Holy Spirit.

        b. The Holy Spirit's direction is always a fresh stigma, injuring our pride and challenging our sophistication.

            (1) 'But God chose the foolish things of the world to shame the wise; God chose the weak things of the world to shame the strong. He chose the lowly things of this world and the despised things – and the things that are not – to nullify the things that are' (1 Cor. 1:27-28).

(2) We must never forget that today's challenge will make us look stupid to most people.

B. This lesson is (very probably) pleasing to charismatic and Pentecostal Christians – and challenging to reformed and evangelical Christians.

1. *Those (by and large) who are most open to the Holy Spirit have been Pentecostals and charismatics.*
   a. Pentecostals: those who generally come from Elim churches and Assemblies of God. They paid the price and bore the stigma for nearly a century.
   b. Charismatics: those who emphasise the gifts of the Spirit (1 Cor. 12:8-10) but across denominational lines, including Anglicans, Baptists and Methodists, and the 'house churches'.

2. *The stress has generally included:*
   a. The gifts of the Spirit – speaking in tongues, prophecy, words of knowledge, healing, etc.
   b. Signs, wonders, miracles.

3. *There have been ecclesiological distinctions, i.e., differences concerning church structure and government:*
   a. Renewal: stay in your denomination, renew it from within.
   b. Restoration: come out of your denomination, go back to the way it was in the New Testament.
   c. Note: there is some overlapping of emphasis and there are some exceptions to the above; this a generalisation.

4. *The Toronto Blessing has appealed largely to the charismatic/ Pentecostal type of Christian.*
   a. Some have rejected it.
   b. But as the gospel was to the Jew 'first', then to the Gentile, it has been accepted by those already markedly associated with the gifts of the Spirit – rather than by the reformed and non-charismatic evangelicals.

5. *Non-charismatic evangelicals have often been repulsed by much that is in the Charismatic Movement.*
   a. Our plea to be open to the Spirit, then, is largely with non-charismatic evangelicals in mind.
   b. It is what I have preached in Westminster Chapel.

C. This lesson will (very probably) please evangelicals but challenge charismatics and Pentecostals. Why?
1. The latter will not see the need of this lesson.
2. They will say that they are already open to God's Word.
3. They may feel insulted at the very idea that they are not open to God's Word.

D. But here is the problem:
1. *Evangelicals feel precisely this way about openness to the Spirit.*
    a. They will probably say one of two things (or both):
        (1) We are open to the Spirit.
        (2) We have the Holy Spirit because we have the Word.
    b. You cannot convince many of them of any need to be open – it is ridiculous, they say, to suggest it.
    c. So they become almost unteachable.
    d. We are at an impasse.

2. *Charismatics and Pentecostals feel much the same way about openness to the Word.*
    a. They will probably say one of two things (or both):
        (1) We are open to the Word.
        (2) We have the Word because we have the Spirit.
    b. You cannot convince many of them of any need to be open to the Word – it is ridiculous, they say, because all we've ever done is to preach the Word.
    c. So they become almost unteachable.
    d. We are at an impasse.

3. Who on either side will become vulnerable and admit need and deficiency?

E. Another problem: questioning the Bible's infallibility.
1. If we doubt the inerrancy of the Word, we are less likely to be open to it.
2. Why be open to the Word if it is not absolutely God's Word?
3. We must be convinced that the Bible is God's own Word. See Wayne Grudem, *Systematic Theology* (Zondervan 1994), pp. 47-140.

F. Why is this lesson important?
  1. *We believe there has been a silent divorce in the church between the Word and the Spirit.*
     a. There are those on the 'Word' side saying:
        (1) The need of the hour is for preaching of the Bible generally and expository preaching particularly.
        (2) We must earnestly contend for the faith once for all entrusted to the saints (Jude 3).
        (3) We need to recover the Reformation heritage – centred on the gospel.
     b. There are those on the 'Spirit' side saying:
        (1) The need today is for signs and wonders.
        (2) The world will not be shaken until we recover apostolic power.
        (3) We need to see healings and prophetic words which will show the world that the church is alive.
     c. What is wrong with either emphasis? Nothing. Both are right.
  2. There is a need for a remarriage of the Word and Spirit.
  3. The combination will mean spontaneous combustion.
  4. Most of the delay in seeing this re-marriage is because neither side will admit to a fault.
  5. I fear that charismatics have been as unteachable and unreachable with regard to openness to the Word as evangelicals have been regarding openness to the Spirit.

I. EVIDENCE THAT SOME CHRISTIANS HAVE NOT BEEN TRULY OPEN TO THE WORD (speaking generally)

A. They seem more interested in God's secret will than they are in his revealed will.
  1. *God's revealed will: the Bible.*
     a. The Old Testament: the Law, Prophets, Psalms (Luke 24:44).
     b. The New Testament: teachings of Jesus, Acts, epistles.
     c. Doctrine.
  2. **God's secret will: direct guidance.**
     a. 'What does God want me to do today?'
     b. 'Whom should I marry? Where should I go to church?'
     c. 'Will I get this job? Should I move house?'

B. They seem more interested in the prophetic word than the preached word.

   1. *Preaching: God's way of saving people and teaching them* (1 Cor. 1:21).

      a. Preaching from the Bible.

      b. Explaining the Bible.

      c. Exploring the Bible.

   2. *Prophetic word: 'Thus saith the Lord.'*

      a. Giving a word of knowledge.

      b. Telling a person what God wants to do for him or her.

      c. Giving specific advice in a critical situation.

C. They seem more interested in manifestations of the Spirit than the gospel.

   1. *Manifestations (how the Spirit shows himself):*

      a. Falling down, laughter.

      b. Signs and wonders.

      c. Unusual prophetic words of knowledge.

   2. *The gospel.*

      a. Who Jesus is and why he came.

      b. What he did on the cross and why.

      c. How people are saved.

D. They seem more interested in the gifts of the Spirit than in the fruit of the Spirit.

   1. Gifts: tongues, prophecy, word of knowledge, etc. (1 Cor. 12:8-10).

   2. Fruit: love, joy, peace, etc. (Gal. 5:22ff).

E. They seem more interested in being edified than in saving the lost.

   1. *Edification (being built up and encouraged).*

      a. Worship and praise.

      b. Feeling the presence of God.

      c. Increase of personal faith.

   2. *Saving the lost.*

      a. Conviction of sin, righteousness and judgment (John 16:7-8).

      b. Reaching the unchurched and leading a soul to Christ.

      c. Conversions.

F. They seem more interested in public worship than in private quiet times.
   1. *Public worship.*
      a. Singing.
      b. Open praying.
      c. Prayer groups.
   2. *Private quiet time.*
      a. Reading the Bible daily.
      b. Time alone with God.
      c. Developing intimacy with God.

G. Here are questions I would put:
   1. Have you ever led another person to Christ?
   2. Do you know how to explain and present the gospel?
   3. How well do you really know your Bible?
   4. How often do you read the Bible – have you really read it through?
   5. How much time do you spend alone with God?
   6. How sensitive are you to grieving the Spirit? (Eph. 4:30).
   7. How concerned are you to dignify God's trials for you? (Jas. 1:2).
   8. Have you totally forgiven those who have hurt you?

II. PROOF THAT WE ARE TOTALLY OPEN TO THE BIBLE

A. We affirm its full inspiration.
   1. *The Holy Spirit wrote the Old Testament*
      a. 'All Scripture is God-breathed and is useful for teaching, rebuking, correcting and training in righteousness' (2 Tim. 3:16).
         (1) 'God-breathed' is a direct reference to the Holy Spirit.
         (2) 'And with that he breathed on them and said, "Receive the Holy Spirit"' (John 20:22).
      b. 'For prophecy never had its origin in the will of man, but men spoke from God as they were carried along by the Holy Spirit' (2 Pet. 1:21).
         (1) The whole of the Bible can be called 'prophecy'.
         (2) All the writers wrote what they did because God prophetically spoke as they wrote under the Spirit's direct guidance.

c. Affirming the scriptures is therefore affirming the prophetic words or word of knowledge that were given to the Old Testament writers.

    (1) Whether it was Moses or David or Isaiah, all had words of knowledge given to them by the Spirit and his leading to put pen to papyrus.

    (2) It is one thing to accept a word of knowledge for someone today – to which we must always be open; it is always safe to accept the scriptures.

2. *The Holy Spirit wrote the New Testament*

  a. The Holy Spirit makes that claim for the New Testament.

    (1) 'He writes the same way in all his letters, speaking in them of these matters. His letters contain some things that are hard to understand, which ignorant and unstable people distort, as they do the other Scriptures, to their own destruction' (2 Pet. 3:16).

    (2) 'For the Scripture says, "Do not muzzle the ox while it is treading out the grain," and "The worker deserves his wages"' (1 Tim. 5:18). Here Paul quotes Jesus' words as found in Luke 10:7 and calls them 'scripture'.

  b. Paul claims this authority for himself. 'If anybody thinks he is a prophet or spiritually gifted, let him acknowledge that what I am writing to you is the Lord's command' (1 Cor. 14:37).

    (1) In 1 Corinthians 7:6 Paul speaks as a concession, not as a command.

    (2) This further shows that, whereas he is stating his godly opinion at places in 1 Corinthians 7, all other places are by 'command' and therefore under the Spirit's inspiration.

B. We esteem the word as the Lord himself does.

1. *The psalmist acknowledges that God has magnified his Word above all his name!* (Ps. 138:2 AV).

  a. This is the literal translation from the Hebrew.

  b. The Living Bible acknowledges this as well.

2. *We could show endlessly how God vindicates his name.*

  a. His name refers to two things:

    (1) Power (Acts 3:16).

    (2) Reputation (Cf. Num. 14:13-16).

b. And yet God magnifies his Word above his power and reputation – why?

   (1) He is more concerned about the truth of his integrity than what people say about him.

   (2) 'You can trust his Word and you can trust his name. Your name is only as good as your word. If you don't keep your word then you won't have a good name. If you do business with somebody and they don't keep their word you'll tell people not to go there, but if they are good you tell people that's where they ought to buy and so forth' (Adonica Howard-Browne).

c. Signs, wonders and miracles were first unveiled in the Bible when God revealed his name to Moses (Ex. 6:3).

d. Yet God wants his Word to be magnified above signs and wonders.

   (1) Salvation is more important than miracles.

   (2) Salvation was unveiled to Abraham (Gen. 15:6; Gal. 3:8), before the era of signs and wonders.

   (3) We are not saved by signs and wonders but by the gospel (Rom. 10:17).

C. We have to be careful to walk in obedience to every word.

1. *Jesus said that 'everything' must be fulfilled that is written about him in the Law, the prophets and the psalms* (Luke 24:44).

   a. 'Not the least stroke of a pen' would be omitted from the fulfilment of the Law (Matt. 5:18).

   b. This shows how clearly and carefully God regards every word he utters.

2. *Paul wanted what he wrote to be acknowledged as the Lord's command* (1 Cor. 14:37).

   a. This means we will give priority to the written Word:

   (1) Over a prophetic word or word of knowledge.

   (2) We will reject any word of knowledge which is contrary to the written word.

   b. We will not go by 'our feelings' or how we 'feel led' if those feelings go against the written Word.

   (1) This could be painful.

   (2) But it will show to what degree we esteem God's own written Word.

D. We will regard a conversion to Christ as the greatest miracle.

    1. *Conversion is a work of the Holy Spirit.*

        a. As much power is needed to convert as to raise the dead or heal the blind or deaf.

        b. After all, that is what conversion does: (1) Raises the dead (Eph. 2:1-8);.(2) Heals the blind (2 Cor. 4:4-5); (3) Heals the deaf (Matt. 13:13-15).

    2. *Conversion takes place because of the preaching of the gospel* (1 Cor. 1:21).

        a. The gospel is the good news that Jesus Christ, the God-man, has paid our debt on the cross.

        b. Many people, even in the church, do not grasp this nor see the implications.

    3. *This presupposes an evangelistic concern.*

        a. We should love evangelism as much as we love seeing other Christians blessed.

        b. We should be as zealous to see the lost saved as some are eager to see their fellow Christians be open to the Spirit.

E. We should desire the fruit of the Spirit as much as we do the gifts of the Spirit. (See 'Gift versus fruits of the Spirit', page 227).

CONCLUSION

Historically Christians have tended towards either a greater emphasis on the Word of God or on the work of the Holy Spirit. Are we prepared to admit we have not been as open to the Word as we should have been? Without in any way questioning the place of the Spirit, we must always be open to God speaking through his Word, the Bible. We will do that if we see it for what it is, God-breathed and inerrant. The Holy Spirit must be fully involved in our study of the Bible as it is only he who can open our eyes to what God is saying through it. We should pray that we will be so equally open to the Word and Spirit that it is impossible to say which excites us more.

5

THE STIGMA OF THE TRINITARIAN GOD

A. **Jonathan Edwards (1703-1752) preached a sermon 'Men are naturally God's enemies'; it could equally be stated that God is naturally man's enemy.**
1. He presented a concept of God and man that seems very alien to the 'popular' God that is heard of nowadays.
2. *The truth is, God is offensive – to the unsaved.*
   a. By referring to God we mean the God of the Bible.
   b. He is not lovable or likable to those who do not have the Holy Spirit.
3. *Some have sought to give God a better 'image' by presenting him in such a manner that nobody would be offended by him.*
   a. Some do this by emphasising one aspect of his nature to the neglect of other aspects of his nature. For example:
      (1) Speaking of his love but not his wrath, or justice.
      (2) Speaking of his tenderness but not his holiness.
      (3) Upholding Jesus but disowning the God of the Old Testament.
   b. Some do this by distorting what the Bible actually says about God:
      (1) Being selective with certain verses in scripture and changing the meaning or denying the existence of others.
      (2) Superimposing a way of interpreting the Bible that is alien to the purpose or understanding of the writers.

B. **In Romans chapter 1 Paul gives us a glimpse of the true God and man's natural response to him.**
1. *The Epistle to the Romans is the most complete statement of the gospel to be found in the New Testament.*
   a. Paul states early on that it is the gospel he will be writing about.

(1) 'The gospel he promised beforehand through his prophets in the Holy Scriptures' (Rom. 1:2).

(2) 'I am not ashamed of the gospel, because it is the power of God for the salvation of everyone who believes: first for the Jew, then for the Gentile' (Rom. 1:16).

b. The reason Romans is the most complete statement is that no apostle had been to Rome and Paul wanted to outline the gospel before his trip there.

(1) The other epistles were written to those who were familiar with his message.

(2) There was no need to say in writing all he had already preached.

2. *The first thing he does, having introduced the gospel, is to refer to God's wrath.*

a. 'The wrath of God is being revealed from heaven against all the godlessness and wickedness of men who suppress the truth by their wickedness' (Rom. 1:18).

b. The gospel itself had been introduced in the context of God's justice, or righteousness (Rom. 1:17).

3. *Then Paul proceeded to show how men rejected the true God:* 'Since what may be known about God is plain to them' (Rom. 1:19).

a. Such people did not accept this God, and 'their thinking became futile and their foolish hearts were darkened' (Rom. 1:21).

b. They rejected the true God and 'created' a god they could be comfortable with. 'And exchanged the glory of the immortal God for images made to look like mortal man and birds and animals and reptiles' (Rom. 1:23).

c. This is what has happened, generally speaking, in our day.

(1) The church has chosen to worship a god that suits her.

(2) Modern theology has mirrored the apostasy of the church. Apostasy (def.): falling away; the view that the church (speaking generally) is fallen, apostate.

C. The God of the Bible is a trinitarian God.

1. *This means God is revealed in three persons:*

   a. God the Father, usually seen as being the first person of the godhead:

      (1) The creator, the architect of providence and salvation (Gen. 1:1).

      (2) The Father of the Lord Jesus Christ (1 John 1:3).

   b. God the Son, the second person of the Trinity.

      (1) Before he became flesh he was known as the Word (John 1:1).

      (2) He is Jesus of Nazareth, born of the virgin Mary, lived for 33 years, died on a cross, rose from the dead, ascended to the right hand of the Father.

   c. God the Spirit, the third person of the Trinity.

      (1) He is eternal (Heb. 9:14) and, like the Father and the Son, has no beginning nor end.

      (2) He, along with the Son, created the world (Gen. 1:2; Col. 1:17) but became manifest as our Comforter or Advocate after Jesus ascended to heaven (John 14:16; Acts 2:1ff).

   d. Note: see 'The Trinity'; chapter 4 in *Understanding Theology, Volume 1.*

2. *The Trinitarian God is offensive to man.*

   a. He is not logically understood.

      (1) No man can logically explain the Trinity.

      (2) This in itself puts us off.

   b. He will have no other God beside himself.

      (1) That means he is all there is – take him or leave him!

      (2) If one opts for a different 'god' it will not be the God 'than which no greater can be conceived' – the only true God.

   c. The only way to God (and to heaven) is through his Son Jesus Christ.

      (1) 'Salvation is found in no-one else, for there is no other name under heaven given to men by which we must be saved' (Acts 4:12).

      (2) 'Jesus answered, "I am the way and the truth and the life. No-one comes to the Father except through me"' (John 14:6).

3. *Stigma (def.): offence.*
    a. Gr. *skandalov*, 'scandal'.
    b. It is used 15 times in the New Testament, e.g., Matthew
        13:41; Romans 9:33; 1 Corinthians 1:23.

D. Why is this study important?

1. *It is a reminder that God is a Trinity.*
    a. Central to orthodoxy (sound doctrine) is the Christian doctrine
        of the Trinity.
    b. This study brings us back to basics – the ABC of theology.

2. *It is a reminder of the sinfulness of man.*
    a. Modern theology, generally speaking, seems to gloss over
        man's depravity and sinfulness.
    b. We are to be reminded that there is that in all of us by nature
        that which is self-righteous and that feels our own
        understanding of God must be 'right'.
        (1) This study makes us face our distorted feelings about God.
        (2) It should help us to put our hands over our mouths, as Job
            did (Job 40:4). 'Surely I spoke of things I did not under-
            stand, things too wonderful for me to know' (Job 42:3).

3. *It lets God be himself.*
    a. As one has put it, 'letting God be God.'
    b. We will look at the character of God – but as he is, in three
        distinct persons.

4. *It shows that each person of the godhead has his own*
    offence.
    a. The Trinity alone is offensive to man.
    b. But we will see that each person is equally offensive; it is
        impossible to say which person of the Trinity is the most
        obnoxious to sinful man!

5. *It will let us see whether we can affirm God as he is and still*
    love him.
    a. A friend is one who knows all about you – and still likes you!
    b. This study will help us to get better acquainted with the true
        God and see whether we still like him!

I. THE STIGMA OF GOD THE FATHER: HIS PREROGATIVE

A. Prerogative (def.): the right or privilege that belongs to the Father.

   1. *God has certain rights or privileges because of who he is.*

      a. Many want to speak of rights, e.g.:

         (1) Human rights.

         (2) Animal rights.

         (3) Rights of certain minorities.

      b. We tend to forget that God has rights of his own.

         (1) The question is, will we give God his rights?

         (2) Will we let him be himself?

   2. *There are basically two ways of doing theology:*

      a. From man's point of view.

         (1) In this case, theology really becomes anthropology (the study of man).

         (2) 'What's in it for me?' governs man's outlook in studying theology.

      b. From God's point of view.

         (1) This aspect of doing theology has been almost completely lost in our generation.

         (2) 'What's in it for God?' should govern our outlook when doing theology.

B. The central theme that underlies a God-centred theology is that God owes man nothing.

   1. *This comes as a shock to many.*

      a. The natural feeling in us is that God has a lot to answer for.

         (1) He created the world without asking us.

         (2) He allowed evil when he could have stepped in.

      b. God surely owes man an explanation.

         (1) He should explain himself to us before he dare ask us to worship and obey him.

         (2) He should come on bended knee to man and apologise for all the suffering he has caused.

   2. *When we let God be God we take a different point of view.*

      a. He is what he is (Heb. 11:6).

         (1) He did not create himself.

         (2) He did not determine what he should be.

b. He is what he is because from everlasting to everlasting he is God (Ps. 90:2). For example:

(1) He is holy because he always was holy.

(2) He is omnipotent (all-powerful) because he always was all-powerful.

c. We therefore must learn to affirm him as he is.

(1) He is the only God there is!

(2) You cannot decide to worship God no. 2 or God no. 3.

3. *As he is in himself he is offensive to us.*

a. Before he ever *does* anything he is obnoxious to sinful man.

b. He therefore is not acceptable to us just because he is *there* and as he *is*.

4. *But the thought that he owes us nothing is indeed too much for us!*

a. Surely he must explain himself.

b. Surely he must apologise.

c. Surely he owes man nothing but happiness in this life and heaven to come.

C. But the offence of offences with God is his prerogative.

1. *In a word: God can give or withhold mercy and still be just.*

a. David Brainerd (1718-1747) sought to know and understand God and the more he searched the angrier he got! Brainerd discerned four things:

(1) God demands perfect righteousness.

    (a)   We can't produce it.

    (b)   This means we need a substitute.

(2) God demands perfect faith.

    (a)   We can't produce it.

    (b)   This means God must give it to us.

(3) God can give faith or withhold it and be just either way.

(4) God can save or damn and be just either way.

b. God said to Moses: 'I will cause all my goodness to pass in front of you, and I will proclaim my name, the LORD, in your presence. I will have mercy on whom I will have mercy, and I will have compassion on whom I will have compassion' (Ex. 33:19).

(1) Paul quoted this. 'I will have mercy on whom I have mercy, and I will have compassion on whom I have compassion' (Rom. 9:15).

(2) This means the word to Moses is applicable to each of us; therefore Paul concluded: 'It does not, therefore, depend on man's desire or effort, but on God's mercy' (Rom. 9:16).

2. *It is God's right, privilege and just decision to do whatever he decides to do.*

   a. According to Paul, God 'works out everything in conformity with the purpose of his will' (Eph. 1:11).

   b. God cannot make a mistake; he is incapable of it.

   (1) From our point of view this is scandalous.

   (2) From his point of view it is just.

   c. Paul anticipated man's reaction and answered it: 'One of you will say to me: "Then why does God still blame us? For who resists his will?" But who are you, O man, to talk back to God? "Shall what is formed say to him who formed it, 'Why did you make me like this?'" Does not the potter have the right to make out of the same lump of clay some pottery for noble purposes and some for common use?' (Rom. 9:19-21).

3. *Jesus affirmed God for being just like he is:* 'At that time Jesus said, "I praise you, Father, Lord of heaven and earth, because you have hidden these things from the wise and learned, and revealed them to little children. Yes, Father, for this was your good pleasure"' (Matt. 11:25-26).

   a. Why did God hide some things and reveal them to little children? For his good pleasure.

   b. Jesus said, 'All that the Father gives me will come to me, and whoever comes to me I will never drive away' (John 6:37).

   (1) Why did not God choose everybody?

   (2) Why did not God stop suffering long ago?

   (3) Why does not God explain himself to us?

   c. The problem is: his prerogative is most offensive to our unregenate minds.

II. THE STIGMA OF THE SON: HIS PROVISION

A. Provision (def.): What is provided, or supplied, for our need.

   1. *In a word: God's Son Jesus Christ is the only provision for our salvation.*

   a. God has provided us with a Saviour.

        (1) This was God's promise to Joseph: 'She will give birth to a son, and you are to give him the name Jesus, because he will save his people from their sins' (Matt. 1:21).

        (2) This pointed to the kind of Saviour the Messiah was predestined to be before he was born.

    b. The reason for his provision is that we are incapable of providing for ourselves.

        (1) God demands perfect righteousness, and we can't produce it.

        (2) It means we need someone to do it for us – a substitute.

2. *God provided this substitute by sending Jesus to die on a cross.*

    a. 'But God demonstrates his own love for us in this: While we were still sinners, Christ died for us' (Rom. 5:8).

        (1) 'Christ died for our sins according to the Scriptures' (1 Cor. 15:3).

        (2) 'He himself bore our sins in his body on the tree, so that we might die to sins and live to righteousness; by his wounds you have been healed' (1 Pet. 2:24).

    b. 'This is love: not that we loved God, but that he loved us and sent his Son as an atoning sacrifice for our sins' (1 John 4:10).

B. The stigma of the Son is two-fold:

  1. He is the only way by which we can come to God (John 14:6) and be saved (Acts 4:12).

  2. *His death on the cross is the only thing that satisfies God's justice.*

    a. His death atones for sin (Rom. 3:25): 'The one who would turn aside his wrath, taking away sin' (NIV margin).

    b. Being justified by his blood we are saved from God's wrath (Rom. 5:9).

C. This nullifies works as being the basis of salvation.

  1. *Paul asked, 'Where, then, is boasting?' The answer: 'It is excluded'* (Rom. 3:27).

    a. God has provided a sacrifice that takes away any opportunity for boasting – except to boast in Christ.

        (1) 'Therefore, as it is written: "Let him who boasts boast in the Lord"' (1 Cor. 1:31).

(2) 'May I never boast except in the cross of our Lord Jesus Christ, through which the world has been crucified to me, and I to the world' (Gal. 6:14).

b. This rules out salvation by any other means than through the blood of the Son:

(1) Every other religion.

(2) Even church membership or baptism.

2. *We are saved by faith alone – the provision of God's Son.*

a. 'This righteousness from God comes through faith in Jesus Christ to all who believe. There is no difference' (Rom. 3:22).

(1) Faith (def.): believing God, or his Word.

(2) We are saved by our persuasion that God's provision of a Redeemer who has done it all is what saves.

b. The bottom line: 'For it is by grace you have been saved, through faith – and this not from yourselves, it is the gift of God – not by works, so that no-one can boast' (Eph. 2:8-9).

D. All this is made more clear by the knowledge that God's provision became our high priest (Heb. 4:14).

1. 'But when this priest had offered for all time one sacrifice for sins, he sat down at the right hand of God' (Heb. 10:12).

2. *We therefore enter into God's presence only 'by the blood of Jesus'* (Heb. 10:19).

a. Our high priest ratified what was done on the cross.

b. He intercedes at the right hand of God for those God gave him.

(1) 'I pray for them. I am not praying for the world, but for those you have given me, for they are yours' (John 17:9).

(2) 'Because of this oath, Jesus has become the guarantee of a better covenant' (Heb. 7:22).

c. The stigma of the Father's prerogative is mirrored by the intercession resulting from the Son's priesthood.

III. THE STIGMA OF THE HOLY SPIRIT: HIS PRESENCE

A. Presence (def.): being present (in place); actually being there.

1. *The Holy Spirit is a person.*

a. He has feelings; he can be grieved or quenched.

(1) 'And do not grieve the Holy Spirit of God, with whom you were sealed for the day of redemption' (Eph. 4:30).

(2) 'Do not put out the Spirit's fire' (1 Thess. 5:19).

    b. It is offensive to us that such a mighty person can be hurt, and withdraw himself like a dove who flies quickly away.

2. *The person of the Spirit demands our respect.*

    a. We must take care not to grieve him.

    b. For him to be present among us is the highest honour ever accorded us.

        (1) Far more honouring than the presence of a monarch is the presence of the Spirit.

        (2) He demands more respect than a monarch dare expect.

B. But this stigma is intensified by the manner in which the Spirit chooses to reveal himself.

    1. *When he poured out himself on the Day of Pentecost the behaviour of the 120 shocked people.*

        a. They were accused of being drunk (Acts 2:13).

        b. That is because they were drunk with the Spirit!

        c. Note: because of the stigma of the Spirit's presence some refuse to invite him to be himself; they only want the Spirit to come so long as he does not disturb or upset us.

    2. *His turning up in power resulted in the sudden death of Ananias and Sapphira* (Acts 5:1-11).

        a. There was great offence in the Spirit doing this.

        b. The result: fear. 'Great fear seized the whole church' (Acts 5:11).

    3. His appearing in power resulted in the very *place* where the disciples assembled being shaken (Acts 4:31).

    4. It is what gave Peter great boldness: 'Then Peter, filled with the Holy Spirit, said to them: "Rulers and elders of the people! If we are being called to account today for an act of kindness shown to a cripple and are asked how he was healed, then know this, you and all the people of Israel: It is by the name of Jesus Christ of Nazareth, whom you crucified but whom God raised from the dead, that this man stands before you healed"' (Acts 4:8-10).

    5. It cost Stephen his life (Acts 7).

    6. It struck Saul of Tarsus to the ground (Acts 9:4).

7. The Spirit gave Peter strange visions (Acts 10).
8. The Spirit led to Gentiles being saved and this offended Jews (Acts 11).
9. Filled with the Spirit Paul told Elymas he would be struck blind (Acts 13:9-11).
10. The Spirit stopped Paul from preaching the gospel in Asia and Mysia (Acts 16:6-8).

C. We may well pray for the Spirit to come down.
1. But are we prepared for him to be himself?
2. Letting God be God applies to the Spirit!

CONCLUSION

Peter and John rejoiced that they were counted worthy to suffer the shame of Jesus' name (Acts 5:41). Anything that is of God carries a stigma or offence to those who are not born again. It would be unnatural for them not to be so offended. The Trinitarian God offends man's understanding as it is not logical that one God is three Persons nor is it seen to be 'fair' that he alone should be worshipped or that his will should be done. The Son of God causes offence by claiming to be the only means of salvation. And the Holy Spirit causes offence because he is the agent of God in the world today. Living the Christian live is not comfortable. We bear the offence of the gospel and should not therefore expect things to be easy for us.

6

THE UNKNOWN AND FORGOTTEN GOD

INTRODUCTION

A. When Paul addressed a group of pagan philosophers on the Areopagus he referred to the inscription 'TO AN UNKNOWN GOD' (Acts 17:23).
   1. Paul took advantage of this to unveil the true God (Acts 17:24-31).
   2. *There is sadly a sense in which this is needed in the church today.*
      a. Perhaps the least known subject in the church today is God himself.
         (1) There is a lot of emphasis on the effects of the Holy Spirit.
         (2) There is a lot of emphasis on worship and experience.
      b. What do we know about God?
         (1) The God of the Old Testament is largely the unknown and forgotten God.
         (2) The God of the New Testament is really not much better known!

B. There are basically two ways of doing theology:
   1. *From man's point of view.*
      a. This is the common approach today.
         (1) We have all been influenced by the 'me' generation and the 'what's in it for me?' era.
         (2) We assume that this is the way to approach God and the study of theology.
      b. Most theology could be more aptly called 'anthro-pology'.
         (1) Anthropology (def.): the study of man.
         (2) Theology that assumes that man must be at its centre is not pure theology at all.
   2. *From God's point of view.*
      a. This is to begin and end with God and see things through his eyes.

(1) When we look at God through our eyes we feel qualified to ask such questions as, 'How could the God of the Bible do this or that?'

(2) The very idea of hell is repugnant to us because we never ask, 'What if, from God's point of view, there is a different way of looking at things?'

b. From God's point of view man does not deserve the explanation man thinks is coming to him.

(1) From man's point of view: God has a lot to answer for and a lot of explaining to do.

(2) From God's point of view: man has a lot to answer for and a lot of explaining to do.

3. *If what has just been stated is offensive to you it proves:*

a. How far you have moved away from the atmosphere displayed in the Bible when God is showing himself.

(1) Yet there were similar eras in biblical history.

(2) It is summed up in the book of Judges, 'Everyone did as he saw fit' (Judg. 21:25).

b. Were God to turn up in power the whole church would have to shift gears quickly.'

(1) The gears would probably be stripped at once!

(2) But all would see why God is seen as 'awesome' ('terrible' AV) (Ps. 99:3).

C. This study is preparation for what is coming.

1. *I really believe a genuine awakening is coming – possibly sooner than any of us thinks.*

a. It will be an unveiling of the true God.

(1) He will be alien to so many.

(2) You may expect people to hate and despise him.

b. The God that unconverted and lukewarm church members think they can get on with is not God at all.

(1) *He* is man's natural enemy as much as man is God's natural enemy (Jonathan Edwards).

(2) We are as far removed from the true God today as was the picture Paul put in Romans chapter 1. 'They exchanged the truth of God for a lie, and worshipped and served created things rather than the Creator – who is for ever praised. Amen' (Rom. 1:25).

2. *This study will attempt to unveil the God who will be revealed in days to come.*

    a. Those who take on board this teaching will be best prepared for what is coming.

    b. They will be best equipped – and will be among God's sovereign vessels.

        (1) John 14:26 tells us that the Holy Spirit reminds us of what was already learned.

        (2) This lesson is a taste of what vessels the Holy Spirit will use.

D. Why is this lesson important?

  1. Most Christians today don't know their Bibles, especially the Old Testament.

  2. Many Christians think the Old Testament God is different from the one depicted in the New Testament.

  3. Many Christians do not know much theology, much less what is truly God-centred theology.

  4. The time is long overdue to remedy this.

  5. Nothing is so edifying or God-honouring as the unveiling of God himself.

I. THE GOD WHO IS JEALOUS FOR HIS OWN GLORY

A. His Name is Jealous (Ex. 34:14).

  1. *Jealousy in fallen man is one of his most unattractive traits.*

    a. It leads to murder (Gen. 4:1-8. Cf. Acts 7:9).

    b. It leads to the demonic taking over (1 Sam. 18:9-10).

        (1) It is what lay behind the enemies of Christ (Matt. 27:18).

        (2) It is what lay behind the enemies of the church (Acts 13:45; 17:5).

  2. *Jealousy in fallen man is what makes us hate God.*

    a. By nature we are jealous of his glory.

        (1) We hate a God who is depicted as he is in the Bible.

        (2) 'How dare God be like that?' the natural man says.

    b. We are naturally hostile to a God like that.

        (1) Before the Fall, being created in God's image, we were devoted to God as he is.

        (2) After the Fall, the capacity for jealousy was corrupted so that instead of loving his glory we resented it.

  3. *Conversion to Christ results in seeing God's glory and loving*
   it (2 Cor. 4:6).
    a. Until conversion we are blind to this (2 Cor. 4:4).
     (1) Satan was jealous of God's glory (Isa. 14:12ff).
     (2) The devil's hatred of God's glory is mirrored by man's
      similar feelings.
    b. If anyone, whether he professes to be a Christian or not,
     finds himself disgusted with the God of the Bible:
     (1) It shows his heart has not been broken (cf. Ps. 51:17).
     (2) The true Spirit of God has not revealed the true God to
      him (1 Cor. 2:14).
  4. *The unconverted man will settle for any 'god' but the God of*
   the Bible.
    a. He wants God to be what he thinks God *ought* to be.
     (1) A god man can control.
     (2) A god who will not punish.
    b. This is what Paul described in Romans 1.
     (1) Man wanted to worship himself (Rom. 1:23-25).
     (2) The result: God gave man up to a depraved mind (Rom. 1:28).

B. God is unashamedly jealous. 'You shall not bow down to them
or worship them; for I, the LORD your God, am a jealous God,
punishing the children for the sin of the fathers to the third and
fourth generation of those who hate me' (Ex. 20:5).
  1. *He will not stand for his people worshipping anything else or*
   anyone else but him.
    a. 'Be careful not to forget the covenant of the LORD your God
     that he made with you; do not make for yourselves an idol
     in the form of anything the LORD your God has forbidden.
     For the LORD your God is a consuming fire, a jealous God'
     (Deut. 4:23-24).
    b. 'Do not follow other gods, the gods of the peoples around
     you; for the LORD your God, who is among you, is a jealous
     God and his anger will burn against you, and he will destroy
     you from the face of the land' (Deut. 6:14-15).
  2. *To prove this he punishes even those who are called by his name.*
    a. Achan (Josh. 7).
    b. King Saul lost his anointing for not obeying totally (1 Sam.
     15:1-29).

      c. Moses was not allowed to enter the Promised Land (Deut. 32:48-52).

      d. The children of Israel died in the wilderness (Heb. 3:16-17).

C. God is jealous because he is a God of glory.

  1. *The glory of God is the sum total of all his attributes.*

    a. Attributes (def.): characteristics or qualities of a person; when of God we refer to his:

      (1) Omnipotence; he is all powerful.

      (2) Omniscience; he is all-wise, he knows everything.

      (3) Omnipresence; he is everywhere.

      (4) Holiness; his purity, or being wholly other (than anything created).

      (5) Justice; he is righteous, he must punish sin.

      (6) Mercy; he doesn't want to punish us.

      (7) Wrath; his anger toward sin.

      (8) Love; his overlooking sin by sending his Son.

    b. The one word that says all of the above: his glory.

      (1) *Kabodh* (Heb.): heaviness, weightiness.

      (2) *Doxa* (Gr.): praise, honour.

  2. *The glory of God is the nearest you get to his 'essence'.*

    a. By nature, then, God is glory.

      (1) It is his brilliance and light (John 1:5).

      (2) It is his sovereign will (Ex. 33:18-19).

    b. When he unveils himself, or manifests himself, it will be a seeing of his glory.

      (1) It is the greatest thing we can aspire to see (Ex. 33:18).

      (2) It is the greatest motive we can wish for (John 5:44).

D. God will not share his glory with another, that is, surrender it by letting a human being be worshipped (Isa. 42:8).

  1. *The worst mistake any person can make is to touch God's glory, that is, take credit for what is God's.*

    a. King Herod soon discovered this (Acts 12:21-23).

    b. So will any of us who could be so foolish.

  2. The only person to have it passed on to him without measure is Jesus Christ (Phil. 2:5-11; Rev. 5:12).

    a. We must bend the knee to him.

    b. We must seek his glory above all else.

(1) The desire for earthly glory may accomplish many things (Eccl. 4:4).

(2) But those God seeks to use aspire only to his glory (John 5:44).

3. *There is therefore no discontinuity between the God of the Old Testament and the God revealed in Christ.*

  a. He is the same God (Mal. 3:6; Heb. 13:8).

  b. Jesus never apologised for the God of the Old Testament.

  (1) Nor should we – ever.

  (2) He is Jesus' Father, and to see Jesus is to see this God (John 14:9).

II. The God whose Word has priority over his Name

A. The Word of God was revealed long before he revealed his Name.

  1. *The Word of God created the heavens and the earth.*

  a. 'And God said, "Let there be light," and there was light' (Gen. 1:3).

  b. In creating all that is, God merely spoke: 'Let...' (Gen. 1:6, 9, 11, 14, 20, 24, 26). And it happened.

  2. *The Word of God was the basis of his revealing himself.*

  a. Adam and Eve heard the 'sound' (AV 'voice') of the Lord God in the Garden (Gen. 3:8).

  b. It was always a case of God speaking (Gen. 3:10).

  (1) To Cain (Gen. 4:1-15).

  (2) To Noah (Gen. 7:1-4; 8:15-18).

  3. *The Word of God was how God manifested himself to the patriarchs.*

  a. To Abraham (Gen. 12:1-3; 15:1-5; 22:1-18).

  b. To Isaac (Gen. 26:24).

  c. To Jacob (Gen. 28:13; 32:28; 46:2-4).

  4. It may have been through a vision, a dream or an angel – but it was always the Word that was communicated.

B. The Name of God was revealed to Moses (c.1300 BC).

  1. *This came in response to Moses' own request, 'What is his name?'* (Ex. 3:13).

  a. God revealed himself to Moses and identified himself as 'the God of your father, the God of Abraham, the God of Isaac and the God of Jacob' (Ex. 3:6).

     b. God ordered Moses, 'So now, go, I am sending you to Pharaoh to bring my people the Israelites out of Egypt' (Ex. 3:10).

     c. It was then that Moses replied, 'Suppose I go to the Israelites and say to them, "The God of your fathers has sent me to you," and they ask me, "What is his name?" Then what shall I tell them?' (Ex. 3:13).

  2. *The reply: 'I AM WHO I AM. This is what you are to say to the Israelites: I AM has sent me to you'* (Ex. 3:14).

     a. 'God also said to Moses, "Say to the Israelites, 'The LORD, the God of your fathers – the God of Abraham, the God of Isaac and the God of Jacob – has sent me to you.' This is my name for ever, the name by which I am to be remembered from generation to generation"' (Ex. 3:15).

       (1) 'The LORD' is the Hebrew of *Yahweh*.

       (2) This was the Name of God, that means 'I am who I am' or 'I will be what I will be.'

     b. Then came the extraordinary statement: 'I appeared to Abraham, to Isaac and to Jacob as God Almighty, but by my name the LORD I did not make myself known to them' (Ex. 6:3).

       (1) This shows that the unveiling of God's name was withheld for hundreds of years, even though God made a covenant with the patriarchs.

       (2) The Word was the primary instrument of revelation.

  3. *The unveiling of God's name was paralleled by a new phenomenon: signs and wonders.*

     a. They began with the burning bush (Ex. 3:3).

     b. They continued with Moses' rod becoming a snake (Ex. 4:1-4).

     c. They increased with the ten plagues in Egypt (Ex. 7-12).

     d. The culmination was the two most extraordinary wonders of the Old Testament.

       (1) The Passover (Ex. 12:13-30).

       (2) The crossing of the Red Sea (Ex. 14:15-31).

C. The priority of the Word over the Name is seen in the New Testament.

  1. *The Second Person of the Godhead was revealed as the Word.*

     a. 'In the beginning was the Word, and the Word was with God, and the Word was God' (John 1:1).

b. It did not say, 'In the beginning was the Name.......'
   (1) The Word (Gr. *logos*) was chosen as the description of Jesus before he was born.
   (2) The Word was in the beginning with God – for he was God.
2. *When the gospel was given its fuller outline (the book of Romans), Paul summed up how to be saved:*
   a. 'But what does it say? "The word is near you; it is in your mouth and in your heart," that is, the word of faith we are proclaiming' (Rom. 10:8).
      (1) This is the way God had revealed himself to Abraham, who was justified by faith alone (Gen. 15:6).
      (2) This became Paul's chief illustration of the doctrine of justification by faith (Rom. 4:1-17).
   b. The gospel is conveyed by preaching.
      (1) 'For since in the wisdom of God the world through its wisdom did not know him, God was pleased through the foolishness of what was preached to save those who believe' (1 Cor. 1:21).
      (2) 'And at his appointed season he brought his word to light through the preaching entrusted to me by the command of God our Saviour' (Tit. 1:3).
3. *The phenomena of Pentecost made room for the Word.*
   a. There were extraordinary signs and wonders when the Spirit fell.
      (1) The violent wind (Acts 2:2).
      (2) The tongues of fire (Acts 2:3).
      (3) The speaking in other tongues (Acts 2:4).
   b. Peter pointed to these only to bring in two things, both of which related to the preaching of the word.
      (1) How it fitted with the Old Testament (Joel 2:28-32; Pss. 16:8-11, 110:1; Acts 2:14-40).
      (2) The preaching of the gospel: the reason for Jesus' death and resurrection and its mandate (Acts 2:22-24,29-33,36,38).
4. *The first great miracle was the occasion to preach the gospel* (Acts 3).
   a. The Name of Jesus was the only explanation for the miracle. 'By faith in the name of Jesus, this man whom you see and

know was made strong. It is Jesus' Name and the faith that comes through him that has given this complete healing to him, as you can all see' (Acts 3:16).

(1) This mirrored the phenomena in Moses' day.

(2) The Name of Jesus was held high because of signs and wonders (cf. Acts 19:17).

b. But the phenomena of signs and wonders that paralleled the power of the Name of Jesus was eclipsed by the gospel.

(1) Peter used the occasion to preach (Acts 3:12-26).

(2) The result of preaching: conversions (Acts 2:41, 4:4).

D. Signs and wonders were never pointed to as ends in themselves.

1. The Word was always magnified above the name.

2. This explains Psalm 138:2: 'You have magnified your word above all your name' (literal translation of the Hebrew).

CONCLUSION

A. There is no discontinuity between the Old Testament and the New Testament.

1. *Discontinuity (def.): a break in a continuous state.*

a. Some think the Old Testament put an end to the God revealed in it.

b. Wrong; the very same God who spoke to the fathers by the prophets spoke by his Son (Heb. 1:1-3).

2. *The New Testament continues the same truth about God.*

a. The Old Testament is the New Testament concealed.

b. The New Testament is the Old Testament revealed.

B. What are we to learn from this?

1. *Our God is the 'God of glory'* (Acts 7:2).

a. Stephen proclaimed the God of glory (Acts 7:2-53).

b. At Stephen's death the glory of God was manifested. 'But Stephen, full of the Holy Spirit, looked up to heaven and saw the glory of God, and Jesus standing at the right hand of God' (Acts 7:55).

2. *The principles of the glory of God are unveiled in Jesus' teachings. For example:*

a. Judging another is an act of self-righteousness. It is transferring to ourselves God's prerogative to judge (Matt. 7:1-2).

        (1) We must never, never, never do this.

        (2) Judging another is touching God's glory.

    b. Vindicating ourselves is the same thing.

        (1) God promises to vindicate (Deut. 32:35).

        (2) When we do it ourselves, it is touching the glory; therefore we are to 'Be merciful, just as your Father is merciful' (Luke 6:36).

3. *However much we may desire to see undoubted signs and wonders (and I do), we must never forget God's own priority.*

    a. Manifestations are never to be sought as an end in themselves.

    b. The gospel (which comes through preaching) is the heart of God.

7

THE MANIFESTATION OF GOD'S GLORY

INTRODUCTION

A. The previous study focused on the God of the Bible who is jealous for his glory.
   1. This study will attempt to apply this teaching.
   2. Theology must be applied; the purpose of theology is to change lives.

B. Since the glory of God is the nearest we can get to his 'essence', it follows that:
   1. *Any manifestation of God's glory will be a manifestation of himself.*
      a. There is a sense in which we could rightly say the glory of God *is* God.
      b. There are of course other ways of looking at God's glory (as we shall see), but the main thing to see is that:
      (1) God's glory is what pleases him.
      (2) The manifestation of his glory is the unveiling of himself.
   2. *The most noble and God-honouring request we can make is to ask God to manifest his glory.*
      a. Manifestation (def.): what is clearly apparent.
      (1) It is when what is unveiled is real and clear.
      (2) What may have been veiled (hidden from us) becomes unmistakeably clear.
      b. To ask God to manifest his glory is doing two things:
      (1) Asking him to show himself.
      (2) Asking him to be himself.
   3. *To ask God to show his glory is to set him free.*
      a. It is the most unselfish request we can make.
      (1) It is not asking him to do this or that for us.
      (2) It is asking him to do what he pleases.
      b. It is what Moses asked of God: 'Show me your glory' (Ex. 33:18).

(1) On the one hand it is a daring, if not almost impertinent request; it is asking God to unveil his heart – to tell all and unveil all.

(2) But it is equally unselfish; for it is not asking God to accommodate a request we may have – e.g., to heal or help out in a situation.

c. Illustration: our congregation's Prayer Covenant.

(1) In 1985 we came up with a Prayer Covenant that included the petition, 'That God would send true revival to Westminster Chapel.'

(2) In 1994 we simply put it, 'The manifestation of God's glory in our midst along with an ever-increasing openness in us to the manner in which he chooses to turn up.'

(3) Praying for revival could be restricting; praying for God to be himself is not.

C. The manifestation of the glory of God may be seen in two basic ways:

1. *Seeing him in what could be a physical way – that is, along the lines of our sense perception, e.g., with our naked eye, hearing or feeling him.*

   a. This could be a demonstration of healing.

   b. This could be seeing his glory as in a cloud.

   c. This could be an individual word of knowledge.

2. *Seeing him in a spiritual way – that is, realising what pleases him, what brings glory to him.*

   a. This could mean accepting the fact that he is pleased to do nothing in a situation – and being content with that.

   (1) The disciples were actually 'kept by the Holy Spirit from preaching the word in the province of Asia' (Acts 16:6).

   (2) They tried to enter Bithynia, 'but the Spirit of Jesus would not allow them to' (Acts 16:7).

   b. It could mean the power of his preached Word – giving insight that cannot be explained naturally.

   (1) 'When the people heard this, they were cut to the heart and said to Peter and the other apostles, "Brothers, what shall we do?"' (Acts 2:37).

   (2) 'Our gospel came to you not simply with words, but

also with power, with the Holy Spirit and with deep
conviction' (1 Thess. 1:5).

D. At the end of the day the manifestation of God's glory is what glorifies him.
   1. Not what may please us.
   2. Not what we may long to see.
   3. *But accepting his sovereign pleasure:*
      a. Not to reveal himself at all.
      b. To reveal himself in a way we had not thought of.

E. Why is this lesson important?
   1. *We are living at a time in which 'manifestations' are often spoken of.*
   2. *Manifestations are often sought or expected along particular lines.*
      a. In some churches 'lines' are literally drawn (or marked with tape) on the floor to keep people apart so they will not fall on top of each other and get hurt!
      b. Falling down is often expected; otherwise they would pray for people sitting where they were.
   3. *Such manifestations could narrow down in people's minds an expectancy which may well be beneath what God himself may want to do.*
      a. Standing in queues to be prayed for is often setting a limit in people's minds.
      b. Though it is often claimed that the manifestations are not the important thing, the fact remains that people in this type of situation don't really expect much beyond what they have clearly seen or heard of.
   4. *A distinction might well be made between 'manifestations' and 'the manifestation' of God's glory.*
      a. 'Manifestations' suggests only what is visible.
      b. 'The manifestation of God's glory' leaves the options entirely to a sovereign God who may have something in mind that exceeds our greatest expectations. 'Now to him who is able to do immeasurably more than all we ask or imagine, according to his power that is at work within us, to him be glory in the church and in Christ Jesus throughout all generations, for ever and ever! Amen' (Eph. 3:20-22).

5. We need to focus on God himself rather than on what he can do for us.

6. *We need to be open to any manner in which he may choose to reveal himself.*

   a. He is sovereign, which means he has the right to make choices – including whether or not to reveal himself at all.

   b. He may do what has been done before; he may do what is unprecedented.

   (1) It may be extremely offensive to us.

   (2) We may be utterly thrilled with what he does.

7. *This study honours the God who is jealous for his glory and whose Word is to be magnified above his Name* (Ps. 138:2,AV).

   a. We must develop a jealousy for his glory.

   b. We must develop a love for his word to be magnified above his name.

I. THE SUPREME MANIFESTATION OF GOD'S GLORY: HIS SON, 'THE RADIANCE OF GOD'S GLORY' (HEB. 1:3).

A. There are three major demonstrations of God's glory in biblical history, all of which centre on Jesus Christ.

   1. *Creation.* 'The heavens declare the glory of God; the skies proclaim the work of his hands' (Ps. 19:1).

   a. 'In the beginning was the Word, and the Word was with God, and the Word was God. He was with God in the beginning. Through him all things were made; without him nothing was made that has been made' (John 1:1-3).

   (1) When God said, 'Let there be light,' (Gen. 1:3), this was the Son speaking as well as the Father.

   (2) The Holy Spirit equally played a part in creation (Gen. 1:2).

   b. For by Jesus Christ 'all things were created. . . . He is before all things, and in him all things hold together' (Col. 1:16-17).

   2. *Redemption.* 'Guaranteeing our inheritance until the redemption of those who are God's possession – to the praise of God's glory' (Eph. 1:14).

   a. This was planned before Creation (Eph. 1:4; 2 Tim. 1:9).

   (1) It was first disclosed in the Garden of Eden (Gen. 3:15).

   (2) It was typified by the way in which Moses led Israel from bondage (Ex. 12:13).

    b. It was unveiled in the fullness of time, when God sent his Son, born of a woman (Gal. 4:4).

      (1) It was completed by Jesus' death on the cross (John 19:30).

      (2) Redemption was vindicated and guaranteed by Jesus resurrection from the dead (Rom. 1:4; 4:25).

3. *Christ's Second Coming.* 'They will see the Son of Man coming on the clouds of the sky, with power and great glory' (Matt. 24:30).

    a. '"Men of Galilee," they said, "why do you stand here looking into the sky? This same Jesus, who has been taken from you into heaven, will come back in the same way you have seen him go into heaven"' (Acts 1:11).

      (1) 'He must remain in heaven until the time comes for God to restore everything, as he promised long ago through his holy prophets' (Acts 3:21).

      (2) 'On the day he comes to be glorified in his holy people and to be marvelled at among all those who have believed' (2 Thess. 1:10).

    b. 'Just as man is destined to die once, and after that to face judgment, so Christ was sacrificed once to take away the sins of many people; and he will appear a second time, not to bear sin, but to bring salvation to those who are waiting for him' (Heb. 9:27-28).

B. The manifestation of God's glory than which no greater can be conceived is the Person of Jesus Christ. 'Anyone who has seen me has seen the Father' (John 14:9).

  1. *When John summed up the privilege of seeing Jesus he put it like this,* 'We have seen his glory, the glory of the One and Only, who came from the Father, full of grace and truth' (John 1:14).

    a. The greatest thing that can be said about God is that he is 'the God of glory' (Acts 7:2).

    b. The greatest thing that can be said about Jesus is that he is the glory of God (Heb. 1:3).

  2. *It is what Satan wants to hide most from men.* 'The god of this age has blinded the minds of unbelievers, so that they cannot see the light of the gospel of the glory of Christ, who is the image of God' (2 Cor. 4:4).

    a. Note: the gospel is 'the gospel of the glory of Christ.'

b. One cannot but fear that this aspect of the gospel, which to Paul was the chief thing, is largely forgotten in our day.

II. THE MANIFESTATION OF GOD'S GLORY TO HIS PEOPLE.

A. There are two words we should be reminded of:

1. *Kabodh* (Heb.): weightiness.

   a. We will have heard the expression 'to throw one's weight around'; that is the idea.

   b. God is 'weighty; and manifesting his glory is throwing his weight around.

2. *Doxa* (Gr.): praise.

   a. Our word 'doxology' comes from this.

   b. It comes from a root word that literally means 'opinion'; in this case, God's opinion.

3. Combining *Kabodh* and *doxa* you have the 'weight of God's opinion'.

   a. This means that his *will* flows from his opinion.

     (1) It may be his opinion that this or that be done.

     (2) When he wills something he reveals his opinion – his glory.

   b. Hence the glory of God may be understood as:

     (1) How he chooses to reveal himself (his presence).

     (2) The dignity of his will (what honours him).

   c. Therefore *any* manifestation of God's glory carries with it the weight of his opinion.

     (1) He does not reveal himself accidentally.

     (2) What he wills to do, he does.

B. One of the first and main ways God manifested his glory in ancient times was by a cloud.

1. *'While Aaron was speaking to the whole Israelite community, they looked towards the desert, and there was the glory of the* LORD *appearing in the cloud'* (Ex. 16:10).

   a. This was a seal of what God had been pleased to do.

     (1) It came as a result of Israel grumbling. 'And in the morning you will see the glory of the LORD, because he has heard your grumbling against him. Who are we, that you should grumble against us?' (Ex. 16:7).

     (2) God promised that they would see his glory by being filled with meat and bread (Ex. 16:12).

      b. The cloud indicated that God was powerfully at work.
  2. *This indicates that the pillar of cloud was how God was pleased to manifest his glory to Israel in guiding them.*
      a. 'By day the LORD went ahead of them in a pillar of cloud to guide them on their way and by night in a pillar of fire to give them light, so that they could travel by day or night' (Ex. 13:21. cf. Ex. 40:36-38).
      b. It was also used as a means of protection against the enemy (Ex. 14:19).
  3. *The same manifestation of God's glory appeared at Sinai.*
      a. 'When Moses went up on the mountain, the cloud covered it, and the glory of the LORD settled on Mount Sinai' (Ex. 24:15-16a).
      b. This was also the case at the Tent of Meeting (Ex. 40:34-35. cf. Num. 16:42).
      c. So too later on in the temple (1 Kings 8:11; cf. 2 Chron. 5:14).

C. The Ark of God

  1. *The Ark of God was an oblong chest overlaid with gold and covered by a slab of solid gold which was called the Mercy Seat* (Ex. 37:1-9).
      a. It was placed in the Most Holy Place, or Holy of Holies (Heb. 9:1-5).
      b. Once a year the Mercy Seat was sprinkled with blood; it was there that atonement took effect (Lev. 16).
      c. One of the reasons the glory appeared at the Tent of Meeting was because the Ark was there.
  2. But when it was later captured (1 Sam. 4:11), it was said that 'The glory has departed from Israel, for the ark of God has been captured' (1 Sam. 4:22).

D. In prophetic visions
  1. Isaiah 6:1-4.
  2. Ezekiel 1:28; 3:23; 10:4; 43:2.

E. Angelic visitation. 'An angel of the Lord appeared to them, and the glory of the Lord shone around them, and they were terrified' (Luke 2:9).

F. The heavenly voice (Matt. 3:16-17; 2 Pet. 1:17).

G. The transfiguration of Jesus (Luke 9:28-36).

H. The miracles of Jesus.
  1. At Jesus' first miracle, in changing the water into wine, it was said, 'He thus revealed his glory' (John 2:11).
  2. We may conclude from this that any such miracle or sign or wonder is a manifestation of God's glory (cf. John 11:40).

I. The inability to believe. 'For this reason they could not believe, because, as Isaiah says elsewhere: "He has blinded their eyes and deadened their hearts, so they can neither see with their eyes, nor understand with their hearts, nor turn – and I would heal them." Isaiah said this because he saw Jesus' glory and spoke about him' (John 12:39-41).
  1. Jesus had just performed miracles (John 12:17).
  2. Thus their being blinded is in one sense a manifestation of God's glory, difficult though this may be for us to accept.

J. Stephen's vision (Acts 7:55).

K. Christ in us, 'the hope of glory' (Col. 1:27).
  1. This is the greatest manifestation of God's glory that any of us can envisage.
  2. *It gives us hope for the present plus the what is to come.*
    a. To be glorified (Rom. 8:30; 1 John 3:2).
    b. To see Christ in his glory (John 17:24).

L. The glory of the Second Coming (Tit. 2:13).
  1. He will come in a cloud with power and glory (Luke 21:27).
  2. He will come in the Father's glory (Matt. 16:27).
  3. He will come in his own glory (Matt. 25:31).

M. The glory of the New Jerusalem (Rev. 21:11,23).

III. THE EFFECT OF GOD'S GLORY ON THOSE WHO EXPERIENCED IT

A. Trembling with fear (Ex. 20:18; Heb. 12:21).

B. Shouting for joy (Lev. 9:23-24; 1 Chron. 15:28).

C. Falling face down (Num. 16:42-45; Ezek. 1:28; 3:23; Rev. 1:17).

D. Being struck dead (1 Sam. 6:19; 2 Sam 6:7).

E. Crying 'Glory!' (Ps. 29:9. cf. 1 Pet. 1:8).

F. Conviction of sin – and obedience (Isa. 6:1-8).

G. Radiant face (Ex. 34:35; Acts 6:15).

H. Blindness (Acts 22:11).

I. Inability to perform normal work (2 Chron. 5:14).

CONCLUSION

Any manifestation of God's glory will be a manifestation of himself. God is manifest in many practical ways: in the history of his dealings with the children of Israel, in answered prayer, the power of the preached Word, healings, guidance etc. But God's glory cannot be more completely manifest than it was in the Person of Christ. Jesus said, 'Anyone who has seen me has seen the Father (John 14:9). Jesus on earth was the personification of the very glory of God.

8

THE REWARDING GOD

INTRODUCTION

A. Many of us are put off by the idea of reward. Why?

1. Some feel it is beneath our dignity to be motivated by reward.
2. Some are so turned off by the prosperity gospel that they resent anything that smacks of it.
3. We like to feel we would be equally motivated to serve God whether or not a reward was involved.
4. Some don't believe the concept of reward is biblical.
5. Some feel it is selfish to think of serving God in terms of reward.
6. Some believe that the grace of the Holy Spirit is sufficient to motivate and that any idea of reward shows contempt for the Holy Spirit's own power.
7. True godliness does not need or want motivation to obey God.
8. The absence of reward lets us completely off the hook if we are wanting to live as we please.

B. The Rewarding God (def.): God's essential nature (as a God of justice) to reward or punish according to man's response to his Word.

1. *Reward (def.): God's blessing in response to faith or obedience.*
   a. To faith, eternal life (John 3:16).
   b. To obedience, blessing (Heb. 11:6).
2. Retribution: deserved punishment due to unbelief or disobedience.
   a. To unbelief, eternal perishing (John 3:16).
   b. To disobedience, withholding of blessing (Gen. 4:13).
3. *Chastening, or disciplining (def.): enforced learning, which may precede or follow our behaviour* (Heb. 12:6).
   a. When chastening precedes: preparation for service (Heb. 12:7-9).
   b. When chastening follows: gracious judgement for our correction but which is preparation none the less (Heb. 12:10-11).

C. God is essentially a God of justice.

1. *The whole concept of Atonement is based upon God's justice.*

   a. Justice (def.): what God determines is fair; righteousness.

   b. Atonement (def.): to make amends for.

      (1) The blood of Jesus atones for our sins. 'God presented him as a sacrifice of atonement, through faith in his blood. He did this to demonstrate his justice because in his forbearance he had left the sins committed beforehand unpunished – he did it to demonstrate his justice at the present time, so as to be just and the one who justifies those who have faith in Jesus' (Rom. 3:25-26).

      (2) We are saved therefore by what he did – on the condition we have 'faith in his blood.' (Rom. 3:25).

2. *God's throne is essentially a throne of justice.*

   a. 'Righteousness and justice are the foundation of your throne' (Ps. 89:14).

   b. 'Then I saw a great white throne and him who was seated on it. Earth and sky fled from his presence, and there was no place for them. And I saw the dead, great and small, standing before the throne, and books were opened. Another book was opened, which is the book of life. The dead were judged according to what they had done as recorded in the books' (Rev. 20:11-12).

3. *God's justice lies behind all his dealings with people prior to the Final Judgement.* 'He is the Rock, his works are perfect, and all his ways are just. A faithful God who does no wrong, upright and just is he' (Deut. 32:4).

   a. 'The LORD within her is righteous; he does no wrong' (Zeph. 3:5).

   b. 'If we confess our sins, he is faithful and just and will forgive us our sins and purify us from all unrighteousness' (1 John 1:9).

4. *God likewise requires justice of us.* 'He has showed you, O man, what is good. And what does the LORD require of you? To act justly and to love mercy and to walk humbly with your God' (Mic. 6:8).

   a. 'Defend the cause of the weak and fatherless, maintain the rights of the poor and oppressed' (Ps. 82:3).

  b. 'The LORD's curse is on the house of the wicked, but he blesses the home of the righteous' (Prov. 3:33. cf. Prov. 11:1).

  c. 'So in everything, do to others what you would have them do to you, for this sums up the Law and the Prophets' (Matt. 7:12. cf. Phil. 4:8).

D. Why is this lesson relevant and important?

  1. It brings us face to face with an aspect of God's nature.

  2. It brings us face to face with our responsibility.

  3. It shows us that God is fair and reasonable.

  4. It makes us face the consequences of obedience and disobedience.

  5. It promotes holiness in our lives.

  6. It motivates us to greater blessing that we might otherwise have missed.

  7. It has serious implications with regard to the Judgement Seat of Christ.

I. THE OLD TESTAMENT PROMISES AND WARNINGS

A. We have been created in God's image (Gen. 1:26-27).

  1. *A sense of God's justice is imprinted on us by nature* (Rom. 1:20).

   a. It is called conscience (Rom. 2:15).

   b. This may be called a sense of fairness.

  2. *We were created with a propensity for motivation.*

   a. Propensity (def.): tendency, or inclination.

   b. This was true even in our pre-fallen state.

    (1) 'And the LORD God commanded the man, "You are free to eat from any tree in the garden; but you must not eat from the tree of the knowledge of good and evil, for when you eat of it you will surely die"' (Gen. 2:16-17).

    (2) This command assumes that man should be motivated by the consequence of his actions.

  3. *In our post-fallen state (the way all of us were born) we can be motivated by reward or fear of punishment.*

   a. God said to Cain, 'If you do what is right, will you not be accepted? But if you do not do what is right, sin is crouching at your door; it desires to have you, but you must master it' (Gen. 4:7).

    b. What Abel did was by faith. 'By faith Abel offered God a better sacrifice than Cain did. By faith he was commended as a righteous man, when God spoke well of his offerings. And by faith he still speaks, even though he is dead' (Heb. 11:4).

  4. *It is essential to our humanity that we are motivated by consequences.*

    a. To deny this is not only to show contempt for the way God made us; it is self-righteous.

      (1) To claim to be motivated by utter unselfishness is arrogance (1 John 1:8).

      (2) We grew up wanting parental approval; we mature in Christ wanting God's approval (Heb. 11:6).

    b. Those who claim to have moved beyond the need for motivation assume they are better then everybody else.

      (1) They implicitly deny the reason God motivates us: that he condescends to our level.

      (2) God motivates us because he knows what we are by nature.

B. The patriarchal period (before the Mosaic Law).

  1. *After this, the word of the* LORD *came to Abram in a vision:* 'Do not be afraid, Abram. I am your shield, your very great reward' (Gen. 15:1).

    a. God initially revealed himself to Abraham as Reward!

    b. Why? All of us need motivation to do the right thing.

    c. Some will say, 'God is my reward, all I need is God himself'.

      (1) True, but how does God bless us if not by what pleases us?

      (2) His presence alone suffices in one sense; but life goes on and we have to live.

      (3) Even heaven contains more than the presence of God; there is the beauty of heaven, the Tree of Life and such things as God will give us alongside his presence! (Rev. 21; 22).

  2. *When Abraham obeyed God by his willingness to sacrifice Isaac, God rewarded him with the oath* (Gen. 22:15-18).

    a. Abraham is a type of the Christian life (John 8:56; Rom. 4).

      (1) The gospel was preached to Abraham (Gal. 3:8).

      (2) We are saved in the same way as Abraham was saved (Gen. 15:6; Rom. 4:1-15).

    b. The writer of Hebrews appeals to Abraham's example that we might inherit the oath as Abraham did (Heb. 6:13-20).

(1) 'God is not unjust; he will not forget your work and the love you have shown him as you have helped his people and continue to help them' (Heb. 6:10).

(2) This is the essential meaning of Hebrews 11:6: 'And without faith it is impossible to please God, because anyone who comes to him must believe that he exists and that he rewards those who earnestly seek him.'

3. *Jacob made a vow at Bethel, that he would faithfully serve God and honour him in order to have God's blessing* (Gen. 28:20-22).

   a. God held Jacob to that vow (Gen. 31:13).

   b. Jacob later testified to God's faithfulness (Gen. 48:15-16).

C. From Moses (c. 1300 BC) until the time of Christ.

1. *The principle that governed the people of God was always this:* 'Those who honour me I will honour, but those who despise me will be disdained' (1 Sam. 2:30).

   a. A promise and a condition lie behind God's blessing:

      (1) 'Delight yourself in the LORD and he will give you the desires of your heart' (Ps. 37:4).

      (2) 'For the LORD God is a sun and shield; the LORD bestows favour and honour; no good thing does he withhold from those whose walk is blameless' (Ps. 84:11).

      (3) 'Wisdom is supreme; therefore get wisdom. Though it cost all you have, get understanding. Esteem her, and she will exalt you; embrace her, and she will honour you' (Prov. 4:7-8).

      (4) 'In all your ways acknowledge him, and he will make your paths straight' (Prov. 3:6).

      (5) 'Honour the LORD with your wealth, with the firstfruits of all your crops; then your barns will be filled to overflowing, and your vats will brim over with new wine' (Prov. 3:9-10).

   b. The warning is the same in reverse:

      (1) God said to Solomon, 'But if you or your sons turn away from me and do not observe the commands and decrees I have given you and go off to serve other gods and worship them, then I will cut off Israel from the land I have given them and will reject this temple I have consecrated for my Name. Israel will then become a

byword and an object of ridicule among all peoples' (1 Kings 9:6-7).

(2) 'The face of the LORD is against those who do evil, to cut off the memory of them from the earth' (Ps. 34:16).

(3) 'I have seen a wicked and ruthless man flourishing like a green tree in its native soil, but he soon passed away and was no more; though I looked for him, he could not be found' (Ps. 37:35-36).

(4) 'Then they will call to me but I will not answer; they will look for me but will not find me. Since they hated knowledge and did not choose to fear the LORD, since they would not accept my advice and spurned my rebuke' (Prov. 1:28-30).

(5) 'Be sure of this: The wicked will not go unpunished' (Prov. 11:21).

2. *The Mosaic covenant is laced with the teaching of reward and punishment depending on obedience.*

  a. 'All these blessings will come upon you and accompany you if you obey the LORD you God' (Deut. 28:2).

    (1) Material blessing was promised (Deut. 28:3-6,8).

    (2) Vengeance against the enemy was promised (Deut. 28:7).

    (3) All people will fear God's people (Deut. 28:10).

    (4) The people of God will be 'at the top, never at the bottom' (Deut. 28:13).

  b. 'However, if you do not obey the LORD your God and do not carefully follow all his commands and decrees I am giving you today, all these curses will come upon you and overtake you' (Deut. 28:15).

    (1) The absence of material blessing (Deut. 28:16-19).

    (2) Plague of diseases will come (Deut. 28:20-22).

    (3) Defeat before God's enemies will take place (Deut. 28:25).

    (4) God's people would be the subject of scorn (Deut. 28:37).

3. *Many in Israel assumed that, owing to the above promises, any withholding of material blessing or presence of disaster or disease was due to sin.*

  a. This is why Job was misunderstood.

  b. The book of Job shows that, despite the intervention of the Mosaic Law, a greater covenant was ultimately to be recognised:

(1) The covenant God made with Abraham.

(2) The Psalmist saw beyond the Mosaic Law, namely the covenant promises in Christ (Ps. 51, 101).

II. THE NEW TESTAMENT PROMISES AND WARNINGS

A. The gospel of Jesus Christ

1. *The gospel ratifies (confirms) God's covenant with Abraham* (John 8:56; Gal. 3:15-18).

    a. The blessings of the gospel are given on the condition of faith (John 3:16; Rom. 3:25).

        (1) This is why Paul spoke of the 'obedience of faith' (AV) or the 'obedience that comes from faith' (Rom. 1:5).

        (2) Paul said to Agrippa, 'I was not disobedient to the vision from heaven' (Acts 26:19).

    b. We are saved by faith, as Abraham (Rom. 4:1-25).

        (1) It is by believing the promise (Gal. 3:6-7).

        (2) This makes us the seed of Abraham (Gal. 3:26-29).

2. Jesus fulfilled the Mosaic Law (Matt. 5:17).

    a. He kept it totally, having never sinned (Heb. 4:15).

    b. He is therefore the 'end of the law so that there may be righteousness for everyone who believes' (Rom. 10:4).

3. We therefore are not under the Law (Gal. 3:13).

    a. We are not under its 'supervision' (Gal. 3:25).

    b. 'So I say, live by the Spirit, and you will not gratify the desires of the sinful nature' (Gal. 5:16).

        (1) We are not saved or kept saved by works (Eph. 2:8-9).

        (2) We are not in danger of losing our salvation by fear of punishment (Gal. 3:10-11).

B. The place of reward and punishment in the light of the gospel:

1. *The unbeliever has no hope beyond the grave* (John 3:16).

    a. The gospel is not what damns (John 3:17).

    b. Those condemned were condemned anyway (John 3:18).

        (1) The condemned will go to eternal Hell (Matt. 25:41-46).

        (2) They will have been judged by their works (Rev. 20:11-16).

2. *The believer is given eternal life* (John 3:16).

    a. This means imputed righteousness (Rom. 4:5).

    b. This means forgiveness of sins (Eph. 1:7).

    c. He cannot lose his salvation (Rom. 8:30).

    d. He will go to heaven when he dies, to be raised up with Christ at his coming (1 Thess. 4:14-18).

C. The place of reward in the Christian life

  1. *Regarding persecution* (Matt. 5:10-12).

    a. 'Great is your reward in heaven' (Matt. 10:12).

    b. Earthly benefit: more power (Acts 4:23-31).

  2. *Regarding tribulation, or trial* (John 16:33).

    a. 'The crown of life' (Jas. 1:12).

    b. Maturity, and the kingdom of God (Jas. 1:2-4; Acts 14:22).

  3. *Regarding financial generosity* (2 Cor. 9:6-8).

    a. 'Treasure in heaven' (Matt. 6:19-21; Phil. 4:17).

    b. 'Having all you need .... supplying the needs of God's people' (2 Cor. 9:8,12).

  4. *On receiving an anointed person* (Matt. 10:41-42).

    a. A prophet's reward (Matt. 10:41).

    b. A righteous man's reward (Matt. 10:41).

    c. Note: 'And if anyone gives even a cup of cold water to one of these little ones because he is my disciple, I tell you the truth, he will certainly not lose his reward' (Matt. 10:42).

  5. *Prayer* (Luke 18:1).

    a. Stored in heaven (Rev. 5:8).

    b. Availing much here below (James 5:16).

  6. *Giving up what is precious, e.g., home, family, possessions* (Matt. 19:27-29).

    a. 'Will receive a hundred times as much.'

    b. Not to mention, 'will inherit eternal life.'

  7. *Holiness or walking in the light* (1 John 1:7; Gal. 6:7-9).

    a. The consciousness of the cleansing blood.

    b. Fellowship with the Father.

  8. *Waiting on God with expectancy* (Luke 12:35-40).

    a. The Lord will serve us (Luke 12:37).

    b. Confidence in waiting 'will be richly rewarded' (Heb. 10:35).

  9. *Loving your enemies* (Matt. 9:43-48).

    a. 'If you love those who love you, what reward have you? (Matt. 7:46).

    b. The obvious conclusion: reward from God comes from loving your enemies (totally forgiving them).

10. *Praying, fasting, giving in secret* (Matt. 6:1-18).

   a. Doing such to be seen: you forfeit your reward.

   b. Doing such not to be seen: a reward from the Father.

D. The place of punishment in the Christian life:

   1. *Death* (1 John 5:16. cf. 1 Cor. 3:17).

      a. Lying to the Holy Spirit (Acts 5:1-11).

      b. Showing contempt at the Lord's Supper (1 Cor. 11:30).

   2. *Illness.*

      a. Unconfessed sin (Jas. 5:15-16).

      b. Showing contempt at the Lord's Supper (1 Cor. 11:31).

   3. Being handed over to Satan (1 Cor. 5:5; 1 Tim. 1:20).

   4. When God swears in his wrath (Heb. 3:11).

      a. The inability to enter God's Rest (Heb. 4:1-7).

      b. The inability to be renewed to repentance (Heb. 6:4-6).

   5. Chastening, or disciplining (gracious judgement) (Heb. 12:5-11).

      a. Internal chastening (through God's Word).

      b. External chastening (through circumstances).

      c. Terminal chastening (when God swears in wrath).

         (1) Death (1 John 5:16).

         (2) Forfeiting God's Rest (Heb. 4:1-6; Heb. 6:6).

E. The Judgement Seat of Christ (1 Cor. 3:10-15; Rom. 14:10-12; 2 Cor. 5:10)

   1. *All who are on the Foundation (Christ) are saved* (1 Cor. 3:11).

      a. The Foundation is Christ.

      b. All in Christ are saved.

   2. *The Foundation is like a superstructure.*

      a. We must make a choice of the materials.

         (1) Gold, silver, costly stones (holiness).

         (2) Wood, hay, straw (disobedience).

      b. The superstructure is visible and it will eventually be 'shown for what it is' (1 Cor. 3:13).

   3. *The Day of Christ will bring the superstructure to light.*

      a. It will be revealed by fire, which will test the quality of everyone's work.

      b. It will be visible for all to see.

4. *If after the fire the superstructure survives, 'the believer will receive his reward.'*
   a. Gold, silver, costly stones will survive.
   b. Wood, hay, straw will be burned up.
5. *The person will suffer loss of reward.*
   a. He will be saved none the less (once saved, always saved).
   b. But he will be saved by fire.

CONCLUSION

Does the idea of reward matter to you? It mattered to Paul. He wanted that reward, the prize, the crown. Yet, as he says in 1 Corinthians 9:25-27, he did not take it for granted: 'No, I beat my body and make it my slave so that after I have preached to others, I myself will not be disqualified for the prize' (1 Cor. 9:27). In 2 Timothy 4:8 he seemed assured of it. 'Now there is in store for me the crown of righteousness, which the Lord, the righteous Judge, will award to me on that day – and not only to me, but also to all who have longed for his appearing.'

The concept of a reward is one that embarrasses some Christians. This should not be the case. It is not something man thought up, it is taught in God's Word. God's people may be rewarded both on earth and in heaven. But we may not assume their reward. Our salvation is for ever secure but that is not true of our reward. The Christian can forfeit his reward by a lack of holy living.

9

THE PATIENCE OF GOD

INTRODUCTION

A. It will be recalled that there are two ways of doing theology:
 1. *From man's point of view – the common way it is done nowadays.*
    a. Most theology today is really anthropology (study of man).
    b. This is a 'What's in it for me?' age.
 2. *From God's point of view – rare these days.*
    a. The Bible is God-centred theology.
    b. It is approaching theology from God's own perspective.

B. We must look at the present subject from God's point of view.
 1. Most of us tend to think of patience in terms of our own interests.
 2. *In this lesson we shall attempt to 'get into God's skin' as it were; to see patience from his perspective:*
    a. How patient he is with us.
    b. How patient he is in waiting for his own vindication.

C. Patience (def.): the ability to wait without speaking or acting.
 1. Gr. *hupomone* from the verb that means 'to wait'; it can also mean 'to expect' or 'to persevere'; used 32 times in the New Testament.
 2. Gr. *makrothumeo*; 'to endure', 'to have patience', the idea being putting up with hardships until the goal is reached.
 3. These words will of course be crucial for how we cope with delay'; but we need to see these meanings from God's point of view.
    a. Romans 15:5 refers to the 'God of patience (*hupomone*)' (AV).
    b. 1 Peter 3:20 says 'God waited patiently (*makrothumia*).'
    c. 2 Peter 3:9: 'He is patient (*makrothumia*) with you.'
    d. 2 Peter 3:15: 'Our Lord's patience (*makrothumia*).'

> **e.** Revelation 1:9: 'The patience of Jesus Christ (*hupomone*)' (AV).

4. *The patience of God is his ability to wait before he acts.*

> **a.** What God will require of us is but a drop in the bucket compared to the kind of patience he has displayed for thousands of years.
>
> **b.** This study hopes to give us but a glimpse of his unlimited patience.

D. Why is this lesson important?

1. It is God-centred, and any theological lesson worth its salt will be precisely that.

2. It focuses on one of God's attributes (characteristics), though less known than the others, such as his omnipotence (unlimited power), omniscience (unlimited knowledge and wisdom) and omnipresence (that God is everywhere).

3. *It gives a glimpse of real suffering.*

> **a.** Do you think you have suffered?
>
> **b.** The truth is, we have gone through nothing compared with what God has endured.

4. It enables us to see afresh how patient God is with us.

5. It is a lesson in vindication (when one's name is cleared); God is the most unvindicated being in all history and he still waits to have his own name cleared.

6. We are going to see something of the patience of Jesus, who in the days of his flesh mirrored his Father's patience.

I. THE PATIENCE OF GOD IN THE OLD TESTAMENT

A. Note: the most neglected part of the Bible for many Christians is the Old Testament.

1. *The Old Testament was Jesus' Bible.*

> **a.** The God of the Old Testament was Jesus' Father.
>
> **b.** Jesus learned the Old Testament as he grew up.
>
> > **(1)** If we are to be like Jesus in every way we should wish to know what he knew before he was launched into his public ministry.
> >
> > **(2)** This for some may open a new vista on how to be more like Jesus.

2. *The Old Testament was the early church's only Bible* (2 Tim. 3:16).

    a. The gospel was to the Jew first (Rom. 1:16).

        (1) To the Jews were given 'the very words of God' (Rom. 3:1-2) (the way Paul saw the Old Testament).

        (2) Israeli history is the Christians' pre-history.

    b. The earliest Christians did not have our New Testament.

        (1) They searched the scriptures to see how Christ was the fulfilment of ancient Israel's expectation.

        (2) I have often suspected that when true revival comes we too will see insights into the Old Testament which the early Christians saw but which may not have been recorded in the Book of Acts.

B. In Noah's day

1. *Wickedness increased as never before.* 'The LORD saw how great man's wickedness on the earth had become, and that every inclination of the thoughts of his heart was only evil all the time' (Gen. 6:5).

    a. The Lord was grieved that he had made man, 'and his heart was filled with pain' (Gen. 6:6).

        (1) Some have offered the opinion that God does not suffer; that he is impassive (incapable of feeling pain).

        (2) Genesis 6:6 refutes this idea.

    b. 'So the LORD said, "I will wipe mankind, whom I have created, from the face of the earth – men and animals, and creatures that move along the ground, and birds of the air – for I am grieved that I have made them"' (Gen. 6:7).

2. *God said, 'My Spirit will not contend with man forever.'* (Gen. 6:3). *'My Spirit shall not always strive with man'* (AV).

    a. This verse shows that, however forbearing, there comes a time when God says, 'Enough is enough.'

    b. 'But Noah found favour in the eyes of the LORD' (Gen. 6:8).

3. *Peter said that 'God waited patiently in the days of Noah while the ark was being built'* (1 Pet. 3:20).

    a. During this time Christ was in Noah by the Spirit and preached to that wicked generation (1 Pet. 3:18-20).

        (1) This is one of the most difficult verses in the Bible.

        (2) The key is in 1 Peter 4:6; those Christ (through Noah) preached to are 'now dead', they are now 'spirits in prison' (1 Pet. 3:19) but they were very much alive in Noah's day.

b. The building of the ark took a lot of time, during this time Noah preached.

   (1) The people rejected Noah.

   (2) God waited until the ark was built and the flood came and destroyed all mankind.

4. *This shows God's ability to wait for years and years and years before he finally demonstrates his wrath.*

   a. We may ask, 'How can God endure the wickedness and blasphemy in our day?'

   b. The answer: he has done it before, and time is on his side.

C. From Abraham to Moses

1. *God saw in advance how long it would be before he would begin to deliver God's people.*

   a. 'Then the LORD said to him, "Know for certain that your descendants will be strangers in a country not their own, and they will be enslaved and ill-treated four hundred years"' (Gen. 15:13).

   b. Paul reckoned that it was 'about 450 years' from the time of this promise until Abraham's seed was back in Canaan (Acts 13:20).

2. *The seed of Abraham came through Isaac, Jacob and his twelve sons.*

   a. It was Joseph's removal to Egypt that led to Israel following him.

   b. The people of Israel, thanks to Joseph and Pharaoh, prospered in Egypt.

3. *But a new king, who owed nothing to Joseph, turned against the Israelites* (Ex. 1:8-14).

   a. The people of Israel became slaves (Ex. 1:11).

   b. The order came for every male child to be killed (Ex. 1:16).

4. *At long last God raised up a deliverer – Moses* (Ex. 2:1ff).

   a. But Israel would still wait a long time before they had the benefit.

   (1) Moses left Pharaoh's palace when he was 40, hoping then to become Israel's deliverer (Acts 7:23. Heb. 11:24-27).

(2) But it was yet another 40 years before Moses was ready
        – at the age of 80!
  b. 'The LORD said, "I have indeed seen the misery of my people
        in Egypt. I have heard them crying out because of their slave
        drivers, and I am concerned about their suffering"' (Ex. 3:7).
  5. *This shows God's patience even when he is working for the*
        good of his people!
    a. And even then Moses had to prove himself – to his own
          people and to Pharaoh.
    b. In a word: God is in no hurry, even when he is at work to
          save his people.

D. Moses and the Children of Israel in the desert
  1. Despite their spectacular deliverance, the people who had been
        redeemed and delivered turned to idolatry (Ex. 32:1-6).
  2. *When given an opportunity to enter Canaan, they chose not to*
        take it (Num. 14).
    a. God swore in his wrath that they would not enter into his
          rest (Heb. 3:11).
    b. They didn't; all but Caleb and Joshua died in the desert
          (Heb. 3:16-19).
  3. *This shows God's patience and his wrath.*
    a. They were forgiven (Num. 14:20). This shows that they
          were a saved people.
    b. But they forfeited their inheritance (Num. 14:23). This shows
          that they would have no reward in heaven.

E. Summary:
  1. 'And he passed in front of Moses, proclaiming, "The LORD, the
        LORD, the compassionate and gracious God, slow to anger,
        abounding in love and faithfulness, maintaining love to
        thousands, and forgiving wickedness, rebellion and sin. Yet
        he does not leave the guilty unpunished; he punishes the
        children and their children for the sin of the fathers to the third
        and fourth generation." Moses bowed to the ground at once
        and worshipped' (Ex. 34:6-8).
  2. God's punishment of his people is 'less then our sins have
        deserved' (Ezra 9:13. cf. Ps. 103:8-13).
  3. 'For he knows how we are formed, he remembers that we are
        dust' (Ps. 103:14).

II. The patience of God in the New Testament

A. No doubt many prophets hoped to see the fulfilment of their words in their own time.

1. What Isaiah saw concerning Jesus (e.g. Is. 53) would take 700 years before its fulfilment.
2. 'For I tell you the truth, many prophets and righteous men longed to see what you see but did not see it, and to hear what you hear but did not hear it' (Matt. 13:17).

B. But God had his own time-plan and schedule.

1. God could have sent Jesus long before he did had he wanted to. Moreover, he could have waited – so that we too could have been in the Old Testament era!
2. *'But when the time had fully come, God sent his Son, born of a woman, born under law, to redeem those under law, that we might receive the full rights of sons'* (Gal. 4:4-5).
   a. This was nearly 400 years after the last Old Testament prophet (Malachi).
   b. This followed much persecution in the inter-testamental period (between Malachi and the coming of John the Baptist).

C. Jesus himself waited 30 years before he began his ministry.

1. *Jesus exhibited extreme patience during the following three years.*
   a. With his enemies. 'He sighed deeply and said, "Why does this generation ask for a miraculous sign? I tell you the truth, no sign will be given to it"' (Mark 8:12).
   b. With his disciples.
      (1) 'But when Jesus turned and looked at his disciples, he rebuked Peter, "Get behind me, Satan!" he said. "You do not have in mind the things of God, but the things of men"' (Mark. 8:33).
      (2) 'Peter said to Jesus, "Rabbi, it is good for us to be here. Let us put up three shelters – one for you, one for Moses and one for Elijah"' (Mark 9:5).
      (3) James and John replied, 'Let one of us sit at your right and the other at your left in your glory' (Mark 10:37).
      (4) Having told Peter he would deny him, Jesus expressed his unconditional love (John 13:37-14:1. cf. Luke 22:31ff).

2. *Patience in his suffering*
   a. All his disciples forsook him and fled (Matt. 26:56).
   b. He had just said to them, 'Could you men not keep watch with me for one hour?' (Matt. 26:40).
   c. He never lost his temper under the most extreme conditions.
      (1) Herod 'plied him with many questions, but Jesus gave him no answer' (Luke 23:9).
      (2) He demonstrated the same control with Pilate (John 19:8-11).
      (3) He prayed for the soldiers who crucified him (Luke 23:34).
      (4) He never retorted once to those around him.
      (5) He never tried to explain to anyone what was really happening (atonement for sin).
   d. His patience was partly motivated by 'the joy set before him' while he endured the cross and scorned its shame (Heb. 12:2).

D. **This patience was also for our sakes, so that he could sympathise with us when he became our great High Priest. (Heb. 4:14-15).**
   1. He was made perfect through suffering (Heb. 2:10. cf. Heb. 5:8).
   2. 'Because he himself suffered when he was tempted, he is able to help those who are being tempted' (Heb. 2:18).
   3. For that reason he can sympathise with our weaknesses (Heb. 4:15).

E. **His patience with Saul of Tarsus**
   1. *Saul witnessed Stephen's defence before the Sanhedrin and his being stoned* (Acts 8:1).
      a. This means he saw Stephen's face shining like an angel. (Acts 6:15).
      b. It made no impact at the time that we know of; Saul guarded the clothes of those who killed Stephen (Acts 22:20).
   2. *He breathed out murderous threats against the disciples* (Acts 9:1).
   3. *He got permission to imprison them* (Acts 9:2).
   4. *He succeeded in getting them into prison* (Acts 26:10).
   5. *He tried to force them to blaspheme* (Acts 26:11).

    a. God might have intervened and struck Saul down.

    b. He did do that in fact, but in mercy!

       (1) The rest is famous history (Acts 9:1-12).

       (2) God decided to exercise patience! 'I was shown mercy' (1 Tim. 1:13).

       (3) 'Here is s trustworthy saying that deserves full acceptance: Christ Jesus came into the world to save sinners – of whom I am the worst. But for that very reason I was shown mercy so that in me, the worst of sinners, Christ Jesus might display his unlimited patience as an example for those who would believe on him and receive eternal life' (1 Tim. 1:15-16).

III. THEOLOGY OF THE PATIENCE OF GOD

A. The explanation for God's patience

    1. *His nature.* 'But do not forget this one thing, dear friends: With the Lord a day is like a thousand years, and a thousand years are like a day' (2 Pet. 3:8).

    a. God lives in the present.

       (1) He 'inhabits eternity' (AV). 'Lives forever' (Isa. 27:15).

       (2) Eternity is an everlasting now.

    b. God by nature is in no hurry

    2. *His satisfied justice* (Isa. 53:11).

    a. The blood of Jesus perfectly and totally satisfied God's justice.

       (1) He looks to no other source than his Son's death.

       (2) Therefore he has no need to punish at the moment.

    b. Since Christ is 'the lamb slain from the creation of the world' (Rev. 13:8) his blood began to work from then.

    3. *His knowledge of the future.* 'I make known the end from the beginning, from ancient times, what is still to come. I say: My purpose will stand, and I will do all that I please' (Isa. 46:10).

    a. God knows his purposes will not be thwarted in the end.

       (1) He sees the end from the beginning.

       (2) He therefore is in no hurry to make things happen now.

    b. What is more, time is on his side.

B. God can wait long before he steps in to convert us.
1. *When the blood cleanses from all sin (1 John 1:7), it does not mean there is no sin in us that does not need correcting.*
   a. Indeed, 1 John 1:8 assures us that we have sin: 'If we claim to be without sin, we deceive ourselves and the truth is not in us.'
   b. It follows that the blood of Christ allows God to use us and bless us despite ourselves.
      (1) Elijah wasn't perfect, but God used him and waited to correct him after his finest hour (1 Kgs. 18:22; 19:18).
      (2) Peter was used on the Day of Pentecost but subsequent events show that Peter had more correction coming (Acts 10. cf. Gal. 2:11-14).
2. *We therefore should never underestimate God's mercy with one individual, neither should we overestimate their piety.*
   a. God can use anybody, often one you and I would reject.
   b. It is not because of how ready or right they are; it is God's patience at work.
   c. This means that there is hope for you and me!

C. God can wait long and invest a lot of time in a person before he or she is used.
1. *Consider how long he waited before helping Israel.*
   a. Joseph waited 22 years before his own vindication.
   b. Moses waited 40 years before he began to lead Israel.
2. *Consider how often we have grieved his Spirit during our own time of preparation.*
   a. When the Spirit is grieved he feels it?
   b. This means the Holy Spirit *feels* it when we are bitter or unforgiving (Eph. 4:30ff).
   c. Yet the Spirit is patient with us!

D. God can be pleased with us and angry with us at the same time.
1. *On what basis is he pleased with us?*
   a. He chose us; he never misfires (Rom. 9:15).
   b. He sees the end from the beginning and deals with us as we will be, not because of what we are (Isa. 46:10).
   c. When we walk in the light the blood of Jesus allows God to fellowship with us (1 John 1:7).

(1) This allows God, little by little, to show us our sin.

(2) As we accept his correction the fellowship continues.

2. *On what basis is he displeased with us?*

    a. He knows what needs correcting and cannot be pleased with our selfishness and greed. 'I was enraged by his sinful greed; I punished him, and hid my face in anger, yet he kept on in his wilful ways' (Isa. 57:17).

        (1) This shows God's efforts to reach us by chastening.

        (2) It shows that it takes time for us to come to terms with what is wrong with us.

    b. But God doesn't give up on us. 'I have seen his ways, but I will heal him; I will guide him and restore comfort to him' (Isa. 57:18).

        (1) He stays with us.

        (2) He remembers that we are dust (Ps. 103:14).

3. *He may even wait until just before the end to deal with us for our most obvious sin!*

    a. We can always see the obvious fault in others.

    b. We are the last to see it in ourselves.

    c. God saw it all along but did not become disillusioned with us at any point along the journey.

        (1) He can wait when he is angry.

        (2) He can wait when he is pleased and not let us know that as well! (Luke 17:10).

CONCLUSION

I have long suspected that the angrier God is, the longer he waits (Rom. 1:21ff). When we get angry, we tend not to hide it for long. God can hide it for a long, long time. 'What if God, choosing to show his wrath and make his power known, bore with great patience the objects of his wrath – prepared for destruction?' (Rom. 9:22). Here are three areas where his anger is delayed: (a) his anger with injustice (Rev. 6:9ff); (b) his anger with nations (Matt. 25:32); (c) his anger with the devil – whose punishment is not described until Revelation 20:10! It is important to remember that our own anger does not stir him into action (Jas. 1:20).

The patience of God is a thread that runs through the entire Bible. In the Old Testament it is evidenced by God's dealings with the children of Israel. The life of Christ also exhibits patience. He waited thirty years before beginning his short public ministry. And at the end of his life of earth, we have the most moving exhibition of patience in the Lord's reaction to his suffering.

God's patience with rebellious mankind, however, is not without end. He says, 'My Spirit will not contend with man forever' (Gen. 3:6).

One day God will clear his name – and ours. He loves to vindicate (2 Thess. 1:5-9). At the end all will see that all God's ways are – indeed – just.

10

THE WISDOM OF GOD

INTRODUCTION

A. In this study we will focus on one of the neglected attributes of God.
    1. Attributes (def.): qualities or characteristics of a person.
    2. *The attributes of God are often described by the three Big O's:*
        a. His omnipotence; he is all-powerful.
        b. His omniscience; he is all-knowing.
        c. His omnipresence; he is everywhere.
    3. *There are of course other attributes of God.*
        a. His sovereignty; his right to do as he pleases.
        b. His holiness; his 'otherness', or hatred of sin.
        c. His justice; his determination to punish sin.
        d. His love; his care over his people.
        e. His mercy; his forgiveness.
    4. *There is a word that sums up the whole of God's attributes: glory.*
        a. It is the sum total of all that can be said about him.
        b. It is the nearest you get to his 'essence', or nature.

B. Wisdom (def.): sound judgement.
    1. In this chapter we will focus on God's wisdom.
    2. *See Chapter 23, The Gift, or Anointing, of Wisdom.*
        a. It is one of the gifts of the Holy Spirit (1 Cor. 12:8).
        b. It is promised to all who ask for it in faith (Jas. 1:5-6).

C. Important distinctions:
    1. *The differences between wisdom and knowledge.*
        a. Knowledge refers to information, or facts.
        b. Wisdom refers to the use of information or facts.
    2. *The differences between cleverness and wisdom.*
        a. Cleverness refers to quickness in learning, and skill.
        b. Wisdom refers to the proper use of skill.
        c. Note: one may be clever but not wise.

3. *The differences between intelligence, intellectual, and being wise.*

    a. Intelligence: how quickly one perceives things.

    b. Intellectual: the power of reasoning and acquiring knowledge.

    c. Wise: showing sound judgement when using reason and knowledge.

D. God's wisdom (def.): the inscrutability of his sound judgement and the ability to get things done.

    1. *God's judgement is perfect and unimprovably sound.*

        a. It is not knowable *a priori* (before it is known).

        b. It is only knowable *a posteriori* (after it is known).

    2. It is always surprising! 'Oh, the depth of the riches of the wisdom and knowledge of God! How unsearchable his judgments, and his paths beyond tracing out! Who has known the mind of the Lord? Or who has been his counsellor?' (Rom. 11:33-34).

E. Why is this study important?

    1. *For our edification – nothing edifies (inspires) more than focusing on God.*

        a. So much theology is really anthropology (study of man) – man-centred.

        b. It is uplifting to get our eyes off ourselves.

    2. *It is encouraging to be reminded that we are all in the hands of a wise God.*

        a. Augustine: 'God loves every person as though there were no-one else to love.'

        b. Each of us is dealt with in inscrutable prudence; we have been 'lavished' with 'all wisdom and understanding' (Eph. 1:8).

    3. *It helps us to lower our voices when, at first, we may be tempted to question God's will.*

        a. When we become more acquainted with his ways it helps us to 'wait and see'.

        b. The way he has dealt with his ancient people is the way he deals with us!

    4. *It humbles our pride.*

        a. We all need more humbling!

        b. When we get a glimpse of God's ways it breeds a respect for his ways and a humbling of our estimate of ourselves.

5. *It glorifies and honours God when we take the time to see something of his ways.*
  a. God lamented of one generation, 'They have not known my ways' (Heb. 3:10).
  b. We can preclude his anger by knowing him better so he won't swear an oath of wrath to us (Heb. 3:11).
  c. We therefore have an opportunity to know him better and save ourselves great sorrow – through this study.

I. THE DESIGN OF GOD'S WISDOM

A. Biblical words or synonyms.
  1. *Old Testament; 'Wisdom' may be used interchangeably with:*
    a. Understanding (Job 39:26; Prov. 23:4).
    b. Insight (Ps. 136:5).
    c. Prudence (Prov. 12:8; Prov. 23:9).
    d. Note: 'Wisdom' in the Old Testament is intensely practical, not theoretical.
      (1) In education knowledge is sometimes divided between 'pure' and 'applied'.
      (2) Wisdom in the Old Testament is applied knowledge.
      (3) It is often the art of being successful, of forming the correct plan to gain the desired results.
  2. *New Testament.*
    a. Gr. *sophia*; by and large it has the same intensely practical nature as in the Old Testament.
    b. However, James uses it in a manner that is essentially like *agape* in 1 Corinthians 13 (Cf. Jas. 3:17-18).
    c. In a word: attain to the love described in 1 Corinthians 13 and you will manifest the wisdom James envisages.

B. Some aspects of God's wisdom:
  1. *The ability to get things done.*
    a. God promised Abraham that his descendants:
      (1) Would be strangers in a country not their own.
      (2) Would be enslaved for four hundred years.
      (3) Would be set free with great possessions.
      (4) Would return to their land (Gen. 15:13-16).

b. God did this:

(1) Through Joseph being sold to the Ishmaelites (Gen. 37:28).

(2) Through Joseph being made Prime Minister of Egypt (Gen. 41:41ff).

(3) Through a Pharaoh who did not know about Joseph (Ex. 1:8).

(4) By raising up Moses and bringing plagues on Egypt (Ex. 3-14).

2. *Hiding the details of his plans until the end.*

a. For example, the above illustrations of Joseph and Moses.

b. Nobody had a clue at the time that there was a plan which was working out perfectly and on time!

c. Like a wise physician who does not reveal all he knows, God gives us bits and pieces – a day at a time.

d. We must remember this:

(1) Regarding how he deals with us individually.

(2) Regarding the future of the church.

(3) Regarding the problem of evil.

3. *Deliberately designed to humble.*

a. 'He catches the wise in their craftiness' (1 Cor. 3:19).

b. His dealings with Nebuchadnezzar:

(1) He said, 'Is not this the great Babylon I have built as the royal residence, by my mighty power and for the glory of my majesty?' (Dan. 4:30).

(2) God had other plans for him!

(3) He then said of the true God: 'All the peoples of the earth are regarded as nothing. He does as he pleases with the powers of heaven and the peoples of the earth. No-one can hold back his hand or say to him: "What have you done?"' (Dan. 4:35).

c. He reveals himself in ways that offend the most sophisticated (2 Kings 5:10).

(1) Paul Cain: 'God offends the mind to reach the heart.'

(2) Isaiah said: 'Therefore once more I will astound these people with wonder upon wonder; the wisdom of the wise will perish, the intelligence of the intelligent will vanish' (Isa. 29:14).

(3) Paul the apostle said, 'But God chose the foolish things of the world to shame the wise; God chose the weak things of the world to shame the strong' (1 Cor. 1:27).

d. He does this by his choice:

(1) To save by preaching. 'For since in the wisdom of God the world through its wisdom did not know him, God was pleased through the foolishness of what was preached to save those who believe' (1 Cor. 1:21).

(2) To choose his elect largely from the ordinary class of people. 'Brothers, think of what you were when you were called. Not many of you were wise by human standards; not many were influential; not many were of noble birth' (1 Cor. 1:26).

(3) To honour the poor (Jas. 1:9; 2:5).

4. *Deliberately taking us by surprise. E.g.:*

a. His choice of King Saul's successor. 'But the LORD said to Samuel, "Do not consider his appearance or his height, for I have rejected him. The LORD does not look at the things man looks at. Man looks at the outward appearance, but the LORD looks at the heart' (1 Sam. 16:7).

b. His way of showing himself even to those highly experienced in his ways. 'The LORD said, "Go out and stand on the mountain in the presence of the LORD, for the LORD is about to pass by." Then a great and powerful wind tore the mountains apart and shattered the rocks before the LORD, but the LORD was not in the wind. After the wind there was an earthquake, but the LORD was not in the earthquake. After the earthquake came a fire, but the LORD was not in the fire. And after the fire came a gentle whisper. When Elijah heard it, he pulled his cloak over his face and went out and stood at the mouth of the cave' (1 Kings 19:11-13a).

c. His way of fulfilling prophecies.

(1) Messiah was to be born in Bethlehem (Mic. 5:2).

(2) Messiah was called out of Egypt (Hos. 11:1).

(3) Nobody could figure it out in advance!

d. In a word: '"For my thoughts are not your thoughts, neither are your ways my ways," declares the LORD. "As the heavens are higher than the earth, so are my ways higher then your ways and my thoughts than your thoughts"' (Isa. 55:8-9).

5. *Attention to detail.*

   a. The Tabernacle. 'See that you make them according to the pattern shown you on the mountain' (Ex. 25:40).

     (1) Every item – the ark, the offerings, the lampstand, the altar – was made with a specific purpose.

     (2) The death and priesthood of Christ fulfilled it all (Heb. 8-10).

   b. His command to King Saul. 'Now go, attack the Amalekites and totally destroy everything that belongs to them. Do not spare them; put to death men and women, children and infants, cattle and sheep, camels and donkeys' (1 Sam. 15:3).

     (1) Saul claimed to have kept the command.

     (2) 'But Samuel said, "What then is this bleating of sheep in my ears? What is this lowing of cattle that I hear?"' (1 Sam. 15:14).

   c. His exposure of Ananias and Sapphira. 'Then Peter said, "Ananias, how is it that Satan has so filled your heart that you have lied to the Holy Spirit and have kept for yourself some of the money you received for the land?"' (Acts 5:3).

   d. The warning regarding our words. 'But I tell you that men will have to give account on the day of judgment for every careless word they have spoken' (Matt. 12:36).

II. THE EXERCISE OF GOD'S WISDOM

A. In creation

1. *Creation is described in Genesis 1.*

2. *But according to the book of Proverbs, creation is the product of God's wisdom.*

   a. The universe (Prov. 3:19ff; Prov. 8:22-31; Jer. 10:12; Ps. 104:24).

   b. Man (Job 10:8-9; Prov. 14:31; Prov. 22:2; Ps. 103:14).

B. In redemption

1. *God created man and planned his redemption in four stages.*

   a. Able to sin.

     (1) God chose to give man free will (Gen. 2:16-17).

     (2) This meant he could sin if he chose to do so.

      b. Not able not to sin.

        (1) Death – physical and spiritual – was the consequence of sin (Rom. 6:23).

        (2) The result: the loss of free will.

      c. Able not to sin.

        (1) This assumes that man has been converted.

        (2) Conversion gives one the power to turn from sin (Acts 26:18).

      d. Not able to sin.

        (1) This will be when we are glorified (Rom. 8:30).

        (2) This condition is irreversible – never again will man sin.

2. *The Fall did not take God by surprise.*

    a. Jesus is the lamb that was chosen from before the world was created (1 Pet. 1:20).

    b. God chose a people before the world was created (2 Tim. 1:9).

3. *In God's timing he sent his Son* (Gal. 4:4).

    a. He might have sent him before or later than he did.

    b. His manner of saving people took everybody by surprise – but it shouldn't have.

      (1) The Law with its sacrificial system paved the way.

      (2) But Israel, who should have known better, rejected Messiah.

4. *God decreed that only believers would be saved.*

    a. God might have let the universality of Christ's death unconditionally save the world.

    b. He chose instead to grant salvation to believers only (Rom. 3:26; John 3:16).

5. *God chose the foolishness of preaching to bring people to faith* (1 Cor. 1:21).

    a. The message was 'foolishness' in man's eyes.

    b. The method also was 'foolishness' in man's eyes.

C. Progressive revelation

    1. *The first major figure to receive the gospel was Abraham* (Gal. 3:8).

      a. God began this in the Garden of Eden (Gen. 3:15,21).

      b. The rudiments of the gospel came to Cain and Abel (Gen. 4:1-7).

    c. God's covenant with Noah pre-figured the covenant he would make with Abraham (Gen. 9:1-17).

  2. *The entrance of the Law*

    a. This came because of the sins of Israel (Gal. 3:19).

    b. This was a temporary measure to prepare for the coming of the Redeemer, to which the Law pointed (Gal. 3:23; Heb. 10:1ff).

  3. *The emergence of prophets*

    a. As the priesthood became corrupt God raised up prophets.

    b. The message of the prophets was two-fold:

      (1) Condemning sin.

      (2) Foretelling the coming of the Redeemer.

  4. *The ministry of Jesus*

    a. His teaching (Matt. 5:17).

    b. His supreme work: his death, resurrection, ascension and intercession.

  5. *The ministry of the Holy Spirit*

    a. He was the infallible interpreter of all that preceded:

      (1) The Old Testament.

      (2) The teachings of Jesus.

    b. He came upon the disciples of Jesus and those who tarried in Jerusalem (Luke 24:49; Acts 2:1-4).

      (1) The reason for Jesus' coming was made clear.

      (2) A further result: the emergence of the Church.

  6. *The teaching of the apostles*

    a. This was God's final and complete revelation.

    b. All that preceded culminated in the teaching of the apostles.

  7. *The Canon of Scripture*

    a. The Old Testament was augmented by writings that were equally inspired – the New Testament.

    b. The revelation of God was now complete.

D. Final Revelation: the Bible

  1. God in his wisdom gave us the Bible.

  2. *The Bible tells us all we need to know about God.*

    a. It may not tell us all we want to know.

    b. It tells us all we need to know.

  3. *It is from the Bible we learn about God's wisdom.*

    a. He knows the end from the beginning (Isa. 46:10).

b. By this we conclude:
  (1) He knows everything.
  (2) He never makes a mistake.

III. WISDOM LITERATURE

A. This is the name given to certain Old Testament books, such as Job, Proverbs and Ecclesiastes.
  1. All of the Bible is 'wisdom literature' – to be sure.
  2. But some books became specifically known as 'wisdom literature'.

B. Wisdom literature is basically of two types:
  1. *Proverbial wisdom, e.g., the Book of Proverbs.*
    a. These are mainly short, pithy sayings.
    b. They are rules for personal happiness and welfare.
  2. *Speculative wisdom, e.g., Job and Ecclesiastes.*
    a. These delve into problems such as the meaning of existence and the relationship between God and man.
    b. This speculative wisdom is practical, not theoretical.
      (1) One does not look for many theological insights.
      (2) It has more to do with living, especially suffering.
    c. This literature is of two kinds:
      (1) Monologues: Ecclesiastes.
      (2) Dialogues: Job.

C. What kind of wisdom do we learn from this literature?
  1. *Note: wisdom literature will not make a lot of sense without our knowledge of the Gospel and the aid of the Spirit.*
    a. The non-Christian can make little sense of it.
    b. The Christian faith alone brings it to fruition.
  2. *Job: why do the righteous suffer?*
    a. Job was a righteous man but suffered terribly.
    b. His 'friends' reflected the 'health and wealth' gospel of their day!
      (1) Their thinking: if one is holy, he will prosper and not suffer.
      (2) Job therefore must be guilty of sin.
    c. Job's 'righteousness' became self-righteousness; God rebuked him.

> **d.** Job was relieved of suffering but not until he repented and prayed for his friends (Job 42:10).
>
> **e.** Message of the Book of Job: God's hidden wisdom regarding suffering and the conclusion of Job that no purpose of God can be thwarted (Job 42:2).

3. *Ecclesiastes: the meaninglessness of life without God.*

> **a.** Written by Solomon who had 'everything' but found all to be 'vanity', e.g., pleasure.
>
> **b.** Behind this vanity are timeless bits of wisdom:
>
>> **(1)** That there is a time for everything; God makes everything beautiful in his way (Eccl. 3:1-11).
>>
>> **(2)** Man is essentially vain; all achievements spring from man's envy of his neighbour (Eccl. 4:4).
>>
>> **(3)** The folly of anger (Eccl. 7:8-9).
>>
>> **(4)** 'Time and chance happen' to all (Eccl. 9:11).
>
> **c.** The bottom line: 'Now all has been heard; here is the conclusion of the matter: Fear God and keep his commandments, for this is the whole duty of man. For God will bring every deed into judgment, including every hidden thing, whether it is good or evil' (Eccl. 12:13-14).

4. *Proverbs: the way to happy living.*

> **a.** The fear of the Lord is the beginning of knowledge, or wisdom (Prov. 1:7).
>
> **b.** The folly of rejecting wisdom (Prov. 1:20-23).
>
> **c.** The folly of adultery (Prov. 5:1-23; 6:20-7:27).
>
> **d.** Most of this book is full of wise and timeless sayings.
>
>> **(1)** Follow these sayings and you will incorporate the very wisdom of God into your daily life.
>>
>> **(2)** We would do well to read a bit of Proverbs *every day*!

CONCLUSION

The gift of wisdom means having the mind of God in a situation. We are all promised this, if we ask for it in faith. It is a source of comfort and assurance that we are in the hands of a God who is infinitely wise. We see God's wisdom in creation, throughout the progressive revelation of the Old Testament, and in redemption. Knowing the Bible to be God's Word, we can therefore rely on its wise counsel.

God's wisdom will be ultimately manifested in the Last Day. All that we have learned about God's wisdom will be unveiled brilliantly that day. We will see how he takes us by surprise and how everything came perfectly into place – including understanding why he allowed evil.

The wisdom of God is continually surprising. When all things seem to 'go wrong', we find at the end of the day we are in the hands of a sovereign God – who has an inscrutable purpose in everything. A special feature of God's surprise: nothing ultimately 'goes wrong' when we acknowledge him in all our ways and lean not on our own understanding (Prov. 3:5-6).

11

THE JEALOUSY OF GOD

A. Jealousy is one of the most unattractive qualities under the sun.
   1. It is usually defined as 'a feeling or showing resentment towards a person one thinks of as a rival' (Oxford dictionary).
   2. We often see it as a symptom of insecurity, and it is usually regarded as a negative rather than a positive trait.

B. Think what you will, God is up front with his self-conscious and open declaration about himself.
   1. *He does not hide the fact that he is a jealous God and he wants everybody to know this!*
      a. 'You shall have no other gods before me. You shall not make for yourself an idol in the form of anything in heaven above or on the earth beneath or in the waters below. You shall not bow down to them or worship them; for I, the LORD your God, am a jealous God, punishing the children for the sin of the fathers to the third and fourth generation of those who hate me, but showing love to a thousand generations of those who love me and keep my commandments' (Ex. 20:3-6).
      b. 'Do not worship any other god, for the LORD, whose name is Jealous, is a jealous God' (Ex. 34:14).
      c. 'For the LORD your God is a consuming fire, a jealous God' (Deut. 4:24).
      d. 'Do not follow other gods, the gods of the peoples around you; for the LORD your God, who is among you, is a jealous God and his anger will burn against you, and he will destroy you from the face of the land' (Deut. 6:14-15).
      e. 'How long, O LORD? Will you be angry for ever? How long will your jealousy burn like fire?' (Ps. 79:5).
      f. 'Then the angel who was speaking to me said, "Proclaim this word: This is what the LORD Almighty says: 'I am very jealous for Jerusalem and Zion'"' (Zech. 1:14).

2. *God's jealousy (def.): God's holy love for us which manifests itself in great anger regarding any rival.*

    a. He cannot abide any rival or competition.

    b. He shows it by anger when he sees any rival or competition.

        (1) It is his hatred toward sin.

        (2) It springs from his holiness and his love for us.

3. *If he were not holy he would not be jealous.*

    a. But he is holy (Lev. 11:44).

    b. 'Your eyes are too pure to look upon evil; you cannot tolerate wrong' (Hab. 1:13).

4. *If he did not love us he would not be jealous.*

    a. But he does love us (Isa. 43:4).

    b. 'The LORD appeared to us in the past, saying: "I have loved you with an everlasting love; I have drawn you with loving-kindness"' (Jer. 31:3).

C. What at first may seem so unattractive about God becomes perhaps the most endearing of his attributes.

    1. *Attributes (def.): characteristics:*

        a. Omnipotent (all-powerful): Luke 1:37; Jeremiah 32:26.

        b. Omniscient (all-knowing): Psalm 139:1-6; Isaiah 46:10.

        c. Omnipresent (everywhere): Psalm 139:7-12; 1 Kings 8:27.

        d. Holy: Exodus 15:11; 1 Peter 1:16.

        e. Invisible: Exodus 33:20; John 1:18.

        f. Just: Genesis 18:25; Exodus 34:7.

        g. Faithful: Lamentations 3:23; I Corinthians 1:9.

            (1) Note: these are but to name a few.

            (2) The sum total of all God's attributes can be put in one word: glory (Acts 7:2).

    2. *God's jealousy is our security.*

        a. It is his rebuke that preserves us.

        b. It is his jealousy that keeps us out of trouble!

D. Why is this lesson important?

    1. *God wants us to know his ways.*

        a. He lamented that Israel 'have not known my ways' (Heb. 3:10).

        b. This is why he swore in his wrath that they would not enter into his rest (Heb. 3:11).

    2. *It explains why he dealt with Israel as he did.*

3. *It explains why he dealt with his people in the New Testament as he did.*

4. *It explains why he deals with us as he does.*

5. *When we come to know him as he is, and love him for being exactly as he is, we will not want:*

   a. To be angry with him.

   b. To apologise for him to others.

I. GOD IS JEALOUS FOR HIS GLORY

A. This lies at the bottom of all he does.

   1. *All that God ever does is for his own glory* (Eph. 1:11-12).

      a. He created us and everything else for his glory.

         (1) 'You are worthy, our Lord and God, to receive glory and honour and power, for you created all things, and by your will they were created and have their being' (Rev. 4:11).

         (2) We therefore, whatever we do, are commanded to do it for his glory (1 Cor. 10:31).

      b. All that happened between Israel and the wicked Pharaoh was for God's glory – and for his getting even more glory!

         (1) 'And I will harden Pharaoh's heart, and he will pursue them. But I will gain glory for myself through Pharaoh and all his army, and the Egyptians will know that I am the LORD' (Ex. 14:4).

         (2) 'I will harden the hearts of the Egyptians so that they will go in after them. And I will gain glory through Pharaoh and all his army, through his chariot and his horsemen' (Ex. 14:17).

         (3) 'The Egyptians will know that I am the LORD when I gain glory through Pharaoh, his chariots and his horsemen' (Ex. 14:18).

   2. *By this we should learn a fundamental lesson: all our disappointments and griefs are for God's glory.*

      a. When we are opposed by the Pharaohs of this world it is for the glory of God.

         (1) God actually said to Pharaoh himself, 'But I have raised you up for this very purpose, that I might show you my power and that my name might be proclaimed in all the earth' (Ex. 9:16).

(2) Paul concluded the doctrine of sovereign election by grace from this account: 'Therefore God has mercy on whom he wants to have mercy, and he hardens whom he wants to harden' (Rom. 9:18).

(3) Paul added that this was for God's glory: 'What if he did this to make the riches of his glory known to the objects of his mercy, whom he prepared in advance for glory?' (Rom. 9:23).

b. Thus behind all of Israel's griefs and hardships was God letting *every single thing* happen for this reason: to gain more glory for himself!

(1) Question: does this bother you? Upset you? Surprise you?

(2) This is the God of the Bible we are talking about – the God and Father of our Lord Jesus Christ!

B. God actually said: his name is Jealous (Ex. 34:14).

1. So it is the glory of his name that is at stake.
2. Therefore when people who are called by his name (2 Chron. 7:14) go off the rails, disobey him, look toward the world or flirt with any or God's competitors:

a. He is angry and will show it.

b. The glory of his name is at stake!

C. Idolatry versus the glory of God.

1. *Ancient Israel sadly turned to the worship of what was visible when they got tired of having to wait on the invisible God.*

a. 'When the people saw that Moses was so long in coming down from the mountain, they gathered round Aaron and said, "Come, make us gods who will go before us. As for this fellow Moses who brought us up out of Egypt, we don't know what has happened to him"' (Ex. 32:1).

b. Then Aaron, wanting to justify himself for going with the people, said, 'So I told them, "Whoever has any gold jewellery, take it off." Then they gave me the gold, and I threw it into the fire, and out came this calf!' (Ex. 32:24).

2. *God raised up prophets who exposed and warned against any kind of idolatry.*

a. God raised up Elijah when King Ahab allowed the prophets of Baal to flourish.

(1) 'When he saw Elijah, he said to him, "Is that you, you
troubler of Israel?" "I have not made trouble for Israel,"
Elijah replied, "But you and your father's family have.
You have abandoned the LORD's commands and have
followed the Baals"' (1 Kings 18:17-18).

(2) 'Elijah went before the people and said, "How long will
you waver between two opinions? If the LORD is God,
follow him; but if Baal is God, follow him"' (1 Kings 18:21).

b. The situation was so bad in Jeremiah's day that he prophesied
that Jerusalem would be destroyed and the people taken
captive to Babylon.

3. *Idolatry today is not so obvious as erecting a pole or a god
of wood or stone.*
   a. The little foxes 'ruin the vineyards' (Song. 2:15).
   b. John said, 'Do not love the world or anything in the world.
   If anyone loves the world, the love of the Father is not in
   him. For everything in the world – the cravings of sinful
   man, the lust of his eyes and the boasting of what he has
   and does – comes not from the Father but from the world'
   (1 John 2:15-16).
   c. The final verse of 1 John is: 'Dear children, keep yourselves
   from idols' (1 John 5:21).
   d. Idolatry (def.): whatever diminishes your zeal for God's
   glory and diminishes intimacy with him.

D. The Ark of the Covenant symbolised God's glory.

1. When the ark was captured, Eli's daughter-in-law named her
son Ichabod – 'The glory has departed' (1 Sam. 4:21).
2. When David tried to bring the Ark to Jerusalem, Uzzah was
struck dead on the spot for merely touching the Ark to keep it
from falling (2 Sam. 6:6-7).
3. The only way David succeeded in bringing the Ark to Jerusalem
was by doing everything 'in the prescribed way', that is,
according to God's Word (1 Chron. 15:13).
   a. God's name was at stake, so too his word.
   b. He magnifies his Word above his name (Ps. 138:2, AV).

II. THE JEALOUSY OF GOD IS MIRRORED IN THE PERSON OF JESUS

A. God is jealous for the glory of his Son.

1. *At his baptism, a voice from heaven said,* 'This is my Son, whom I love; with him I am well pleased' (Matt. 3:17).

2. *Peter foolishly suggested three shelters when the Lord's glory was manifested to the inner circle* (Matt. 17:4).
   a. 'While he was still speaking, a bright cloud enveloped them, and a voice from the cloud said, "This is my Son, whom I love; with him I am well pleased. Listen to him!"' (Matt. 17:5).
   b. 'When they looked up, they saw no-one except Jesus' (Matt. 17:8).

3. *God said, 'I am the LORD; that is my name! I will not give my glory to another or my praise to idols'* (Isa. 42:8).
   a. But he shared that glory with Jesus, because Jesus is God.
   b. He gave Jesus his name! (Phil. 2:9-11).

B. From the right hand of God the jealousy of the Lord Jesus was disclosed to John on the Isle of Patmos.

1. Jesus was seen with eyes 'like blazing fire' (Rev. 1:14).

2. *His message to the seven churches in Asia revealed his jealousy over each church.*
   a. He was grieved that the church at Ephesus had forsaken its 'first love' (Rev. 2:4).
   b. He was angry with Pergamum for its faulty teaching (Rev. 2:14ff).
   c. He was angry with Thyatira for its immorality and idolatry (Rev. 2:20ff).
   d. He was angry with Sardis for its misleading reputation (Rev. 3:1).
   e. He was angry with the Laodiceans for their lukewarmness (Rev. 3:14ff).

3. *Note: this is a grim reminder that the Lord Jesus is aware of* everything *going on in every church that is called by his name.*
   a. What do you suppose the Lord would say to your church?
   b. Would we be surprised by his words to us today?

C. The Lord is utterly impartial and will not bend the rules for any of us.

   1. Close though he was to Peter, he actually said to him, 'Get behind me, Satan! You are a stumbling-block to me; you do not have in mind the things of God, but the things of men' (Matt. 16:23).

   2. *Bearing in mind Peter's denial, Jesus said to him, 'Simon, son of John, do you truly love me more than these?'* (John 21:15).

   a. Peter avowed his love.

   b. But Jesus asked him a third time 'Simon, son of John, do you love me?' (John 21:17).

   c. Question: how many times have we affirmed our love for the Lord: 'O Jesus, I have promised to serve Thee to the end.'

   (1) The issue is not so much how we feel in church.

   (2) What matters is our lives – public and private – seven days a week!

D. The glory of the Lord is likewise mirrored in the person of the Holy Spirit.

   1. *When he was lied to in a revival situation, people were struck dead just as quickly as Uzzah when he touched the ark of the covenant.*

   a. Peter accused Ananias of lying to the Holy Spirit.

   (1) He did this by withholding the full price of the property he sold while claiming he had donated it all.

   (2) There was no law that Ananias had give everything.

   (3) But when he did this under the Holy Spirit's power in the church he 'lied to the Holy Spirit' (Acts 5:3).

   b. Sapphira was given an opportunity to come clean.

   (1) 'About three hours later his wife came in, not knowing what had happened. Peter asked her, "Tell me, is this the price you and Ananias got for the land?" "Yes," she said, "that is the price"' (Acts 5:7-8).

   (2) 'Peter said to her, "How could you agree to test the Spirit of the Lord? Look! The feet of the men who buried your husband are at the door, and they will carry you out also"' (Acts 5:9).

   (3) 'At that moment she fell down at his feet and died. Then the young men came in and, finding her dead, carried her out and buried her beside her husband. Great fear

seized the whole church and all who heard about these events' (Acts 5:10-11).

c. The jealousy of God and the jealousy of the Spirit are one and the same.

2. *When the Lord's Supper is not honoured in a revival situation the jealousy of God may become apparent at once.*

   a. This is what happened at Corinth.

   b. Paul said, 'Therefore, whoever eats the bread or drinks the cup of the Lord in an unworthy manner will be guilty of sinning against the body and blood of the Lord' (1 Cor. 11:27).

      (1) 'For anyone who eats and drinks without recognising the body of the Lord eats and drinks judgment on himself' (1 Cor. 11:29).

      (2) 'That is why many among you are weak and sick, and a number of you have fallen asleep' (1 Cor. 11:30).

   c. All this is because of the jealousy of the Holy Spirit at the Lord's table.

      (1) I suspect many have repeated the sin of Corinth.

      (2) But there is no evidence of sickness or premature death – very possibly because we are not yet in a revival situation.

      (3) Question: do we want revival after all?

3. *For the sake of the church God may likewise visit those in authority with a manifestation of his jealousy.*

   a. When Herod allowed the people to shout to him, 'This is the voice of a god, not a man,' God himself decided to step in.

   b. 'Immediately, because Herod did not give praise to God, an angel of the Lord struck him down, and he was eaten by worms and died' (Acts 12:23).

4. *The jealousy of the Spirit is at work in our relationship to him.*

   a. This is why we are warned:

      (1) 'And do not grieve the Holy Spirit of God, with whom you were sealed for the day of redemption' (Eph. 4:30).

      (2) 'Do not put out the Spirit's fire' (1 Thess. 5:19).

    b. When we grieve the Spirit:

        (1) We lose presence of mind and power.

        (2) We are left to operate in our own strength.

    c. When we quench the Spirit:

        (1) We forfeit what God would have done in manifesting his glory.

        (2) We continue on in our dead traditions.

    d. Remember: God will bend the rules for none of us.

E. Because we are bought with a price – Christ's own blood – God has complete rights over all of us (1 Cor. 6:20).

    1. *Our bodies are consequently temples of the Holy Spirit.*

        a. This has mainly to do with sexual conduct (1 Cor. 6:18).

        b. 'Do you not know that your body is a temple of the Holy Spirit, who is in you, whom you have received from God? You are not your own; you were bought at a price. Therefore honour God with your body' (1 Cor. 6:19-20).

    2. *God gets particularly angry when his people do not conform to his moral code revealed in scripture.*

        a. 'It is God's will that you should be sanctified: that you should avoid sexual immorality' (1 Thess. 4:3).

        b. 'The Lord will punish men for all such sins. . . Therefore, he who rejects this instruction does not reject man but God, who gives you his Holy Spirit' (1 Thess. 4:6-8).

III. THERE IS A POSITIVE SIDE TO GOD'S JEALOUSY

A. Remember that God's jealousy is his holy love for us.

    1. *This is what lies behind that interesting verse: 'The Spirit he caused to live in us envies intensely'* (Jas. 4:5).

        a. The jealous Holy Spirit lives in us!

        b. Although he can be grieved he none the less brings us back to himself when we slip.

        (1) Were it not for that, we'd never come back!

        (2) This is why James added, 'But he gives us more grace' (James 4:6).

    2. This alone explains God's chastening, or disciplining (Heb. 12:5-11).

        a. Here are the principles:

(1) Every Christian will be disciplined (Heb. 12:6-10).

(2) Being disciplined is painful (Heb. 12:11).

(3) It is to lead us to holiness (Heb. 12:10-11).

b. It is because God is jealous that he chastens.

(1) Jonah learned this (Jonah 2).

(2) David learned this (2 Sam. 12).

B. God steps in on behalf of hurting people.

1. *He rebuked the people of the Jerusalem church for neglecting the poor.*

    a. They wanted to go 'up market' and showed preference to those who gave the appearance of being affluent (Jas. 2:1-5).

    b. James would not let them get away with it (Jas. 2:6ff).

2. *He came to the aid of Christians who were mistreated by their employers* (Jas. 5).

    a. Their cries reached the ears of the Lord (Jam. 5:4).

    b. These Christian capitalists were roundly rebuked (Jas. 5:5).

3. The 'mature' Christian who overlooks the weaker Christian is rebuked (Rom. 14:10-15. cf. 1 Cor. 8:9-13).

CONCLUSION

Because jealousy is an unattractive human quality, we can find it hard to cope with the idea of God being jealous. But God is totally open about his jealousy. 'I, the LORD your God, am a jealous God' (Ex. 34:14). God is jealous for his glory. If we attribute glory to anyone or anything other than the Triune God, we make that person or object an idol. Idolatry makes God jealous and provokes him to anger.

God wants control over our lives – to the minutest detail. Since we have been bought by the shed blood of Christ, God has complete rights over us and is jealous when we do not treat our bodies as his temple. God's jealousy is the measure of his love for us. But remember that we are being cared for by holy love.

12

DOES GOD LOVE EVERYBODY?

INTRODUCTION

A. The answer to this question is surely 'yes'.

1. *This would appear to be the case in the light of several plain verses in the New Testament:*

   a. John 3:16, which Martin Luther called, 'The Bible in a nutshell.' 'For God so loved the world that he gave his one and only Son, that whoever believes in him shall not perish but have eternal life.'

   b. 2 Peter 3:9, which many evangelicals quote: 'The Lord is not slow in keeping his promise, as some understand slowness. He is patient with you, not wanting anyone to perish, but everyone to come to repentance.'

   c. 2 Corinthians 5:19, which is given in the context of Christ's atonement ('He died for our sins' – v. 15): 'That God was reconciling the world to himself in Christ, not counting men's sins against them. And he has committed to us the message of reconciliation.'

2. *Summed up:*

   a. God loves the world.

   b. God wants all to be saved.

   c. Christ died for all and reconciled the world to God.

B. However, there are verses in the Bible that suggest the answer is 'No'.

1. *This would appear to be the case in the light of several verses:*

   a. Romans 9:13, which quotes Malachi 1:2-3: 'Just as it is written: "Jacob I loved, but Esau I hated."'

   b. John 17:9, the words of Jesus whose high priestly prayer says: 'I pray for them. I am not praying for the world, but for those you have given me, for they are yours.'

   c. 1 Peter 2:8, which quotes Isaiah 8:14 and gives Peter's commentary: 'And, "A stone that causes men to stumble and a rock that makes them fall." They stumble because they disobey the message – which is also what they were destined for.'

2. *It would seem that:*
a. God loves some, hates others.
b. Christ does not intercede for everybody after all.
c. Those who do not believe were destined for stumbling.

C. Does the Bible contradict itself?

1. *Does Jesus contradict himself?*
a. In the same Gospel of John he says two things:
(1) God loves the world.
(2) But Jesus does not pray for the world.
b. Peter says two things:
(1) God wants all to be saved.
(2) Some are destined for the contrary.

2. *It follows, then, that one of the following is true:*
a. God contradicts himself.
b. Jesus contradicts himself.
c. The Bible is not infallible, showing contrary views, therefore an inerrant inspiration.
d. That God is behind all the aforementioned New Testament quotations; that there is a solid explanation with and that there are no contradictions after all.
(1) But if there is no contradiction, how are these verses reconciled?
(2) If there is a true contradiction, the Bible is untrustworthy.

D. There is a further issue implicit in this study.

1. *God's wrath toward the believer*
a. David prayed: 'O LORD, do not rebuke me in your anger or discipline me in your wrath' (Ps. 6:1).
b. Yet he was a man after God's own heart (1 Sam. 13:14).
c. Does God love David or not?

2. *God's willingness to heal*
a. In some places Jesus healed everybody. 'Jesus went through all the towns and villages, teaching in their synagogues, preaching the good news of the kingdom and healing every disease and sickness' (Matt. 9:35).

b. He refused to do so elsewhere. 'And he did not do many miracles there because of their lack of faith' (Matt. 13:58).

3. *The promise to answer prayer*

   a. 'You may ask me for anything in my name, and I will do it' (John 14:14).

   b. 'Three times I pleaded with the Lord to take it away from me' (2 Cor. 12:8).

4. *God's love for Israel*

   a. 'The LORD appeared to us in the past, saying: "I have loved you with an everlasting love; I have drawn you with loving-kindness"' (Jer. 31:3).

   b. '"Therefore I tell you that the kingdom of God will be taken away from you and given to a people who will produce its fruit' (Matt. 21:43).

5. *God's protection over his own*

   a. 'A thousand may fall at your side, ten thousand at your right hand, but it will not come near you. You will only observe with your eyes and see the punishment of the wicked' (Ps. 91:7-8).

   b. 'It was about this time that King Herod arrested some who belonged to the church, intending to persecute them. He had James, the brother of John, put to death with the sword' (Acts 12:1-2).

E. At bottom in this study is the issue of suffering and God allowing evil.

   1. God is all powerful. 'I am the LORD, the God of all mankind. Is anything too hard for me?' (Jer. 32:27).

   2. God is love and 'full of compassion and mercy' (Jas. 5:11; 1 John 4:16).

   3. *And yet we read:*

   a. Because of the birth of Jesus, all boys in Bethlehem under the age of two were killed (Matt. 2:16).

   b. Because Peter was miraculously delivered from prison, the guards of the prison were executed (Acts 12:19).

F. Why is this study important?

   1. *The Christian faith ought to teach a person how to think.*

   a. These are extremely difficult issues; the most difficult of all.

   b. We need to show we have faced these issues.

2. *Non-Christians often think that we haven't looked at obvious questions, such as: why does God allow evil and suffering?*

    a. We have opportunity to show we have the same questions.

    b. Peter said, 'But in your hearts set apart Christ as Lord. Always be prepared to give an answer to everyone who asks you to give the reason for the hope that you have. But do this with gentleness and respect' (1 Peter 3:15).

3. *Christians need to believe simultaneously in the sovereignty of God and the mercy of God.*

    a. It will not do to run from obvious teachings.

    b. Many reject out of hand what they find unpleasant but which the Bible teaches.

4. *If the Word and the Spirit are going to come together in our day, surely a beginning point is to be utterly open to both.*

    a. An important part of the Word is God's sovereignty.

    b. Many who are open to the Spirit do not seem to have a place for God's sovereignty.

5. *Coming to grips with issues like these will make us strong and increase our faith.*

    a. It will put 'meat on our bones'.

    b. In times of trouble we can emerge triumphantly all the more quickly when we have absorbed these truths.

I. The heart of God and the inscrutable will of God

A. The heart of God

1. *Arthur Blessitt refers to the 'heartbeat' of God; God's desire for each of us to see every person saved and for us to try to see them converted.*

    a. Among the last words of Jesus are:

        (1) 'Go and make disciples of all nations' (Matt. 28:19).

        (2) 'Go into all the world and preach the good news to all creation' (Mark 16:15).

    b. It was Peter's heartbeat on the day of Pentecost. 'With many other words he warned them; and he pleaded with them, "Save yourselves from this corrupt generation"' (Acts 2:40).

    c. It was the heartbeat of all believers not just apostles.

        (1) 'All except the apostles were scattered throughout Judea and Samaria' (Acts 8:1).

(2) 'Those who had been scattered preached the Word
wherever they went' (Acts 8:4).

d. Paul took advantage of every opportunity to preach. 'So he
reasoned in the synagogue with the Jews and the God-
fearing Greeks, as well as in the marketplace day by day
with those who happened to be there' (Acts 17:17).

e. Paul accommodated himself to people as they were. 'To the
weak I became weak, to win the weak. I have become all
things to all men so that by all possible means I might save
some' (1 Cor. 9:22).

2. *Every revival is characterised by an increase in conversions.*
   a. This shows the will of the Holy Spirit.
   b. It follows, then, that this is the heartbeat of God.
   c. Note: at the Cane Ridge Revival (1801), eye-witnesses said
   that acute theological differences which previously divided
   the church disappeared for a while – until the Revival
   subsided.

3. *Jesus represented the heartbeat of God.*
   a. He said that anyone who sees him sees the Father (John
   14:9).
   b. He invited us to come to him. 'Come to me, all you who are
   weary and burdened, and I will give you rest' (Matt. 11:28).
   c. No-one was rejected who came to him; not even a leper
   (Matt. 8:1ff).
   d. He said he did not come to condemn the world but that the
   world might be saved through him (John 3:17).

4. *Peter perhaps summed up the heart of God when he said
that God was not willing that any should perish but that all
should come to repentance* (2 Pet. 3:9).

5. *God said long before Jesus came that he took no pleasure in
the death of the wicked.* 'Do I take any pleasure in the death
of the wicked? declares the Sovereign LORD. Rather, am I not
pleased when they turn from their ways and live?' (Ezek.
18:23).

**B. Behind all the above lie the undoubted statements that seem
to modify or contradict such verses.**
   1. *If nothing is too hard for the Lord, why does he not exercise his
   power to save all?*

a. He did it with Saul of Tarsus (Acts 9:1-12).

    (1) Saul was not on his way to a prayer meeting in Damascus.

    (2) He was in the process of killing Christians (Acts 26:10-11).

b. But God stopped him suddenly.

    (1) A bright light intervened.

    (2) Saul became immediately compliant (Act 22:10).

c. In a word: if God saved Saul, he could save anybody.

2. *The same Jesus who said that God loved the world also said things which revealed God's sovereignty and inscrutability.*

  a. Definitions:

    (1) Sovereignty of God: his prerogative to do what he pleases with anyone at any time.

    (2) Inscrutability of God: the impossibility of fully understanding God or figuring him out.

  b. Jesus said:

    (1) 'All that the Father gives me will come to me, and whoever comes to me I will never drive away' (John 6:37).

    (2) 'All things have been committed to me by my Father. No one knows the Son except the Father, and no one knows the Father except the Son and those to whom the Son chooses to reveal him' (Matt. 11:27).

    (3) 'No one can come to me unless the Father who sent me draws him, and I will raise him up at the last day' (John 6:44).

  c. Paul said:

    (1) Quoting Moses, 'I will have mercy on whom I have mercy, and I will have compassion on whom I have compassion' (Rom. 9:15).

    (2) 'And we know that in all things God works for the good of those who love him, who have been called according to his purpose' (Rom. 8:28).

    (3) 'For we know, brothers loved by God, that he has chosen you' (1 Thess. 1:4).

  d. Luke summarised why some believed and others did not. 'When the Gentiles heard this, they were glad and honoured the word of the Lord; and all who were appointed for eternal life believed' (Acts 13:48).

II. THE MYSTERY OF GOD AND HIS DEALINGS WITH HIS PEOPLE

A. Chastening, or disciplining

1. *When God does this he is said to be angry* (Ps. 6:1; 38:1).

   a. David, the man after God's own heart, said: 'Remove your scourge from me; I am overcome by the blow of your hand. You rebuke and discipline men for their sin; you consume their wealth like a moth – each man is but a breath' (Ps. 39:10-11).

   b. 'I was enraged by his sinful greed; I punished him, and hid my face in anger, yet he kept on in his wilful ways' (Isa. 57:17).

2. *But this is actually a sign of God's love and tenderness.*

   a. 'Because the Lord disciplines those he loves, and he punishes everyone he accepts as a son' (Heb. 12:6).

   b. 'I have seen his ways, but I will heal him; I will guide him and restore comfort to him' (Isa. 57:18).

3. *In a word: it is simultaneous wrath and mercy.*

   a. These are contradictory.

   b. But both are true.

B. Healing

1. *Jesus had compassion and healed people.*

   a. Sometimes every single person was healed.

   b. Only exception: when there was unbelief.

      (1) But could he have overcome this and created faith? Yes.

      (2) And yet this shows God's displeasure with any unbelief and cynicism.

2. *Jesus is the same today as yesterday* (Heb. 13:8).

   a. He is still full of compassion (Heb. 4:15).

   b. But people today by and large are unhealed when prayed for.

   c. Does this mean Jesus does not love everybody?

3. In a word: God is sovereign when it comes to healing as well as in salvation.

C. Prayer

1. Jesus told us to pray and not give up (Luke 18:1).

2. He said that anything asked for in his name would be granted (John 14:14).

    3. Paul – a chosen vessel – had to endure a 'thorn in the flesh' (2 Cor. 12:7-9).

    4. Note: prayer is a great mystery, but at the end of the day God will only answer that which is according to his will (1 John 5:14-15).

D. God and Israel

    1. Israel was God's chosen nation and people.

    2. The Israelites loved with an everlasting love.

    3. *But by and large they rejected the Messiah.*

        a. Could not God have overruled this and created faith in every Jew? Yes.

        b. But the true Israel, it turns out, was spiritual rather than physical.

            (1) That means being a Jew by procreation is not what makes one a child of God.

            (2) So Paul said, 'It is not as though God's word had failed. For not all who are descended from Israel are Israel' (Rom. 9:6).

    4. In a word: only the elect are saved and not all of the physical seed of Israel were chosen of God (Rom. 9:11).

E. God's protection

    1. *This is the most difficult of all.*

        a. God promises protection for those who trust him.

            (1) 'You will only observe with your eyes and see the punishment of the wicked' (Ps. 91:8).

            (2) 'He will not let your foot slip – he who watches over you will not slumber' (Ps. 121:3).

        b. These promises have as their only connection: our trust in God.

    2. *But the common testimony of all of us is often to the contrary.*

        a. Christians have accidents – lose use of limbs and eyes, etc..

        b. Christians get hurt – including being raped and robbed.

        c. Illnesses can also cause permanent loss of physical abilites.

        d. Are those who experience adversity not loved by God?

    3. *Big issue: problem of evil.*

        a. Bad things happen to good people – God's own.

        b. Good things happen to bad people – even evil men.

        c. The problem of evil is not a general, hypothetical problem; it touches the best of people.

III. Some reflections and tentative answers

A. Note: we do not intend to gloss over or underestimate the difficulty this lesson poses.

1. We are dealing ultimately with the greatest theological-philosophical problem that ever existed: the problem of evil.
2. Only a fool would claim to have the answer to this.

B. However there are some possible, if only tentative (not definite) explanations:

1. *God's own language as expressed by Isaiah:* '"For my thoughts are not your thoughts, neither are your ways my ways," declares the LORD. "As the heavens are higher than the earth, so are my ways higher than your ways and my thoughts than your thoughts"' (Isa. 55:8-9).

    a. This is God's hint that we should not try to, or expect to understand everything.

    (1) 'Who has understood the mind of the Lord, or instructed him as his counsellor?' (Is. 40:13).

    (2) 'Oh, the depth of the riches of the wisdom and knowledge of God! How unsearchable his judgments, and his paths beyond tracing out!' (Rom. 11:33).

    b. We must let God be himself and uphold the privilege that is his not to tell us all he knows.

2. *The nature of faith.* 'Now faith is being sure of what we hope for and certain of what we do not see' (Heb. 11:1).

    a. God has decreed that he would be known by faith (Hab. 2:4).

    b. That which makes faith faith is that we believe without the empirical evidence.

    (1) Man's nature: to see, then believe (Mark 15:32).

    (2) What pleases God: believing him without seeing (Heb. 11:6).

    c. If we knew all the answers, we wouldn't need faith.

3. *The antinomy (def.): parallel principles which seem contradictory but both being equally true.*

    a. God loves everybody; he doesn't love everybody equally.

    (1) Jacob have I loved, Esau I have loved less – a meaning of 'hate' which many scholars affirm.

    (2) God obviously has the right to choose some and not all.

    b. So much that is true in Christian theology is best explained in terms of antinomy.

      (1) Jesus is God and man.

      (2) The Christian is simultaneously a saint and a sinner.

4. *The name of God*

    a. The name refers to God's identity and power.

    b. Part of God's identity is that he has a will of his own.

      (1) Praying in Jesus' name is to acquiesce to his will.

      (2) That seems to cover John 14:14.

5. *Any misunderstanding regarding unanswered prayer may be cleared up – in at least two ways:*

    a. God has a better idea than our personal requests (John 11).

    b. Paul's spiritual development was more important than having his 'thorn' removed (2 Cor. 12:9-10).

6. *God's love for the world shows his intention and purpose but is manifested by his further provision.*

    a. God's love is manifested to those who believe (John 3:16).

    b. Christ died for all but intercedes only for those who have been chosen and who come to him (John 17:9; Heb. 7:25).

7. *The burning bush* (Ex. 3:1-6)

    a. Moses wanted to see precisely why the bush didn't burn up.

    b. God said, 'Stop! Don't come any closer.'

CONCLUSION

Does God love everybody? '"Do I take any pleasure in the death of the wicked?" declares the Sovereign LORD. "Rather, am I not pleased when they turn from their ways and live"' (Ezek. 18:23) would tend to show that God does love everybody. But if he does, why does he not turn everyone from their wicked ways and freely give them the gift of life? It is clear from other parts of Scripture that God does not love everybody with the same degree of love. God's love is a mystery tied up with the fact of his sovereignty. But the extent of it and its limitations are beyond our understanding.

13

THE NAME OF JESUS

A. What a glorious opportunity to explore the greatest and sweetest name on earth!

  1. God – the Father of Jesus – gave his Son a name.

  2. *And yet his parents each had a hand in officially giving him his name.*

    a. 'But after he had considered this, an angel of the Lord appeared to him in a dream and said, "Joseph son of David, do not be afraid to take Mary home as your wife, because what is conceived in her is from the Holy Spirit. She will give birth to a son, and you are to give him the name Jesus, because he will save his people from their sins"' (Matt. 1:20-21).

    b. 'But the angel said to her, "Do not be afraid, Mary, you have found favour with God. You will be with child and give birth to a son and you are to give him the name Jesus"' (Luke 1:30-31).

B. In ancient times a person's name provided two things:

  1. *Identification.*

    a. It is what distinguished one person from another.

    b. If a person's name was the same as another's:

      (1) His name would be linked with his father's for further identification.

      (2) E.g., Simon Peter was known as Simon Barjona, son of Jonah (Matt. 16:17).

  2. *Index to their character or calling.*

    a. Abraham's new name (from Abram) meant 'father of a great multitude'.

    b. Sarah's new name (from Sarai) meant 'princess'.

    c. Isaac means 'laughter'.

d. Jacob meant 'supplanter' but he was given the name Israel which means 'he who strives with God' or 'soldier of God'.

C. Jesus is the Greek form of Joshua (cf. Acts 7:45; Heb. 4:8).

1. *Whether in the long form* yeshua *('Yahweh is salvation') or one of the short forms* yesua *('Yahweh saves', Neh. 7:7) the name:*
   a. Identifies the son of Mary and Joseph; it would be the way he would be known forever and ever.
   b. Refers to his character and calling: Saviour.
2. *Joshua, Moses' successor, was chosen to lead the people of Israel from the desert to the promised land* (Josh. 3-4).
   a. This means also that Joshua was a type of Christ.
   b. But there was another Joshua in the Old Testament.
      (1) Joshua the high priest, contemporary of Zerubbabel (Ezra 2:2; Neh. 7:7).
      (2) But instead of referring to either of these Joshuas, the angel explains the significance of the name by referring to Psalm 130:8: 'He himself will redeem Israel from all their sins.'

D. All the above should be put in the context of what we know about the name of God (see *Understanding Theology*, Volume 1, chapter 9).

1. *One of the most startling verses in the Old Testament is Exodus 6:3:* 'I appeared to Abraham, to Isaac and to Jacob as God Almighty, but by my name the LORD I did not make myself known to them.'
   a. Yahweh literally means 'I am who I am' or 'I will be what I will be' (Ex. 3:14).
   b. This came in reply to Moses' request, 'Suppose I go to the Israelites and say to them, "The God of your fathers has sent me to you," and they ask me, "What is his name?" Then what shall I tell them?' (Ex. 3:13).
2. *Parallel with the fresh understanding of the meaning of God's name came a new phenomenon: signs and wonders.*
   a. Signs and wonders were virtually unknown in the era of the Patriarchs (Abraham, Isaac and Jacob).
      (1) Not missing of course was God's extraordinary providence.

   (2) One must not forget the unusual birth of Isaac.

  b. But with the emergence of the significance of God's name came an extraordinary series of signs, wonders and miracles.

   (1) The first was the burning bush (Ex. 3:2-6).

   (2) Then came the wonder of Moses' rod, the ten plagues in Egypt, the pillar of cloud and fire, the crossing of the Red Sea and the manna.

 3. *The two main ways God revealed himself in the Old Testament were by his word and his name.*

  a. The Psalms declared that God magnified his word above all his name (Ps. 138:2 AV – the literal translation of the Hebrew; see the Living Bible margin).

  b. But in the name of Jesus one has both.

   (1) Jesus is the word that was made flesh (John 1:14).

   (2) His name was the basis of the miracles (Acts 3:16).

E. Why is the lesson important?

 1. As we have seen, names are significant in the Bible.

 2. The greatest and sweetest name of all is Jesus.

 3. His name is an index to his calling but also to his power.

 4. We need to see how faith joined to his name can bring salvation and healing.

 5. It is essential to our understanding of prayer.

I. OTHER TITLES AND NAMES OF JESUS

A. Lord Jesus Christ

 1. *'Lord' refers to Jesus being God.*

  a. It is bringing all that was true of Jahweh to the person of Jesus.

  b. Essential to our profession of faith is our affirmation that Jesus is God.

   (1) 'That if you confess with your mouth, "Jesus is Lord," and believe in your heart that God raised him from the dead, you will be saved' (Rom. 10:9).

   (2) 'Therefore I tell you that no-one who is speaking by the Spirit of God says, "Jesus be cursed," and no-one can say, "Jesus is Lord," except by the Holy Spirit' (1 Cor. 12:3).

2. *The word 'Christ' refers to Jesus being the Messiah.*

    a. Messiah and Christ can be used interchangeably.

        (1) Messiah means the Anointed One.

        (2) Anointed is the Greek equivalent of Messiah.

    b. Anointed comes from *chrio* (Gr.) that means to smear with an ointment.

        (1) Messiah was the long expected fulfilment of the Old Testament prophecies.

        (2) Lord Jesus Christ embodies three things in the title:

            (a) The 'human' name – Jesus.

            (b) The Deity of Jesus – Lord.

            (c) His being the Jews' Messiah, or Anointed One – Christ.

B. Son of God

1. *Jesus had no earthly father.*

    a. Joseph and Mary had no sexual relations until after Jesus was born (Matt. 1:25).

    b. Mary was a virgin and became pregnant by the Holy Spirit (Luke 1:34-36).

2. *He was therefore literally God's own Son.*

    a. He was God's 'one and only' Son (John 3:16; 1:18).

    b. God could never have a 'second' Son.

        (1) The fullness of the Godhead lived in Jesus (Col. 2:9).

        (2) The Eternal Word (Gr. *logos*), the Second Person of the Godhead, became flesh – Jesus (John 1:14).

            (a) The Father, the first Person of the Godhead, did not become flesh.

            (b) The Holy Spirit, the Third Person of the Godhead, did not become flesh.

C. Son of Man

1. *An expression that comes from Ezekiel and Daniel 7:13-14, Jesus used this expression of himself more than any other.*

    a. It occurs 81 times in the gospels – 64 in the synoptics; it refers to:

        (1) The apocalyptic Son of Man who comes at the end of the age.

        (2) The suffering and dying Son of Man.

        (3) The earthly Son of Man.

b. Rudolf Bultmann claimed Jesus never used the title of himself but of another figure coming in the future!

2. *Don Carson thinks that Jesus used the term because it was ambiguous; it could conceal as well as reveal.*

    a. It could temporarily hide his Messianic identity, for the term Son of Man was regarded as the God-like figure Daniel referred to.

    b. It none the less revealed Jesus' self-conscious identity of himself – that he was the one Daniel meant.

    c. The expression captures both authority and suffering and the phrase may have been 'mystified after the cross' (Carson).

D. Son of David (Matt. 1:1).

1. This refers to his kingship and genealogy traced to King David (cf. Luke 2:4).

2. 'Christ' was understood by many Jews as being the son of David (Matt. 22:41-42).

3. Bartimaeus cried out, 'Jesus, Son of David, have mercy on me!' (Mark 10:47).

E. Other titles

1. Immanuel ('God with us'): Matthew 1:23; Isaiah 7:14.

2. Saviour: Luke 2:11; Acts 5:31.

3. Word: John 1:1,14; Revelation 19:13.

4. Lamb of God: John 1:29,35; Revelation 5:6.

5. Mediator: Galatians 3:19; 1 Timothy 2:5.

6. Lord of glory: 1 Corinthians 2:8; James 2:1.

7. King of kings, Lord of lords: Revelation 19:16.

8. Prophet: Matthew 21:11.

9. Priest: Hebrews 4:14.

10. King: 1 Timothy 1:17.

II. The sound of Jesus' name

A. What the sound of Jesus' name does to the Father.

1. *At the natural level there is a certain pride and satisfaction which parents feel in their children's names.*

    a. The parent has the privilege of naming their son or daughter.

b. We therefore are affirmed in a certain measure when we hear people addressing or referring to our children's names.
  (1) We had our own reasons for the names we chose.
  (2) Our reasons are in a sense fulfilled in the sound of their names.

2. *How much more with the Father who gave his Son his name.*
  a. God is pleased with his Son.
    (1) 'And a voice from heaven said, "This is my Son, whom I love; with him I am well pleased"' (Matt. 3:17).
    (2) 'While he was still speaking, a bright cloud enveloped them, and a voice from the cloud said, "This is my Son, whom I love; with him I am well pleased. Listen to him!"' (Matt. 17:5).
  b. The sound of the name Jesus gives us immediate access to the Father.
    (1) 'Jesus answered, "I am the way and the truth and the life. No-one comes to the Father except through me"' (John 14:6).
    (2) 'Salvation is found in no-one else, for there is no other name under heaven given to men by which we must be saved' (Acts 4:12).
  c. To be saved therefore we must call on the name of Jesus.
    (1) 'For, "Everyone who calls on the name of the Lord will be saved"' (Rom. 10:13).
    (2) The name of the Lord is Jesus; God waits to hear the sound of that name!
      (a) The name of Jesus gets the Father's attention.
      (b) That name therefore must be uttered – confessing with your mouth, 'Jesus is Lord' (Rom. 10:9).

3. *It is likewise essential to all effective prayer.*
  a. The Lord's Prayer (Matt. 6:9-13) presupposes the name of Jesus.
    (1) Some claim this Prayer omits the name of Jesus.
    (2) Wrong; the moment we say, 'Our Father in heaven,' we declare Jesus' name.
      (a) The only reason we can call God 'Father' is because he revealed himself that way by sending his Son.
      (b) Therefore the Lord's Prayer assumes Jesus!

b. When we pray therefore we ask in Jesus' name.

    (1) 'And I will do whatever you ask in my name, so that the Son may bring glory to the Father. You may ask me for anything in my name, and I will do it' (John 14:13-14).

    (2) The object of the prayer is the Father.

      (a) It is he to whom we pray.

      (b) We come to the Father on the basis of Jesus' name.

c. Two examples of such praying:

    (1) The prayer that resulted in the very place being 'shaken' was 'through the name of your holy servant Jesus' (Acts 4:24-31).

    (2) Paul's prayer for the Ephesians was prefaced by 'In him [Christ Jesus our Lord] and through faith in him [Gr.: through the faith of him] we may approach God. . . . For this reason I kneel before the Father. . . . ' (Eph. 3:12-21).

B. What the sound of Jesus' name does for sinners.

'How sweet the name of Jesus sounds
In a believer's ear;
It soothes his sorrows, heals his wounds,
And takes away his fear.'

John Newton

1. *The name Jesus embodies all Jesus was to sinners.*

a. Jesus said:

    (1) 'I have not come to call the righteous, but sinners' (Matt. 9:13).

    (2) 'It is not the healthy who need a doctor, but the sick' (Luke 5:31).

b. Isaiah said of him:

    (1) 'A bruised reed he will not break, and a smouldering wick he will not snuff out' (Isa. 42:3; Matt. 12:20).

    (2) 'He has sent me to bind up the broken-hearted, to proclaim freedom for the captives and release from darkness for the prisoners' (Isa. 61:1; Luke 4:18).

c. Ananias said to Saul of Tarsus:

    (1) 'And now what are you waiting for? Get up, be baptised and wash your sins away, calling on his name' (Acts 22:16).

    (2) What saved – baptism? No! 'Calling on his name.'

2. *The name of Jesus embodies all Jesus was to the sick.*

   a. 'When Jesus had entered Capernaum, a centurion came to him, asking for help. "Lord," he said, "my servant lies at home paralysed and in terrible suffering" (Matt. 8:5-6).

      (1) Jesus' response: 'I will go and heal him' (Matt. 8:7).

      (2) Jesus' response to the begging leper who pleaded, 'Lord, if you are willing, you can make me clean,' was: 'I am willing. Be clean' (Matt. 8:2-3).

   b. People brought all their sick to him. 'And begged him to let the sick just touch the edge of his cloak, and all who touched him were healed' (Matt. 14:36).

      (1) At one place 'The power of the Lord was present for him to heal the sick' (Luke 5:17).

      (2) A paralysed man was instantly healed. 'Everyone was amazed and gave praise to God. They were filled with awe and said, "We have seen remarkable things today' (Luke 5:26).

   c. Peter and John saw a forty year old man who had been crippled from birth.

      (1) 'Then Peter said, "Silver or gold I do not have, but what I have I give you. In the name of Jesus Christ of Nazareth, walk"' (Acts 3:6).

      (2) 'By faith in the name of Jesus, this man whom you see and know was made strong. It is Jesus' name and the faith that comes through him that has given this complete healing to him, as you can all see' (Acts 3:16).

   d. The signs, wonders and miracles that emerged with the disclosing of God's name (Ex. 6:3) characterised the name of Jesus!

3. *What the name of Jesus does for the poor.*

   a. 'The common people heard him gladly' (Mark 12:37 AV).

   b. When John the Baptist had second thoughts and sent word to Jesus, 'Are you the one who was to come, or should we expect someone else?' Jesus replied:

      (1) 'Go back and report to John what you have seen and heard: The blind receive sight, the lame walk, those who have leprosy are cured, the deaf hear, the dead are raised, and the good news is preached to the poor' (Luke 7:22).

(2) 'Listen, my dear brothers: Has not God chosen those who are poor in the eyes of the world to be rich in faith and to inherit the kingdom he promised those who love him?' (Jas. 2:5).

c. Jesus' mandate and mission was this: 'The Spirit of the Lord is on me, because he has anointed me to preach good news to the poor. He has sent me to proclaim freedom for the prisoners and recovery of sight for the blind, to release the oppressed, to proclaim the year of the Lord's favour' (Luke 4:18-19).

(1) Note: there is no promise that the poor would become prosperous (as the sick might be healed).

(2) What is the purpose, then, of Jesus' name and the poor?

    (a) The poor are affirmed, they are given acceptance and status.

    (b) They have equal rights with anyone else in the Kingdom of God.

C. What the sound of Jesus' name does to Satan.

1. *The devil instantly recognised Jesus and knew who he was.*

    a. 'What do you want with us, Jesus of Nazareth? Have you come to destroy us? I know who you are – the Holy One of God!' (Mark 1:24).

    (1) '"Be quiet!" said Jesus sternly. "Come out of him!" The evil spirit shook the man violently and came out of him with a shriek' (Mark 1:25-26).

    (2) 'The people were all so amazed that they asked each other, "What is this? A new teaching – and with authority! He even gives orders to evil spirits and they obey him"' (Mark 1:27).

    b. A demon-possessed man saw Jesus; 'He cried out and fell at his feet, shouting at the top of his voice, "What do you want with me, Jesus, Son of the Most High God? I beg you, don't torture me!"' (Luke 8:28).

    (1) Jesus cast the demons out; sent them to the pigs.

    (2) Jesus said to the man, 'Return home and tell how much God has done for you' (Luke 8:39).

2. *What Jesus did when confronting evil powers has been transferred to his very name!*

    a. Paul faced a demon-possessed slave girl who had a spirit by which she predicted the future.

      (1) She was a nuisance to Paul and others for several days.

      (2) He finally turned to the girl 'and said to the spirit, "In the name of Jesus Christ I command you to come out of her!"' (Acts 16:18).

    b. Some men found they were out of their depth when they tried to play around with the demonic and Jesus' name.

      (1) They would say, 'In the name of Jesus, whom Paul preaches, I command you to come out' (Acts 19:13).

      (2) 'One day, the evil spirit answered them, "Jesus I know, and I know about Paul, but who are you?" Then the man who had the evil spirit jumped on them and overpowered them all. He gave them such a beating that they ran out of the house naked and bleeding' (Acts 19:15-16).

'There is power in the name of Jesus;
We believe in his name.
We have called on the name of Jesus;
We are saved! We are saved!
At his name the demons flee,
At his name the captives are freed.
For there is no other name that is higher
Than Jesus.'   *Noel Richards*

D. God gave Jesus his own name! (Phil. 2:9-11).

CONCLUSION

God gave Jesus his name, and in so doing marked his fatherhood of the infant Saviour. The name also indicated the Lord's character and calling. Jesus means 'Saviour'. Jesus was given several other titles, all of them marking an aspect of his person or mission.

The name of Jesus is essential to all effective believing prayer. It is the name that thrills the heart of Christians. The right use of the name of Jesus gives the believer power over Satan. The Devil is afraid of the name of Jesus. A warning – there are conditions that are attached to the name of Jesus before power is manifested. There is no promise that suggests that the name of Jesus has automatic power in and of itself. The following must be joined to that name.

Faith: 'By faith in the name of Jesus, this man whom you see and know was made strong. It is Jesus' name and the faith that comes through him that has given this complete healing to him, as you can all see' (Acts 3:16). Had there been no faith there could have been no healing.

God's will. 'This is the confidence we have in approaching God: that if we ask anything according to his will, he hears us. And if we know that he hears us – whatever we ask – we know that we have what we asked of him' (1 John 5:14-15). This principle obviously must lie behind the promise of John 14:14: 'You may ask me for anything in my name, and I will do it.'

Also God is sovereign and does not deposit power in his Son's name that can be used indiscriminately like the sons of the Jewish priest in Acts 19:14. We must simultaneously bow down to the name of Jesus and to the sovereignty of God. But when these two coalesce the outcome is awesome.

14

MARY THE MOTHER OF JESUS

INTRODUCTION

A. It is always right to consider the character of Mary, the mother of our Lord.

    1. *This is the way her cousin Elizabeth (six months pregnant with her own baby) referred to Mary the mother of Jesus before he was born.* 'But why am I so favoured, that the mother of my Lord should come to me?' (Luke 1:43).

        a. At that time Mary had only been pregnant for a day or two.

        b. She wasted no time after submitting to the will of God (Luke 1:38-39).

    2. *As soon as Elizabeth heard Mary's greeting her own child – who was John the Baptist – leaped in her womb* (Luke 1:41).

        a. Elizabeth was immediately filled with the Holy Spirit.

        b. 'In a loud voice she exclaimed: "Blessed are you among women, and blessed is the child you will bear! But why am I so favoured, that the mother of my Lord should come to me?"' (Luke 1:42-43).

B. The phrase 'mother of our Lord' was extended to 'Mother of God' in ancient church history.

    1. *Is there a difference between calling Mary the 'mother of our Lord' and 'Mother of God'?*

        a. Is not 'the Lord' the same as 'God'?

        b. If so, what is wrong with calling Mary the 'Mother of God'?

    2. *Elizabeth was filled with the Spirit when she called Mary 'the mother of my Lord'.*

        a. That much we know, and this we must also do.

        b. But does it follow that we call her the Mother of God?

C. Why is this subject important?

1. *Roman Catholics call Mary the 'Mother of God' and even pray, 'Hail Mary, Mother of God, pray for us sinners now and at the hour of our death.'*

   a. We should know the correct response to this.

   b. If this is not right to do, why?

2. *Protestants have sometimes overreacted and shown little or nor respect for Mary at all.*

   a. It seems some are fearful of sounding too much like those they feel are in error.

   b. Is this overreaction justified?

3. We need to see exactly what is the correct biblical, spiritual and theological understanding of Mary the mother of Jesus.

4. We must never forget the importance of the virgin birth of Christ.

5. A look at ancient church history is interesting and gives us an opportunity to see how the worship of Mary developed.

6. Peter said, 'But in your hearts set apart Christ as Lord. Always be prepared to give an answer to everyone who asks you to give the reason for the hope that you have. But do this with gentleness and respect, keeping a clear conscience, so that those who speak maliciously against your good behaviour in Christ may be ashamed of their slander' (1 Pet. 3:15-16).

7. The only way to know what to believe is by a careful review of what the scriptures tell us.

I. THE BIRTH OF JESUS

A. Old Testament prophecy

1. *The first prophecy of Jesus is Genesis 3:15:* 'And I will put enmity between you and the woman, and between your offspring and hers; he will crush your head, and you will strike his heel.'

   a. It was a word to the serpent.

   b. The reference to 'hers' is to the woman – Eve – who had sinned.

2. *The most explicit prophecy of Jesus' birth is Isaiah 7:14:* 'Therefore the Lord himself will give you a sign: The virgin will be with child and will give birth to a son, and will call him Immanuel.'

    a. A virgin will become pregnant.

       (1) Heb. *Almah* literally means 'maiden' or 'young woman'.

       (2) But a young woman in those days was always assumed to be a virgin.

    b. The child would be male – 'a son'.

    c. He would be called 'Immanuel', which means 'God with us'.

3. *Isaiah elaborated on this in Isaiah 9:6:* 'For to us a child is born, to us a son is given, and the government will be on his shoulders. And he will be called Wonderful Counsellor, Mighty God, Everlasting Father, Prince of Peace.'

    a. A child would be 'born'.

    b. A son is 'given'.

    c. He would be a ruler: 'government will be on his shoulders'.

    d. He would have supreme wisdom: 'Wonderful Counsellor'.

    e. He would be God: 'Mighty God'.

    f. He is the eternal God: 'Everlasting Father'.

    g. His achievement would be bringing peace: 'Prince of Peace'.

B. New Testament fulfilment

1. *Matthew's account – from Joseph's perspective* (Matt. 1:18-25).

    a. Mary was pledged to be married to Joseph.

       (1) This was like engagement today.

       (2) However, it was probably stronger than that; to be 'pledged' meant no turning back.

    b. Joseph and Mary did not sleep together.

       (1) Unlike so many today, this was unthinkable.

       (2) Mary therefore remained a virgin.

    c. Mary 'was found to be with child through the Holy Spirit' (v.18).

       (1) Matthew gives no further details how this came about.

       (2) Presumably Mary told Joseph what had happened (as told by Luke).

    d. Joseph was apparently not cheered by the news.

       (1) He had a good reputation – 'a righteous man'.

       (2) He respected her reputation – 'did not want to expose her to public disgrace'.

       (3) He decided to break the engagement – a bond so strong that the word 'divorce' was used: 'he had in mind to divorce her quietly' (v.19).

   e. An angel of the Lord intervened: 'But after he had considered
   this, an angel of the Lord appeared to him in a dream and
   said, "Joseph son of David, do not be afraid to take Mary
   home as your wife, because what is conceived in her is
   from the Holy Spirit"' (Matt. 1:20).
   (1) This gave the scenario an aura of infallibility.
   (2) He was addressed by name, together with his genealogy.
   (3) He was told not to be afraid.
   (4) He was told to take her home – and to be her husband.
   (5) The whole matter is what the Holy Spirit had done.
   (6) In a word: Mary was vindicated (cf. Luke 1:35).

   f. At this point God's purpose in this was unveiled: 'She will
   give birth to a son, and you will give him the name Jesus,
   because he will save his people from their sins' (Matt. 1:21).
   (1) The child in her is male.
   (2) Joseph had the privilege of naming the son Jesus.
   (3) The son's mission was to save God's people.

   g. Matthew tied the matter to Isaiah's prophecy: 'All this took
   place to fulfil what the Lord had said through the prophet:
   "The virgin will be with child and will give birth to a son,
   and they will call him Immanuel" – which means "God
   with us"' (Matt. 1:22-23).
   (1) The quotation is from the LXX (Septuagint).
   (2) Here the Greek word *parthenos* was used, a word that
   can only mean 'virgin', which shows how the ancient
   rabbis understood the Hebrew *almah*.

   h. The unsung hero of Christmas is Joseph.
   (1) He submitted to the stigma of being accused of fathering
   the child out of wedlock. 'When Joseph woke up, he
   did what the angel of the Lord had commanded him and
   took Mary home as his wife' (Matt. 1:24).
   (2) His life would never be the same again (cf. John 6:42).

   i. There would be no conjugal relationship until after Jesus
   was born. 'But he had no union with her until after she
   gave birth to a son' (Matt. 1:25).
   (1) The implication is clear: a conjugal relationship would
   begin after Jesus' birth.
   (2) This is verified by John 7:3-5 (cf. Mark 3:31ff).
   (3) Paul explicitly calls James 'the Lord's brother' (Gal. 1:19).

2. *Luke's account – from Mary's perspective which in terms of actual time obviously preceded the event described by Matthew* (Luke 1:26-56).

    a. Gabriel was sent to Nazareth to visit Mary (v.26).

        (1) She is said to be a virgin (v.27).

        (2) She was engaged to Joseph, a descendent of David (v.27).

    b. The angel's greeting was this: Mary is 'highly favoured', as 'the Lord is with you' (v. 28).

        (1) Mary could not grasp what was happening (v.29).

        (2) Mary was told not to be afraid (v.30).

    c. Then came the purpose of the visit. 'You will be with child and give birth to a son, and you are to give him the name Jesus. He will be great and will be called the Son of the Most High. The Lord God will give him the throne of his father David, and he will reign over the house of Jacob for ever; his kingdom will never end' (Luke 1:31-33).

        (1) Mary was further bewildered.

        (2) '"How will this be," Mary asked the angel, "since I am a virgin?"' (Luke 1:34).

    d. The answer and explanation: 'The angel answered, "The Holy Spirit will come upon you, and the power of the Most High will overshadow you. So the holy one to be born will be called the Son of God"' (Luke 1:35).

        (1) The Holy Spirit would do the work.

        (2) The child would be male and would be the Son of God.

    e. As for the incredulity of all this: 'For nothing is impossible with God' (Luke 1:37).

    f. Mary agreed:

        (1) 'I am the Lord's servant'.

        (2) 'May it be to me as you have said' (v.38).

        (3) At that moment Mary became pregnant. 'Then the angel left her' (v.38).

    g. It was at that time Mary went to see Elizabeth (v.39ff).

        (1) As soon as she greeted Elizabeth the six-month old child leaped in Elizabeth's womb, and Elizabeth was filled with the Holy Spirit (v.41).

        (2) 'In a loud voice she exclaimed: "Blessed are you among women, and blessed is the child you will bear!"' (Luke 1:42).

h. This is when Elizabeth referred to Mary as the mother of her Lord. 'But why am I so favoured, that the mother of my Lord should come to me?' (Luke 1:43).

i. Elizabeth also marvelled that Mary's submission to the angel's words was an act of faith: 'Blessed is she who has believed that what the Lord has said to her will be accomplished' (Luke 1:45).

    (1) This is a fact some might overlook.

    (2) Mary had to believe before all the above took place.

j. In a word: She, like the rest of us, had to be justified by faith.

k. Mary then prophesied (Luke 1:46-55).

    (1) She saw that she would be honoured from now on: 'From now on all generations will call me blessed.'

    (2) This is significant: 'blessed' is the way the Spirit foresaw the proper respect due to Mary.

    (3) 'Blessed' means 'happy' and implies an anointing – nothing more.

II. THE RISE AND DEVELOPMENT OF THE CULT OF MARY

A. The denial of the virgin birth

1. *A certain Cerinthus (late first century) said that Jesus was not born of a virgin but was the son of Joseph and Mary, like other men.*

    a. But he was superior to all others in justice, prudence and wisdom.

    b. 'Christ' descended on Jesus at his baptism in the form of a dove but flew back in the end leaving Jesus to suffer.

2. *Certain Jews called 'Ebionites'.*

    a. They believed Jesus fulfilled the Jewish law and God chose him to be Messiah.

    b. But he was only the son of Joseph and Mary; they denied the virgin birth.

3. *Gnosticism generally denied the virgin birth.*

    a. While it stressed the deity of Christ, it denied that Jesus as a man in the flesh was the Christ.

    b. Christ in the flesh was not born of the virgin.

4. *The Apostles' Creed was designed largely to refute Gnosticism and to affirm Jesus' humanity and virgin birth. The Creed includes these lines:*

      a. 'Who was born of the Holy Spirit and the Virgin Mary.'

      b. 'Who was crucified, dead and buried.'

B. The 'theotokos' controversy

  1. *Cyril (d.444 AD) became the bishop of Alexandria in 412 AD.*

    a. He called Mary *theotokos* (Gr. 'God-bearer').

      (1) This phrase preceded this time.

      (2) But Cyril became a champion and campaigner for this phrase.

    b. It had been used by Athanasius and others.

  2. *Nestorius (c.428 AD), bishop of Constantinople, denied that the Virgin Mary was* theotokos.

    a. It was Jesus the man who was born of Mary, not God the Word.

    b. 'I could not call a baby two or three months old "God".'

  3. *Cyril objected to Nestorius' teaching.*

    a. He wrote Nestorius a firm letter urging Nestorius to accept *theotokos*.

    b. Nestorius refused.

  4. *Cyril maintained that God the Word, who is eternally begotten or born of God the Father, was in time born of the Virgin Mary as man.*

    a. Therefore Mary is *theotokos*.

    b. Because the man Jesus born of her was God.

  5. Nestorianism was regarded as heresy by the Western church.

  6. *Whereas* theotokos *literally means* God-bearer, *it became known in Latin, and subsequently in English, as* Mother of God.

    a. Cyril won the day.

    b. But many feel that Nestorius was orthodox and misunderstood.

      (1) He was wrong to say that baby Jesus was not God.

      (2) He only felt that a human mother could not give the divine nature to the *Logos* (Word), hence Christ's deity did not originate from Mary.

C. The Immaculate Conception

  1. Duns Scotus (1265–1307) is the first major advocate of Mary's immaculate conception: the idea that she was conceived without any sin – that she was pure and sinless from the moment of her conception.

2. This was widely held by many before him but people like Thomas Aquinas (d.1274) held that she was freed from sin *after* her conception.

3. With Duns Scotus' position the way was opened for the concept that Mary did not need redemption.

4. Duns Scotus won the day and this was defined as dogma in 1854 by Pope Pius IX.

5. This was reaffirmed by Vatican II (1962-65).

D. The veneration of Mary

1. Irenaeus (d.200 AD) suggested that Mary was the Second Eve. 'The knot of Eve's disobedience was loosened by the obedience of Mary.'

2. Tertullian (c.200 AD) asserted her perpetual virginity.

3. With the rise of monasticism the Virgin became the ideal.

4. She became foremost among all saints.

5. *She eventually virtually took the place of her Son.*

   a. At Vatican II, some wanted her to be defined as 'Co-Redemptrix' – the one who, together with Jesus Christ, redeemed the world.

   b. After all, her consent was needed for the Incarnation.

      (1) She co-operated actively in the work of human salvation.

      (2) She gave life to the world.

   c. 'Death through Eve, life through Mary.'

      (1) She was united with Jesus in suffering as he died on the cross.

      (2) Mary is the Mediatrix, who mediates between us and God.

III. Proper respect for Mary

A. Is she rightly to be called the 'Mother of God'?

1. *Martin Luther said, 'Yes; it is not wrong to say that God was born of Mary.'*

   a. It would be the same as if we said, 'This woman has given birth to a child; the child's soul, however, is not of her nature but of God, and therefore she cannot be the mother of the child.'

   b. But, says Luther, a woman is the mother of the entire child including the soul, although the soul, in a special sense, has its origin from God.

2. For this reason, Luther argues, we are justified in saying that Mary is the Mother of God.

B. I answer: this is unnecessary and invites idolatry.

  1. *It is simply taking logic beyond what the scriptures explicitly say.*

    a. I could say, Jesus is God, Mary is the mother of Jesus; therefore Mary is the Mother of God.

    b. But that is simply carrying logic beyond what the scriptures actually say.

  2. *But is not 'the mother of my Lord' and 'mother of God' the same thing?*

    a. Logically, yes.

    b. But that is not what Elizabeth, filled with the Spirit, said.

  3. *Although 'God' and 'the Lord' equally refer to the Deity (Godhead), the term 'Lord' is more personal and intimate.*

    a. In Hebrew this is *Elohim* (God) and *Yahweh* (Lord).

      (1) *Elohim* is general Deity – referring to his power and transcendence.

      (2) *Yahweh* is the specific name of God – referring to his involvement with us; the Father gave Jesus this name (Phil. 2:11).

    b. The word 'God' immediately suggests his various attributes – omniscience, omnipotence, omnipresence, etc..

      (1) To call Mary the Mother of God is unnecessarily inviting the worship of her that followed in the Roman Catholic church.

      (2) It implies Mary is eternal and gave birth to the God who made us.

CONCLUSION

We are none the less required to give Mary due honour and call her 'blessed' (Luke 1:48). She did in a sense truly restore dignity to womanhood. This is implied in I Timothy 2:15: 'But women will be saved through childbearing – if they continue in faith, love and holiness with propriety' ('saved' here means 'restored', see NIV footnote). Mary did this in giving birth to the Son of God.

Mary's suffering and self-denial were very deep and significant. 'A sword will pierce your own soul,' Simeon said to Mary. This was fulfilled when Jesus died (see John 19:25). Mary kept secret a thousand things most people would have soon revealed about Jesus. 'His mother treasured all these things in her heart' (Luke 2:51). Her reward in heaven will be wonderful beyond our ability to fathom. Her heart must be grieved in heaven, if possible, should she know that people venerate her and pray to her.

15

CHRISTMAS AND THE GLORY OF GOD

INTRODUCTION

A. Christmas has always had its critics.
   1. *These criticisms come partly from the world.*
      a. Some people hate Christmas because of its Christian basis.
      b. Some people hate Christmas because it makes them feel lonely.
         (1) More suicides take place during the Christmas season than at any other time.
         (2) This is partly because of memories that haunt lonely people.
      c. Some hate Christmas because they feel obligated to celebrate.
         (1) They have to buy presents.
         (2) Their schedules are disrupted.
   2. *These criticisms come partly from those of non-Christian religions:*
      a. Jews sometimes resent Christmas.
         (1) It reminds them of what Christians think about the Old Testament.
         (2) They don't like to feel they have gone wrong regarding Messiah.
      b. Muslims largely resent Christmas.
         (1) If given control over a nation, they would abolish it.
         (2) They resent the thought that Jesus is the Son of God.
      c. Jehovah's Witnesses hate Christmas.
         (1) They refuse to call Jesus God.
         (2) They resent the teaching that we are saved by Christ's life and death.
   3. *These criticisms come partly from Christians:*
      a. They point out that Christmas is derived largely from Roman Catholism.
         (1) 'Christmas' means Christ and mass.
         (2) That Roman Catholics make so much of Christmas is sufficient reason not to observe it, some say.

    b. They point out that Jesus was probably not born in December.

    c. There is no biblical suggestion that we should celebrate Christ's birth.

    d. Christmas is so commercial.

        (1) People buy presents that people don't want or need.

        (2) We sometimes buy things for people we don't like.

        (3) Someone said, 'We spend money we don't have for people we don't like on presents they don't need.'

4. *Some would add: Jesus came to bring peace on earth but that peace does not exist in many places.*

    a. This means, they say, Jesus' coming has proved false.

    b. Why should we celebrate such a date?

5. *Many people did not even grasp the point of the Millennium.*

    a. The year 2,000 is 2,000 AD (anno domini – the year of our Lord).

    b. But many resent any reference to the fact of Christ's coming two thousand years ago.

        (1) Incidentally, Christ may have been born in 4 BC or before.

        (2) If so, the Millennium should have been celebrated in 1996!

B. The question is: does Christmas bring glory to God?

    1. Is God glorified by the celebration of the birth of his Son?

    2. Is God glorified by non-Christians celebrating Christmas?

    3. Is God glorified by the commercialism of Christmas?

C. But there are other questions we may ask:

    1. Are we better off to ignore Christmas?

    2. Does the actual date of Jesus' birth determine one way or the other whether his birth is honoured?

    3. Are Christians who do not celebrate Christmas more spiritual?

    4. In a day in which the family unit is under ever-increasing attack, are we better off to cease coming together as families in a traditional way?

    5. Should Christians surrender Christmas to pagans just because it is commercial?

    6. Does not the celebration of Christmas make a statement of the fact of Christ's coming two thousand years ago?

    7. Is it not a good thing that Muslims and Jews are forced to reckon with Christmas every year knowing full well its origin refers to the birth of Jesus?

D. Why is this lesson important?

1. All the above questions are worth answering.
2. Any investigation into a Christian event can be edifying to Christians and a witness to non-Christians.
3. There is an inseparable connection between the glory of God and the birth of Jesus; that alone is worth looking into.
4. Regarding the Millennium, we need to be bold and unafraid of the most important date in world history – the coming of the God-man into the world.
5. We need to ask, as honestly as possible, is there not a way forward for us by which Christmas can truly glorify God?

I. THE BIRTH OF JESUS AND THE GLORY OF GOD

A. As a number of our studies focus on the glory of God some observations will inevitably overlap with other chapters:

1. *The Hebrew word* kabodh *translates 'glory'.*
   a. It means 'heaviness', or 'weightiness'.
   b. We sometimes refer to a person who 'throws his weight around' because of one's position or stature.
      (1) That is the general idea of *kabodh*.
      (2) God is of the highest stature, he is 'weighty'.
   c. Note: many testimonies coming from revival situations tell of this 'heaviness' that drove them to the floor helplessly – and that they couldn't get up for a while.

2. *The Greek word* doxa *translates 'glory', or 'praise'.*
   a. Ephesians 1:14 refers to the 'praise of his glory'.
      (1) Here *epainos* translates 'praise'.
      (2) 'Blessing' is the translation of *doxa*.
   b. *Doxa* comes from a root word that means 'opinion'.
      (1) The *doxa* of God is not only the praise of God but also the opinion of God.
      (2) This is why the will of God is inseparably connected to *doxa*, for its context in Ephesians 1:14 shows the 'plan of him who works out everything in conformity with the purpose of his will...for the praise of his glory' (Eph. 1:11-12).

3. *When we combine* kabodh *with* doxa *we come up with an
   understanding of glory that suggests the following:*
   a. It is the dignity of God's will.
   b. It is the praise of his will.

4. *However,* kabodh *is often connected with light and
   brightness.*
   a. Isaiah prophesied of the glory that would come to Zion.
      (1) 'Arise, shine, for your light has come, and the glory of
          the LORD rises upon you. See, darkness covers the earth
          and thick darkness is over the peoples, but the LORD rises
          upon you and his glory appears over you. Nations will
          come to your light, and kings to the brightness of your
          dawn' (Isa. 60:1-3).
      (2) The glory of the Lord making an 'appearance' shows
          that it can be visible.
   b. The concept of shekinah glory emerged in ancient Israel
      with this in mind.

5. *The glory became associated with a cloud, or smoke.* 'While
   Aaron was speaking to the whole Israelite community, they
   looked toward the desert, and there was the glory of the LORD
   appearing in the cloud' (Ex. 16:10).
   a. The first hint of this was in Egypt after the Passover. 'Then
      the angel of God, who had been travelling in front of Israel's
      army, withdrew and went behind them. The pillar of cloud
      also moved from in front and stood behind them, coming
      between the armies of Egypt and Israel. Throughout the
      night the cloud brought darkness to the one side and light
      to the other side; so neither went near the other all night
      long' (Ex. 14:19-20).
   b. This phenomenon appeared at the Tent of Meeting. 'As
      Moses went into the tent, the pillar of cloud would come
      down and stay at the entrance, while the LORD spoke with
      Moses' (Ex. 33:9).
   c. It was seen after Solomon brought the Ark into the Temple.
      'When the priests withdrew from the Holy Place, the cloud
      filled the temple of the LORD. And the priests could not
      perform their service because of the cloud, for the glory of
      the LORD filled his temple' (1 Kings 8:10-11).

6. *The coming of the Messiah was to be associated with the glory of God being revealed.*

   a. 'And the glory of the LORD will be revealed, and all mankind together will see it. For the mouth of the LORD has spoken' (Isa. 40:5).

   b. The Lord would suddenly come into his Temple (Mal. 3:1).

   (1) The result would be conviction of sin. '"See, I will send my messenger, who will prepare the way before me. Then suddenly the Lord you are seeking will come to his temple; the messenger of the covenant, whom you desire, will come," says the LORD Almighty. But who can endure the day of his coming? Who can stand when he appears? For he will be like a refiner's fire or a launderer's soap. He will sit as a refiner and purifier of silver; he will purify the Levites and refine them like gold and silver. Then the LORD will have men who will bring offerings in righteousness' (Mal. 3:1-3).

   (2) This was the effect of the glory upon Isaiah. '"Woe to me!" I cried. "I am ruined! For I am a man of unclean lips, and I live among a people of unclean lips, and my eyes have seen the King, the LORD Almighty"' (Isa. 6:5).

7. *In a word: the glory is the sum total of all God's attributes.*

   a. The one word that encompasses all that God is: glory.

   b. Consider the attributes of God:

   (1) Omnipotence: he is all-powerful.

   (2) Omniscience: he is all-knowing.

   (3) Omnipresence: he is everywhere.

   (4) Holiness.

   (5) Justice.

   (6) Wrath.

   (7) Love.

   (8) Mercy.

   (9) Truth.

   (10) Wisdom.

   c. The glory of God says it all.

   (1) In Acts 7:2 Stephen referred to 'the God of glory'.

   (2) In Acts 7:55 Stephen saw the glory of God.

B. What happened when Jesus was born?

1. *Prophecy was fulfilled.*
   a. A virgin conceived (Isa. 7:14).
      (1) Luke 1:26-28.
      (2) Matthew 1:18-25.
   b. Apparently contradictory prophecies coalesced.
      (1) Micah 5:2. cf. Matthew 2:5ff.
      (2) Isaiah 9:1-7. cf. Luke 2:1-7.
   c. Kings came to worship (Matt. 2:1ff. cf. Is. 60:3).
   d. Those in power were completely by-passed.
      (1) This was the dignity of God's will.
      (2) 'And the LORD said, "I will cause all my goodness to pass in front of you, and I will proclaim my name, the LORD, in your presence. I will have mercy on whom I will have mercy, and I will have compassion on whom I will have compassion"' (Ex. 33:19).
      (3) This followed Moses' request, 'Show me your glory' (Ex. 33:18).
      (4) God by-passed:
         (a) Herod.
         (b) Chief priests (Matt. 2:4).
         (c) Teachers of the law (Matt. 2:4).
         (d) 'All Jerusalem' (Matt. 2:3).
         (e) Caesar Augustus (Luke 2:1).
         (f) Quirinius (Luke 2:2).
         (g) The people of Nazareth and Bethlehem (Luke 2:4).
         (h) Those who owned the inn in Bethlehem (Luke 2:7)

2. *Those who were let in on the Event: Angels as well as:*
   a. The Magi; 'wise men', probably kings.
   b. Shepherds (Luke 2:8).
   c. It began as a day of 'small things' (Zech. 4:10).
   d. In the making: Isaiah's prophecy 'root out of dry ground' (Is. 53:2).
   e. Joseph and Mary lived with a carefully guarded secret:
      (1) They were found by the Magi (Matt. 2:11).
      (2) They were found by the shepherds (Luke 2:16).
      (3) They fled to Egypt (Matt. 2:13-15).
      (4) Note: 'But Mary treasured up all these things and pondered them in her heart' (Luke 2:19).

3. *The glory of God was manifested to the shepherds.* 'And there were shepherds living out in the fields nearby, keeping watch over their flocks at night. An angel of the Lord appeared to them, and the glory of the Lord shone around them, and they were terrified' (Luke 2:8-9).

  a. They were not seeking the glory of God, as far as we can tell.

    (1) God may come to those who seek him (Jer. 29:13).

    (2) God may reveal himself 'to those who did not seek me' (Isa. 65:1).

    (3) When the glory of God is at stake it is because of the dignity, or weightiness, of his will.

    (4) Note: we never know to whom or where God may suddenly manifest his glory; this is so that nobody can take any credit. 'So that no one may boast before him' (1 Cor. 1:29).

  b. The glory of the Lord 'shone around them'.

    (1) This refers to his brightness.

    (2) This refers to his omnipresence – 'around them'.

      (a) God is always everywhere. 'The whole earth is full of his glory' (Isa. 6:3).

      (b) But he manifests himself nonetheless in special ways.

      (c) God's omnipresence is seen in that there was no visible 'origin', that is, like a light that came from heaven to earth as a beam; rather, it was around them. There would have been no shadows (Jas. 1:17).

  d. This began with an angel, culminating in 'a great company of the heavenly host' appearing with the angel (Luke 2:13).

    (1) One angel came to the shepherds, possibly the same angel that appeared to Mary and perhaps Zechariah. (If so, it was Gabriel. Cf. Daniel 9:21.)

    (2) God loves to do the extraordinary with the most ordinary people; that is his style.

  e. The emotional reactions of the shepherds.

    (1) Fear. 'They were terrified' (Luke 2:9).

    (2) Excitement. 'When the angels had left them and gone into heaven, the shepherds said to one another, "Let's go to Bethlehem and see this thing that has happened, which the Lord has told us about"' (Luke 2:15).

    (3) cf. 2 Samuel 6:8-9,14.

4. *The event was climaxed by a celebration of the glory of God.* 'Glory to God in the highest, and on earth peace to men on whom his favour rests' (Luke 2:14).

   a. All the above brought glory to God.

   b. All the above was a manifestation of the glory of God.

   c. All the above means that we too must bring glory to God.

II. CAN WE BRING GLORY TO GOD OUT OF CHRISTMAS?

A. Behind this possibility is the principle of grace abounding.

   1. *Even if Christmas has pagan origins, God can overrule.*

      a. He makes the wrath of men to praise him. 'Surely your wrath against men brings you praise, and the survivors of your wrath are restrained' (Ps. 76:10).

      b. God can get glory out of anything!

   2. *The Plan of Redemption had its origins in the Fall of Man.*

      a. But, said Paul, 'Where sin increased, grace increased all the more' (Rom. 5:20).

      b. So too with Christmas.

B. The teaching of all the above brings glory to God.

   1. *This lesson is about the glory of God.*

   2. *Were it nor for Christmas, might we have thought of this lesson?*

      a. God instituted the Lord's Supper to keep us in continual remembrance of Christ's death.

      b. Who can deny that God allowed Christmas to emerge, in order that we give attention to Christ's birth which might otherwise have received less attention?

C. How then might Christmas bring glory to God?

   1. *When we honour the birth of his Son.*

   2. *When we remind people of the reason for Christmas.*

   3. *When we take non-Christian friends to church.*

   4. *When we worship God in thanksgiving for the birth of his Son:*

      a. For the way it was ordained.

      b. For the way it was prophesied.

      c. For the way prophecy was fulfilled.

   5. *When we remember why Christ came.*

      a. He was born a Saviour (Luke 2:11).

      b. His name was called Jesus for he would save his people from their sins (Matt. 1:21).

6. *When we remember the Cross.*
   a. The Son of God was born to die.
   b. His death is what explained his designation as Saviour.
      (1) Messiah was not to be a political figure.
      (2) Messiah was to shed his blood and bear our sins (Isa. 53:6).
7. *When we concentrate on the words of the great carols.*
   a. Charles Wesley's theology in 'Hark the herald angels sing' is an unfolding of brilliant theology.
8. *When we remember the lonely.*
   a. This is an opportunity to open our homes to lonely people.
   b. We can shower them with presents that they otherwise would never receive.
9. *When we can be thankful for family and friends.*
   a. We may not always have what we now have in the way of family.
   b. Make the most of days that we will treasure.
10. When we receive a present, remember God's gift to us: his Son.

CONCLUSION

Christmas has its critics from those within the church, those outside of it and followers of other religions. But an annual festival celebrating the birth of Jesus can be used to bring glory to God and therefore be acceptable to him. God's glory was manifest at the birth of Jesus, who is the personification of his glory. He was also glorified by the angels, the shepherds and the magi. Christmas can be used as the basis of outreach though which God is glorified in the conversion of sinners. However, there is much about Christmas that is dishonouring to God, such as its commercialism and hypocrisy.

16

THE SIGNIFICANCE OF PALM SUNDAY

INTRODUCTION

A. The original event of Palm Sunday is mentioned in all four gospels in the New Testament.
   1. *Synoptic gospels.*
      a. Matthew 21:1-17.
      b. Mark 11:1-11.
      c. Luke 19:28-40.
   2. Gospel of John 12:12-19.

B. This event is foretold in the Old Testament.
   1. *'Rejoice greatly, O Daughter of Zion! Shout, Daughter of Jerusalem! See, your king comes to you, righteous and having salvation, gentle and riding on a donkey, on a colt, the foal of a donkey'* (Zech. 9:9).
      a. Matthew and John refer to Zecheriah 9:9.
      b. Mark and Luke do not mention it.
   2. *'Blessed is he who comes in the name of the LORD. From the house of the LORD we bless you'* (Ps. 118:26).
      a. All four gospels refer to this verse.
      b. Three of the gospels add to this:
         (1) 'Blessed is the coming kingdom of our father David' (Mark 11:10).
         (2) 'Peace in heaven and glory in the highest!' (Luke 19:38).
         (3) 'Blessed is the King of Israel!' (John 12:13).

C. Three of the gospels use the term 'Hosanna':
   1. Matthew 21:9: 'Hosanna to the Son of David! . . . Hosanna in the highest!'
   2. Mark 11:10: 'Hosanna in the highest!'
   3. *John 12:13: 'Hosanna!'*
      a. Hosanna means 'save!' or 'he saves' or 'salvation'.
      b. Luke does not mention this.

D. The synoptic gospels each refer to Jesus' order to go to a village, find a donkey, untie it and bring it to him.

1. Mark and Luke show that the disciples were asked why they were taking the colt (Mark 11:4ff; Luke 19:33ff).
2. Matthew refers to a donkey and a colt; the disciples were to bring 'them' to Jesus (Matt. 21:2).
3. Mark and Luke refer only to a colt.
4. John says that Jesus 'found a young donkey and sat upon it' (John 12:14).

E. How Palm Sunday got its name.

1. *The event took place five days before the Passover.*
   a. Passover that year was on Good Friday (14th Nisan).
   b. Jesus arrived at Bethany 'six days before the Passover' (John 12:1).
   c. 'The next day' – which would have been the first day of the week – 'the great crowd that had come for the Feast heard that Jesus was on his way to Jerusalem' (John 12:12).
   d. In a word: it was Sunday.
2. John then says, 'They took palm branches and went out to meet him, shouting, "Hosanna!" "Blessed is he who comes in the name of the Lord!" "Blessed is the King of Israel!"' (John 12:13).
3. *Hence, we call that day Palm Sunday.*
   a. It was the first day of what we now call Holy Week.
   b. It was the beginning of the last week of Jesus' life on earth.

F. Never in history had there been any event so promising that ended in such despair.

1. *When Jesus began his descent from the Mount of Olives into Jerusalem, the crowds were thrilled.*
   a. The disciples felt vindicated that they had left all to follow Jesus.
   b. The multitudes were convinced that the long-awaited Messiah had come.
      (1) Many were present who knew about Jesus' raising Lazarus from the dead (John 12:17ff).
      (2) Anybody who could perform a miracle like that would have little difficulty in overthrowing Rome.
2. *But by the time Passover had arrived, everything had changed.*
   a. Jesus was betrayed by Judas Iscariot (John 18:2; Matt. 26:48-55).

   b. All the disciples deserted him and fled (Matt. 26:56).
   c. Jesus was condemned by the Sanhedrin (Matt. 26:65-66).
   d. Peter denied that he knew Jesus (Matt. 26:69-75).
   e. Pontius Pilate ordered the crucifixion (Matt. 27:26).
   f. Jesus was crucified (Matt. 27:35).

G. What is the significance of Palm Sunday?
   1. It must be important; it was foretold in the Old Testament.
   2. All four gospels give it in detail.
   3. But nothing turned out as the people hoped.

I. THE LORD JESUS HIMSELF WAS THE ARCHITECT OF THE WHOLE AFFAIR

A. That in itself makes it important.
   1. If God is in something, it is significant, regardless of the outcome.
   2. That something doesn't have what appears to be a happy ending is no proof that God wasn't behind it.

B. Jesus ordered it and the smallest details fell into place.
   1. 'As they approached Jerusalem and came to Bethphage on the Mount of Olives, Jesus sent two disciples, saying to them, "Go to the village ahead of you, and at once you will find a donkey tied there, with her colt by her. Untie them and bring them to me. If anyone says anything to you, tell him that the Lord needs them, and he will send them right away"' (Matt. 21:1-3).

   2. *They did as Jesus said, found what he said would be there.*
      a. They found the colt.
      b. People asked, 'What are you doing, untying that colt?' (Mark 11:5).
      c. They answered as Jesus had told them to, and the people let them go (Mark 11:6).

II. PROPHECY WAS BEING FULFILLED

A. God honours his own prophetic word.
   1. Matthew says, 'This took place to fulfil what was spoken through the prophet' (Matt. 21:4).
   2. Zechariah 9:9 gives no hint what the words meant.

B. Any event that the New Testament takes seriously is important in God's sight, therefore must be in ours.
   1. Palm Sunday was God's idea.
   2. This is why it was told in advance and given so much attention in the New Testament.

III. THE HUMILITY OF ISRAEL'S KING

A. Normally a king would ride on a horse.
   1. A king lives in a palace.
   2. He wears 'fine clothes' (Matt. 11:8).
   3. The Old Testament kings rode in chariots driven by horses.

B. Jesus came into Jerusalem not in a chariot but riding on a donkey.
   1. This ought to have sent a signal to the crowds.
   2. The same Jesus who had 'no place to lay his head' (Luke 9:58) was not changing his lifestyle at the last minute.
   3. *He was a servant king!*
      a. The disciples however still didn't understand. 'Also a dispute arose among them as to which of them was considered to be greatest' (Luke 22:24).
      b. 'Jesus said to them, "The kings of the Gentiles lord it over them; and those who exercise authority over them call themselves Benefactors. But you are not to be like that. Instead, the greatest among you should be like the youngest, and the one who rules like the one who serves. For who is greater, the one who is at the table or the one who serves? Is it not the one who is at the table? But I am among you as one who serves' (Luke 22:25-27).
         (1) 'After that, he poured water into a basin and began to wash his disciples' feet, drying them with the towel that was wrapped around him' (John 13:5).
         (2) 'I have set you an example that you should do as I have done for you. I tell you the truth, no servant is greater than his master, nor is a messenger greater than the one who sent him' (John 13:15-16).

IV. How God welcomes praise

A. Even if we praise God for the wrong reasons.

1. *The reason the people were so excited.*

   a. They felt that Jesus would unveil his Messiahship.

   b. They felt that Jesus would overthrow Rome.

2. *They thought that Jesus' entry into Jerusalem was paving the way for this.*

   a. So they cried, 'Hosanna!'

   b. Their praise was nonetheless honouring to God.

   (1) Jesus affirmed it (Matt. 21:16).

   (2) "'I tell you," he replied, "if they keep quiet, the stones will cry out"' (Luke 19:40).

B. God welcomed the praise and participation of children!

1. *Children are often overlooked, even by those who think they are so close to Jesus* (Matt. 19:13).

   a. Perhaps the disciples wanted Jesus all to themselves.

   b. Perhaps they thought Jesus wouldn't want to be bothered.

   c. They didn't know Jesus as well as they thought! 'Jesus said, "Let the little children come to me, and do not hinder them, for the kingdom of heaven belongs to such as these"' (Matt. 19:14).

2. Children getting excited about Jesus have always made religious people indignant. 'But when the chief priests and the teachers of the law saw the wonderful things he did and the children shouting in the temple area, "Hosanna to the Son of David," they were indignant' (Matt. 21:15).

3. Jesus welcomed and defended the praise of the children. "'Do you hear what these children are saying?" they asked him. "Yes," replied Jesus, "have you never read, 'From the lips of children and infants you have ordained praise'?"' (Matt. 21:16).

V. How God feels when we miss what could have been ours

A. The servant king was a weeping king.

1. *It was a fact: Jesus wept* (John 11:35).

   a. This was at the graveside of Lazarus.

   (1) Mary and Martha each felt hurt that Jesus showed up four days after the funeral.

(2) '"Lord," Martha said to Jesus, "if you had been here, my brother would not have died' (John 11:21 cf). 'When Mary reached the place where Jesus was and saw him, she fell at his feet and said, "Lord, if you had been here, my brother would not have died"' (John 11:32).

b. Jesus' response: he wept – for one reason: he cared.

  (1) He didn't scold or moralise.

  (2) Even though he knew he would be raising Lazarus from the dead in moments, he wept.

2. *Jesus wept on Palm Sunday.*

a. While others were shouting, Jesus was weeping.

  (1) 'As he approached Jerusalem and saw the city, he wept over it' (Luke 19:41).

  (2) That is how our Lord feels about a city that does not want to know him.

b. Why did Jesus weep on Palm Sunday?

  (1) Because what was rightfully theirs was being forfeited. 'And said, "If you, even you, had only known on this day what would bring you peace – but now it is hidden from your eyes' (Luke 19:42).

  (2) Because of what would happen as a result of their rejection of him. 'The days will come upon you when your enemies will build an embankment against you and encircle you and hem you in on every side' (Luke 19:43).

  (3) Because they did not recognise the day of answered prayer. 'You did not recognise the time of God's coming to you' (Luke 19:44).

B. God feels deeply over what we miss out on.

1. *This is the way he felt about ancient Israel.*

a. 'How can I give you up, Ephraim?' (Hosea 11:8).

b. 'Say to them, "As surely as I live, declares the Sovereign LORD, I take no pleasure in the death of the wicked, but rather that they turn from their ways and live. Turn! Turn from your evil ways! Why will you die, O house of Israel?"' (Ez. 33:11).

2. Jesus mirrored this feeling on Palm Sunday.

VI. THE PATTERN FOR REVIVAL

A. Every revival in church history has a cycle.
1. There is a beginning, a continuation, an ending.
2. *When it is over, it is over.*
   a. Continuing good followed, but all revivals come to an end.
   b. When Palm Sunday was over, it was over.

B. The pattern of revival on Palm Sunday.
1. *The origin: the word of Christ.*
   a. It began with the command: 'go'. 'Saying to them, "Go to the village ahead of you, and just as you enter it, you will find a colt tied there, which no one has ever ridden. Untie it and bring it here' (Mark 11:2).
   b. It began with a few: Jesus sent two disciples.
2. *Affirming the smallest thing* (cf. Luke 16:10).
   a. They were to look for a colt. Why? They didn't know then.
   b. They found the colt and soon found out why!
      (1) It made no sense at first.
      (2) They risked being misunderstood; taking a colt that didn't belong to them! (Mark 11:2-3).
   c. When their fears were lifted, they were prepared for more!
3. *The Lord became openly involved.*
   a. Up to now, the Lord was behind the scenes.
   b. When the disciples obeyed and had their strength renewed, the Lord himself came openly into the picture. 'Many people spread their cloaks on the road, while others spread branches they had cut in the fields. Those who went ahead and those who followed shouted, "Hosanna!" "Blessed is he who comes in the name of the Lord!"' (Mark 11:8-9).
4. The emphasis was on Jesus and salvation (Mark 11:9-10).
5. Vindication of the Scripture (Mark 11:9-10).
6. It included everybody, including children (Matt. 21:15).
7. It brought opposition (Matt. 21:15).
8. The whole city was stirred (Matt. 21:10).
9. It caused people to ask, Who is Jesus? (Matt. 21:10).
10. The cleansing of the church. 'Jesus entered the temple area and drove out all who were buying and selling there. He overturned the tables of the money changers and the benches of those selling doves' (Matt. 21:12).

11. Signs and wonders. 'The blind and the lame came to him at the temple, and he healed them' (Matt. 21:14).

VII. Delayed appreciation

A. Palm Sunday was not appreciated or understood at first.
1. There was such a high expectancy at the beginning of the day.
2. *Then it was all over.* 'At first his disciples did not understand all this. Only after Jesus was glorified did they realise that these things had been written about him and that they had done these things to him' (John 12:16).
   a. Many times we fail to capture the significance of a moment God is in – only to realise later how precious it was.
   b. Jacob: 'Surely the LORD is in this place, and I was not aware of it' (Gen. 28:16).

B. Why was it not appreciated at the time?
1. *The crowds began to outnumber those initially involved.*
   a. It began with two disciples, then (presumably) the Twelve.
   b. But soon came the crowds, partly as a result of Lazarus being raised from the dead.
   c. Note: revival will likely result in people coming out of nowhere, thoroughly enjoying it, though not initially involved.
2. *The incongruity of a king on a donkey.*
   a. This did not fit the pattern they were comfortable with.
   b. Spontaneous worship broke out that didn't follow tradition.
3. *Were they afraid?* It is written: 'Do not be afraid, O daughter of Zion' (John 12:15).
   a. Note: often God's work begins in a manner that is unimpressive – like a root out of dry ground (Isa. 53:2).
   b. Spirituality (def.): closing the time gap between the appearance of God's glory and our appreciation of it.

VIII. God's estimate of the place of prayer

A. After Jesus entered the temple area and overturned the tables of the money changers, '"It is written," he said to them, " 'My house will be called a house of prayer,' but you are making it a 'den of robbers'"' (Matt. 21:13).

    1. It is interesting that he calls the temple 'my house'.

    2. He regarded it as his!

B. The idea of the temple being a house of prayer seemed not to have entered anybody's mind.

    1. The temple had lost its meaning.

    2. Jesus restored the meaning.

C. Jesus showed the importance of his house being a place of prayer.

    1. It should include individuals praying.

    2. *It means corporate prayer.*

        a. It assumes intercessory prayer (Acts 12:5).

        b. This means standing in the gap (Ps. 106:23).

D. The very design of the temple and the sacred items in it showed the temple was erected around prayer.

    1. Blood sacrifice of the altar.

    2. Basin: clean consciences to pray.

    3. Table: fellowship with the Lord.

    4. Lampstand: illumination as one enjoys fellowship with God.

    5. Altar of incense: its smell passed through the curtain.

IX. THE DISAPPOINTING TURN JESUS TOOK

A. Everything hinged upon a turn Jesus took, after he entered the city of Jerusalem.

    1. It was a turn that surprised and disappointed everybody.

    2. *After he entered Jerusalem, he had two choices:*

        a. To turn to the left: temple area.

        b. To turn to the right: governor's palace.

B. Picture Jesus coming down from the Mount of Olives; he walks through the eastern gate.

    1. A turn to the right: he would confront Rome.

    2. A turn to the left: he would confront religious people.

    3. He took the left; he confronted religious people.

C. What did this mean?

    1. God is more interested in religion than in politics.

    2. God is more interested in souls than in governments.

3. God is more interested in prayer than in government.

4. God is more interested in fulfilling his word than in the traditional expectations of men.

X. How to cope with disappointment

A. Issue: dream versus reality.

1. A dream can be based on unrealistic expectations.

2. The reality is what God actually did.

B. The people had to cope with the fact that Palm Sunday did not come up to expectations.

1. The truth can be disappointing at first.

2. The truth turned out to be transforming.

   a. The eventual result: the cross and resurrection.

   b. One week later Jesus' followers had no regrets.

      (1) God always does it like this.

      (2) He sanctifies to us our deepest distress.

CONCLUSION

The events of Palm Sunday were the fulfilment of Old Testament prophecy. Jesus made the arrangements for the day, arrangements that illustrate his humility. He entered Jerusalem riding on a donkey, rather than on a horse as a king would have done. Jesus' kingship was not of this world. His entry was however triumphal and he accepted the praise of the crowd. Even if people praised God at the time with minimal understanding of what they were doing, Jesus affirmed it.

The Lord wept on Palm Sunday, deeply moved by the fact that although he longed to draw the people of Jerusalem under his care, they were unprepared to submit to him. Such was the compassion of the King of Kings. Only he knew what was ahead. He still knows, but what he does will be absolutely right – and eventually appreciated.

17

THE BLOOD OF JESUS

INTRODUCTION

A. I always know I am on safe territory in God's sight when I preach, teach or focus in any way on the blood of Jesus.

   1. *We are talking about the very blood which Jesus shed when he was crucified nearly 2,000 years ago.*

      a. The first evidence of Jesus shedding his blood was in the Garden of Gethsemane. 'And being in anguish, he prayed more earnestly, and his sweat was like drops of blood falling to the ground' (Luke 22:44).

      b. The second time Jesus shed blood was after his flogging by Pilate's order (Matt. 27:26. cf. John 19:1).

      c. The third would have followed the Roman soldiers' having set a crown of thorns on his head (Matt. 27:29. cf. John 19:2).

      d. The fourth and main part of Jesus' shedding of blood was the act of crucifixion itself.

         (1) They nailed spikes through his hands and feet into the wooden cross.

         (2) This cross was hoisted upwards and dropped into a hole in the ground.

         (3) While hanging in extreme agony the blood dripped to the ground. flowing from his brow, his hands and feet – and possibly other parts of his body from the flogging.

      e. The fifth evidence of shedding blood, immediately following this death, was when a soldier 'pierced Jesus' side with a spear, bringing a sudden flow of blood and water' (John 19:34).

   2. *We are therefore referring to the actual blood that came from the body of the Son of God.*

      a. Abel's blood, shed at the hands of his brother Cain, dripped to the ground and cried out to God from the ground (Gen. 4:10-11).

    b. Jesus' blood, shed on the cross, would also have fallen to the ground; it too cried out to God.

3. *This blood was precious in God's sight.*

    a. Jesus was God's beloved Son who was very pleasing to him (Matt. 3:17. cf. Matt. 17:5).

    b. How precious was that blood to the Father – and to us (1 Pet. 1:19).

4. *We therefore can be sure that any respect and honour we show to the blood of Jesus will be honouring and pleasing to God.*

    a. The man I was named after, Dr R T Williams, used to counsel young ministers, 'Honour the blood, and honour the Holy Ghost.'

    b. I fear that the rising number of ministers in this country who have either avoided or poked fun at the blood of Christ shows no sign of abating.

        (1) If Bible-denying liberals despise this teaching, it must be right.

        (2) If the devil hates this teaching, it must be right.

5. We are on safe and solid ground.

B. The purpose of this lesson is not only to redress the balance but also to clarify the meaning of the blood of Jesus in our day.

    1. *We will deal with these questions:*

        a. What is the meaning of the blood of Jesus?

            (1) Is it a phrase that simply refers to the cross, or Jesus' death?

            (2) Is there value in the literal blood of Jesus itself?

        b. What does the blood of Jesus do:

            (1) For God?

            (2) To Satan?

            (3) For us?

    2. We will also deal with the meaning of Atonement, how the work of Christ on the cross is applied to our lives and its relevance in spiritual warfare.

C. Why is this study important?

    1. It focuses on the greatest event in the history of mankind: the death of Jesus on the cross.

    2. It focuses on the meaning and purpose of Christ's death: atonement.

3. It comes to terms with a phrase or word ('the blood of Jesus', 'the blood', etc.) which appears no fewer than thirty-five times in the New Testament.
4. It shows the connection between the Old Testament and the New Testament.
5. It shows what is the basis of our fellowship with the Father.
6. It shows what must be preached and taught in a generation that knows so little about Christ's atonement.
7. It brings us face to face with one of the most essential ingredients in spiritual warfare.

I. THE MEANING OF BLOOD IN THE OLD TESTAMENT

A. Why would we go to the Old Testament before speaking directly about the blood of Jesus? Answer:

1. *The gospel is for the Jew first* (Rom. 1:16).
   a. Every Jew would have an understanding of blood, based on the teaching he or she would have received already.
   b. There would be little need to say more, once it was understood that the blood of Jesus took the place of the blood shed by sacrifices under the Old Covenant.
2. *There is no discontinuity between the Old Testament and the New Testament.* (See *Understanding Theology*, Chapter 11, on the Covenant.)
   a. Every new convert would know that the faith of Christ had its roots in the God of Israel.
   b. Therefore the teaching about the blood shed in ancient Israel would underlie the Atonement of Christ and all its implications.
3. How blood shed was understood in ancient times would find its fulfilment in Christ (Heb. 10:1).

B. The 'law of first mention'.

1. *A time-honoured hermeneutical method is especially relevant for the teaching on the subject of blood.*
   a. Hermeneutics (def.): the science of biblical interpretation.
   b. Many Bible teachers consider this fundamental to much theological interpretation.
2. *The 'law of first mention' (def.): the way a word is first used in the Bible will be the way this word is largely understood thereafter. For example:*

    a. Sin (Gen. 4:7). Sin, not doing what is right, leads to mastery over us.

    b. Covenant (Gen. 6:18). Its first use was to be the way it would be generally understood thereafter: what God promises to do.

    c. Faith (Gen. 15:6). Faith is essentially believing God.

    d. Tears (2 Kgs. 20:5). God takes special note of our tears.

C. The first use of 'blood': 'The LORD said, "What have you done? Listen! Your brother's blood cries out to me from the ground"' (Gen. 4:10).

    1. Abel's blood cried out to God.

    2. It was an appeal for God to act.

    3. It was literal blood, which fell into the ground.

    4. God heard the cry.

    5. The blood continued to make its own appeal, even though the person whose blood it was had died.

D. When God first required blood from a sacrifice (Ex. 12).

    1. *Literal blood was required, not just the taking of life.* 'Then they are to take some of the blood and put it on the sides and tops of the door-frames of the houses where they eat the lambs' (Ex. 12:7).

        a. Each man was to take a lamb for his family (Ex. 12:3).

        b. The lamb was to be slaughtered (Ex. 12:6).

        c. The blood was to be visibly sprinkled on the sides and tops of door frames with a bunch of hyssop (Ex. 12:22).

    2. *The blood was a sign.* 'The blood will be a sign for you on the houses where you are' (Ex. 12:13).

        a. It was visible to one another; the community had a common identity – the blood of a lamb.

        b. It was a testimony against false gods. 'On that same night I will pass through Egypt and strike down every firstborn – both men and animals – and I will bring judgment on all the gods of Egypt. I am the LORD' (Ex. 12:12).

    3. *The blood was visible to God.* 'When I see the blood' (Ex. 12:13).

        a. This is what God would look for when the destroyer passed through Egypt.

    b. Note: it did not say, 'When *you* see the blood,' but rather, 'When *I* see the blood.'

4. *The blood was protection.* 'When I see the blood, I will pass over you. No destructive plague will touch you when I strike Egypt' (Ex. 12:13).

    a. It was protection from God's wrath. 'I will pass over you.'

    b. It was protection from the destroying angel. 'When the LORD goes through the land to strike down the Egyptians, he will see the blood on the top and sides of the door-frame and will pass over that doorway, and he will not permit the destroyer to enter your houses and strike you down' (Ex. 12:23).

    c. Note: The destroyer was the Lord but a distinction is made between him and the destroying angel; 'He [the Lord] will not permit the destroyer to enter your houses and strike you down.'

      (1) We may infer that the destroying angel (1 Cor. 10:10) was the devil.

      (2) The devil was given the power of death (Heb. 2:14).

      (3) The devil was often God's instrument to do his work. See (2 Sam. 24:1 and 1 Chron. 21:1).

5. *The blood set God free from doing what otherwise he would have done.*

    a. He would have killed all the firstborn living in Egypt, including those of Israel. 'On that same night I will pass through Egypt and strike down every firstborn – both men and animals – and I will bring judgment on all the gods of Egypt. I am the LORD' (Ex. 12:12).

    b. But because of the blood he was set free not to destroy the firstborn of Israel. 'No destructive plague will touch *you* when I strike Egypt' (Ex. 12:13).

6. *The blood took the place of those who otherwise would have been killed.*

    a. It was a substitute for the lives of those who were under the threat of death.

    b. Their sole hope was the blood that intervened.

7. The blood was a covering. 'Blessed is he whose transgressions are forgiven, whose sins are covered' (Ps. 32:1).

E. The sprinkling of the blood
1. *The blood of the covenant* (Ex. 24)
    a. Young bulls were sacrificed as offerings to the Lord (Ex. 24:5).
       (1) One half of the blood was put in bowls by Moses.
       (2) The other half was sprinkled on the altar (Ex. 24:6).
    b. The Book of the Covenant was read to the people.
       (1) They responded, 'We will do everything the Lord has said; we will obey' (Ex. 24:7).
       (2) This is when the people, not God, took the Oath.
    c. The blood was then sprinkled *on the people*. 'Moses then took the blood, sprinkled it on the people and said, "This is the blood of the covenant that the Lord has made with you in accordance with all these words"' (Ex. 24:8).
       (1) All that was seen above pertaining to the blood at Passover is to be understood here.
       (2) What the blood did then was needed again, only this time being sprinkled not on what was material but on their very persons.
2. *Consecration of priests* (Ex. 29)
    a. A ram's blood was sprinkled on the altar (Ex. 29:16).
    b. Another ram was slaughtered and some of its blood was placed:
       (1) On the lobes of the right ears.
       (2) On the thumbs of the right hands.
       (3) On the big toes of the right feet (Ex. 29:19-21).
3. *The offerings*
    a. The burnt offering (Lev. 1).
    b. The fellowship offering (Lev. 3).
    c. The sin offering (Lev. 4 and 5).
    d. The guilt offering (Lev. 7).
4. *The Mercy Seat: the Day of Atonement* (Lev. 16)
    a. The High Priest went into the Holy of Holies once a year, but never without blood, which he offered for himself and for the sins the people had committed in ignorance (Heb. 9:7).
    b. He took the blood of a bull and a goat (Lev. 16:14-15).
    c. He sprinkled it with his finger seven times on the cover, or lid, of the Ark of the Covenant (called the Mercy Seat). 'He is to take some of the bull's blood and with his finger

sprinkle it on the front of the atonement cover; then he shall sprinkle some of it with his finger seven times before the atonement cover' (Lev. 16:14).

d. The purpose of this ritual was to cleanse the sanctuary (Lev. 16:18), the priest and his household (Lev. 16:6) and the people. 'Because on this day atonement will be made for you, to cleanse you. Then, before the LORD, you will be clean from all your sins' (Lev. 16:30).

5. The prayer of David, the returning backslider: 'Cleanse me [by sprinkling] with [a bunch of] hyssop and I shall be clean; wash me and I shall be whiter than snow' (Ps. 51:7).

II. THE BLOOD OF JESUS

A. Sometimes the term 'blood' merely denotes *death* by shedding blood.

1. The death of the prophets (Matt. 23:30,35).
2. Death by martyrdom (Heb. 12:4. cf. Acts 22:20).
3. The death of Jesus (Matt. 27:4,24-25; Acts 5:28).
4. Note: some want to make the phrase 'the blood of Christ' refer symbolically to the death of Christ – meaning the way he died, by shedding his blood (Acts 20:26; Rom. 3:25; 5:9; 1 Cor. 10:16; Eph. 1:7; 2:13; Col. 1:14 (margin), 20; Rev. 1:5; 5:9).

B. The pre-history that we have examined from the Old Testament shows how the phrase 'blood of Christ' was intended to be understood.

1. More than the blood of the animal was required; the blood was collected and sprinkled (applied).
2. *To the Jewish mind the reference to Christ's blood meant:*
   a. His death by shedding bis blood on the cross.
   b. The importance of the blood that was shed.
3. *The way the blood of Christ is treated in so many places – where it meant more than Jesus' mere death – are enough to indicate how the references to his blood were meant to be understood:*
   a. His death on a cross.
   b. The value of the blood that was spilt.

C. The epistle to the Hebrews

1. *The reference to the Day of Atonement.*

   a. 'But only the high priest entered the inner room, and that only once a year, and never without blood, which he offered for himself and for the sins the people had committed in ignorance' (Heb. 9:7).

   b. Comparison to the blood of animals. 'He did not enter by means of the blood of goats and calves; but he entered the Most Holy Place once for all by his own blood, having obtained eternal redemption' (Heb. 9:12).

   c. The reference to cleansing. 'How much more, then, will the blood of Christ, who through the eternal Spirit offered himself unblemished to God, cleanse our consciences from acts that lead to death, so that we may serve the living God!' (Heb. 9:14).

2. *The comparison of the two covenants.*

   a. The first covenant was 'not put into effect without blood' (Heb. 9:18).

   b. We will recall how the blood was collected and then sprinkled on the people. 'When Moses had proclaimed every commandment of the law to all the people, he took the blood of calves, together with water, scarlet wool and branches of hyssop, and sprinkled the scroll and all the people' (Heb. 9:19).

   c. There is no way these references to Christ's blood could be euphemisms for his death; special attention and application of the *blood* was required.

      (1) The blood was sprinkled on the very premises of the tabernacle. (Heb. 9:21).

      (2) 'In fact, the law requires that nearly everything be cleansed with blood, and without the shedding of blood there is no forgiveness' (Heb. 9:22).

D. The sprinkling

1. *The Greek* rantizo *(to sprinkle) or* rantismos *(sprinkling) mean 'to spray or sprinkle something with something.'*

   a. It may refer to any liquid: water, oil, blood.

   b. The second word (for sprinkling) is not found in ancient literature outside the Bible.

   2. *It is used five times in Hebrews*: (Heb. 9:13,19,21; 10:22 and
      12:24).
      a. These references compare Christ's death to the Day of
         Atonement; how the blood is *applied*.
      b. Hebrews 12:24 can only refer to the Mercy Seat, or its
         equivalent in heaven: 'To Jesus the mediator of a new
         covenant, and to the sprinkled blood that speaks a better
         word than the blood of Abel.'
   3. *Peter used it once:* 'Through the sanctifying work of the Spirit,
      for obedience to Jesus Christ and sprinkling by his blood' (1
      Pet. 1:2b,c,d).
      a. This refers to blood that has been *applied*.
         (1) The blood was sacrificed on the altar, so Jesus died on
            the cross.
         (2) The blood was sprinkled on the Mercy Seat; Jesus
            entered heaven itself with his blood.
      b. This is Peter's meaning: the sanctifying Spirit applies the blood.
   4. *It is implied in 1 John 1:7:* 'But if we walk in the light, as he is
      in the light, we have fellowship with one another, and the blood
      of Jesus, his Son, purifies us from all sin.'

E. The Lord's Supper: in two parts
   1. *The bread symbolises the body.* 'While they were eating, Jesus
      took bread, gave thanks and broke it, and gave it to his disciples,
      saying, "Take and eat; this is my body"' (Matt. 26:26).
   2. *The cup symbolises the blood.* 'Then he took the cup, gave
      thanks and offered it to them, saying, "Drink from it, all of you.
      This is my blood of the covenant, which is poured out for many
      for the forgiveness of sins"' (Matt. 26:27,28).
      a. Prayer of thanks preceded each act of worship.
      b. This demonstrates how special recognition was given to the
         blood.
         (1) If the term 'blood of Christ' only meant Christ's death,
            the eating of the body would have been sufficient for
            the Lord's Supper.
         (2) But the separate reference to the blood distinguishes it.

F. 'Christ, our Passover lamb' (1 Cor. 5:7)
   1. This 'throw away' comment by Paul proves that Passover pre-
      figured Christ's death.

2. *We may therefore see how Jesus' hanging on the cross, set against the sprinkled blood at Passover, brings to mind those glorious words: 'When I see the blood, I will pass over you.' This means:*

a. The literal blood of Jesus.

b. It was a sign – to us and to God.

c. It was protection.

d. It set God free to save us.

e. It took our place.

f. It is our covering.

CONCLUSION

Every Jew knew the significance of blood. Old Testament religion was based on the concept of blood sacrifice, teaching that there was no redemption without the shedding of blood. The blood of Jesus is of infinitely more value than the blood shed by sacrifices under the Old Covenant. Jesus' shedding of his blood instituted the New Covenant. Full and final atonement was made at Calvary. We may therefore conclude that the blood of Jesus satisfies God's justice (Rom. 3:25-26), defeats Satan (See Rev. 12:11), and cleanses us (1 John 1:7). No wonder that Peter called Christ's blood 'precious' (1 Pet. 1:19).

18

THE LAW OF GOD AND
THE CROSS OF CHRIST

INTRODUCTION

A. A few years ago I was accused of being an Antinomian.

    1. *Antinomianism (def.): literally, 'against law'.*

        a. It is a term that emerged as a result of the teaching of Johann Agricola, a follower of Martin Luther.

        b. Agricola claimed that the Law of God had no relevance in the life of the believer.

            (1) Some believe he was the best exponent of Luther's teaching.

            (2) Others believe he went too far and he is, at any rate, seen as the father of Antinomianism.

            (3) Luther himself apparently coined the term and disavowed Agricola's teaching.

    2. *Antinomianism became synonymous with the teaching that, if we are saved, the Law has no relevance for Christian living; therefore it does not matter how we live.*

        a. My book *Once Saved, Always Saved* led some to charge me with being Antinomian.

        b. It is an unfair charge, although I do believe we are eternally saved – apart from works.

    3. *Many Puritans believed that our assurance of salvation is grounded in the works of the Law.*

        a. They do not believe we are saved by works.

        b. They do believe we are assured by works.

            (1) I disagree; our assurance of salvation is not to be based on works other than as a secondary basis.

            (2) The primary basis of our assurance of salvation is Christ alone.

B. In this lesson we will examine the Law of God and how Jesus fulfilled the Law.

  1. *The Law of God was given to Moses at Mount Sinai in approximately 1300 BC.*

    a. The Law was 'put into effect through angels by a mediator' (Gal. 3:19).

      (1) This probably means that angels were the instruments of the 'finger of God' (cf. Deut. 9:10).

      (2) The mediator in this case was Moses.

    b. The Law is generally thought to be in three parts:

      (1) The Moral Law – the Ten Commandments.

      (2) The Civil Law – how the people of God would govern themselves.

      (3) The Ceremonial Law – how the people of God should worship.

  2. *In the Sermon on the Mount Jesus said,* 'Do not think that I have come to abolish the Law or the Prophets; I have not come to abolish them but to fulfil them' (Matt. 5:17).

    a. Jesus knew some might think that he had indeed come to do away with the Law.

      (1) Gr. *katalusai*: to abrogate, to nullify.

      (2) That would have rendered the Law useless and irrelevant.

    b. Some no doubt hoped Jesus would nullify the Law.

      (1) There were revolutionary people who thought Messiah would do away with the Law, and start all over.

      (2) Some people love the overturning of tradition of any kind.

    c. If there were those present who hoped that Jesus would nullify the Law, their hopes were dashed.

      (1) Jesus certainly had the authority to do this sort of thing had he wanted to.

      (2) But no; 'I have not come to abolish' the Law.

  3. *He added: 'I have come. . . to fulfil' the Law.*

    a. By saying this he was announcing a new era.

    b. Jesus sent a signal to all who hoped he would abolish the Law.

      (1) Far from there being any discord between his teaching and the Law, there was continuity between his teaching and the Law.

(2) This sent an ominous signal to anybody who did not want
the Law abolished; whatever did it mean that he would
'fulfil' the Law?

   c. Dr Lloyd-Jones reckons it was the most stupendous claim
that Jesus ever made.

4. The purpose of this lesson is to examine that claim.

C. Why is this lesson important?

1. *It is fundamental to the whole teaching of the Bible.*
   a. 'The Law and the Gospel' is a way of summarising the Bible.
   b. 'For the law was given through Moses; grace and truth came
   through Jesus Christ' (John 1:17).

2. *It is to examine two great events:*
   a. The giving of the Law.
   b. The coming of Christ.

3. *It is to understand the meaning and purpose of these two events.*
   a. The meaning of the Law – and why it came.
   b. What Jesus meant by fulfilling the Law.

4. *It is to make us good theologians!*
   a. Martin Luther said:
   (1) 'Whoever knows how to skilfully distinguish between
   the Law and the Gospel, by the grace of God he also
   knows how to be a theologian.'
   (2) 'Anybody who wishes to be a theologian. . . must
   distinguish between the Law and the Gospel'
   (3) 'There's no man living on earth who knows how to
   distinguish between the Law and the Gospel.'
   b. This lets us know we will have to do a lot of thinking!

I. THE LAW: A PARENTHESIS (BRACKETS) BETWEEN ITS ORIGIN AND FULFILMENT

A. When Jesus said he would 'fulfil' the Law it meant:

1. *The end of an era, namely, that of the Law's rule.*
   a. A sentence with a parenthesis (brackets) can be read without
   quoting the contents of the brackets.
   b. The brackets however make the meaning of the sentence clearer.

2. *The beginning of an era, namely, all that was entailed in the
   meaning of the Law being fulfilled.*

a. Gr. *plerosai*, to fulfil – the opposite of destroy.

(1) It does not mean to supplement or enlarge.

(2) It does not mean to keep going or continue.

(3) It does not mean to obey.

b. This means to bring about the event to which the Law was pointing.

(1) The Law pointed beyond itself.

(2) The Law had not been fulfilled.

c. No one had ever really kept the Law. 'Now then, why do you try to test God by putting on the necks of the disciples a yoke that neither we nor our fathers have been able to bear?' (Acts 15:10).

d. The very content of the Law showed it was incomplete.

3. *The fulfilment of the Law meant that some person and event were the object toward which it pointed.*

a. In Matthew 5:17 Jesus is actually saying:

(1) 'I am that person.'

(2) 'My coming is that event.'

b. It was therefore a prophetic statement.

(1) It had not been done yet; he had perhaps another two or three years to live and to do it.

(2) But it was a promise that he would do what no other person had ever done.

B. Why did the Law emerge in the first place? 'What, then, was the purpose of the law? It was added because of transgressions until the Seed to whom the promise referred had come. The law was put into effect through angels by a mediator' (Gal. 3:19).

1. *Why does Paul say 'added'?*

a. Note: 'The law was added so that the trespass might increase. But where sin increased, grace increased all the more' (Rom. 5:20).

b. This shows that Paul's comment in Galatians 3:19 was no unguarded comment; it was carefully worded and thought through.

2. *Answer: it was never meant to replace the gospel.*

a. The gospel was first preached to Abraham some four hundred years before the law was given, circa 1700 BC. 'Understand, then, that those who believe are children of

Abraham. The Scripture foresaw that God would justify the Gentiles by faith, and announced the gospel in advance to Abraham: "All nations will be blessed through you." So those who have faith are blessed along with Abraham, the man of faith' (Gal. 3:7-9).

(1) The gospel did not begin with Moses but Abraham.

(2) This is why Jesus said, 'Your father Abraham rejoiced at the thought of seeing my day; he saw it and was glad' (John 8:56).

b. The Law was 'added', that is, it came alongside.

(1) It was extra.

(2) It paralleled the gospel that had emerged 400 years before.

c. The Law was never permanent in the first place.

(1) It had not come to replace the promise to Abraham.

(2) It only came alongside until it be fulfilled: 'Until the Seed [that is, Jesus Christ] to whom the promise [to Abraham] referred had come' (Gal. 3:19).

3. *Had it not been for the transgression of the Children of Israel the implication is: the Law need never have come at all.*

a. But the people needed a restraint.

(1) They began complaining.

(2) They were prone to idolatry.

b. God stepped in – and gave the Law.

(1) It restrained the people from further sin by fear of punishment.

(2) It did not produce the righteousness the Law required.

C. In a word: the Law was temporary from the beginning.

1. *It pointed beyond itself by its very content.*

2. *All it waited for: fulfilment.*

3. *Jesus went on to say,* 'I tell you the truth, until heaven and earth disappear, not the smallest letter, not the least stroke of a pen, will by any means disappear from the Law until everything is accomplished' (Matt. 5:18).

a. This was a way of saying that he knew his work was truly cut out for him!

b. It shows what would have to be done.

(1) Not merely keeping the Ten Commandments.

(2) Also: over 2,000 verses of legislation to be found in Exodus, Leviticus, Numbers, Deuteronomy.

D. The content of the Law, which shows the work cut out for Jesus to fulfil.

1. *The statutes of the Law – all of its rules and regulations.*

   a. This meant all the Law: Moral, Civil, Ceremonial.

   b. This meant the minutiae of the Law: 2,000 verses of legislation in addition to the Ten Commandments.

2. *The Law in all its strictures had to be kept.*

   a. It required the highest possible level of pure living – in thought, word, deed.

   b. It demanded total obedience without the slightest deviation.

   (1) Circumcision on the eighth day after birth.

   (2) Keeping the Sabbath (Saturday).

   (3) All the feasts and holy days.

   (a) The 'new moons'.

   (b) The 'seventh year'.

   (c) Passover.

   (d) Feast of Unleavened Bread.

   (e) Feast of Tabernacles.

   (f) Feast of Trumpets.

   (g) Day of Atonement.

   (4) Dietary restrictions, eg not cooking 'a young goat in its mother's milk' (Ex. 23:19).

   (5) Dress codes, eg not to wear 'clothing woven of two kinds of material' (Lev. 19:19).

   (6) Agricultural restrictions, eg 'Do not mate different kinds of animals. Do not plant your field with two kinds of seed.' (Lev. 19:19).

   c. Sacrifices of the Law, various animals being slaughtered for the shedding of blood.

II. THE MISSION OF JESUS: TO CLOSE THE PARENTHESIS AND FULFIL THE LAW

A. What was expected of one who would fulfil the Law and the Prophets?

1. He would be born of a virgin (Isa. 7:14).

2. He would be a prophet like Moses (Deut. 18:15).

3. He would keep the details of the Law (above).

4. He would be a priest after the order of Melchizedek (Ps. 110:4).

5. He would be of the tribe of Judah and lineage of David (Acts 2:30).

6. He would be born in Bethlehem (Micah 5:2).

7. He would dwell in Galilee (Is. 9:1ff).

B. What did Jesus actually do?

1. *He upheld the standard of the Law.*

    a. Some hoped he would abolish it.

    b. He upheld it and by doing so maintained the moral standard of righteousness.

2. *He was born under the Law and submitted to it.* 'But when the fullness of the time was come, God sent forth his Son, made of a woman, made under the law' (Gal. 4:4).

    a. He did not put himself above the Law.

    b. He took not on himself the nature of angels but the seed of Abraham, being bone of our bone and flesh of our flesh (Heb. 2:14-17).

    c. His parents kept the Law for him, including seeing that he was circumcised the eighth day. Luke 2:21. 'And when they had performed all things according to the law of the Lord, they returned into Galilee, to their own city Nazareth' (Luke 2:39).

3. *He lived without sin.* 'For we do not have a high priest who is unable to sympathise with our weaknesses, but we have one who has been tempted in every way, just as we are – yet was without sin' (Heb. 4:15. cf. I Pet. 2:22).

    a. He kept the Ten Commandments.

        (1) He worshipped only the Father (John 5:19,31).

        (2) He never abused his Father's name.

        (3) He kept the Sabbath.

        (4) He never stole or lied.

        (5) He never coveted.

    b. In a word: he practised what he preached.

        (1) He never retaliated when they mocked him.

        (2) He never complained or murmured.

C. How did Jesus fulfil the Law?

1. *By being our substitute*

    a. All he ever did was doing what was required of us.

b. He took our place, ensuring that whatever was required of us he had already done for us.

(1) His baptism was our baptism (Matt. 3:15).

(2) His keeping the Law was our keeping the Law (1 Cor. 1:30).

(3) His obedience was our obedience (Rom. 5:15,19).

2. *By suffering for us*

a. The penalty of the Law was Christ's death sentence in order to pay the penalty of our capital crimes.

(1) Our murdering became his.

(2) Our adultery became his.

b. He suffered death for us.

(1) 'God made him who had no sin to be sin for us, so that in him we might become the righteousness of God' (2 Cor. 5:21).

(2) 'We all, like sheep, have gone astray, each of us has turned to his own way; and the Lord has laid on him the iniquity of us all' (Is. 53:6).

c. This literally happened when, on Good Friday, 'About the ninth hour Jesus cried out in a loud voice, "Eloi, Eloi, lama sabachthani?"- which means, "My God, my God, why have you forsaken me?"' (Matt. 27:46).

(1) No man suffered as Jesus did.

(2) We may never know how much.

> 'We may not know, we cannot tell
> What pains he had to bear;
> But we believe it was for us
> He hung and suffered there.'
> *Cecil Francis Alexander*

3. *He fulfilled the requirements of the sacrificial system.*

a. He was the seed of the woman (Gen. 3:15).

b. He became our Passover lamb (1 Cor. 5:7).

(1) All the Old Testament sacrifices were 'shadows'. 'The law is only a shadow of the good things that are coming – not the realities themselves. For this reason it can never, by the same sacrifices repeated endlessly year after year, make perfect those who draw near to worship' (Heb. 10:1).

(2) He was the fulfilment of all the animals – bulls, goats, lambs, pigeons.

c. Those sacrifices had to be repeated daily and annually.

 (1) Note: that alone ought to have been sufficient hint to ancient Israel that they were not doing the job very well!

 (2) It shows that there must be more; that someone must put an end to all the sacrifices.

d. But on Good Friday, after living a sinless life for 33 years – and three years of public ministry:

 (1) Jesus became God's Lamb (John 1:29).

 (2) He was the ultimate fulfilment of everything both the Law and the Prophets anticipated.

e. Once he uttered the words, 'It is finished' (John 19:30):

 (1) The veil in the Temple was torn in two from top to bottom.

 (2) Bodies of the saints rose and walked around Jerusalem.

4. *The Divine Justice was totally satisfied.*

a. Jesus met – therefore fulfilled – the requirements of the Law.

 (1) Enoch walking with God did not do it.

 (2) Noah walking with God did not do it.

 (3) Abraham, Isaac and Jacob did not fulfil the Law.

 (4) Moses was faithful but did not fulfil the Law.

 (5) David loved the Law but didn't keep it.

 (6) The prophets did not do it.

b. The blood of Jesus did it.

 (1) He lived a perfect life.

 (2) His death sealed all he had done.

c. In a word: Mission Accomplished!

III. The ongoing fulfilment of the Law by us

Jesus died 'in order that the righteous requirements of the law might be fully met in us, who do not live according to the sinful nature but according to the Spirit' (Rom. 8:4).

A. Having said what he would do, Jesus made another astonishing statement: 'For I tell you that unless your righteousness surpasses that of the Pharisees and the teachers of the law, you will certainly not enter the kingdom of heaven' (Matt. 5:20).

1. No one had ever heard such an utterance.
2. *No one believed that ordinary people in Galilee even came up to the standard set by the teachers of the Law and the Pharisees.*
   a. Surely they had a 'corner on the market'!
   b. Surely they were head and shoulders above everybody when it came to righteousness.
3. *But their righteousness was in fact superficial.*
   a. They did everything outwardly.
   b. They did everything to be seen of men.

B. Jesus gave an interpretation of various commandments that showed how one might indeed 'surpass' the righteousness of the Scribes and Pharisees.

1. *Murder was a matter of the heart.* 'You have heard that it was said to the people long ago, "Do not murder, and anyone who murders will be subject to judgment." But I tell you that anyone who is angry with his brother will be subject to judgment. Again, anyone who says to his brother, 'Raca,' is answerable to the Sanhedrin. But anyone who says, 'You fool!' will be in danger of the fire of hell' (Matt. 5:21-22).
   a. The Pharisees thought they were sinless because they had not committed outward murder.
   b. Jesus showed that if we hate or hold grudges we have violated the sixth commandment.
   c. He went on to say, 'But I tell you: Love your enemies and pray for those who persecute you' (Matt. 5:44).
      (1) This is a real possibility.
      (2) Doing this fulfils the Law, for Paul said that love is the fulfilment of the Law (Rom. 13:10).
2. *Adultery is a matter of the heart.* 'You have heard that it was said, "Do not commit adultery." But I tell you that anyone who looks at a woman lustfully has already committed adultery with her in his heart' (Matt. 5:27-28).
   a. The Pharisees thought they were sinless because they had not committed the physical act of adultery.
   b. Jesus showed that lust violates the seventh commandment.
   c. The Greek is intentionally ambiguous, meaning:
      (1) Lusting so as to be obsessed in the thoughts.
      (2) Causing another to lust.

3. *Misusing God's name was not merely swearing by his name.*
'Again, you have heard that it was said to the people long ago,
"Do not break your oath, but keep the oaths you have made to
the Lord." But I tell you, Do not swear at all: either by heaven,
for it is God's throne; or by the earth, for it is his footstool; or by
Jerusalem, for it is the city of the Great King. And do not swear
by your head, for you cannot make even one hair white or
black. Simply let your 'Yes' be 'Yes,' and your 'No,' 'No';
anything beyond this comes from the evil one' (Matt. 5:33-37).

   a. The Pharisees thought they could be without sin as long as
they kept their vows.

   b. Jesus said that we must not swear by a greater authority
every time we open our mouths but must tell the truth all
the time!

**C. Note: the above examples are but the beginning of how the
Law is continued to be fulfilled by walking in the Spirit (Gal.
5:16).**

CONCLUSION

Jesus came not to destroy the law but to fulfil it. In the eternal plan of
God the law was temporary, always pointing beyond itself to Christ.
Jesus fulfilled the law by upholding it, by being born under it and
submitting to it and by living a sinless life. In no point did Jesus break
the law of God. The Lord was our substitute and fulfilled the legal
requirements of the sacrificial system by being himself the sacrifice
on Calvary.

The parenthesis of the law is closed and completed. Christians are
not under the law (Gal. 5:18). At the same time they outclass the
Law by walking in the Spirit.

19

HOW THE EARLY CHURCH COPED WITH JESUS' CRUCIFIXION

INTRODUCTION

A. **The crucifixion of Jesus was an unimaginable shock to the earliest disciples of Jesus.**
1. *Having received the Gospel of the Kingdom, the disciples could not cope with the thought of Jesus' crucifixion, though warned by him in advance* (Luke 18:31ff).
   a. 'Jesus turned and said to Peter, "Get behind me, Satan! You are a stumbling-block to me; you do not have in mind the things of God, but the things of men"' (Matt. 16:23).
   b. 'Then Jesus said to his disciples, "If anyone would come after me, he must deny himself and take up his cross and follow me"' (Matt. 16:24).
2. *Moses and Elijah 'spoke about his departure' when they appeared with Jesus on the Mount of Transfiguration* (Luke 9:31).
   a. But this apparently made no impact on the disciples.
   b. They had fixed, preconceived ideas about Jesus' messianic role.

B. **For us today who have received the gospel in the light of all that has preceded us, we tend to forget how the crucifixion affected the disciples.**
1. *As they were very sleepy at the Transfiguration* (Luke 9:32), *so too were they at Gethsemane.*
   a. They did not grasp the seriousness of the hour.
   b. Peter had earlier proclaimed his undying allegiance to Christ (Matt. 26:33).
   c. Jesus suffered alone in the Garden. 'Sleep on now, and take your rest' (Matt. 26:45 AV).

2. Peter denied Christ (Matt. 26:69-75).

3. *In the meantime, all his disciples forsook him and fled* (Matt. 26:56).

   a. The feeling of many was summed up in these words: 'We had hoped that he was the one who was going to redeem Israel' (Luke 24:21a).

   b. They were demoralised and disillusioned by the Cross.

C. The Roman crucifixion was the capital punishment of its day.

   1. It was the cruellest and most painful way to die.

   2. It was reserved for the lowest of the low.

   3. *Its shame and horror cannot be exaggerated.*

   a. For this to happen to the man they thought was God's Messiah was unthinkable.

   b. It never crossed their minds that this was God's own idea for his Son and all for us – from the beginning.

D. The question we ask: how did they cope?

   1. How did the early church come to see the crucifixion?

   2. What do the four gospels seek to convey, having been written several years after the event?

E. Why should this subject be dealt with? Why is it important?

   1. It shows how the disciples leaned on the Old Testament to grasp what was going on.

   2. It shows how they would have understood little or nothing without the Holy Spirit.

   3. It helps us appreciate the kind of persecution the early church felt – if Jesus is alive, where is he?

   4. It focuses on God's finest hour: the giving of his Son for our redemption.

   5. It is right to do so.

I. THE PRE-PENTECOSTAL MIND-SET OF THE DISCIPLES

A. There is the old spiritual:

Were you there when they crucified my Lord? Were you there?
Were you there when he rose up from the grave? Were you there?

   1. *No-one present at the Cross on Good Friday seemed to have perceived what was happening.*

    a. Paul said that 'God was reconciling the world to himself in Christ, not counting men's sins against them' (2 Cor. 5:19).

    b. In a word: atonement was taking place.

        (1) To atone (def.): to make amends, to make up for some error or deficiency.

        (2) Christ was making amends for our sins by shedding his blood.

    c. But no-one knew this at the time, as far as we know.

    d. Therefore to have been physically present at the scene of the crucifixion would not have brought one any closer to an understanding of what was happening.

        (1) There appeared to be no purpose in what was happening.

        (2) As for the chief priests who ordered the crucifixion, they had clear consciences: 'We considered him stricken by God, smitten by him, and afflicted' (Isa. 53:4).

2. *Even after Jesus was raised from the dead, no-one who saw him seemed to have been any closer to an understanding of why he died or why he was raised from the dead!*

    a. Mary Magdalene did not have a clue why he was raised from the dead, even though she saw him. 'Jesus said, "Do not hold on to me, for I have not yet returned to the Father. Go instead to my brothers and tell them, 'I am returning to my Father and your Father, to my God and your God'"' (John 20:17).

    b. When Jesus appeared to ten of the disciples they were 'overjoyed' (John 20:20), yet they still had little or no understanding of why he died on the cross.

    c. Thomas's confession 'My Lord and my God!' (John 20:28) proves nothing more than what Peter had previously confessed (Matt. 16:16).

    d. Indeed, his physical appearance did not remove all doubt: 'When they saw him, they worshipped him; but some doubted' (Matt. 28:17).

B. Even after the resurrection they did not know why Jesus died or why he arose.

    1. *They were still thinking in the traditional manner about Messiah.*

        a. Convinced though they were that Jesus was the Messiah, their vision of Messiah had not changed.

b. They expected a great political or military leader who would do at least two things:

(1) Restore Israel to its ancient glory.

(2) Set them free from Rome.

2. *This came out by their question – which had been on their minds from the first day: 'Lord, are you at this time going to restore the kingdom to Israel?'* (Acts 1:6).

    a. After all his teaching, Jesus was still being fitted into the traditional Messiah mould!

    b. After he was raised from the dead, they still expected their views to be vindicated.

II. THE POST-PENTECOSTAL UNDERSTANDING OF THE EARLY CHURCH

A. Jesus had said to them, when introducing the Holy Spirit:

    1. *The Spirit would remind them of what Jesus taught.* 'But the Counsellor, the Holy Spirit, whom the Father will send in my name, will teach you all things and will remind you of everything I have said to you' (John 14:26).

    2. *The Spirit would guide them into all truth.* 'But when he, the Spirit of truth, comes, he will guide you into all truth. He will not speak on his own; he will speak only what he hears, and he will tell you what is yet to come' (John 16:13).

    3. *The Spirit would make Jesus as real to them at the spiritual level as he had been real to them at the natural level.*

        a. This is implied in John 14:16, that the Father would give them 'another Counsellor to be with you forever.'

        (1) Gr. *parakletos*, one who comes alongside.

        (2) Jesus had been that for three years; now the Holy Spirit would be – 'another' Counsellor.

        b. This is explicit in his words, 'In a little while you will see me no more, and then after a little while you will see me' (John 16:16).

        (1) When he was taken to heaven, they could not see him.

        (2) When the Spirit came down, they saw him – but in the Spirit.

        (3) He was so real to Peter that he quoted Psalm 16:8, 'I saw the Lord always before me' (Acts 2:25).

B. For the first time, then, the disciples finally understood why Jesus died, arose and ascended to heaven: by the Spirit.

1. *Why he died. It was:*
   a. By God's set purpose and foreknowledge (Acts 2:23).
   b. For the forgiveness of our sins (Acts 2:38).
   c. That people accept him by repenting (Acts 2:38).

2. *He arose, because:*
   a. It was impossible for death to keep its hold on him (Acts 2:24).
   b. He was the Son of God, the 'Holy One' who could see no decay (Acts 2:27).
   c. The scriptures, which referred to Christ and not to David, had to be fulfilled (Acts 2:29-31).

3. *He ascended, not to be seen visibly by all but:*
   a. Exalted to the right hand of God (Acts 2:33).
   b. To make his enemies a footstool for his feet (Acts 2:34-35).
   c. To be acclaimed as Lord and Messiah (Acts 2:36).

C. The resurrection and ascension became a part of the offence of the Cross.

1. The stigma of the cross spoke for itself.

2. *But if Jesus was raised from the dead, where is he now?*
   a. 'God has raised this Jesus to life, and we are all witnesses of the fact' (Acts 2:32).
   b. And yet it is one thing for Peter to say that he personally saw Jesus; where is he now?
   (1) Exalted to the right hand of God.
   (2) But where is the proof of that?

3. *The ascension was based entirely upon scripture.*
   a. The disciples could say that they saw Jesus disappear behind the clouds (Acts 1:9).
   b. But what authority did they have for claiming he was in heaven at God's right hand? Only scripture: 'For David did not ascend to heaven, and yet he said, "The Lord said to my Lord: 'Sit at my right hand'"' (Acts 2:34). 'The LORD says to my Lord: "Sit at my right hand until I make your enemies a footstool for your feet"' (Ps. 110:1).

    (1)They appealed to common sense: David had not been resurrected; 'his tomb is here to this day' (Acts 2:29).

    (2)David himself pointed to the only explanation: Messiah was to die, be raised from the dead and made to ascend to heaven.

D. At the end of the day, then, all who affirm Christ do so by faith – and that by the Spirit.

    1. It was not being physically present that made one a believer.

    2. It is by the Spirit who imparts faith (Eph. 2:8).

    3. *We today therefore can get as close to the event as those in the earliest church – by faith.*

        a. We should not feel deprived that we were not alive 2,000 years ago. Rather, be glad that God has visited us by his Spirit – bringing us as near to Christ as the disciples were!

III. The Gospels' depiction of Good Friday mirrors the way the early church came to view the glorious event of that day.

A. Having received the Spirit the gospel writers were able to look back on events and see their biblical significance.

    1. *Palm Sunday.* 'At first his disciples did not understand all this. Only after Jesus was glorified did they realise that these things had been written about him and that they had done these things to him' (John 12:16).

        a. What was it they later understood? That the event of Jesus riding on a donkey into Jerusalem was clearly foretold in the Old Testament: (1) Psalm 118:25,26; John 12:13; (2) Zecheriah 9:9; John 12:15.

        b. It is interesting that each gospel describes this event. Matthew 21:1-16; Mark 11:1-10; Luke 19:28-44; John 12:12-19.

            (1)All find support in the Old Testament.

            (2)Jesus quoted Psalm 8:2 to justify the children's role (Matt. 21:15-16).

    2. *Israel's rejection of Messiah.* 'Therefore I tell you that the kingdom of God will be taken away from you and given to a people who will produce its fruit' (Matt. 21:43).

        a. This was the purpose of the Parable of the Tenants (Matt. 21:33-46).

        b. Jesus applied Psalm 118:22-23 to his own death (cf. Acts 4:11).

3. *The disciples' forsaking Jesus.* 'Then Jesus told them, "This very night you will all fall away on account of me, for it is written: 'I will strike the shepherd, and the sheep of the flock will be scattered'"' (Matt. 26:31. cf. Zech. 13:7).

4. *Judas Iscariot's betrayal* (Matt. 27:9. cf. Zech. 11:12). Indeed the whole scenario of Jesus' betrayal and arrest 'has all taken place that the writings of the prophets might be fulfilled' (Matt. 26:56).

5. *The crucifixion*

   a. 'It is written: "And he was numbered with the transgressors"; and I tell you that this must be fulfilled in me. Yes, what is written about me is reaching its fulfilment' (Luke 22:37. cf. Is. 53:12). This was fulfilled when Jesus was crucified between two criminals (Luke 23:32-33).

   b. 'When they had crucified him, they divided up his clothes by casting lots' (Matt. 27:35). This fulfilled Psalm 22:18: 'They divide my garments among them and cast lots for my clothing' (cf. John 19:24).

   c. 'About the ninth hour Jesus cried out in a loud voice, "*Eloi, Eloi, lama sabachthani?*" – which means, "My God, my God, why have you forsaken me?"' (Matt. 27:46). This fulfilled Psalm 22:1. Note: Psalm 22 is a Messianic psalm that reflects Christ's sufferings.

   d. 'Later, knowing that all was now completed, and so that the Scripture would be fulfilled, Jesus said, "I am thirsty"' (John 19:28. cf. Ps. 69:21).

   e. They did not break Jesus' legs (John 19:33), which was a fulfilment of Exodus 12:46, Numbers 9:12 and Psalm 34:20, John 19:36.

   f. John also quoted Zecheriah 12:10 to show prophecy fulfilled in the crucifixion of Jesus: 'They will look on the one they have pierced' (John 19:37).

6. *The burial*

   a. Joseph of Arimathea, 'a rich man', got permission from Pilate to bury Jesus in his tomb (Matt. 27:57-61).

   b. This fulfilled Isaiah 53:9: 'He was assigned a grave with the wicked, and with the rich in his death, though he had done no violence, nor was any deceit in his mouth.'

B. Other ways the Old Testament was used by the early church.

1. That Jesus was the prophet of whom Moses spoke. 'For Moses said, "The Lord your God will raise up for you a prophet like me from among your own people; you must listen to everything he tells you' (Acts 3:22. cf. Deut. 18:15,18,19).

2. 'Indeed, all the prophets from Samuel on, as many as have spoken, have foretold these days. And you are heirs of the prophets and of the covenant God made with your fathers. He said to Abraham, "Through your offspring all peoples on earth will be blessed"' (Acts 3:24-25. Cf. Gen. 22:18).

3. Peter's use of Psalm 118:22: 'He is "the stone you builders rejected, which has become the capstone"' (Acts 4:11).

4. The early church's intercessory prayer quoted Psalm 2:1-2 (Acts 4:25-26).

5. Stephen's defence before the Sanhedrin (Acts 7).

6. Philip's use of Isaiah 53 (Acts 8:31-35).

IV. The work of the Holy Spirit and the supernatural on Good Friday

A. Where was the third person of the Trinity on Good Friday?

1. Possibly the most neglected aspect of Good Friday is the work of the Holy Spirit.

2. But Hebrews 9:14 tells us that Jesus did what he did by the Holy Spirit: 'How much more, then, will the blood of Christ, who through the eternal Spirit offered himself unblemished to God, cleanse our consciences from acts that lead to death, so that we may serve the living God!'

   a. Jesus had the Spirit without limit (John 3:34).

   b. Paul says that Jesus was vindicated by the Spirit (1 Tim. 3:16).

      (1) This means that Jesus was vindicated from within, that is, he got his approval from the Father not from people (cf. John 5:44).

      (2) This means also that we vindicate Jesus by our confession of him – for we do it by the Spirit.

   c. This in part explains the fruit of the Spirit in the person of Jesus on Good Friday (and before):

      (1) The absence of self-pity (Luke 23:28).

(2) Refusal to retort when they said, 'He saved others, but he can't save himself. . . . come down now from the cross, that we may see and believe' (Mark 15:31-32).

(3) Refusal to vindicate himself (Luke 23:8ff).

(4) His care for his mother (John 19:25-27).

(5) Forgiving those who crucified him (Luke 23:34).

B. Supernatural manifestations.

1. *The sovereign conversion of one of the thieves.*

   a. There is no greater miracle than that of conversion.

   b. His reply to the thief who prayed, 'Jesus, remember me when you come into your kingdom,' was, 'Today you will be with me in paradise' (Luke 23:42-43).

2. *Supernatural darkness.* 'From the sixth hour until the ninth hour darkness came over all the land' (Matt.27:45).

   a. What caused this darkness? 'Were you there when the sun refused to shine, were you there?'

      (1) It was definitely *not* an eclipse of the sun; it was Passover, there was a full moon. All accounts indicate that it was unusual – darkness from noon until 3 o'clock.

   b. It was the cloud of glory that caused this darkness.

      (1) 'The LORD said to Moses: "Tell your brother Aaron not to come whenever he chooses into the Most Holy Place behind the curtain in front of the atonement cover on the ark, or else he will die, because I appear in the cloud over the atonement cover"' (Lev. 16:2).

      (2) 'When the priests withdrew from the Holy Place, the cloud filled the temple of the LORD. And the priests could not perform their service because of the cloud, for the glory of the LORD filled his temple. Then Solomon said, "The LORD has said that he would dwell in a dark cloud"' (1 Kings 8:10-12).

3. *The curtain in the temple 'was torn in two from top to bottom'* (Matt. 27:51).

   a. This was the veil, or curtain, that separated the Holy Place from the Holy of Holies.

   b. Inside the Holy of Holies was the Mercy Seat.

      (1) God supernaturally ripped the curtain in two, signalling the end of the ancient sacrificial system.

(2) The darkness over the land showed that the sphere of divine action centred on the work of God's Son on the Cross.

4. *The earthquake.* 'The earth shook and the rocks split' (Matt. 27:51).
   a. This indicated the authority of Christ over all nature.
   b. The preaching of the Cross commands all nature to respect the power of Jesus' blood.

5. *People being raised from the dead.* 'The tombs broke open and the bodies of many holy people who had died were raised to life. They came out of the tombs, and after Jesus' resurrection they went into the holy city and appeared to many people' (Matt. 27:52-53).
   a. The Cross signalled the death of death (Heb. 2:14).
   b. As a token certain people were earmarked for being raised from the dead.
   c. God may yet honour the preaching of the Cross with signs and wonders (1 Cor. 2:2-5).

CONCLUSION

To the disciples of Jesus his crucifixion was an unimaginable shock. There had remained a mindset which looked for a human kingly Messiah, and the death of Jesus took away the last possibility for him to fit that mould.

Despite the supernatural manifestations surrounding the death of Christ his followers did not really begin to understand the significance of his sacrifice until after Pentecost. Following the coming of the Holy Spirit their eyes were opened to see Christ as the fulfilment of Old Testament prophecy and this became the basis of the early church's proclamation of the gospel.

20

THE HOLY SPIRIT
IN THE OLD TESTAMENT

INTRODUCTION

A. The prominence of the Holy Spirit in the New Testament is undoubted.
   1. The Holy Spirit was involved in the birth of Jesus. 'The angel answered, "The Holy Spirit will come upon you, and the power of the Most High will overshadow you. So the holy one to be born will be called the Son of God"' (Luke 1:35).
   2. John the Baptist was filled with the Spirit from his mother's womb (Luke 1:15,41).
   3. John said that Jesus would baptise with the Spirit (Matt. 3:11).
   4. The Spirit came on Jesus at his baptism (Matt. 3:16).
   5. Jesus had the Spirit without any limit (John 3:34).
   6. Jesus told us to ask for the Holy Spirit (Luke 11:13).
   7. Jesus cast out devils by the Spirit (Matt. 12:28).
   8. *Jesus referred to the Spirit as the one who would replace him* (John 14:16).
      a. He is called the Spirit of truth (John 14:17).
      b. He would remind us of what we learned (John 14:26).
      c. He would testify about Jesus (John 15:26).
      d. He would convict of sin, righteousness and judgment (John 16:8).
      e. He would guide into all truth (John 16:13).
   9. The disciples were urged to wait for the Spirit (Luke 24:49; Acts 1:4).
   10. The Holy Spirit came in power on the day of Pentecost (Acts 2).

B. The apostle Paul explained Jesus' words: 'I have much more to say to you, more than you can now bear' (John 16:12).
   1. *The Holy Spirit is a sensitive person.*
      a. He can be grieved (Eph. 4:30).
      b. He can be quenched (1 Thess. 5:19).

2. There are gifts of the Spirit (1 Cor. 12:8-10. cf. Rom. 11:29).
3. There are fruits of the Spirit (Gal. 5:22ff).
4. We should seek to be filled with the Spirit (Eph. 5:18).
5. There is a sealing of the Spirit (Eph. 1:13).

C. **Hebrews 9:14 says that the Holy Spirit is eternal.**
1. The Lord is the Spirit who was operative in Moses' day (2 Cor. 3:15-17).
2. The Holy Spirit is God (Acts 5:3-5).

D. **If the Spirit is eternal (having no beginning or ending), and if the Holy Spirit is God, he must have been present in the Old Testament – but where?**
1. How prominent is the Holy Spirit in the Old Testament?
2. *How do we find him, where do we look for him?*
   a. Hebrew *rûah* is a word that means 'wind', also 'spirit'.
   b. So Jesus said, 'The wind blows wherever it pleases. You hear its sound, but you cannot tell where it comes from or where it is going. So it is with everyone born of the Spirit' (John 3:8).

E. **Why is this study important?**
1. We should want to know whether the Spirit functioned in the Old Testament as he did in the New Testament.
2. Did people in the Old Testament have the Holy Spirit dwelling in them?
3. Did people in the Old Testament have assurance; if so, how did they know this?
4. Does the teaching of 'Once saved, always saved' apply to them?
5. How did the appropriate the benefit of Christ's death?

I. THE NEW TESTAMENT CLAIMS THAT THE HOLY SPIRIT WAS PRESENT IN THE DAYS OF THE OLD TESTAMENT

A. **The Holy Spirit was responsible for the formation of the Old Testament.**
1. According to Jesus, David wrote by the Holy Spirit. 'He said to them, "How is it then that David, speaking by the Spirit, calls him 'Lord'? For he says, 'The Lord said to my Lord: "Sit at my right hand until I put your enemies under your feet"'"' (Matt. 22:43-44. cf. Ps. 110:1).

2. The early church affirmed the same thing. 'You spoke by the Holy Spirit through the mouth of your servant, our father David: "Why do the nations rage and the peoples plot in vain? The kings of the earth take their stand and the rulers gather together against the Lord and against his Anointed One"' (Acts 4:25-26).

3. *The breath of God is the Holy Spirit.*
   a. 'All Scripture is God-breathed and is useful for teaching, rebuking, correcting and training in righteousness' (2 Tim. 3:16).
   b. 'And with that he breathed on them and said, "Receive the Holy Spirit"' (John 20:22).

4. Consequently, Peter wrote, 'Above all, you must understand that no prophecy of Scripture came about by the prophet's own interpretation. For prophecy never had its origin in the will of man, but men spoke from God as they were carried along by the Holy Spirit' (2 Peter 1:20-21).

B. The Holy Spirit was present in creation.
   1. 'In the beginning God created the heavens and the earth. Now the earth was formless and empty, darkness was over the surface of the deep, and the Spirit of God was hovering over the waters' (Gen. 1:1-2).
   2. *God said, 'Let us make man in our image, in our likeness.'* (Gen. 1:26).
      a. This shows the plurality of the Godhead; one God in three persons.
      b. 'In the beginning was the Word, and the Word was with God, and the Word was God' (John 1:1).

C. Peter explores the ministry of the prophetic in the Old Testament in terms of the Holy Spirit in them. 'Concerning this salvation, the prophets, who spoke of the grace that was to come to you, searched intently and with the greatest care, trying to find out the time and circumstances to which the Spirit of Christ in them was pointing when he predicted the sufferings of Christ and the glories that would follow' (1 Pet. 1:10-11).
   1. The Holy Spirit was not only present but was also the explanation of what they prophesied.
   2. Their ministry was to point to the sufferings of Messiah (cf. Isa. 53).

D. When Jesus first revealed his mission he quoted from Isaiah 61:1. 'He went to Nazareth, where he had been brought up, and on the Sabbath day he went into the synagogue, as was his custom. And he stood up to read. The scroll of the prophet Isaiah was handed to him. Unrolling it, he found the place where it is written: "The Spirit of the Lord is on me, because he has anointed me to preach good news to the poor. He has sent me to proclaim freedom for the prisoners and recovery of sight for the blind, to release the oppressed, to proclaim the year of the Lord's favour." Then he rolled up the scroll, gave it back to the attendant and sat down. The eyes of everyone in the synagogue were fastened on him, and he began by saying to them, "Today this scripture is fulfilled in your hearing." All spoke well of him and were amazed at the gracious words that came from his lips. "Isn't this Joseph's son?" they asked' (Luke 4:16-22).

E. The writer of Hebrews claims that the Holy Spirit was behind both the warning and the swearing of the oath in wrath regarding the children of Israel in the desert.
   1. Introducing Psalm 95:7-11, 'as the Holy Spirit says' (Heb. 3:7).
   2. *Psalm 95 refers to the children of Israel in the desert.*
      a. The warning: 'Today, if you hear his voice.'
      b. The oath: 'So I declared on oath in my anger, "They shall never enter my rest"' (Ps. 95:11).

F. What God was doing in the formation of the Tabernacle in the desert (and all in it – lampstand, table, bread, the Most Holy Place, altar of incense, the ark) was under the direct leadership of the Holy Spirit.
   1. 'The Holy Spirit was showing by this that the way into the Most Holy Place had not yet been disclosed as long as the first tabernacle was still standing' (Heb. 9:8).
   2. No wonder, then, that the writer of Hebrews could speak of the Spirit as being eternal. 'How much more, then, will the blood of Christ, who through the eternal Spirit offered himself unblemished to God, cleanse our consciences from acts that lead to death, so that we may serve the living God!' (Heb. 9:14).

G. The writer of Hebrews goes into great detail to explain that the people of the Old Testament did what they did by faith (ch. 11).

    1. Faith is no New Testament innovation; it is the explanation for the extraordinary accomplishments by sovereign vessels of the Old Testament. 'This is what the ancients were commended for' (Heb. 11:2).

    2. *Faith is only possible by the Holy Spirit!* (2 Thess. 2:13; Eph. 2:1-8).

        a. 'A man can receive only what is given him from heaven' (John 3:27).

        b. 'The Spirit gives life; the flesh counts for nothing. The words I have spoken to you are spirit and they are life' (John 6:63).

        c. Conclusion: the Holy Spirit is the only explanation for faith, whether then or now.

II. HOW WERE PEOPLE IN THE OLD TESTAMENT SAVED?

A. All people who ever lived must come under the judgment of God.

    1. *God has declared the whole world guilty.*

        a. Jews and Gentiles alike are 'all under sin' (Rom. 3:9).

        b. 'Now we know that whatever the law says, it says to those who are under the law, so that every mouth may be silenced and the whole world held accountable to God' (Rom. 3:19).

        c. What about those not under the Law? They too will be judged.

            (1) 'The wrath of God is being revealed from heaven against all the godlessness and wickedness of men who suppress the truth by their wickedness, since what may be known about God is plain to them, because God has made it plain to them. For since the creation of the world God's invisible qualities – his eternal power and divine nature – have been clearly seen, being understood from what has been made, so that men are without excuse' (Rom. 1:18-20).

            (2) 'Indeed, when Gentiles, who do not have the law, do by nature things required by the law, they are a law for themselves, even though they do not have the law, since they show that the requirements of the law are written on their hearts, their consciences also bearing witness, and their thoughts now accusing, now even defending them' (Rom. 2:14-15).

2. *All will stand before God.*

    a. 'This will take place on the day when God will judge men's secrets through Jesus Christ, as my gospel declares' (Rom 2:16).

    b. 'Just as man is destined to die once, and after that to face judgment' (Heb. 9:27).

    c. 'And I saw the dead, great and small, standing before the throne, and books were opened. Another book was opened, which is the book of life. The dead were judged according to what they had done as recorded in the books. The sea gave up the dead that were in it, and death and Hades gave up the dead that were in them, and each person was judged according to what he had done' (Rev. 20:12-13).

B. Faith is the only way to salvation.

1. All the people in the Old Testament were saved the same way all people today are saved: by faith.

    a. The children of Israel were saved by believing Moses.

        (1) 'And they believed. And when they heard that the Lord was concerned about them and had seen their misery, they bowed down and worshipped' (Ex. 4:31).

        (2) When Moses gave explicit instructions regarding a Passover – an unprecedented occurrence – the people 'bowed down and worshipped. The Israelites did just what the LORD commanded Moses and Aaron' (Ex. 12:27-28).

        (3) 'They were all baptised into Moses in the cloud and in the sea' (1 Cor. 10:2).

    b. 'The law was given through Moses; grace and truth came through Jesus Christ' (John 1:17).

        (1) It was not keeping the law that saved them; it was faith in God's word that came through Moses.

        (2) 'The law is only a shadow of the good things that are coming – not the realities themselves. For this reason it can never, by the same sacrifices repeated endlessly year after year, make perfect those who draw near to worship' (Heb. 10:1).

        (3) The law pointed to Christ the 'end of the law so that there may be righteousness for everyone who believes' (Rom. 10:4).

2. *The faith that saved the ancient people was embryonic faith.*
  a. This means it was barely formed, undeveloped – but real none the less.
  b. Calvin called it 'implicit faith' (*Institutes* III:ii:4-5).
    (1) It was in Jesus' disciples before they attained full enlightenment.
    (3) People who believed that Christ was the Messiah, 'although they had not been given even a trace of the gospel, are graced with the title "faith"; yet it was only the beginning of faith' (Calvin, *ibid*).
  c. This is the best explanation for what the ancient Israelites experienced.
    (1) 'Whoever can be trusted with very little can also be trusted with much, and whoever is dishonest with very little will also be dishonest with much' (Luke 16:10).
    (2) By the people in the Old Testament believing the little to which they were exposed, they showed they would therefore believe the much had they been given the opportunity.

C. The same Holy Spirit who creates faith in us is the Spirit who enabled them to believe.
  1. The writer of Hebrews makes it clear that it was none other then the Holy Spirit at work then. 'The Holy Spirit was showing by this that the way into the Most Holy Place had not yet been disclosed as long as the first tabernacle was still standing' (Heb. 9:8).
  2. *The only difference: the degree of revelation that they had.*
    a. They saw only the types and shadows, but their faith saved because of what these types and shadows represented.
    b. We see the fulfilment – the complete revelation.
    c. In either case, our ability, or enablement, to believe is by the Holy Spirit. There is no other explanation.

III. MANIFESTATIONS OF THE SPIRIT

A. Communion with the Spirit, or gifts of the Spirit.
  1. *Adam and Eve, before the Fall.*
    a. God spoke to them (Gen. 1:28-30; 2:16-18).
      (1) No person has seen God directly (John 1:18).
      (2) God therefore communicated with them by the Spirit.

b. Even after they sinned, God spoke (Gen. 3:8-19).

(1) God provided a sacrifice for their sin (Gen. 3:21).

(2) They were none the less driven from Eden (Gen. 3:23ff).

2. *Enoch walked with God* (Gen. 5:24).

a. He did this by faith (Heb. 11:5).

b. He had the witness that he pleased God (Heb. 11:5).

c. This was only possible by the Spirit.

3. *David prayed for a restoration of the joy of salvation* (Ps. 51:12).

a. Having sinned, he prayed: 'Do not cast me from your presence or take your Holy Spirit from me' (Ps. 51:11).

b. David was conscious of the Spirit's presence, especially when he lost this for a time.

4. *Samson was given an unusual anointing: strength.*

a. He sinned by revealing the secret of this strength to Delilah (Jud. 16:18).

b. The Lord 'left' him, that is, the anointing left him (Jud. 16:20).

c. He prayed for a second chance – and got it (Jud. 16:28).

(1) This shows he still had the Spirit in him.

(2) When his hair grew back, the anointing of strength returned.

5. *Job was said to be blameless* (Job 1:1).

a. He showed himself none the less to be self-righteous (Job 40:4).

b. He prayed for his 'friends'; the former state was restored (Job 42:10).

6. *Saul was changed into another person* (1 Sam. 10:9).

a. He was given an unusual prophetic gift (1 Sam. 10:11).

b. The Spirit of the Lord departed from Saul and yet he retained the gift of prophecy (1 Sam. 16:14; 19:24. cf. Rom. 11:29).

7. *Jonah disobeyed God* (Jonah 1:2-3).

a. Jonah repented (Jon. 2).

b. The Lord came to him a second time and he obeyed (Jonah 3:1ff).

8. *Observations from the above:*

a. The Holy Spirit dealt with these people.

b. Some of these people lost their anointing in some sense, yet God did not desert them utterly. David, Samson and Jonah were restored.

c. Saul is an example of one who would be saved but by fire (1 Cor. 3:15).

        (1) He was given a new heart – he was saved.

        (2) He would be with Samuel after he died (1 Sam. 28:19).

    d. The teaching of 'Once saved, always saved' is true in the Old Testament.

B. Assurance of salvation

  1. *The gospel was given to Abraham* (Gal. 3:8).

    a. He was justified by faith (Gen. 15:6).

    b. He saw the Lord Jesus Christ in his day (John 8:56).

    c. God swore an oath to him (Gen. 22:16).

  2. *The gospel was still in force after the Law came in* (Gal. 3:19-22).

    a. Those under the Law (from Moses until the time of Christ) were not saved by keeping the Law.

    b. They were saved by believing the word – faith alone.

  3. *This is why God did not delight in the types and shadows during the whole time the Law was in force.*

    a. 'You do not delight in sacrifice, or I would bring it; you do not take pleasure in burnt offerings. The sacrifices of God are a broken spirit; a broken and contrite heart, O God, you will not despise' (Ps. 51:16-17).

    b. 'Even though you bring me burnt offerings and grain offerings, I will not accept them. Though you bring choice fellowship offerings, I will have no regard for them' (Amos 5:22).

    c. 'For I desire mercy, not sacrifice, and acknowledgement of God rather than burnt offerings' (Hosea 6:6).

  4. *Note: the children of Israel were saved by faith because they were under a covenant of grace.*

    a. Personal assurance of salvation was not something they would always be conscious of as we are.

    b. Their faith was an embryonic, or implicit, faith; assurance was likely in a minute degree.

    c. And yet there were probably also exceptions:

        (1) Sovereign vessels, like Abraham or David, enjoyed a high level of assurance at times (Ps. 18).

        (2) People generally were given great joy over what God would do at special times (Neh. 8:10; 2 Chron. 30).

        (3) 'He regarded disgrace for the sake of Christ as of greater value than the treasures of Egypt, because he was looking ahead to his reward' (Heb. 11:26).

(a) The reference to Christ was the way Moses felt about his relationship with God, long before he had a fuller understanding of God.

(b) This shows that he had a degree of assurance even before he understood very much about God.

d. Peter says that Christ was the Lamb that was slain, chosen from before the world (1 Pet. 1:19-20).

(1) It does not follow that the priests who offered the sacrifices in the Old Testament understood all that these sacrifices were pointing to.

(2) People were saved not by these sacrifices but by their obedience to the word – which God honoured.

(3) Even after Christ came and died, the New Testament labours to show believers at the time what this actually meant!

(4) In a word: the believers in the Old Testament appropriated Christ's death by the embryonic faith they had at the time.

e. The full revelation of Jeremiah's prophecy was only understood later.

(1) '"No longer will a man teach his neighbour, or a man his brother, saying, 'Know the Lord,' because they will all know me, from the least of them to the greatest," declares the Lord. "For I will forgive their wickedness and will remember their sins no more"' (Jer. 31:34).

(2) The writer of Hebrews quotes this to prove that the first covenant (Law) was imperfect. Heb. 8:7-12.

C. Supernatural work of the Spirit

1. 'On the day the tabernacle, the Tent of the Testimony, was set up, the cloud covered it. From evening till morning the cloud above the tabernacle looked like fire' (Num. 9:15).

2. 'As soon as you hear the sound of marching in the tops of the balsam trees, move quickly, because that will mean the LORD has gone out in front of you to strike the Philistine army' (2 Sam. 5:24).

3. 'When the priests withdrew from the Holy Place, the cloud filled the temple of the LORD. And the priests could not perform their service because of the cloud, for the glory of the LORD

filled his temple. Then Solomon said, "The LORD has said that he would dwell in a dark cloud' (1 Kings 8:10-12).

4. 'And Elisha prayed, "O LORD, open his eyes so he may see." Then the LORD opened the servant's eyes, and he looked and saw the hills full of horses and chariots of fire all around Elisha' (2 Kings 6:17).

5. 'As they began to sing and praise, the LORD set ambushes against the men of Ammon and Moab and Mount Seir who were invading Judah, and they were defeated' (2 Chron. 20:22).

D. Prophecies concerning the fullness of the Spirit

1. Pertaining to the Lord Jesus Christ, the root of Jesse (Isa. 11:1-2).
2. Pertaining to the Lord Jesus Christ, the servant of the Lord (Isa. 42:1-4).
3. Pertaining to the Lord Jesus Christ, the Messiah (Isa. 61:1-2).
4. The Spirit to be poured out on all (Joel 2:28-32).

CONCLUSION

While the Holy Spirit is often referred to in the New Testament, he is more rarely mentioned in the Old. However, this does not indicate that he was inactive. The Holy Spirit was present at creation (Gen. 1:2). He was at work throughout Old Testament times. The early church affirmed this: 'You spoke by the Holy Spirit through your servant, our father David' (Acts 4:25). Old Testament believers came to faith through the agency of the Holy Spirit, there is not and never has been any other means.

Once we understand the person of the Holy Spirit and his ways, it is easy to see him at work in the Old Testament. Even the Sermon on the Mount does not explicitly mention the Holy Spirit; yet understanding it in terms of the realm of the Spirit is the only explanation of the Kingdom of Heaven that makes sense. We therefore should not be surprised that the Holy Spirit is not always mentioned by name in the Old Testament, but he is the only explanation of how people believed and accomplished great things.

21

OPENNESS TO THE HOLY SPIRIT

INTRODUCTION

A. We have seen that the stigma (offence) of the Holy Spirit is his very presence.
   1. In other words, the stigma of the Spirit is the Spirit himself.
   2. *He by nature offends; all that is offensive about the Father and the Son is embodied in the person of the Holy Spirit.*
      a. When one is offended by the Spirit it is because one is offended by God.
         (1) It is not possible to find God to be pleasant but find the Holy Spirit offensive.
         (2) It is not possible to affirm all that Jesus Christ was and did, then turn around and reject the Holy Spirit.
      b. The persons of the Godhead are united.
         (1) Equally each has his own stigma.
         (2) The Holy Spirit mirrors the other persons of the godhead; therefore how we respond to the person of the Spirit shows what we really feel about either the Father or the Son.

B. But since the Spirit can be offensive, why should we be open to him?
   1. Are we not foolish or irrational if we deliberately open ourselves to one who is offensive and who offends?
   2. *Answer: we must affirm God as he is; the Holy Spirit is God.*
      a. When our hearts are truly right with God we will find that God is not offensive at all!
      b. We will instead find him glorious!
   3. But we must take God as he is and be prepared to affirm the presence of the Holy Spirit – however God may sovereignly choose to reveal himself.

C. Sometime ago I pleaded with a fellow minister, 'Stay open to the Holy Spirit.'

    1. He replied, 'I don't know what you mean by that.' I don't know whether he was sincere or cynical in his reply, I want to show in this chapter what openness to the Holy Spirit is.

        a. It is humility; the recognition that I don't have everything, I don't know everything.

        b. It is the awareness that I need more of the Holy Spirit.

        c. It is the self-conscious desire to find God wherever he is, to recognise him as soon as he appears and to miss nothing that could be received from him.

        d. It is knowing that God is willing to give me so much more as long as I admit my poverty as opposed to saying 'I do not need a thing' (Rev. 3:17).

D. It is one thing for the Holy Spirit to open our hearts or our understanding; it is another for us to be open to him instead of challenging him to open us first.

    1. Admittedly, we have to be changed by God himself (by his sovereign power) before we are going to listen and obey.

    2. *But is there not a case for our remaining open to the same Holy Spirit, having been converted, that we miss nothing he would say to us?*

        a. Answer: yes.

        b. The underlying problem of the Hebrew Christians, to whom Hebrews is addressed, was that they had become 'hard of hearing' (Gr. – Heb. 5:11 AV).

            (1) This means they had become closed to the point of not even being able to hear God any more.

            (2) They felt no need to be open.

E. Why is this lesson important?

    1. *The only link between us and the Throne of Grace is the Holy Spirit.*

        a. If he is quenched or grieved we have cut off the only link that will let us know how God is moving today.

        b. We must therefore maintain the best possible relationship to the Spirit

    2. *Although God is the same yesterday, today and forever, and therefore unchanging in his nature, he does not always*

reveal himself in one generation as he did in another.
  a. We must therefore be open to the Spirit lest we miss the way in
     which this God sovereignly chooses to manifest his glory.
  b. This is why Jonathan Edwards taught us that the task of
     every generation is to discover in which direction the
     Sovereign Redeemer is moving, then move in that direction.
3. *If we are closed (our minds fully made up) to whatever God
  may wish to do or say today we will miss his glory just as
  Israel missed recognising the Messiah when he appeared.*
  a. You could never have convinced the scribes, the priests or
     Pharisees that God's chosen Messiah would appear before
     their eyes – and they not see him!
  b. But this *is* what happened!
4. *If we are truly open to the Holy Spirit (because we are
  prepared to pay the price that goes with whatever the stigma
  may be) there is probably more likelihood that we will not
  miss his glory when it is unveiled.*
5. *How one accepts this lesson is a fairly good indicator
  whether we truly love God and his Word.*

**I. Every generation has its stigma by which the believer's faith
is tested**

A. It is not so difficult to believe what God did yesterday.
  1. *But what God did yesterday was highly offensive at the time.*
     a. We may say, 'I wouldn't have objected had I been alive then.'
     b. But the only proof that we would have accepted what God
        did in a previous generation is our affirming what God is
        doing in ours.
  2. *Even the Pharisees felt themselves very pious because they
     affirmed yesterday's men!*
     a. Jesus confronted them on this very issue. 'And you say, "If
        we had lived in the days of our forefathers, we would not
        have taken part with them in shedding the blood of the
        prophets"' (Matt. 23:30).
     b. But by rejecting the equivalent offence – rejecting Jesus
        Christ himself – in their own day Jesus said to them, 'So
        you testify against yourselves that you are the descendants
        of those who murdered the prophets. Fill up, then, the
        measure of the sin of your forefathers!' (Matt. 23:31-32).

(1) It is sometimes said that the good is the enemy of the best; a church that is reasonably prosperous doesn't want revival.

(2) It is often true that the greatest enmity toward what God is doing today comes from those who became a part of what God was doing yesterday.

c. It would not be surprising for followers of Whitefield and Spurgeon today to have rejected them when they were alive!

B. The offence in what God is doing in the present is usually changed sufficiently, from what he did previously, in order to test one's love of God and true openness to the Spirit.

1. *Not a single person listed in Hebrews 11 had the luxury of stepping into the stigma created by yesterday's man or woman of faith.*

a. Enoch 'walked with God' (Gen. 5:24).

b. Noah 'walked with God' (Gen. 6:9).

(1) Noah might have concluded: I have proved that I please God as much as Enoch did since I am doing what Enoch did.

(2) The result of Enoch's openness to the Spirit was that he was translated – God took him so that he did not see death (Gen. 5:24; Heb. 11:5).

(3) But Noah walked with God and was not translated (as he might well have wished) but had to endure a terrific stigma: maintaining it was going to rain (unprecedented) and that judgement was coming on the earth.

(4) 'By faith Noah, when warned about things not yet seen, in holy fear built an ark to save his family. By his faith he condemned the world and became heir of the righteousness that comes by faith' (Heb. 11:7).

c. Abraham was not allowed to do what Noah did.

(1) Perhaps there would have been little stigma to building another ark!

(2) But Abraham's stigma was different. 'By faith Abraham, when called to go to a place he would later receive as his inheritance, obeyed and went, even though he did not know where he was going' (Heb. 11:8).

    d. That is not all; Abraham had to embrace a far greater challenge later. 'By faith Abraham, when God tested him, offered Isaac as a sacrifice. He who had received the promises was about to sacrifice his one and only son' (Heb. 11:17).

        (1) He might have said, 'I've paid my dues. I've shown I love God – no more bearing of the cross for me!'

        (2) Sometimes we may feel we've done enough for God – enough for a lifetime.

        (3) But Abraham had to bear yet another offence!

2. *All those described in Hebrews 11 were faced with a new and unprecedented stigma in their own generation.*

    a. If you ask: How can I know I would qualify for a place in Hebrews 11 had I been living in ancient times?

    b. I answer: if you embrace today's stigma you would have embraced whatever stigma there was in a previous day.

        (1) You may say, 'I could never die like the martyrs of old.'

        (2) I say: You would if you show today that you bear the stigma God puts before you. 'Whoever can be trusted with very little can also be trusted with much, and whoever is dishonest with very little will also be dishonest with much' (Luke 16:10).

II. WHY BE OPEN TO THE HOLY SPIRIT?

A. Because God still speaks today. 'Today, if you hear his voice' (Ps. 95:7).

But did this refer to the Holy Spirit? Yes. 'So, as the Holy Spirit says: "Today, if you hear his voice, do not harden your hearts as you did in the rebellion, during the time of testing in the desert, where your fathers tested and tried me and for forty years saw what I did. That is why I was angry with that generation, and I said, 'Their hearts are always going astray, and they have not known my ways.' So I declared on oath in my anger, 'They shall never enter my rest'"' (Heb. 3:7-11).

B. Some will say: surely the Bible is the infallible, inerrant and unchanging word of God, and this was given yesterday.

    1. *I answer:*

        a. God's Word – the Bible – is infallible, inerrant and unchanging.

        b. God gave us the Bible yesterday.

        c. But the Holy Spirit *applies it today*.

2. *The application of God's Word by the Holy Spirit will be to focus on an aspect of that Word which will be the offence of today.*

    a. The Holy Spirit continues to speak – clearly, directly and immediately; through:

        (1) Prophecy.

        (2) Word of knowledge.

        (3) Vision.

        (4) Audible voice.

    b. But he will never, never, never conflict with or contradict anything in the Bible but only make it clearer!

        (1) The Holy Spirit speaking today is *not* new revelation or in competition with the Bible (like the Book of Mormon – or the Koran – which contradict the Word of God).

        (2) The proof of the Holy Spirit's voice or manifestation will be that it vindicates and magnifies the Bible.

C. Openness to the Holy Spirit is what will put us in good stead not to miss what God is doing today.

    1. *There is no great stigma (speaking generally) in defending what Athanasius (4th century) stood for.*

        a. He stood alone – and won.

        b. But nobody will be ridiculed (that is, in the church) for saying that Jesus Christ is truly God – co-eternal and co-substantial and co-equal with the Father.

    2. *There is no great stigma in defending justification by faith alone today – even with some Roman Catholics.*

        a. Martin Luther (1413-1546) stood alone.

        b. But he won the day; today Christians grant that we are saved by faith alone in Christ's work on the cross.

    3. *The stigma* may *repeat itself:*

        a. Creation over against evolution brings offence.

        b. Hell over against annihilation brings offence.

        c. So one must not rule out that a challenge to an ancient truth once vindicated could re-emerge as a new battle that must be won.

        d. Remember however that the rule of thumb will be that the new stigma will be a *stigma* and it won't be easy to accept and stand for.

4. *The Holy Spirit will not deceive us.*

    a. If we are on good terms with him, we will know what he is *in* and *behind* and what he is *doing* and *saying*.

    b. He is not likely to let those in whom he dwells ungrieved in large measure miss what is on the cutting edge (in heaven's eyes).

III. WHAT IS OPENNESS TO THE SPIRIT? HOW MAY WE KNOW WE ARE OPEN?

A. That we are open in our hearts as well as our heads.

    1. It was Lydia's *heart* that the Lord opened (Acts 16:14).

    2. *It is possible to be theoretically open (that is, we give intellectual assent) but closed in our hearts.*

        a. Why would we be open in the head but not the heart?

        b. Because we may accept the validity of, say, a study like this one – yet remain afraid.

    3. *The chief impediment to openness to the Spirit is fear.* 'For God did not give us a spirit of timidity, but a spirit of power, of love and of self-discipline' (2 Tim. 1:7).

B. We must become vulnerable.

    1. Vulnerable (def.): able to be hurt; unprotected against attacks.

    2. *Becoming vulnerable means that:*

        a. We are willing to be hurt – or embarrassed.

        b. We cease protecting ourselves with things such as:

            (1) Defence mechanisms (setting up defences in our minds).

            (2) Excuses why we should not be involved.

            (3) Worrying about our reputation with friends – even closest friends.

C. That we are extremely sensitive to the Spirit.

    1. *The Holy Spirit is a person who can be grieved* (Eph. 4:30) *or quenched* (1 Thess. 5:19).

        a. We grieve him chiefly by bitterness – having an unforgiving spirit (which is why we slander people) (Eph. 4:30ff).

        b. We quench the Spirit chiefly by:

            (1) Protecting ourselves from vulnerability.

            (2) Speaking against what God is presently doing – supposing God *couldn't* be doing *that*!

2. *When the Spirit is (1) unquenched and (2) in us in large measure (which means we cultivate our relationship with him by giving him time and walking in the light* (1 John 1:7):

    a. We will go with the Spirit's flow.

    b. We will feel it when we are displeasing him.

    c. We will recognise what he is doing and saying.

3. *NB: 'Extremely' sensitive.*

    a. The Spirit is easily grieved.

    b. Only a high level of sensitivity to the Spirit will recognise the Spirit elsewhere:

        (1) In the Word that is preached.

        (2) In the prophetic word.

        (3) In various manifestations.

D. How *can* we become open if we fear we are not open but want to be open?

1. Be sure there is no unconfessed sin in our lives (John 1:9).

2. Be sure there is no bitterness or grudge against anyone (Eph. 4:31ff).

3. Be sure we do not speak against anyone (Jas. 3).

4. Be sure we have a solid prayer and Bible reading life (Luke 18:1; 2 Tim. 2:15).

5. Walk in all the light God gives us (1 John 1:7).

6. Learn to know the Spirit's voice (Heb. 3:7-8).

7. Develop a familiarity with his ways and the ability to recognise his presence (Heb. 3:10-11).

CONCLUSION

Some warnings. First, do not assume you are open to the Spirit today just because you may have been yesterday. Our relationship with the Holy Spirit must be current.

Secondly, do not assume you are open because you have taken a strong stand on some valid issue. For example you can take a stand on specific issues, such as abortion, inspiration of scripture or sound teaching, and not be necessarily open to the Spirit. You could have the gifts of the Spirit and not be open; after all, they are irrevocable (Rom. 11:29).

Thirdly, do not assume you are open to the Spirit because God is blessing *you.* You may be prospering, you may have a good job, you may know God's guidance, you may have been healed, but still not be open to the Spirit.

The consequence of not being open to the Spirit is horrendous; it means probably: you cannot enter God's rest (Heb. 3:7-11); you cannot hear him speak again (Heb. 5:11ff). But if you are open to the Spirit and able to recognise him at work, you will be at peace with yourself and are not likely to miss what he is doing.

Openness to the Spirit is an admission of need. It is also the desire to recognise him however he presents himself, to increase in knowledge of him, and to make ourselves available to do whatever he gives us to do and to go wherever he leads.

22

GIFTS VERSUS FRUITS OF THE SPIRIT

INTRODUCTION

A. There is a lot of interest in the Holy Spirit today.
1. One publisher told me not long ago that he knew of fifty books in print on the subject of the Holy Spirit; only three on Jesus.
2. Publishers tend to come out with books that 'sell' rather than what people need.

B. Whereas we are looking at the subject of the Holy Spirit, we believe we are focussing on a needed emphasis.
1. *What are the aspects of the Spirit people seem to be interested in? Probably these:*
    a. The baptism of the Spirit.
    b. The gifts of the Spirit.
2. *Why is it that Christians today, speaking generally, are more interested in the Holy Spirit than in Jesus? Probably because:*
    a. People assume they already know enough about Jesus.
    b. The gospel is a mere assumption with many people, hence there is no great need to keep going over it.
    c. The rise of Pentecostalism, which has been somewhat upstaged by the Charismatic Movement, has drawn attention to the Holy Spirit, especially the gifts of the Spirit.
3. *The gifts of the Holy Spirit have largely been ignored by most churches until the emergence of the aforementioned movements.*
    a. It almost goes without saying that the gifts of the Spirit have not been in prominent operation in most denominations until recent times.
        (1) Were it not for these movements, there is every reason to assume that these gifts would have continually been ignored.

        (2) We ought to thank God for those who have called our attention to what has been ignored.

        (3) We should thank God for John Wimber who has put 'signs and wonders' on the map!

   b. Some well-meaning Christians have come up with a convenient theological rationale for ignoring the gifts of the Spirit: it is called 'cessationism'.

        (1) This is the idea that the gifts of the Spirit, as well as all signs and wonders, 'ceased' with the early church and the completion of the New Testament.

        (2) In a word: the gifts of the Spirit are unavailable today – and have been for 1900 years.

        (3) Cessationism would not refer to the fruits of the Spirit, however, only the gifts.

        (4) As for the biblical basis for cessationism: there is none.

        (5) Cessationism was a convenient explanation for the relative absence of the miraculous in church history.

        (6) Today it serves as a cop-out.

        (7) To those who embrace cessationism (and make it an article of faith) there is no choice but to claim that anything that is supernatural such as signs, wonders, miracles or gifts of the Spirit, are either of the flesh or demonic.

C. But a notable turn of events has taken place: with the current interest in the gifts of the Spirit there is now a neglect of the fruits of the Spirit.

   1. The gifts of the Spirit were ignored for centuries.

   2. Now it is the fruits of the Spirit which are (I fear) greatly neglected.

D. Why is this study important?

   1. It helps redress the imbalance of emphasis that we know is too true today.

   2. It will show the importance of both the fruits and the gifts of the Spirit.

   3. It will show what is the difference between them.

   4. It will show how each is available.

   5. It will show which may well be the more important.

I. IDENTIFYING THE GIFTS OF THE SPIRIT

A. There are generally speaking, three passages of scripture that demonstrate the gifts of the Spirit.

1. *Romans 12:3-8*

    a. They are referred to here as 'measure of faith' rather than as gifts of the Spirit. 'For by the grace given me I say to every one of you: Do not think of yourself more highly than you ought, but rather think of yourself with sober judgement, in accordance with the measure of faith God has given you' (Rom. 12:3).

        (1) 'Measure of faith' refers to the limit of our faith.

        (2) Each of us has a measure of the Spirit which results in having so much, but only so much, of the Spirit.

        (3) Only Jesus had the Spirit without any limit, which means that he had all of the Holy Spirit there is! 'For the one whom God has sent speaks the words of God, for God gives the Spirit without limit' (John 3:34).

        (4) Paul's point in Romans 12:3-8: learn to accept the limit of your faith and live within that limit; do not claim a gift you don't really have.

    b. The gifts he mentions are:

        (1) Prophesying (v.6).

        (2) Serving (v.7).

        (3) Teaching (v.7).

        (4) Encouraging (v.8).

        (5) Contributing to others' needs (v.8).

        (6) Leadership (v.8).

        (7) Showing mercy (v.8).

    c. Although Paul doesn't call them 'gifts of the Spirit', that is obviously what they are since some of them overlap with the gifts of the Spirit in 1 Corinthians 12.

        (1) 'We have different gifts,' says Paul, the same language used in 1 Corinthians 12; cf. Romans 12:6, and 1 Corinthians 12:4.

        (2) Some want to refer to the gifts in Romans 12 as motivational gifts, the idea being that each person – whether by temperament, nature or the Spirit – finds he is in one of the seven categories of Romans 12:3-8.

2. *Ephesians 4:7-13*

   a. Here the ascended Lord is said to have given 'gifts to men' (v.8).

   b. These gifts however largely refer to offices or functions in the church. (See offices in The Church, p. 307.)

3. *1 Corinthians 12*

   a. They are called 'gifts' or 'manifestations' of the Spirit (vv. 4, 7).

      (1) Gr. *charismata* – grace-gifts.

      (2) Gr. *phanerosis* – manifestations.

      (3) I like to call them 'anointings' of the Spirit.

   b. Paul lists nine of these in verses 8 to 10:

      (1) Wisdom.

      (2) Knowledge; the AV 'word of knowledge'.

      (3) Faith.

      (4) Healing.

      (5) Miracles.

      (6) Prophecy.

      (7) Discerning of spirits.

      (8) Tongues.

      (9) Interpretation of tongues.

   c. Later on he mentions more (in v. 28) not in the previous list:

      (10) Helps (AV), those able to help others, which is much like 'encouraging' in Romans 12:8.

      (11) Gifts of administration, probably much like 'leadership' in Romans 12:8.

   d. This lets us know that the list is endless; there are as many gifts in the body of Christ as there are Christians in the body of Christ.

      (1) Each one of us is unique.

      (2) This makes our gift unique.

   e. All that the list in 1 Corinthians 12 intended to do was to give examples.

B. The apostle makes some important observations about the gifts.

   1. We should come to terms with the gift or gifts we have and not move outside them (Rom. 12:3,6).

   2. *Each of them is sovereignly given by God.*

    a. 'All these are the work of one and the same Spirit, and he gives them to each one, just as he determines' (1 Cor. 12:11).

    b. 'But in fact God has arranged the parts in the body, every one of them, just as he wanted them to be' (1 Cor. 12:18).

3. The gifts, or anointings, are for the 'common good' of the church.

4. The Spirit that enables us to confess 'Jesus is Lord' is the same Spirit that enables the gifts to function (1 Cor. 12:3-4).

5. We should not be jealous of another's gift (1 Cor. 12:12-26).

6. No-one has all the gifts and functions that are in the church (1 Cor. 12:28-30).

7. We should eagerly desire the greater gifts, which shows some are greater than others (1 Cor. 12:31).

II. IDENTIFICATION OF THE FRUITS OF THE SPIRIT

A. These are found literally throughout the New Testament.

    1. *For example, the Sermon on the Mount shows how the Law is fulfilled by the Spirit, including:*

      a. Loving your enemies (Matt. 5:44).

      b. Humility in selfless acts (Matt. 6:1-18).

        (1) When we give, not to be seen by men.

        (2) When we pray, not to be seen by men.

        (3) When we fast, not to be seen by men.

      c. Forgiving others (Matt. 6:14).

      d. Not judging others (Matt. 7:1-5).

    2. *Romans 13–15 is an unfolding of how the Spirit fulfils the Law.*

    3. *1 Corinthians 13 elaborates on the primary fruit of the Spirit.*

    4. *Galatians 5:22-23 explicitly lists some of the fruits of the Spirit:*

      a. Love. **b.** Joy. **c.** Peace.

      d. Patience. **e.** Kindness. **f.** Goodness.

      g. Faithfulness. **h.** Gentleness. **i.** Self-control.

      j. Note: the nine fruits of the Spirit are only examples – note that there are only nine, not unlike 1 Corinthians 12:8-10.

    5. *Ephesians 4:31-32 shows implicitly by use of the negative and practical.* 'Get rid of all bitterness, rage and anger, brawling

and slander, along with every form of malice. Be kind and
compassionate to one another, forgiving each other, just as in
Christ God forgave you' (cf. Eph. 5:1-7).

    a. There are more: 'Speak to one another with psalms, hymns
and spiritual songs. Sing and make music in your heart to
the Lord, always giving thanks to God the Father for
everything, in the name of our Lord Jesus Christ' (Eph.
5:19-20).

    b. The husband-wife relationship is to be the outworking of
the fruits of the Spirit.

        (1) Wives are to submit to their husbands (Eph. 5:22-24).

        (2) Husbands are to love their wives (Eph. 5:25-33).

6. Philippians 2 stresses that we should be devoid of selfish ambition
and therefore 'consider others better than yourselves' (Phil. 2:1-
4) whereupon Paul tells us to do as Jesus did in not holding on to
the glory he had before he became flesh (Phil. 2:5-8).

7. Colossians ('the little book of Ephesians') says the same thing
again (Col. 3).

8. What Paul calls 'love' James calls 'wisdom' (Jas. 3:13-18).

9. *Peter's counsel is the same.*

    a. The husband-wife relationship (1 Pet. 3:1-7).

    b. He explains what he means by loving as brothers: 'Do not
repay evil with evil or insult with insult, but with blessing,
because to this you were called so that you may inherit a
blessing' (1 Pet. 3:9).

    c. 'For this very reason, make every effort to add to your faith
goodness; and to goodness, knowledge; and to knowledge,
self-control; and to self-control, perseverance; and to
perseverance, godliness; and to godliness, brotherly
kindness; and to brotherly kindness, love. For if you possess
these qualities in increasing measure, they will keep you
from being ineffective and unproductive in your knowledge
of our Lord Jesus Christ' (2 Pet. 1:5-8).

10. The epistles of John elaborate Jesus' teaching on love as found
in John's gospel (John 13:34):

    a. Love one another (1 John 3:11).

    b. 'There is no fear in love. But perfect love drives out fear,
because fear has to do with punishment. The one who fears
is not made perfect in love' (1 John 4:18).

III. THE SIMILARITIES AND DIFFERENCES BETWEEN GIFTS AND FRUITS OF THE SPIRIT

A. Wherein they are the same.
1. *They come from the same Spirit.*
   a. There is not a Holy Spirit who dispenses gifts and another Spirit who gives the fruits.
   b. It is the same Holy Spirit in both.
      (1) 'There are different kinds of gifts, but the same Spirit. There are different kinds of service, but the same Lord. There are different kinds of working, but the same God works all of them in all men' (1 Cor. 12:4-6).
      (2) 'For this reason I kneel before the Father, from whom his whole family in heaven and on earth derives its name. I pray that out of his glorious riches he may strengthen you with power through his Spirit in your inner being, so that Christ may dwell in your hearts through faith. And I pray that you, being rooted and established in love, may have power, together with all the saints, to grasp how wide and long and high and deep is the love of Christ, and to know this love that surpasses knowledge—that you may be filled to the measure of all the fullness of God' (Eph. 3:14-19).

2. *The same Spirit is in all Christians.*
   a. All Christians have the Holy Spirit.
      (1) 'If anyone does not have the Spirit of Christ, he does not belong to Christ.'
      (2) 'For we were all baptised by one Spirit into one body— whether Jews or Greeks, slave or free—and we were all given the one Spirit to drink' (1 Cor. 12:13).
   b. Note: the term 'baptism of the Holy Spirit' is used two ways in the New Testament.
      (1) According to 1 Corinthians 12:13, all Christians have been baptised by the Spirit – at conversion.
      (2) According to Acts 8:15-17, there is a sense in which some Christians have not been baptised by the Spirit.
   c. The best way to understand this is probably to see a twofold operation of the Spirit in believers.

   (1) The Holy Spirit comes unconsciously when we are born
        again, although some feel a conscious power.
   (2) There is a subsequent filling for many which seems more
        powerful than at conversion.
   d. Note: any Christian can have either the gifts or the fruits of
        the Spirit without the subsequent operation of the Spirit,
        although it is likely that those who have experienced this
        will manifest both gifts and fruits more powerfully.

3. *Both are important in the body of Christ.*
   a. The gifts enable us to serve others by signs and wonders
   b. The fruits enable us to edify others by a gentle and loving
        heart.

B. Wherein they are different

1. *The gifts of the Spirit are sovereignly meted out.*
   a. God sovereignly grants gifts.
   b. The fruits are inherent in every Christian.
2. *There is no command to have a gift of the Spirit, e.g., 'You must
    receive the gift of tongues.'*
   a. No-one is required to manifest a gift of the Spirit.
   b. We are all required to manifest the fruits of the Spirit.
3. *We all have (and we do) one gift but we are required to have
    all the fruits.*
   a. 'Do all speak with tongues?' Answer: no.
   b. But we are to have all the fruits.
4. *Gifts do not prove spirituality; the fruits do.*
   a. The Corinthians thought they were spiritual because of their
        gifts, especially tongues.
   b. 'No,' thunders Paul; the proof of spirituality is love (1 Cor.
        13).
5. *You are not likely to lose a gift, but you can lose the fruits.*
   a. 'For God's gifts and his call are irrevocable' (Rom. 11:29).
   b. 'What has happened to all your joy? I can testify that, if you
        could have done so, you would have torn out your eyes and
        given them to me' (Gal. 4:15).
6. *Gifts are more likely to engender pride than the fruits.*
   a. We can get very proud (if not careful) over having one of the
        gifts of the Spirit – or any function or office in the church.
   b. The reason for the fruits: to negate pride.

7. A gift may not always be working but the fruits may be there day and night. This is part of the meaning of 1 Corinthians 13:8: 'Love never fails. But where there are prophecies, they will cease; where there are tongues, they will be stilled; where there is knowledge, it will pass away.'

IV. THE ADVANTAGES OF EACH

A. The gifts:

1. *They perform a direct service to the body of Christ.*
   a. The gift of healing speaks for itself.
   b. The prophecy or word of knowledge can do one of two things: (1) encourage; (2) warn.
2. *They can serve as an evangelistic tool.*
   a. They provide a platform for the gospel (e.g. Acts 9:35,42).
   b. It leaves people without further excuse (Acts 4:16).
3. *They authenticate the message of the gospel.*
   a. People – if honest – must conclude that there is a God.
   b. When signs and wonders accompany our preaching it can add credibility to what we preach and teach.
4. *It is by the fruit that we come to terms with our own gifts – to avoid jealousy* (cf. 1 Cor. 12:21-26).

B. The fruits:

1. *They edify others.*
   a. Love sets others free.
   b. Love keeps you from a judgmental spirit.
2. *They edify the people who have them.*
   a. There is no greater joy than what comes from the Holy Spirit.
   b. They show how we fulfil the Law (Rom. 13:10).
3. *They show that the Spirit is ungrieved – which sets him free to work powerfully.* The Holy Spirit can be grieved (Eph. 4:30). When he is not grieved, he moves in us and around us more freely.
4. They may lead to the receiving of the gifts.

V. THE AVAILABILITY OF EACH

A. The gifts

1. Every Christian has the Spirit, therefore the potential for the gifts is endless.

2. We are told to covet the greater gifts; God would not encourage us in this direction if they cannot be had.

3. In all probability, true revival would result in a wider manifestation of the gifts.

B. The fruits

1. They are available because we have the Spirit.

2. Unlike the gifts, we are commanded to exhibit the fruits of the Spirit; it follows that we can do so.

3. *The increase of the fruits is up to us; we make a choice, for example, whether or not to forgive.*

    a. Love is the chief fruit of the Spirit.

    b. If we show love, the others are likely to follow.

CONCLUSION

From time to time there seems to be more interest in the gifts of the Spirit than in the fruit of the Spirit. We are living in such a time. Scripture lists the gifts of the Spirit. These include prophesying, serving, teaching, encouraging. The gifts are God's to give. Love, joy, peace, patience, kindness, goodness, faithfulness, gentleness and self-control are the fruit of the Spirit, and result from having received the Holy Spirit.

Paul called 'love' the most excellent way (1 Cor. 12:31). This is Paul's way of saying: it is better to show love than to have the gifts of the Spirit. By showing love God may grant the desire of your heart in giving you spiritual gifts!

23

THE GIFT OF WISDOM

A. In this chapter we will study the wisdom of God.
   1. *There are two ways this may be done:*
      a. Taking James 1:5, which is a universal promise to every believer: 'If any of you lacks wisdom, he should ask God, who gives generously to all without finding fault, and it will be given to him.'
      b. Taking 1 Corinthians 12:8, which is a particular promise to those sovereignly blessed: 'To one there is given through the Spirit the message of wisdom'.
   2. There is not one of us who would not desire this wisdom.

B. We want also to deal with the connection between the gift of wisdom and that of knowledge.
   1. 1 Corinthians 12:8 goes on to say: 'To another the message of knowledge by means of the same Spirit'.
   2. What is the difference between the gift of wisdom and the 'word of knowledge' (AV) as it is so often referred to?

C. Why is this study important?
   1. The ever-increasing interest in the gifts of the Spirit calls for a clear and sober look at the subject generally.
   2. The first in Paul's 'list' of the gifts is that of wisdom – but strangely the most neglected!
   3. What is more 'sensational' (e.g. gift of healing, miracles or even prophecy) may not be the most needed.
   4. When we recall how pleased God was with Solomon's request for wisdom (1 Kgs. 3:9-10), we may conclude that God is still pleased with those who want this!
   5. At the end of the day it may well be that Paul's putting this at the top of his list is a hint that it is what we today need more than anything else.

D. The gift of wisdom (def.): the ability to see in advance what is the right course of action.

    1. *There are other valid definitions of wisdom:*

        a. It is the intelligent use of knowledge.

            (1) Wisdom and knowledge are not always the same thing.

            (2) One may have knowledge and abuse it.

            (3) One may be clever and not wise.

        b. It is discernment.

            (1) To discern means to judge by making a distinction between choices. Wisdom, then, is sound judgement.

    2. *The wisdom God gives will be an impartation of his own wisdom to us.*

        a. We saw that God's wisdom is not only sound judgement but is unpredictable.

        b. He (or she) who has this wisdom will have a discernment that is often as surprising as what God shows.

        c. But this means that wisdom will sometimes be misunderstood or underestimated at the time.

        d. He (or she) who possesses this wisdom must be prepared to wait a while (sometimes a good while) for vindication.

        e. Sometimes wisdom will be immediately apparent; sometimes it will not be so welcome.

I. THE ANOINTING OF THE SPIRIT

A. The term 'anointing' of the various 'gifts' may be a better one to use in the long run, for four reasons:

    1. *There are three Greek words that emerge in 1 Corinthians 12:4-6:*

        a. Gr. *charismata*; 'there are different kinds of *gifts*, but the same Spirit' (v.4).

            (1) The word 'charismatic' comes from this.

            (2) This is a particular 'grace', or 'gift'.

        b. Gr. *diakonia*; 'there are different kinds of *service*, but the same Lord' (v.5).

            (1) This is essentially what the word 'deacon' comes from.

            (2) It means 'ministry', or 'service'.

        c. Gr. *energemata*; 'there are different kinds of *working*, but the same God works all of them in all men' (v.6).

            (1) We get the word 'energy' from this.

            (2) It refers to the power of the Spirit in this case.

    d. The word 'anointing' best fits all the above.

        (1) From 1 Corinthians 12:4-8 it is obvious that they can be used interchangeably in this context.

        (2) For such flows from the anointing of the Spirit.

2. *The anointing is what each of us has by being Christians.*

    a. Gr. *chrisma*. Note these distinctions:

        (1) It is not the same as *charismata*.

        (2) It is not *charisma*, which is sometimes used to try to describe one's unusual personality.

    b. It is the root word for Christ, or Messiah.

        (1) Gr. *chrio*, 'to smear as with an ointment'.

        (2) It is that which give rise to Christ's own anointing (Luke 4:18).

    c. It is used in 1 John and refers to all Christians.

        (1) 'But you have an anointing from the Holy One, and all of you know the truth' (1 John 2:20).

        (2) 'As for you, the anointing you received from him remains in you, and you do not need anyone to teach you. But as his anointing teaches you about all things and as that anointing is real, not counterfeit – just as it has taught you, remain in him' (1 John 2:27).

3. *In the above Paul also calls 'manifestations' of the Spirit:* 'Now to each one the manifestation of the Spirit is given for the common good' (1 Cor. 12:7).

    a. It may mean either differences, distinctions, distributions, apportionings or dealings out.

    b. We therefore may see there are many words that fit.

4. *There are as many 'anointings' as there are people!*

    a. Some hastily refer to the so-called 'nine gifts of the Spirit' in 1 Corinthians 12:8-10.

        (1) They forget that Paul continues the list in 1 Corinthians 12:28-30.

        (2) Thus you must add: the anointing of helping others (AV – 'helps') and 'gifts of administration'.

    b. The big point Paul makes in 1 Corinthians 12:4-7 is not the difference between the gifts as much as the difference between people who have the Holy Spirit.

        (1) It is not the gift God uses, it is you.

        (2) Every Christian is different – unique.

B. Paul introduces this section by flattening the distinction between the charismatic and the non-charismatic. Why?

    1. *One must not underestimate the considerable overlapping between the natural and the supernatural.*

        a. A gift, or anointing, of the Spirit can be quite unspectacular; for example, helping others.

        b. One may have a natural predisposition to do certain things.

    2. *One may have a certain anointing by common grace.*

        a. We must never underestimate the overlapping between common grace and special grace in the gifts or the Spirit.

        b. One may have a natural endowment of wisdom, for example, that is applied by the Holy Spirit.

    3. *Jackie Pullinger: 'To the spiritual person the supernatural seems natural.'*

        a. The result: it is effortless.

        b. The anointing (def.): what comes easily. (1) You don't have to 'work it up'. (2) It is either there or it isn't.

II. THE ANOINTING OF WISDOM

A. Wisdom is a life-style (Jas. 1:5; 3:13-18).

    1. *This is universally offered to believers.*

        a. 'If any of you lacks wisdom, he should ask God, who gives generously to all without finding fault, and it will be given to him' (Jas. 1:5).

        b. But it is offered to believers only! 'But when he asks, he must believe and not doubt, because he who doubts is like a wave of the sea, blown and tossed by the wind' (Jas 1:6).

    2. *This wisdom is both 'vertical' and 'horizontal' in its application.*

        a. Vertical – toward God, to know his ways.

            (1) When we fall into 'trials of many kinds' (Jas. 1:2) we may not understand the reason at first; if we dignify the trial (not murmuring or rushing through it) we get to know intimacy with God.

            (2) The goal: 'that you may be mature and complete, not lacking anything' (Jas. 1:4).

        b. Horizontal – toward others, to show selfless concern.

            (1) This comes to the same thing as the *agape* love of 1 Corinthians 13; it is humility and is the opposite of 'envy and selfish ambition' (Jas. 3:13-14).

(2) It is the life-style of Christian love which is 'first of all pure; then peace-loving, considerate, submissive, full of mercy and good fruit, impartial and sincere' (Jas. 3:17-18).

3. *This we should desire before God more than anything else.*
   a. It is a life-style.
   b. To those who have this already will more likely come the special anointing of wisdom.
      (1) Paul shows that the best way to attain to the various gifts, or anointings, of the Spirit is by the 'most excellent way' of love (1 Cor. 12:31–13:13).
      (2) One should not ask for the special ability to show the wisdom of God who does not preeminently desire the brokenness and humility displayed in 1 Corinthians 13.

B. Wisdom as a special gift

1. *It is the objective wisdom of God imparted to the mind, when needed, whereby one functions naturally with it.*
   a. It is God's own wisdom 'in miniature'.
      (1) All that God is in his inscrutable wisdom is, in measure, put into one's mind and heart.
      (2) He therefore mirrors, when it is operating, the very kind of awesomeness that characterises God.
      (3) Solomon displayed this in 1 Kings 3:16-28 – 'they held the king in awe' – and he apparently had it often. Cf. 1 Kings 10:1-6. Note: even Solomon did some very foolish things as well (1 Kgs. 11:1-10), so let no-one think that the gift is a permanent endowment that remains unconditionally apart from one's life-style.
   b. It is presence of mind.
      (1) It is the mind of the Spirit. 'But when they arrest you, do not worry about what to say or how to say it. At that time you will be given what to say, for it will not be you speaking, but the Spirit of your Father speaking through you' (Matt. 10:19-20).
      (2) It is what characterised Stephen before the Sanhedrin: 'they could not stand up against his wisdom or the Spirit by whom he spoke' (Acts 6:10). Note: behind this wisdom lay a heart devoid of bitterness (Acts 7:60).

(3) It is the sort of thing that may come in an emergency; nobody has it all the time; it is given as urgently needed.

c. It is impartial (cf. Jas. 3:17).

(1) One's personal feelings will not get in the way when one is displaying this wisdom (Jude 3).

(2) Jesus was fond of Peter but had to say to him on one occasion, 'Get behind me, Satan! You are a stumbling block to me; you do not have in mind the things of God, but the things of men' (Matt. 16:23).

d. It is required of deacons (Acts 6:3).

2. *It is 'given': handed over by the Spirit in a time of need.*

a. Gr. *didotai* (present, indicative, passive): handed over; 'given through the Spirit' (1 Cor. 12:8).

b. Solomon's example shows that it is not given to the extent one could never err again.

c. This should keep one humble.

(1) If one automatically had it all the time he would be conceited (Rom. 12:16).

(2) Let no-one say 'I have the gift of wisdom'; this shows at once one doesn't have wisdom!

(3) Joseph had an amazing gift – regarding dreams; but he didn't have wisdom; he was guilty of throwing 'pearls to pigs'! (Matt. 7:6; Gen. 37:5ff).

(4) This means that one could have another anointing (e.g., tongues) and not have wisdom in exercising it.

d. It will therefore manifest the qualities of the Holy Spirit when being exercised (Gal. 5:22ff).

(1) The one displaying wisdom will not be drawing attention to himself.

(2) He will consider the feelings and self-esteem of the other person. A good example of this is Galatians 6:1: 'Brothers, if someone is caught in a sin, you who are spiritual should restore him gently. But watch yourself, or you also may be tempted.'

(3) God knows 'what to say next'; when the Spirit is given one will know exactly what to say.

c. One proceeds no further than what is *warranted* by the Spirit.

(1) This means there are certain principles in operation.

(2) One literally follows the Spirit and speaks when the Spirit gives permission.

(3) The Golden Rule will always be in operation. 'Do to others as you would have them do to you' (Luke 6:31).

(4) When one is truly being guided under that anointing of wisdom he will feel a 'check' (a negative impulse) when not to speak.

(5) Likewise one proceeds under that anointing by way of the freedom, or peace, to say this or that.

(6) God may be anointing you to say nothing (Matt. 21:27; Luke 23:8-9. cf. Acts 16:6-7).

(7) It may be as wise and courageous to say nothing as to speak on some occasions.

3. *A perfect example of the anointing of wisdom in speech is Paul's little letter to Philemon; sheer brilliance is displayed.*

a. This was the 'Holy Spirit's twisting of the arm'.

b. Philemon was enabled to 'save face' while having to comply with Paul's request.

4. *It may be given for you to exercise unconsciously.*

a. Moses did not know that his face was aglow (Ex. 34:29).

b. Likewise we may not be conscious that we are exercising this.

(1) Possibly for our good!

(2) One of the greatest life-changing moments in my life came from a man who, I'm certain, exercised this gift to me – but he didn't know it.

III. THE WORD OF KNOWLEDGE

A. This is listed second in order following the anointing of wisdom.

1. The NIV translates *logos* as 'message'; the AV as 'word'.

2. *Either will do – it comes to the same thing.*

a. It may be a message or word of knowledge from God to us.

b. It may be a message or word of knowledge from us to another.

3. *Note: at bottom in any anointing is revelation.*

a. No gift of the Spirit functions without revelation.

(1) We are not talking about adding to scripture.

(2) Revelation here means the mind of the Spirit.

    b. The anointing of a word of knowledge touches one's revelatory gift.

       (1) This lay behind the miracle of Acts 3:1ff.

       (2) Peter and John knew what God was going to do!

B. It is spiritual knowledge that is meant.

  1. Knowledge is essentially information.

  2. *The word of knowledge will bring spiritual information.*

    a. The Holy Spirit is not likely to impart algebra or physics to one who has no prior training in such.

    b. This therefore somewhat limits the kind of knowledge referred to.

       (1) We are therefore not referring to common grace.

       (2) One may be a brilliant scientist and know nothing of this spiritual gift.

  3. *Spiritual knowledge (def.): Divine information to help us spiritually as Christians.*

    a. There are essentially two kinds of spiritual knowledge:

       (1) Theological knowledge. This very course should add to one's potential in this area.

       (2) Edifying (inspirational) knowledge. This may come via the pulpit or on a one to one basis.

    b. Whether theological or inspirational, all will cohere with the analogy of faith (Rom. 12:6).

       (1) Analogy of faith: comparing scripture with scripture.

       (2) No word of knowledge from God will go contrary to scripture.

C. There are two ways this anointing may be applied:

  1. *Raw knowledge: what is given without any application.*

    a. The Holy Spirit may give one word and the recipient will know what it means.

       (1) It may be a scripture that comes to one's mind.

       (2) It could be a vision.

    b. The person who gives the word to another may not understand the meaning which the recipient will grasp.

       (1) A prophetic word may be raw knowledge.

       (2) The person giving it may have little or no understanding of what he is giving to another by a mere word or insight.

  2. *Refined knowledge: information mixed with application.*

    a. This is largely what preaching is.

(1) A minister may not know how his preaching will be received.

(2) Often the hearer 'knows' it is an immediate word from God for him or her.

b. This often overlaps with a prophetic word.

(1) It is often difficult to tell what the difference is between a prophetic word and the word of knowledge.

(2) The hearer will often know better than anyone how pertinent it is.

CONCLUSION

The anointing of wisdom and word of knowledge are valuable gifts to the church and are available today. Scripture encourages us to recognise our need for the gift of wisdom and to ask God for it. Wisdom operates in two directions, vertically towards God, as we seek to know his ways, and horizontally towards others, as we exercise it in our relationships and dealings. The 'word of knowledge' is also a gift. It should be tested by Scripture as God will never contradict himself.

24

THE GIFT OF GIVING

A. Giving is a gift
1. 'It is more blessed to give than to receive' (Acts 20:35).
2. *Yet giving is a gift.*
   a. It is not specifically listed as one of the gifts of the Spirit, unless it is 'those able to help others', what the AV calls 'helps' (1 Cor. 12:28).
   b. Paul lists 'contributing to the needs of others' among other gifts (Rom. 12:8).
3. *But is it a gift we would covet, or eagerly desire, as 1 Corinthians 12:31 puts it?*
   a. Not all have these gifts mentioned in 1 Corinthians 12 or Romans 12.
   b. But the gift of giving is offered to all of us!

B. There are two levels of giving.
1. Giving to God what is already his – the tithe (def: one-tenth of your income).
2. *Giving beyond the tithe – which may be given directly to God, or to others.*
   a. There is a sense in which tithing is not giving; it is merely handing over to God what is his already.
      (1) We *give* it, yes.
      (2) But it is really *returning* it – to him.
   b. The gift of giving really comes into its own when we begin to help by giving *above* or *beyond* the tithe.
      (1) For many, sadly, tithing has not been consistently practised – which is robbing God.
      (2) For some, hopefully, we will explore the area of true generosity – going beyond the one-tenth that is God's.

C. Why is this study important?

1. We need to know what the Bible has to say about tithing and giving.
2. Many sincere Christians have never been taught even to tithe, much less to give beyond the tithe.
3. *Most British Christians do not tithe.*
    a. If all Methodists are tithing it means they are only earning an average £1,800 a year.
    b. If all the Anglicans in Essex were made redundant and started tithing their dole money the church's income could increase by 65%.
4. Very few ministers teach and preach tithing.
5. The financial condition of the church generally is deplorable, and is a poor testimony to the world.
6. Christians who do not tithe are impoverished but don't know it; this study will, hopefully, help to change this condition.
7. Christians who don't tithe are under God's judgement but often don't know it because nobody told them.
8. Giving is a wonderful gift and those who exercise this gift are blessed more than those who are on the receiving end of it.
9. Giving gives great joy; learning this will lead to a fruit of the Spirit.
10. The church generally will be set free to do much, much more for God's Kingdom when its members accept their responsibility in this area.

I. THE TITHE IS THE LORD'S 'A tithe of everything from the land, whether grain from the soil or fruit from the trees, belongs to the LORD; it is holy to the LORD' (Lev. 27:30).

A. This is why not tithing is robbing God: 'Will a man rob God? Yet you rob me. But you ask, "How do we rob you?" In tithes and offerings' (Mal. 3:8).

1. *If I earn £10,000 a year and do not give at least £1,000 to God, I have robbed him.*
    a. If I gave £500 to him I still owe him £500.
    b. If I have no intention of giving the other £500, or never get around to it, the Bible says I have stolen it.
    c. That means I am using stolen money.

2. *Malachi uncovered part of Israel's problem by pointing this out to them.*
   a. Could this be true with you?
   b. If there is a defect (something wrong) in your own life and you are not tithing, you may have the answer right under your nose!

B. **Many are quick to point out that tithing is commanded by a Mosaic Law (Lev. 27:30) and we are not under the Law (Gal. 5:18).**
   1. What they overlook is that tithing emerged as a pattern *before* the Law came.
   2. *Moses legalised what had been done out of gratitude.*
      a. Adultery did not become sin suddenly because God gave Moses the Ten Commandments.
      b. Adultery was sin long before the Law ever came (Gen. 39:9).

C. **The first known tither was Abraham (Gen. 14).**
   1. *The story is this:*
      a. Lot, Abraham's nephew, got caught in the cross-fire of a war between the king of Sodom and other kings.
      b. Lot lost both his possessions and his freedom.
      c. Word of this got back to Abraham who proceeded to rescue his nephew.
      d. Abraham (with 318 of his trained men) had phenomenal success.
         (1) Abraham subdued the kings and plundered hem.
         (2) He rescued Lot and got everything back.
   2. *Out of the blue, as it were, Melchizedek, King of Salem and priest of God Most High brought out bread and wine and blessed Abraham.*
      a. It is at this point that tithing comes into the picture.
      b. So grateful was Abraham that he gave Melchizedek 'a tenth of everything' (Gen. 14:20).

D. **Observations:**
   1. There is no indication that Abraham was told to tithe by Melchizedek himself.
   2. Abraham was not keeping any prescribed command or law of God.

3. Abraham did what he did voluntarily and gratefully.

4. He gave a tenth of the plunder (Heb. 7:4).

5. The Law came 430 years later (Gal. 3:17) and simply enforced tithing; by doing so it sanctioned what may be justly called *true righteousness*.

6. Abraham gave not only voluntarily but also systematically.

    a. This required calculation, taking care.

    b. It meant looking over all that God had given and carefully working out what one-tenth was.

7. Abraham is seen in the New Testament as a prototype (first example) of the Christian.

    a. It was Abraham to whom the gospel came (Gal. 3:8).

    b. Abraham was Paul's chief example of the doctrine of justification by faith alone (Rom. 4).

    c. Jesus could say that Abraham 'rejoiced at the thought of seeing my day; he saw it and was glad' (John 8:56).

    d. We are children of Abraham by faith and truly exemplify him by doing what he did (Rom. 4:12).

8. Almost everything the Pharisees did Jesus either criticised or made light of – but not with regard to tithing!

    a. He rebuked them for neglecting justice, mercy and faithfulness.

    b. And yet he upheld their careful practice of tithing (Matt. 23:23).

    c. This was Jesus' explicit endorsement of tithing.

9. The whole background of tithing lay behind Paul's statement: 'On the first day of every week, each one of you should set aside a sum of money in keeping with his income, saving it up, so that when I come no collections will have to be made' (1 Cor. 16:2).

    a. 'In keeping with his income' is the exact principle that Abraham carried out – and which the Law commanded.

    b. There is no New Testament abolishing of tithing – rather the assumption of its continued practice by grateful Christians, as is the case of all forms of righteousness (Rom. 13:10).

10. There is no hint of a promise to Abraham that he would be blessed by tithing.

    a. Tithing was his privilege; it was the gift of giving in operation.

   b. Ironically it is Malachi, who prophesied during the 1,300
      years' parenthesis of the Law, who promised blessing by
      tithing! '"Bring the whole tithe into the storehouse, that there
      may be food in my house. Test me in this," says the LORD
      Almighty, "and see if I will not throw open the floodgates of
      heaven and pour out so much blessing that you will not have
      room enough for it"' (Mal. 3:10).
   c. This principle coheres with other words, from both Testaments:
      (1) 'Honour the LORD with your wealth, with the firstfruits
         of all your crops; then your barns will be filled to
         overflowing, and your vats will brim over with new
         wine' (Prov. 3:9-10).
      (2) 'Remember this: Whoever sows sparingly will also reap
         sparingly, and whoever sows generously will also reap
         generously....You will be made rich in every way so that
         you can be generous on every occasion, and through us
         your generosity will result in thanksgiving to God' (2 Cor.
         9:6,11).

II. TO WHOM SHOULD WE GIVE OUR MONEY?

A. The tithe should go to the church – and the church only.
   1. *The tithe 'belongs to the LORD'* (Lev. 27:30).
      a. Abraham gave it to the 'priest of the God Most High' (Gen.
         14:18-20).
         (1) There was no church or temple to which or through
            which Abraham could express his feelings of gratitude.
         (2) When Melchizedek emerged with bread and wine (fore-
            shadowing the Lord's Supper), Abraham knew exactly
            how to express his gratitude.
      b. When the Law made tithing legal and binding, it was the
         Levitical priesthood to whom tithes were to be paid. 'I give
         to the Levites all the tithes in Israel as their inheritance in
         return for the work they do while serving at the Tent of
         Meeting' (Num. 18:21).
         (1) As Abraham paid tithes to Melchizedek the priest so
            Moses required tithes to be paid to Levi.
         (2) Tithes were paid to support the work which the priests
            did in the tabernacle for the services of God's worship
            and work.

2. *The prophet Malachi applied the nickname 'storehouse' to the service of God* (Mal. 3:10).

   a. Then it meant the Temple, or synagogue.

   b. The New Testament equivalent is the church.

      (1) Those who preach the gospel 'should earn their living from the gospel' (1 Cor. 9:14).

      (2) 'For the Scripture says, "Do not muzzle the ox while it is treading out the grain," and "The worker deserves his wages"' (1 Tim. 5:18).

   c. Tithes therefore should be solely and exclusively for the work of the gospel.

      (1) The storehouse is the ecclesiastical service of God.

      (2) When the church does not receive its members' tithes, everybody loses.

3. *If every church member in Britain would honour this principle from this day forward, here is what would happen:*

   a. Every giver would enjoy the fruit of the gift of giving – you will be 'made rich in every way' (2 Cor. 9:11).

      (1) It doesn't necessarily mean financial wealth, although Malachi even hints at this (Mal. 3:10-12).

      (2) It certainly means you will be enriched – fulfilled.

   b. The church would have to look for ways to spend the money.

   c. Every minister and member of staff would be paid with dignity.

   d. Missionary enterprises, which should get their money from churches rather than from individuals, would be supported more than ever.

   e. The church would have funds to care for the poor.

B. What is beyond the tithe should go either to the church or other worthy Christian causes (Rom. 12:8).

   1. *Sometimes the church puts on special appeals for funds, e.g.:*

      a. Redecoration of premises; refurbishing.

      b. Missions.

      c. New areas of ministry.

   2. *Para-church organisations, e.g.:*

      a. Missionary societies.

      b. TEAR Fund.

      c. Gideons.

d. Christian colleges.

e. Needs in eastern Europe.

3. *Directly to worthy or hurting people.*

    a. The poor.

    b. Needy ministers or missionaries.

4. *It is in this category that the gift of giving truly begins to flourish.*

    a. Sadly many never have experienced this; they don't even tithe!

    b. Not all are able to do this however; this is why Romans 12:8 is listed as a special gift.

        (1) Those who have above average incomes ought to explore this area – if they haven't already done so.

        (2) Those who have 'double-tithed' can testify to the blessing from this kind of giving.

C. Remember: the church is the apple of God's eye.

1. He loves the church (Eph. 5:25).

2. We honour God by honouring the church.

3. 'Those who honour me I will honour' (1 Sam. 2:30).

III. THE BLESSING OF GIVING

A. Why don't Christians tithe?

1. They have not been taught.

2. They have a misunderstanding of the Law.

3. They refuse to do so. (I was like this for years.)

B. Why should we tithe?

1. Because of what it will do for God's work on earth.

2. Because of what it will do for God in heaven; it pleases him.

3. Because of what it will do for us.

    a. We will be no worse off for doing so; God may even prosper us (this shouldn't surprise us).

    b. We will be enriched as a person – it could lead to our greatest spiritual breakthrough.

        (1) Any area of disobedience affects the whole of us.

        (2) Likewise when we walk in the light the blood cleanses from 'all sin' (1 John 1:7).

4. The nearest the Bible comes to proving God is in Malachi 3:10 (AV): 'Prove me now herewith, saith the LORD of hosts, if I will not open you the windows of heaven, and pour you out a blessing, that there shall not be room enough to receive it.'

a. This is God's own Word.

b. He did not need to motivate us like this – but he did! Why?

(1) He stoops to our weakness.

(2) All of us need motivation.

(3) Obedience in the Bible is always rewarded in some manner.

CONCLUSION

Scripture's guide for giving is the tithe, and that has been so since the time of Abraham. Jesus endorsed the giving of a tithe in that he criticised the Pharisees for their interpretation of many of the laws, but did not criticise their adherence to tithing. The tithe belongs to God, and when we give it to him we are only giving what is his own. The tithe should be worked out carefully and given cheerfully. And it should all be given to the work of the church. Givings over and above the tithe can be given at the discretion of the giver, e.g., to missionary organisations, other good causes and individuals in need.

> There was a man,
> Some called him mad;
> The more he gave
> The more he had.   *John Bunyan*

At the end of the day, however, tithing is a Christian duty. We shouldn't exercise the gift of giving because it 'works', rather we must give cheerfully, whether or not it 'works'; but because it is right (2 Cor. 9:7).

Frequently asked questions:

1. *Should we tithe the 'gross' or the 'net'?* I answer: (a) the gross if we are on salary; (b) the net (after expenses) if we are in business. Note: what is deducted from our gross pay is for our own good; in fact we get it back.

2. *Why tithe if my income is so small?* Because it is right to do; God will bless you as much, if not more, than those who are rich.

3. *What if I cannot afford to tithe?* You cannot afford not to.

4. *When should I begin?* Now. Ask God to forgive you for waiting so long. It may be you can give a large offering as a gesture of

repentance! The only way to do it: take 10% 'from the top'; consider it hot money – get rid of it; don't pay it after other bills are paid; put God first.

5. *Should I tithe when I am in debt?* Yes. You will be in debt a year from now, ten years from now (in all probability) if you don't tithe.

Remember this principle: *you can never out-give the Lord*. When this teaching grips you, you will see it truly as a gift – God's gift to you – to let you be a giver. Who knows, it may be, when we get to heaven, we will find that the gift of giving was of more value to the Kingdom than any of the spiritual gifts.

25

THE GIFT OF DISCERNING OF SPIRITS

INTRODUCTION

A. In 1 Corinthians 12:8-10 Paul lists nine gifts of the Spirit:
'To one there is given through the Spirit the message of wisdom, to another the message of knowledge by means of the same Spirit, to another faith by the same Spirit, to another gifts of healing by that one Spirit, to another miraculous powers, to another prophecy, to another distinguishing between spirits, to another speaking in different kinds of tongues, and to still another the interpretation of tongues.'

   1. The so-called 'nine gifts of the Spirit' is complicated by yet more in 1 Corinthians 12:28, where other gifts are added: 'those able to help others' and 'gifts of administration.'

   2. In Romans 12:6-8 still more gifts are listed: serving, encouraging, contributing to the needs of others, leadership and showing mercy.

   3. *We may therefore conclude: there are many gifts of the Spirit not listed in 1 Corinthians 12.*

      a. All Paul does in 1 Corinthians 12:8-10 is to list certain examples of how the Holy Spirit functions in the body of Christ.

      b. Indeed, a careful study leads to this conclusion: there are as many gifts in the body of Christ as there are people.

         (1) No two people are the same.

         (2) No two gifts are the same.

B. These gifts are even more aptly called 'anointings'.

   1. It is the anointing of the Spirit as a person that enables him to function.

   2. *Not all have all the gifts all the time!*

      a. They are given as needed.

      b. All who have the Holy Spirit have the potential to exercise any of the above gifts.

C. All these gifts are important, and some overlap with others.

　　1. The gift of prophecy overlaps with 'message of knowledge'.

　　2. The gifts of healings and miracles overlap.

　　3. So too: wisdom and the gifts of discerning of spirits.

D. The anointing to discern the spirits is very important, especially in a time of revival.

　　1. Why? Jonathan Edwards said that when the church is revived, so is the devil!

　　2. The devil is the great counterfeiter; he may appear as a 'angel of light' (2 Cor. 11:14).

E. Discerning of spirits (def.): the ability to tell the difference between the counterfeit and the Holy Spirit.

　　1. Gr. *diakriseis*: judging, making a distinction.

　　2. *You can see how the gift of wisdom and discernment overlap.*

　　　　a. Solomon in requesting wisdom prayed, 'So give your servant a discerning heart to govern your people and to distinguish between right and wrong. For who is able to govern this great people of yours?' (1 Kings 3:9).

　　　　b. We should pray for this every day.

F. Why is this study important?

　　1. *Wisdom is the greatest of the gifts, and we have seen that the gift of discerning of spirits overlaps with wisdom.*

　　2. *This gift, or anointing, will be needed in a revival atmosphere.*

　　　　a. I for one believe that true revival is coming.

　　　　b. Revival solves problems; it also creates problems.

　　　　　　(1) This is why many fear revival.

　　　　　　(2) Revival never comes in a neat and tidy package that coheres with folk religion.

　　　　　　(3) One can expect every 'weirdo', 'flaky' person and strange manifestation to appear as revival gets closer and closer.

　　　　c. The gift of discernment will be invaluable at such time; we should begin praying for it now.

　　3. *This gift is needed in a revolutionary age.*

　　　　a. Jonathan Edwards taught us that the task of every generation is to discern in which direction the Sovereign Redeemer is moving, then move in that direction.

      b. Edwards' teaching can be paraphrased into a warning: the task of every generation is to discern in which way Satan turns up and to move in the opposite direction.

         (1) What is Satan up to in our day?

         (2) With the collapse of Marxism has Satan gone to sleep?

         (3) You can be sure he will try to keep one step ahead of us to thwart God's purposes, if possible.

      c. New Age is but one manifestation of Satan in our day.

   4. *The greatest need of all is to be able to recognise the Holy Spirit himself.*

      a. Many hastily assume that the gift of discerning of spirits is limited to the recognition of the demonic. Wrong. It is far more important to be able to recognise what is genuine.

I. ANGELS

A. Angels are 'spirits'. 'Are not all angels ministering spirits sent to serve those who will inherit salvation?' (Heb. 1:14).

   1. This means they are invisible; you cannot normally see an angel.

   2. *There are exceptions.*

      a. Sometimes God allows an angel to be visible.

         (1) An angel appeared to Gideon (Judg. 6:11ff).

         (2) An angel appeared to Manoah's wife, Samson's mother (Judg. 13:3).

      b. Sometimes an angel is visible but not at first recognisable as an angel. 'Do not forget to entertain strangers, for by so doing some people have entertained angels without knowing it' (Heb. 13:2).

      c. One reason angels are invisible is to keep us from focusing on them or even worshipping them. Even John fell down to worship the angel (Rev. 22:8-9).

B. There are two kinds of angels.

   1. Fallen angels, those who entered into Satan's revolt.

   2. *Unfallen angels, those who did not enter into Satan's revolt.*

      a. These are called 'elect angels' (1 Tim. 5:21).

      b. They have known terrific temptation.

         (1) You can be sure Satan attempted to recruit every angel in God's universe.

         (2) He succeeded with some, failed with others.

C. The angelic spirits referred to at this stage are aptly called 'heavenly' spirits.

1. *They have resisted Satan's revolt against God.*

    a. This is good to know when you consider that God has already dispatched an angel to your side. 'The angel of the LORD encamps around those who fear him, and he delivers them' (Ps. 34:7). Your angel is experienced in spiritual warfare.

2. We may therefore conclude that heavenly spirits are around us; the more we are in the company of God's people, the more heavenly spirits will be around us.

D. Question: is it possible to discern heavenly spirits?

1. *Elisha did.*

    a. Those around him were motivated by a spirit of fear.

    b. '"Don't be afraid," the prophet answered, "Those who are with us are more than those who are with them." And Elisha prayed, "O LORD, open his eyes so that he may see." Then the LORD opened the servant's eyes, and he looked and saw the hills full of horses and chariots of fire all round Elisha' (2 Kings 6:16-17).

2. It would be safe to say that a good feeling in a very spiritual atmosphere is best explained by the presence of angels.

3. *What is the advantage of such discernment?*

    a. Courage. To know that those who are with us are more than those who are with the enemy!

    b. To keep us from panic. When we know that God has sent angels to our side we know God is with us, and that knowledge will keep us calm.

II. DEMONIC SPIRITS

A. These are the fallen angels that went along with Satan's revolt (Isa. 14:12-15).

1. 'For if God did not spare angels when they sinned, but sent them to hell, putting them into gloomy dungeons to be held for judgment' (2 Pet. 2:4).

2. 'And the angels who did not keep their positions of authority but abandoned their own home – these he has kept in darkness, bound with everlasting chains for judgment on the great Day' (Jude 6).

B. C S Lewis, *The Screwtape Letters*, shows a hierarchy of demonic spirits.
   1. *There is something to this.*
      a. Satan is like the 'general'.
      b. Other demonic spirits vary in power and intelligence.
   2. *If there is a hierarchy of angels (cf. Jude 9), it follows that such exists in the demonic realm.*
      a. They know their destiny (Matt. 8:29; Luke 8:31).
      b. Satan knows his time is short (Rev. 12:12).

C. The 'distinguishing between spirits' of 1 Corinthians 12:10 includes the ability to discern the demonic presence.
   1. *We should know two things from the start:*
      a. What demonic spirits are like:
         (1) They are liars (John 8:44).
         (2) They accuse (Rev. 12:10).
         (3) They deceive (2 Cor. 11:3).
         (4) They hate (John 8:44).
            (a) They hate God, his Kingdom, his people and all righteousness.
            (b) They engender hate; they play into any unforgiving spirit in us, to magnify others' faults and cause more strife (James 3:11ff).
         (5) They intimidate. 'Be self-controlled and alert. Your enemy the devil prowls around like a roaring lion looking for someone to devour' (1 Pet. 5:8).
            (a) They create fear.
            (b) They make you think you are 'finished' before you've had time to consider things calmly.
      b. What they try further to do:
         (1) To oppress a believer, coming from outside. 'Those who oppose him he must gently instruct, in the hope that God will grant them repentance leading them to a knowledge of the truth, and that they will come to their senses and escape from the trap of the devil, who has taken them captive to do his will' (2 Tim. 2:25-26).
         (2) To possess, so as to exercise control over a person.

D. The anointing of discernment of spirits enables one to do the following:

  1. *To tell the difference between the divine presence and the 'angel of light'.*

  a. The divine presence gives peace. 'But the wisdom that comes from above is first of all pure; then peace-loving, considerate, submissive, full of mercy and good fruit, impartial and sincere' (Jas. 3:17).

  b. The demonic promotes envy and disorder. 'For where you have envy and selfish ambition, there you find disorder and every evil practice' (Jas. 3:16).

  c. Note: this assumes a good knowledge of the Bible and sound theology (2 Tim. 2:15).

  (1) One must be fairly sharp theologically to see the heresy that lurks behind an otherwise 'good' representative of God.

  (2) Remember that Satan will play into our sense of indignation and self-righteousness when he turns up.

  (3) Many do not realise the surprising people who can be an 'angel of light'.

  2. *To tell the difference between the demonic and the flesh.*

  a. A person may be in the flesh but not necessarily be demonic.

  (1) When Peter said, 'Lord, it is good for us to be here. If you wish, I will put up three shelters – one for you, one for Moses and one for Elijah' (Matt. 17:4).

  (2) God's presence may be powerful and yet a good person get in the flesh!

  b. Sometimes a person can be in the flesh and the devil take over. 'Jesus turned and said to Peter, "Get behind me, Satan! You are a stumbling-block to me; you do not have in mind the things of God, but the things of men"' (Matt. 16:23).

  (1) Peter did not like Jesus saying that he would be crucified, then raised from the dead.

  (2) Satan rode on top of Peter's fears.

  (a) Peter was not conscious that the devil got in.

  (b) But Jesus was; we too must be like Jesus in this way when this happens.

  (3) Satan will use 'good' people to prevent the ongoing work of the Spirit.

3. *To tell the difference between oppression and possession.*

    a. 'Oppression' is when Satan plays into our weaknesses, especially fear.

        (1) Some people are governed day and night by a spirit of fear (2 Tim. 1:7).

        (2) It is because they listen to the devil rather then trust God and his word.

        (3) They will sometimes believe they are possessed when all they need do is resist the devil (Jas. 4:7).

    b. 'Possession' is when Satan has control.

        (1) Such a person will not confess that Jesus Christ is come in the flesh (1 John 4:2-3).

        (2) They are not able to resist the devil; they need another person to cast out the demon.

        (3) Any person who can confess from his heart that Jesus Christ is God's one and only Son who has come in the flesh, and who will pray 'Jesus, cover me by your blood,' is not demon possessed.

4. *Note: beware of elevating yourself to the level of your incompetence!* (See Acts 19:13-16).

III. THE FLESH

A. This too comes under 'discernment of spirits' since the human being has a soul, or spirit.

    1. *Two distinctions are therefore needed:*

        a. Whether a person is in the flesh or the Holy Spirit.

        b. Whether a person is in the flesh or being led by the devil.

    2. *The only remedy here, as always, is for us to be full of the Holy Spirit.*

        a. Human intelligence is not enough.

        b. We must be full of God's Holy Spirit.

B. There are various levels of the flesh, which may be neither demonic nor the Holy Spirit.

    1. An innocent comment (Matt. 17:4).

    2. When one 'feels led' to do this or that, when it is fleshly (1 Cor. 14:6-17).

    3. When one is biased, his mind is made up (Acts 15:37-39).

4. Legalistic bondage (Gal. 5:1; 2 Cor. 3:17).

5. Bitterness (Prov. 18:19. cf. Eph. 4:30ff).

C. When one has the gift of discernment he or she can see what is really going on.

1. A lot of biblical knowledge, maturity and experience are required.

2. Every church leader needs this anointing.

IV. THE HOLY SPIRIT

A. The greatest need of all is the ability to recognise God.

1. *It is the highest level within the limits of this gift.*

2. *Not to see the demonic but the genuine.*

   a. Sometimes one sees later: 'That really was God.'

   b. Jacob had this delayed discernment (Gen. 28:16).

3. *A high degree of spirituality is required to recognise the Holy Spirit, especially if there is a mixture of activities.*

   a. One should be able to see if God is generally at work, even if the counterfeit lurks here and there.

   b. One should be able to see the rough diamond before it is cut and polished.

4. *I fear many good people overestimate their ability to discern and are too proud to admit to getting it wrong.*

B. If the Holy Spirit is in me, he will recognise himself in another person.

1. *If the ungrieved Spirit is in me, I will recognise the Holy Spirit – wherever he is.*

2. *The problem is: if I have bitterness or an unforgiving spirit, I will not be able to discern!*

   a. Therefore for the gift of discerning of spirits to be functioning it is required that I am on good terms with the Holy Spirit!

   b. Intelligence, Bible knowledge and experience are not enough!

   c. If the Holy Spirit were completely withdrawn from the church today (speaking generally), ninety per cent of the work of the church would continue as though nothing had happened.

CONCLUSION

The gift of discerning the spirits allows the believer to distinguish between counterfeit spirits and the Holy Spirit. The exercise of this gift is important because Satan tries to replicate any work of God's Spirit for his own evil ends. To discern the spirits requires that we know the Holy Spirit and are filled with him and that we know how not to grieve him.

Proper discernment of the spirits helps Christians to be courageous in danger and calm in crises. This gift also helps Christians to recognise brothers and sisters in Jesus and not to be fooled by false professions of faith. The highest use of this gift is the discernment of God, the ability to recognise him whatever the circumstances in which he is working.

26

THE TRUTH ABOUT PREDESTINATION

A. Our subject this time is more edifying to some than to others.
1. My purpose is to try to make it edifying to everybody.
2. I have my work cut out for me, and I shall do my best.

B. I happen to believe that a strong dose of the biblical doctrine of predestination needs to be injected into the thinking of many Christians today.
1. *I grant that there are some who don't need this injection; I know some who are almost 'diseased' by predestination flowing through their theological veins!*
    a. Some see predestination in almost every verse in the Bible and cannot finish a sermon without it or enjoy a sermon that is not filled with it.
    b. I fear that people like them have put others off the subject – driving them to an opposite point of view.
2. *But there is, if anything, speaking generally – as I survey contemporary Christianity – a move away from any notion of the biblical teaching of predestination.*
    a. *The Openness of God*, written by Clark Pinnock and other theologians in North America, took many by storm – and they showed signs of embracing it. The position of this book, stated briefly, is:
        (1) God does not know the future.
        (2) God waits for our choices in order to know what he will do next.
        (3) The future is open because God is open – to us and our decisions.
        (4) The only unchanging feature of God is that his nature is to change.
    b. This book is essentially 'process theology' in evangelical dress.

(1) Process theology is a kind of pantheism (all is God) or, as some prefer, panentheism (all is *in* God).

(2) Nature determines God's will; man is at the centre of nature.

(3) What God was doing in a previous day may be contradicted by what he is doing today – since it is God's nature to change.

(4) The architects of process theology never for a moment saw themselves as evangelical; a new breed of men have wanted to show that it is essentially biblical given some corrections and embellishments.

   c. That this book would be embraced by some respected men is a symptom of how far the present Christian scene has drifted from a biblical doctrine of God.

     (1) This study will not be a critique of the aforementioned book or the view it expresses.

     (2) I simply refer to the book because it shows how far removed many are from a biblical understanding of God generally and predestination particularly.

C. What I propose to do is to show the truth about predestination and help you to love it.

  1. *Do not be afraid of the word predestination even though the perversions of it have been used of the devil to conspire against the greatness and glory of God.*

    a. Islam is a perversion of predestination as it is a perversion of Jesus Christ and of the true God: 'Whatever happens, Allah wills it.'

    b. Or as some put it, 'What is to be will be whether it happens or not.'

  2. *The best of God's people in history have done a disservice to the teaching by making it absolutely central to the doctrine of salvation.*

    a. We saw in an earlier study that certain Puritans centred everything on the premiss that a certain number are foreordained to heaven and a certain number are foreordained to hell – and God gets equal glory from either.

    b. This way of looking at predestination is letting logic rather than scripture determine our belief.

    3. *The alternative to a harsh or extreme view of predestination is not adopting a God who does not know the future.*

        a. There is nothing awesome about a God who makes up his mind on the basis of my choices.

        b. A God who has *all* power and *all* knowledge is one I fear and worship.

    4. All that matters: what does the Bible say?

D. Definitions:

    1. *Predestination: God's self-conscious purpose and ability to carry out his will without man's aid or interference.*

        a. It means God has a will of his own. 'In him we were also chosen, having been predestined according to the plan of him who works out everything in conformity with the purpose of his will' (Eph. 1:11).

        b. It means he can do anything. 'For nothing is impossible with God' (Luke 1:37).

        c. Nothing can stop him from doing what he truly wants to do. 'I make known the end from the beginning, from ancient times, what is still to come. I say, "My purpose will stand, and I will do all that I please"' (Isa. 46:10).

    2. *The secret will of God: the knowledge he keeps to himself until such time he is pleased to unveil it.*

        a. He is beyond our understanding.

            (1) 'Oh, the depth of the riches of the wisdom and knowledge of God! How unsearchable his judgments, and his paths beyond tracing out!' (Rom. 11:33).

            (2) '"For my thoughts are not your thoughts, neither are your ways my ways," declarers the LORD. "As the heavens are higher than the earth, so are my ways higher than your ways, and my thoughts than your thoughts."' (Is. 55:8-9).

        b. He does not have to explain himself. 'Who has known the mind of the Lord? Or who has been his counsellor?' (Rom. 11:34).

            (1) Why he permits evil.

            (2) Why he lets good things happen to bad people and bad things happen to good people.

        c. The secret will of God consists of matters such as:

            (1) Who will be saved.

            (2) Where I will be ten years from now.

E. Why is this subject so important?

1. The word 'predestined' *is* in the Bible and one ought to ask: why is it there and what does it mean?

2. *It is what lets God be God.*

   a. In Romans 1:18-25 Paul shows how unregenerate men hated the true God and decided to create a 'God' they could be comfortable with.

   b. 'For although they knew God, they neither glorified him as God nor gave thanks to him, but their thinking became futile and their foolish hearts were darkened' (Rom. 1:21).

      (1) They came up with images of man. (Rom. 1:23).

      (2) They then came up with images of 'birds and animals and reptiles' (Rom. 1:23).

      (3) 'They exchanged the truth of God for a lie, and worshipped and served created things rather then the Creator – who is forever praised. Amen.' (Rom. 1:25).

   c. Take predestination from theology and you end up vindicating Fuerbach: 'God is nothing more than man's projection on the backdrop of the universe.'

3. *It produces a true fear of God.*

   a. When I know God is all-powerful and sovereign, I want to get on good terms with him.

   b. A God who waits on me before he makes up his mind is hardly a God I will fear.

4. It makes me want to bow down and worship.

5. *It is a key to understanding God and his Word.*

   a. It is not the only key – the mistake some make.

   b. But it is what will give you a world-view, a perspective of God and history when you read either the Old or New Testament.

I. PREDESTINATION AND SCRIPTURE

A. Gr. *proorizo*, used six times in the New Testament.

1. *It means 'to foreordain', 'to predestinate'.*

   a. *Orizo* means 'to limit', 'to set the limit', 'to fix', 'to appoint'. 'This man was handed over to you by God's set purpose and foreknowledge; and you, with the help of wicked men, put him to death by nailing him to the cross' (Acts 2:23).

b. *Orizo* with *pro* means 'to set beforehand'.

2. *It is what God does: he determines in advance.*

a. Concerning the crucifixion; 'They did what your power and will had decided beforehand should happen' (Acts 4:28).

b. Concerning being like Christ; 'For those God foreknew he also predestined to be conformed to the likeness of his Son, that he might be the firstborn among many brothers' (Rom. 8:29).

c. Concerning people; 'And those he predestined, he also called; those he called, he also justified; those he justified, he also glorified' (Rom. 8:30).

d. Concerning God's secret will; 'No, we speak of God's secret wisdom, a wisdom that has been hidden and that God destined for our glory before time began' (1 Cor. 2:7).

e. Concerning our adoption; 'He predestined us to be adopted as his sons through Jesus Christ, in accordance with his pleasure and will' (Eph. 1:5).

f. Concerning purpose; 'In him we were also chosen, having been predestined according to the plan of him who works out everything in conformity with the purpose of his will' (Eph. 1:11).

B. Gr. *tasso*, used 8 times in the New Testament.

1. It means 'to appoint', 'to order', 'to arrange'.

2. *It is used more than one way:*

a. Jesus appointed the eleven, telling them where to go (Matt. 28:16).

b. The centurion was a man set under authority (Luke 7:8).

c. There is no authority except what God has established (Rom. 13:1).

3. It is Luke's word to describe why some believed: 'When the Gentiles heard this, they were glad and honoured the word of the Lord; and all who were appointed for eternal life believed' (Acts 13:48).

C. Predestination implied without using the word.

1. *God's response to Moses' request to see his glory.* 'And the LORD said, "I will cause all my goodness to pass in front of you, and I will proclaim my name, the LORD, in your presence. I will have mercy on whom I will have mercy, and I will have compassion on whom I will have compassion"' (Ex. 33:19).

a. This shows God's sovereign right to do as he pleases.

b. This became Paul's own rationale for the doctrine of election (Rom. 9:15).

(1) Paul had quoted 'Jacob I loved, but Esau I hated,' from Malachi 1:2-3 after concluding: 'Yet, before the twins were born or had done anything good or bad – in order that God's purpose in election might stand' (Rom. 9:11).

(2) Paul never said however that God predestines some to damnation; only that he had the right if he so chose. 'What if God, choosing to show his wrath and make his power known, bore with great patience the objects of his wrath – prepared for destruction?' (Rom. 9:22).

2. Jesus' choice of his disciples.

a. Of all of them generally. 'You did not choose me, but I chose you and appointed you to go and bear fruit – fruit that will last. Then the Father will give you whatever you ask in my name' (John 15:16).

b. Of Nathanael particularly. '"How do you know me?" Nathanael asked. Jesus answered, "I saw you while you were still under the fig-tree before Philip called you"' (John 1:48).

3. *The origin of our calling and conversion.* 'Who has saved us and called us to a holy life – not because of anything we have done but because of his own purpose and grace. This grace was given us in Christ Jesus before the beginning of time' (2 Tim. 1:9).

a. God's choice of Israel. 'Here is my servant, whom I uphold, my chosen one in whom I delight; I will put my Spirit on him and he will bring justice to the nations' (Isa. 42:1).

b. God's choice of the Gentiles. 'I revealed myself to those who did not ask for me; I was found by those who did not seek me. To a nation that did not call on my name, I said, "Here am I, here am I"' (Isa. 65:1).

4. *The origin of special calling (e.g. to service).*

a. The call of Jeremiah: 'Before I formed you in the womb I knew you, before you were born I set you apart; I appointed you as a prophet to the nations' (Jer. 1:5).

b. The call of John the Baptist: 'For he will be great in the sight of the Lord. He is never to take wine or other fermented drink, and he will be filled with the Holy Spirit even from birth' (Luke 1:15).

c. The call of Paul:

(1) He was a chosen vessel (Acts 9:15. cf. Acts 22:14).

(2) He was separated from birth (Gal. 1:15).

5. *Foreknowledge of those who would believe* (1 Pet. 1:2).

  a. Of those in Corinth. 'I have many people in this city' (Acts 18:10).

  b. Those Jesus prayed for. 'My prayer is not for them alone. I pray also for those who will believe in me through their message' (John 17:20).

  c. Promise to Abraham. 'I will make you into a great nation and I will bless you; I will make your name great, and you will be a blessing' (Gen. 12:2).

6. The choice of preaching. (1 Cor. 1:21; Tit. 1:3).

7. The choice of foolishness to confound the wise (1 Cor. 1:27-28).

8. The choice of ordinary people (1 Cor. 1:26; Jas. 2:5).

9. The choice of David (1 Sam. 13:14; 16:1-13; Ps. 78:70).

10. The choice of Jesus Christ (1 Pet. 2:6).

D. Caution: do not go beyond scripture.

1. The problem is 'solved' if you let the scriptures speak for themselves; let God be God.

2. Don't try to be too logical; stay with the scriptures.

3. When we speak of 'those predestined' we must resist thinking of those 'not predestined.'

4. *It is like the dark side of the moon, which no man has seen.*

  a. It is but the conceptual completion of logic in our minds.

  b. Keep predestination positive; do not try to see the dark side of the moon! (cf. John 21:21-22).

II. PREDESTINATION AND PROPHECY

A. It could be safely argued that the greatest proof of predestination is prophecy.

1. Not all prophecy is predictive; sometimes God prophesies what is going on in the present and what his will is now.

2. *But a great element of prophecy is the given knowledge of what is yet to be.*

    a. How could God give his servants knowledge of the future if he did not know what is to come?

    b. If what is to come is definite, it can only be predestined.

        (1) God knew it would happen.

        (2) God made sure it happened!

B. Old Testament examples

1. *God told Abraham that his descendants would be enslaved and mistreated for four hundred years* (Gen. 15:13).

    a. Liberal critics of the Bible claim that Genesis was written long after the event and that it was easy to say then that this would happen.

    b. But if we believe in an infallible Bible it follows that this is what God said to Abraham before it happened.

2. God's word to Rebekah before the birth of her twins (Gen. 25:23).

3. The dreams to Joseph that his brothers would bow to him (Gen. 37:7,9).

4. God's word to Moses concerning Pharaoh's hardness (Ex. 7:3; 9:12; 14:4).

5. *Messianic prophecies.*

    a. Isaiah 7:14. cf. Matthew 1:23.

    b. Isaiah 9:7. cf. Matthew 1:18-25; 4:16.

    c. Isaiah 53. cf. Acts 8:32ff.

        (1) Sometimes prophecies are cryptic, awaiting the outcome before it is obvious – as Isaiah 53.

        (2) Sometimes prophecies are explicit, giving names in advance.

            (a) The reference to Cyrus (Isa. 45:1).

            (b) The reference to Bethlehem (Micah 5:2).

    d. The resurrection of Jesus (Ps. 16:8-11. Cf. Acts 2:25ff).

    e. The priesthood of Jesus (Ps. 110).

6. *Daniel's prophecies of the rise and fall of nations* (Dan. 2, 7, 8).

    a. Though cryptic all acknowledge they referred to events now fulfilled.

    b. For this reason liberal critics insist that Daniel was written after the events!

7. *Jeremiah's prophecy of the Babylonian captivity.*
   a. He stood alone in his claim that the Babylonians would capture Jerusalem.
   b. He stood alone in his claim that the captivity would last 70 years (Jer. 29:10)

C. New Testament prophecies.
   1. The world famine (Acts 11:27ff).
   2. Paul's capture in Jerusalem (Acts 21:10-11).
   3. We will leave prophecies concerning eschatology for the present.

III. PREDESTINATION AND TRIALS

A. Did you know that our trials are predestined by God? They are!
   1. *Paul said we should not be unsettled by trials*: 'You know quite well that we were destined for them' (1 Thess. 3:3).
      a. The reason they knew 'quite well': Paul had taught them.
      b. It was part of his pastoral theology: 'I ask you, therefore, not to be discouraged because of my sufferings for you, which are your glory' (Eph. 3:13).
   2. Paul preached, 'We must go through many hardships to enter the kingdom of God' (Acts 14:22).

B. This is why James said, 'Consider it pure joy, my brothers, whenever you face trials of many kinds' (Jas. 1:2).
   1. God does not grant trials indiscriminately but only to those who are able to bear them (1 Cor. 10:13).
   2. *Consider it a compliment from God when you fall into trials; God knows you are up to it.*
      a. It is the way we grow; 'The testing of your faith develops perseverance' (Jas. 1:3).
      b. God does not lead us directly from A to Z, but from A to B, B to C. The route includes trials of many kinds, all sovereignly given by God.

C. Does Satan not cause the trial? Answer:
   1. *Only by God's permission.*
      a. Before the devil could get at Job he had to go to God for permission (Job 1:9-12).
      b. And yet God initiated the matter of Job (Job 1:8).

2. *Paul regarded his 'thorn in the flesh' as being 'a messenger of Satan'* (2 Cor. 12:7).

   a. Knowing as Paul did this was from God, he none the less 'pleaded with the Lord to take it away' (2 Cor. 12:8).

   b. God's reply: 'My grace is sufficient for you, for my power is made perfect in weakness' (2 Cor. 12:9).

D. Because trials are predestined Peter said, 'Do not be surprised at the painful trial you are suffering' (1 Pet. 4:12).

   1. Such suffering is 'according to God's will' (1 Pet. 4:19).

   2. He granted that some trials we do bring on ourselves. 'If you suffer, it should not be as a murderer or thief or any other kind of criminal, or even as a meddler' (1 Pet. 4:15).

   3. But when it comes passively (without our bringing it on), take it as from God himself – and rejoice!

CONCLUSION

Predestination is God's self-conscious purpose and ability to carry out his will without man's aid or interference. It is therefore an offence to man's pride. However, it is a great source of comfort. The God whose purposes will assuredly be carried out is the One of whom it was said, 'Will not the Judge of all the earth do right?' (Gen 18:25).

I find tremendous encouragement in the doctrine of predestination, even although I don't know the difference between God's predestined will and his permissive will, nor do I know why God has not chosen all, or why he has chosen me. I only know I am so grateful to God, it is what causes me to worship with awe – I am utterly and totally and eternally indebted to him.

27

THE TRUTH ABOUT FREE WILL

INTRODUCTION

A. **It is not a little presumptuous to try in two successive chapters to give the truth about two of the most difficult and controversial subjects in the history of the Christian church!**
   1. *We sought to unveil last time a bit of what the Bible tells us about predestination.*
      a. This subject could go on and on.
      b. We gave a glimpse of what the scriptures have to say on this vast but comforting teaching.
   2. *If anything, the subject this time is more difficult!*
      a. Whereas the word 'predestination' (and equivalent terms) are found in the Bible, the term 'free will' is not found at all.
      b. The phrase 'free will of man' is an assumption many have without looking very deeply into the subject.

B. **Theology is not the only field in which the issue of man's free will comes into the picture.**
   1. *It is at the heart of any philosophical pursuit.*
      a. Theology can be generally summarised like this:
         (1) Theology – is there a God?
         (2) Anthropology – was man created or did he evolve?
         (3) Soteriology – does man need to be redeemed? If so, how?
         (4) Eschatology – is there life beyond the grave?
      b. Philosophy can be generally summarised:
         (1) Epistemology – what is true?
         (2) Metaphysics – what is real?
         (3) Axiology – what has value?
      c. To wrestle with these three philosophical issues is to come face to face with determinism and free will.
         (1) Determinism refers to what causes a person to react in a certain way – to what extent things lie outside himself.

(2) Free will refers to whether man truly is free to react in a different manner from another human being given the same circumstances.

2. *The same is true in psychology.*
   a. The psycho-analytic movement (beginning with Sigmund Freud) believes behaviour is caused by our childhood experiences.
      (1) The ego is one's self-consciousness.
      (2) The superego is one's conscience (formed by parents or stimuli from authority figures).
      (3) The subconscious is what is beneath our consciousness, what may be forgotten or perhaps repressed (denied).
   b. Freudianism is a very deterministic system which in effect denies that man is truly free.
   c. Behavioursim (championed by B F Skinner) is, if anything, even more deterministic.
      (1) Man's reaction to stimuli is predictable.
      (2) Man is basically an animal, like Pavlov's dogs, which could be trained along predictable lines.
      (3) In a word: people react in much the same way when conditions are the same; man is not really free.
   d. Humanistic psychology (championed by Abraham Maslow and Carl Rogers) seeks to deny Freud and Skinner, claiming that man *is* free.
      (1) The issue here is not whether man is free.
      (2) The point: the issue of free will is not only a theological matter!

C. Definitions:
1. *Free will: man is autonomous (self-governing) and has the power to determine his heart, life and destiny.*
   a. Martin Luther wrote a treatise *Bondage of the Will*; Jonathan Edwards wrote a treatise *Freedom of the Will*.
      (1) Luther argued against freedom of the will; that man is enslaved by sin and to sin.
      (2) Edwards said that man is free to do what he wants to do; but what does he want to do? He loves darkness rather than light; man hates God and will always choose the path contrary to God.

   b. A distinction needs to be made between man as he was before the Fall and as he is after the Fall.

     (1) Before the Fall he was autonomous and had the power to choose (Gen. 2:16).

     (2) After the Fall he was said to be a dying man (Gen. 2:17).

2. *Antinomy: parallel truths that are irreconcilable but both true. For example:*

   a. Jesus is God; Jesus is man (John 1:1,14).

     (1) Jesus is not 50% man and 50% God.

     (2) He is 100% man and 100% God.

   b. We love God; we fear God.

     (1) We cry 'Abba, Father,' feeling his love (Rom. 8:15).

     (2) We fear the Lord and try to persuade men (2 Cor. 5:11).

D. Why is this study important?

1. *It teaches us to wrestle with profound issues.*

   a. It helps teach us how to think.

   b. Many (sadly) never dip below the surface of subjects like this and make up their minds before they look at the deeper issues – not to mention scripture.

2. *It makes us face man as he was (in the Garden of Eden before the Fall) and now as he is (after the Fall).*

   a. If man as he is is like man as he was, man is autonomous and free.

   b. If man as he is is as Adam became, the issue is more complex.

   c. Therefore this study makes us face the fall of man.

3. It shows how the responsibility of man coheres with the truth about predestination.

4. It shows what is the Christian's responsibility regarding obedience.

5. It shows what our responsibility is concerning the lost.

I. WHAT DO THE SCRIPTURES ACTUALLY SAY?

A. Those which tend to suggest man is not free:

1. *Man is dead (spiritually).* 'As for you, you were dead in your transgressions and sins' (Eph. 2:1. cf. Col. 2:13).

   a. If man is dead it assumes he cannot move or feel unless life is imparted to him first.

b. This is why he must be 'quickened' (AV). 'For just as the Father raises the dead and gives them life, even so the Son gives life to whom he is pleased to give it' (John 5:21. cf. 6:63).

2. *Man is blind.* 'The god of this age has blinded the minds of unbelievers, so that they cannot see the light of the gospel of the glory of Christ, who is the image of God' (2 Cor. 4:4).

a. This means that, in addition to man's condition of being spiritually dead, Satan has done *his* dirty work on man as well.

b. It presupposes a powerful, supernatural work to heal this blindness. 'For God, who said, "Let light shine out of darkness," made his light shine in our hearts to give us the light of the knowledge of the glory of God in the face of Christ' (2 Cor. 4:6).

3. *Man is unable to come to Christ.* 'No-one can come to me unless the Father who sent me draws him, and I will raise him up at the last day' (John 6:44).

a. This reveals man's helplessness in his own salvation.

b. Unless the Father draws him – the work of the Holy Spirit – man will never come to Christ. 'There is no-one who understands, no-one who seeks God' (Rom. 3:11).

4. *Man is rebellious.* 'This is the verdict: Light has come into the world, but men loved darkness instead of light because their deeds were evil' (John 3:19).

a. Most of the Hebrew words for sin can be summed up in one word: rebellion.

b. This is why man will reject God's offer, something which makes no sense unless one sees it is part of man's nature to be like this. 'You diligently study the Scriptures because you think that by them you possess eternal life. These are the Scriptures that testify about me, yet you refuse to come to me to have life' (John 5:39-40).

5. *Man is under judgement.* 'For this reason they could not believe, because, as Isaiah says elsewhere: "He has blinded their eyes and deadened their hearts, so they can neither see with their eyes, nor understand with their hearts, nor turn – and I would heal them"' (John 12:39-40).

a. All the above regarding man is true because God himself has judged man, rendering him incapable of receiving the truth about Christ.

b. This is why Jesus taught in parables. 'This is why I speak to them in parables: "Though seeing, they do not see; though hearing, they do not hear or understand"' (Matt. 13:13).

B. Those which tend to imply that man is free:

1. *Man is called to make a choice.* 'But if serving the LORD seems undesirable to you, then choose for yourselves this day whom you will serve, whether the gods your forefathers served beyond the River, or the gods of the Amorites, in whose land you are living. But as for me and my household, we will serve the LORD' (Josh. 24:15).

  a. Had Israel been incapable of making the right choice, Joshua is mocking them in requiring such a choice.

  b. Elijah assumed the same thing when confronting the prophets of Baal. 'Elijah went before the people and said, "How long will you waver between two opinions? If the LORD is God, follow him; but if Baal is God, follow him." But the people said nothing' (1 Kings 18:21).

2. *Man is called to repent.* 'In the past God overlooked such ignorance, but now he commands all people everywhere to repent' (Acts 17:30).

  a. Repenting is apparently something we are required to do; otherwise God would not put it to us.

  b. Peter called for this on the Day of Pentecost. 'Peter replied, "Repent and be baptised, every one of you, in the name of Jesus Christ for the forgiveness of your sins. And you will receive the gift of the Holy Spirit' (Acts 2:38).

3. *Becoming a Christian is the result of being persuaded.* 'Since, then, we know what it is to fear the Lord, we try to persuade men. What we are is plain to God, and I hope it is also plain to your conscience' (2 Cor. 5:11).

  a. The root word in the Greek for faith (*pistis*) is *peitho* that means persuasion.

  b. Agrippa could see that Paul was trying to persuade him. 'Then Agrippa said to Paul, "Do you think that in such a short time you can persuade me to be a Christian?"' (Acts 26:28).

4. *Jesus wept over Jerusalem* (Luke 19:41) *because they should have accepted him but did not.* 'O Jerusalem, Jerusalem, you who kill the prophets and stone those sent to you, how often I have longed to gather your children together, as a hen gathers her chicks under her wings, but you were not willing' (Matt. 23:37).

a. What was offered to Israel was rightfully theirs.

b. But it was their steadfast refusal that led to their blindness. 'All the people answered, "Let his blood be on us and on our children!"' (Matt. 27:25).

5. *It a person is lost it is because he rejected what was on offer to him.* 'But when the Jews opposed Paul and became abusive, he shook out his clothes in protest and said to them, "Your blood be on your own heads! I am clear of my respon-sibility. From now on I will go to the Gentiles"' (Acts 18:6).

a. The Jews were given the first opportunity to believe.

b. Their repeated rejection was of their own will. 'But concerning Israel he says, "All day long I have held out my hands to a disobedient and obstinate people"' (Rom. 10:21).

C. Note: we have given an equal number of points and texts in support of two contrary views; many, many more could be printed (we have not intentionally left out any 'difficult' verse that may seem more weighty for a particular view).

1. *Are we prepared to state that we are dealing with an antinomy?*

a. Man is not a free moral agent.

(1) He is not free – he is under the dominion of sin.

(2) He is not moral – he chooses darkness not light.

(3) He is not the agent – that is the work of the Holy Spirit.

b. Man is free and responsible for his own decisions.

(1) He has the responsibility to choose to serve the Lord.

(2) He is responsible to receive and not reject the gospel.

(3) He can be persuaded or can resist what he hears.

2. *These are contradictory principles and propositions but both are equally true.*

a. We are dealing with an antinomy.

b. But this antinomy did not apparently exist before the Fall.

(1) Man sinned; death set in (Rom. 6:23).

(2) The offspring of Adam did not inherit a pre-Fallen condition, as if God started all over again every time a person was born.

(3) One man started it all; we inherit his sin. 'Therefore, just as sin entered the world through one man, and death through sin, and in this way death came to all men, because all sinned' (Rom. 5:12).

II. GOD HAS LONG BEEN IN THE BUSINESS OF COMMISSIONING OR ALLOWING MAN TO MAKE THINGS HAPPEN AS THOUGH APART FROM HIS SOVEREIGNTY

A. Abraham and Isaac (Gen. 22)

1. *Abraham was told by God to sacrifice Isaac.* 'Then God said, "Take your son, your only son, Isaac, whom you love, and go to the region of Moriah. Sacrifice him there as a burnt offering on one of the mountains I will tell you about"' (Gen. 22:2).

   a. Note: sometimes God requires us to do things which make no sense at the time.

   b. He often gives instructions little by little, leaving final instructions until after we have begun to obey – 'on one of the mountains I *will* tell you about.'

2. *Isaac was the only link between God, promises to Abraham and their fulfilment – and yet Abraham proceeded to carry out God's command.*

   a. He inwardly concluded that God would raise Isaac from the dead! (Heb. 11:19).

   b. Abraham was just about to slay his son – and was unexpectedly stopped by God himself, calling to him. '"Do not lay a hand on the boy," he said, "Do not do anything to him. Now I know that you fear God, because you have not withheld from me your son, your only son"' (Gen. 22:12).

      (1) This language looks like it implies that God did not know until then whether or not Abraham feared him.

      (2) It was Abraham's sheer obedience, which Hebrews 11:17 says was carried out 'by faith'.

B. Rebekah and her twin sons (Gen. 25, 27)

1. *Rebekah was given a prophetic word while she was pregnant.*

   a. 'The LORD said to her, "Two nations are in your womb, and two peoples from within you will be separated; one people will be stronger than the other, and the older will serve the younger"' (Gen. 25:23).

b. Paul took this up and made it a basis for the doctrine of election. 'Yet, before the twins were born or had done anything good or bad – in order that God's purpose in election might stand' (Rom. 9:11).

2. *Whether she kept quiet about this to her husband (Isaac) or to Jacob (whom she clearly preferred) we do not know.*

  a. Jacob manipulated Esau into selling his birthright.

    (1) But what Esau did was by his own choice.

    (2) He had to live with that choice.

  b. Rebekah urged Jacob to trick Isaac so that Jacob would receive the Patriarchal Blessing (Gen. 27:5-10).

    (1) Jacob deceived his father Isaac (Gen. 27:19-29).

    (2) But the writer of Hebrews puts the blame squarely on Esau! 'See that no-one is sexually immoral, or is godless like Esau, who for a single meal sold his inheritance rights as the oldest son. Afterwards, as you know, when he wanted to inherit this blessing, he was rejected. He could bring about no change of mind, though he sought the blessing with tears' (Heb. 12:16-17).

C. Saul and David

1. *Against God's wishes Israel demanded a king 'as all the other nations have'* (1 Sam. 8:5).

  a. God told Samuel to let them have their king (1 Sam. 8:7).

  b. God in turn helped Samuel find the king – as if God were totally behind it! (1 Sam. 9).

2. *Saul did not turn out well despite a brilliant start* (cf. 1 Sam. 11).

  a. Saul displeased the Lord (1 Sam. 13:13ff; 1 Sam. 15).

  b. God had the next king in mind, a man 'after his own heart' (2 Sam. 13:14).

  c. Saul lost his inheritance – of his own will (1 Sam. 26:21).

3. *And yet Hosea sums up the whole scenario*: 'So in my anger I gave you a king, and in my wrath I took him away' (Hos. 13:11).

D. The crucifixion of Jesus

1. *Judas and his betrayal.*

  a. Jesus knew of him from the beginning (John 6:70-71).

  b. He was a thief all along (John 12:6).

  c. He betrayed Jesus of his own will, albeit with the help of Satan (Matt. 26:14-16. cf. John 13:27).

(1)He was a fulfilment of prophecy (Zech. 11:12).

(2)It did not take Jesus by surprise (John 17:12).

2. *The wickedness of men.*

   a. The envy of the Jewish leaders (Matt. 27:18).

   b. The cowardice of Pilate (John 19:8-16).

   c. The choice of the crowd (Matt. 27:21).

3. *How all the above was later perceived:*

   a. 'This man was handed over to you by God's set purpose and foreknowledge; and you, with the help of wicked men, put him to death by nailing him to the cross' (Acts 2:23).

   b. 'Indeed Herod and Pontius Pilate met together with the Gentiles and the people of Israel in this city to conspire against your holy servant Jesus, whom you anointed. They did what your power and will had decided beforehand should happen' (Acts 4:27-28).

E. Evangelism

1. *Jesus' last words in Matthew included the mandate 'to go and made disciples of all nations'* (Matt. 28:19).

   a. He had earlier said, 'As my Father has sent me, I am sending you' (John 20:21).

   b. We are to be witnesses 'to the ends of the earth' (Acts 1:8).

2. *These words are put to us as though evangelising were entirely up to us.*

   a. Granted that this enabling was by the power of the Spirit; nonetheless, 'We cannot help speaking about what we have seen and heard' (Acts 4:20).

   b. When threatened Peter and John replied, 'We must obey God rather than men!' (Acts 5:29).

3. *In a word: it was up to them to get on with it; it is equally up to us.*

   a. We should evangelise as if another's destiny were in his hands – and ours.

   b. Those who proceed like that are the movers and shakers of this world, insofar as God's kingdom is concerned.

F. Prayer

1. *The old spiritual, 'Every time I feel the Spirit moving in my heart I'll pray,' is misleading.*

   a. If I waited until I felt 'led', I fear I'd pray very little.

   b. I just do it!

2. *Jesus' own encouragement that we should 'always pray and not give up'* (Luke 18:1) *is probably the strongest verse in the Bible for keeping on praying.*

    a. Paul said, 'Pray continually' (1 Thess. 5:17).

    b. Jesus said, 'Ask and it will be given to you' (Luke 11:9), the context of which urges to *keep on asking.*

3. *Prayer is perhaps the greatest mystery of all, insofar as the present subject is concerned.*

    a. Does our prayer change things?

    b. Did God lead us to pray because he is prepared to work?

        (1) John Wesley: 'God does nothing but in answer to prayer.'

        (2) All I know is that I am prepared to intercede as though it was entirely up to me. 'So he said he would destroy them – had not Moses, his chosen one, stood in the breach before him to keep his wrath from destroying them' (Ps. 106:23).

G. Inheritance (reward). See Colossians 3:24.

1. Paul feared most that he would lose his reward (even though he would make it to heaven): 'No, I beat my body and make it my slave so that after I have preached to others, I myself will not be disqualified for the prize' (I Cor. 9:27).

2. *It is possible to lose a reward and still be saved* (1 Cor. 3:15).

    a. Another can cause us to lose our reward (Rev. 3:11).

    b. And yet we are responsible for not letting this happen. (2 John 8).

3. Whereas sanctification is by the Spirit (2 Thess. 2:13), it is up to us to resist the world, the flesh and the devil (1 John 2:15-16).

4. We are fools if we take this lightly.

CONCLUSION

This subject of free will highlights an apparent contradiction in Scripture. Some verses seem to indicate that man is a free moral agent able to decide on his own salvation, while others appear to show that he is not free, not moral and not the agent, who is the Holy Spirit. This is one of Scripture's paradoxes. Any thinking on the subject has to bear in mind the sovereignty of God.

Those who obey God and work for him as though it were entirely up to them tend to be those God uses most! But if we can work equally hard as the most zealous of men and women, and hold to the robust teaching of God's sovereignty, we are all the better for it. Why? Because we honour the truth. We glorify God most when we believe his word and also become doers and not hearers only (Jas. 1:22-27).

28

THE KINGDOM OF HEAVEN

INTRODUCTION

A. There are few biblical subjects as vast and controversial as the present one.
   1. It is folly to think we can cover this in much depth, but we will try.
   2. There are widely held differing views, both in the course of church history and among the best of Christian leaders at the present time.

B. For openers, here is the frequency of use of relevant terms in the Bible.
   1. The word 'kingdom' is found no fewer the 184 times in the Old Testament; 162 times in the New Testament.
   2. *There are various uses of the term, e.g.:*
      a. Kingdom of priests (Ex. 19:6).
      b. Kingdom of Sihon (Num. 32:33).
      c. Kingdom of Israel (1 Sam. 24:20).
      d. Kingdom of the Lord (2 Chron. 13:8).
      e. Everlasting kingdom (Ps. 145:13).
      f. Sinful kingdom (Amos 9:8).
   3. *The phrase Kingdom of Heaven is found 28 times in the New Testament; all in Matthew.*
      a. Synoptic gospels.
         (1) Matthew, no fewer than 28 times.
         (2) Mark, none; but the Kingdom of God no fewer than 15 times.
         (3) Luke, none; but the Kingdom of God no fewer than 32 times.
      b. Johannine literature.
         (1) John uses the phrase Kingdom of God twice (John 3:3,5).
         (2) Book of Revelation uses the Kingdom of God once (Rev. 12:10).

4. *The phrase Kingdom of God is found 68 times in the New Testament – 5 times in Matthew.*

    a. 49 times in Mark, Luke and John.

    b. 7 times in the book of Acts.

    c. Pauline literature 9 times, plus Kingdom of Christ (Eph. 5:5) Kingdom of the Son (Col. 1:13).

    d. 'Your kingdom' (Heb. 1:8); 'Eternal kingdom of our Lord' (2 Pet. 1:11).

C. Is there a difference between the Kingdom of Heaven and the Kingdom of God? Answer: no.

  1. *Proof: they are used interchangeably:*

    a. The same parables in which Matthew referred to the Kingdom of Heaven, Mark and Luke relate referring to the Kingdom of God.

      (1) 'Jesus told them another parable: "The kingdom of heaven is like a man who sowed good seed in his field"' (Matt. 13:24).

      (2) 'Again he said, "What shall we say the kingdom of God is like, or what parable shall we use to describe it?"' (Mark 4:30).

    b. What Jesus refers to as the secrets of the kingdom:

      (1) 'He replied, "The knowledge of the secrets of the kingdom of heaven has been given to you, but not to them"' (Matt. 13:11).

      (2) 'He told them, "The secret of the kingdom of God has been given to you. But to those on the outside everything is said in parables"' (Mark 4:11).

    c. The announcement of the Kingdom:

      (1) 'From that time on Jesus began to preach, "Repent, for the kingdom of heaven is near"' (Matt. 4:17).

      (2) '"The time has come," he said. "The kingdom of God is near. Repent and believe the good news!"' (Mark 1:15).

  2. *It would seem that the terms 'heaven' and 'God', perhaps during the intertestamental period [between the Old and New Testaments], came to be understood interchangeably when referring to God's kingdom.*

    a. Heaven was known as the dwelling place of God (cf. 1 Kings 8:27).

b. Jesus said we should pray, 'Our Father in heaven' (Matt. 6:9).

c. For reasons we cannot fully understand only Matthew uses the term Kingdom of Heaven.

d. It is thought that the Aramaic (which Jesus spoke) might also be understood either way.

D. Definitions of terms

1. *Kingdom is translated from the Greek* basileia.

    a. It refers to realm, dimension, principality or empire.

    b. It presupposes a monarch – a king or queen.

2. It may refer to a country ruled by a monarch.

3. *Kingdom of heaven: the rule of God.*

    a. It is said of Her Majesty the Queen: she does not rule; she reigns.

    b. The kingdom of heaven is the rule of God.

        (1) However, there is a sense in which he reigns and not rules, that is, insofar as the world being in utter subordination (under control) to God's rule. 'In putting everything under him [Jesus], God left nothing that is not subject to him. Yet at present we do not see everything subject to him' (Heb. 2:8).

        (2) The complete and total rule of God will come when, in the future, 'the kingdom of the world has become the kingdom of our Lord and his Christ' (Rev. 11:15).

        (3) But this total submission is to be experienced now by those who receive Jesus Christ as Saviour and Lord.

    c. Note: other definitions will emerge below as we see some of the ways the term 'Kingdom of God' is used.

E. Why is this lesson important?

1. Any word or phrase used as often as Kingdom of God is worthy of careful study.

2. *We must see the connection between the Kingdom of God and the New Birth.*

    a. 'In reply Jesus declared, "I tell you the truth, no one can see the kingdom of God unless he is born again"' (John 3:3).

    b. 'Jesus answered, "I tell you the truth, no one can enter the kingdom of God unless he is born of water and the Spirit"' (John 3:5).

3. We must see the connection between the Kingdom and God and suffering. 'Strengthening the disciples and encouraging them to remain true to the faith. "We must go through many hardships to enter the kingdom of God," they said' (Acts 14:22).
4. There is a connection between the Kingdom of God and our inheritance. 'For of this you can be sure: No immoral, impure or greedy person – such a man is an idolater – has any inheritance in the kingdom of Christ and of God' (Eph. 5:5).
5. *There is an obvious eschatological (doctrine of last things) significance to the Kingdom of God.*
    a. 'In the presence of God and of Christ Jesus, who will judge the living and the dead, and in view of his appearing and his kingdom, I give you this charge' (2 Tim. 4:1).
    b. 'The seventh angel sounded his trumpet, and there were loud voices in heaven, which said: "The kingdom of the world has become the kingdom of our Lord and of his Christ, and he will reign for ever and ever"' (Rev. 11:15).
6. Jesus assumed that the Kingdom is 'near' (Matt. 4:17). What did this mean?
7. Why did Jesus refer to the Kingdom of Heaven (or God) in connection with the parables?
8. Is there a difference between the Kingdom and the Church?
9. Does the presence of the Kingdom mean the appearance of signs and wonders?
10. Is the Gospel of Christ the same thing as the good news of the Kingdom?

I. THE NEARNESS (BUT INVISIBILITY) OF THE KINGDOM

A. The earliest references to the Kingdom of Heaven are connected to repentance (Gr. *metanoia*, change of mind).
1. 'And saying, "Repent, for the kingdom of heaven is near"' (Matt. 3:2).
2. *'From that time on Jesus began to preach, "Repent, for the kingdom of heaven is near"'* (Matt. 4:17).
    a. It is said that 'Jesus went throughout Galilee, teaching in their synagogues, preaching the good news of the kingdom, and healing every disease and sickness among the people' (Matt. 4:23. cf. Matt. 9:35; 24:14).

b. The next reference is in the opening statement of the Sermon on the Mount. 'Blessed are the poor in spirit, for theirs is the kingdom of heaven' (Matt. 5:3).

c. Jesus talked about people being 'the least' and 'great' in the Kingdom of Heaven (Matt. 5:19).

d. He then spoke of entering it (Matt. 5:20. cf. John 3:5).

e. He told us to pray for it. 'This, then, is how you should pray: "Our Father in heaven, hallowed be your name, your kingdom come, your will be done on earth as it is in heaven"' (Matt. 6:9-10).

f. He told the Twelve to announce that it was near (Matt. 10:7).

g. He spoke of the Kingdom in the parables (Matt. 13:11-13), and throughout the Synoptic Gospels.

h. Jesus gave the 'keys of the Kingdom of Heaven' to Peter (Matt. 16:19).

i. The disciples asked, 'Who is the greatest in the Kingdom of Heaven?' (Matt. 18:1).

j. He spoke of the Kingdom of God being taken from Israel (Matt. 21:43).

k. He spoke of shutting the Kingdom (Matt. 23:13).

l. He spoke of inheriting the Kingdom (Matt. 25:34).

m. He spoke of drinking of the fruit of the vine with us (Matt. 26:29).

B. The assumption of the disciples – before and after Jesus' death and resurrection – was that the Kingdom was visible.

1. There is nothing in the verses above that says the Kingdom would be visible.

2. *Jesus even stipulated (insisted on as part of the argument) that the Kingdom to which he was referring was not visible.*

   a. He knew they thought it was visible here on earth.

   b. But he said, 'The kingdom of God does not come with your careful observation, nor will people say, "Here it is," or "There it is," because the kingdom of God is within you' (Luke 17:20-21).

3. *They never got the message!*

   a. After the resurrection of Jesus the Kingdom and its restoration was uppermost in their minds.

     (1) They assumed all along that Messiah would restore the

Kingdom to be what it was, say, in David's or Solomon's day; this meant the overthrow of Rome.

(2) They asked, 'Lord, are you at this time going to restore the kingdom to Israel?'

(3) It was an ill-posed question; Jesus never said this would happen in the first place.

b. Jesus' only answer was:

(1) 'It is not for you to know the times or dates the Father has set by his own authority. But you will receive power when the Holy Spirit comes on you; and you will be my witnesses in Jerusalem, and in all Judea and Samaria, and to the ends of the earth' (Acts 1:7-8).

(2) 'I am going to send you what my Father has promised; but stay in the city until you have been clothed with power from on high' (Luke 24:49).

C. But the Kingdom was near

1. *Jesus' very presence meant it was near.*

a. He was a Monarch of the Kingdom.

b. He admitted this before Pilate (John 18:37) but said, 'My kingdom is not of this world. If it were, my servants would fight to prevent my arrest by the Jews. But now my kingdom is from another place' (John 18:36).

2. *The evidence of the Kingdom's nearness was in what Jesus did for people.*

a. He healed. 'Jesus went throughout Galilee, teaching in their synagogues, preaching the good news of the kingdom, and healing every disease and sickness among the people' (Matt. 4:23).

b. He forgave sin. 'When Jesus saw their faith, he said, "Friend, your sins are forgiven"' (Luke 5:20).

3. *The next step forward was the coming of the Holy Spirit.*

a. The Spirit came on people on the Day of Pentecost (Acts 2:1-4).

b. It then 'clicked' what Jesus had been teaching all along, but it took the Spirit to make this clear (cf. John 16:13).

(1) They saw why Jesus came; why he died and rose.

(2) They experienced the Kingdom: the Spirit was in them.

4. *There are thus two comings of the Kingdom:*

a. The coming of Christ which culminated (reached its high point) in the coming of the Spirit.

    b. The future coming of Christ which will mean Final Judgment.

        (1) 'Just as man is destined to die once, and after that to face judgment, so Christ was sacrificed once to take away the sins of many people; and he will appear a second time, not to bear sin, but to bring salvation to those who are waiting for him' (Heb. 9:27-28).

        (2) 'In the presence of God and of Christ Jesus, who will judge the living and the dead, and in view of his appearing and his kingdom, I give you this charge' (2 Tim. 4:1).

        (3) This Kingdom will be visible! 'Look, he is coming with the clouds, and every eye will see him, even those who pierced him; and all the peoples of the earth will mourn because of him. So shall it be! Amen' (Rev. 1:7).

II. THE KINGDOM AND THE HOLY SPIRIT

A. Jesus spoke of entering the Kingdom (Matt. 7:21; 19:23).

    1. *It necessitated being 'born again'* (John 3:3,5).

        a. This required the work of the Holy Spirit (John 3:8).

        b. This is also called regeneration or being 'made alive' (Eph. 2:5).

    2. *This was also called being 'saved'.*

        a. 'That if you confess with your mouth, "Jesus is Lord," and believe in your heart that God raised him from the dead, you will be saved' (Rom. 10:9).

        b. 'For it is by grace you have been saved, through faith – and this not from yourselves, it is the gift of God – not by works, so that no one can boast' (Eph. 2:8-9).

    3. *The New Birth, or being saved, is preceded by the preaching of the gospel* (Rom. 10:14).

        a. This is what Peter did on the Day of Pentecost (Acts 2:14-36).

        b. From that time on their understanding of the Kingdom cohered with what Jesus taught (cf. Acts 14:22): 'Strengthening the disciples and encouraging them to remain true to the faith. "We must go through many hardships to enter the kingdom of God," they said.'

B. It will be recalled that the first statement concerning the Kingdom of Heaven was connected to repentance (Matt. 3:1).

    1. *Both John the Baptist and Jesus introduced the Kingdom of Heaven with the need for repentance.*

        a. Repentance means 'change of mind'.

           (1) Agreeing with God.

           (2) Saying, 'I was wrong'.

        b. This has not changed since Peter mentioned it after he preached on the Day of Pentecost. 'Peter replied, "Repent and be baptised, every one of you, in the name of Jesus Christ for the forgiveness of your sins. And you will receive the gift of the Holy Spirit"' (Acts 2:38).

           (1) They had to correct their view about Jesus.

           (2) They needed to be sorry for their sin.

    2. *When Jesus began the Sermon on the Mount, he said,* 'Blessed are the poor in spirit, for theirs is the kingdom of heaven' (Matt. 5:3).

        a. This meant a broken spirit (Ps. 51:17).

        b. This meant asking God for mercy (Luke 18:13).

C. The Sermon on the Mount and the parables show Jesus' doctrine of the Holy Spirit.

    1. *At this stage a clearer definition of the Kingdom of Heaven emerges: it is the realm of the ungrieved Spirit.*

        a. The Kingdom means a realm which is ruled by a Monarch.

        b. The Monarch of the Kingdom of Heaven is Jesus.

           (1) The Holy Spirit took Jesus' place (John 14:16-17).

           (2) Jesus went to the right hand of God (Acts 2:33).

        c. Jesus rules his people by his Spirit.

           (1) The Holy Spirit is a person as Jesus is a person.

           (2) He is called 'another' advocate, comforter, counsellor. Gr. *parakletus*, one who comes alongside.

        d. The rule of Jesus in us is effectual to the extent the Holy Spirit is utterly himself in us.

           (1) He can be grieved (Eph. 4:30).

           (2) He can be quenched (1 Thess. 5:19).

    2. *The realm of the ungrieved Spirit is that dominion in which the Spirit is all that he is.*

        a. He is himself.

        b. He is 'at home'.

3. *The beatitudes show how the anointing works.*

    a. The beatitudes (beginning with 'blessed') show a logical sequence, or progression.

    b. Each beatitude represents a stage that shows a slightly higher level of anointing.

4. *The parables likewise show what it is like for the anointing of the Spirit to function in us.*

    a. The parables make no sense when you try to apply them to a visible or material world.

    b. They show how the Christian life works, as well as how God is at work in the world.

D. Overlapping of the Kingdom of Heaven and the Church.

1. *The Kingdom of Heaven is the realm of the ungrieved Spirit.*

2. *The church is the 'called out' (Gr. ekklesia; called out).*

    a. It refers to a people, not a building.

    b. The people are visible but the Spirit in them is not.

3. *The church is visible, the Kingdom is invisible.*

    a. You can be in the church but not in the Kingdom.

       (1) False profession may get you into the church.

       (2) Baptism without saving faith may get you into the church.

    b. But if you are in the Kingdom you will want to be in the church.

       (1) 'If anyone is ashamed of me and my words in this adulterous and sinful generation, the Son of Man will be ashamed of him when he comes in his Father's glory with the holy angels' (Mark 8:38).

       (2) Being in the Kingdom but not a part of the church is unthinkable!

III. THE KINGDOM OF HEAVEN (OR GOD) AND INHERITANCE

A. There is an intimate and inseparable connection between the Kingdom of God and our inheritance.

1. *It is no accident that the strongest admonitions to believers appear in the context of inheriting the Kingdom.*

    a. 'Do you not know that the wicked will not inherit the kingdom of God? Do not be deceived: Neither the sexually immoral nor idolaters nor adulterers nor male prostitutes nor homosexual offenders nor thieves nor the greedy nor

drunkards nor slanderers nor swindlers will inherit the
kingdom of God' (1 Cor. 6:9-10).

   b. 'The acts of the sinful nature are obvious: sexual immorality,
impurity and debauchery; idolatry and witchcraft; hatred,
discord, jealousy, fits of rage, selfish ambition, dissensions,
factions and envy; drunkenness, orgies, and the like. I warn
you, as I did before, that those who live like this will not
inherit the kingdom of God' (Gal. 5:19-21).

   c. 'But among you there must not be even a hint of sexual
immorality, or of any kind of impurity, or of greed, because
these are improper for God's holy people. Nor should there
be obscenity, foolish talk or coarse joking, which are out
of place, but rather thanksgiving. For of this you can be
sure: No immoral, impure or greedy person – such a man is
an idolater – has any inheritance in the kingdom of Christ
and of God' (Eph. 5:3-5).

2. *That is why we have what would otherwise seem like a strange
verse,* 'We must go through many hardships to enter the
kingdom of God' (Acts 14:22, AV: 'We must through much
tribulation enter the Kingdom of God.')

   a. Is one saved by suffering? No.

   b. Is one saved by holy living? No.

   c. Then why these verses which may be taken to suggest such?

**B. The Kingdom of God is unfolded in the New Testament at
no fewer than three levels.**

1. First level: conversion (John 3:3; Col. 1:13).

2. *Second level: inheritance. See verses just quoted above.*

   a. Inheritance experienced below: an 'earnest' (Eph. 1:14, AV).

   b. Inheritance in heaven: reward (1 Cor. 3:14; Col. 3:24).

3. Third level: Second Coming of Christ (1 Cor. 15:24; 2 Tim. 4:1).

**C. Note: Those verses which appear to some to disprove the
doctrine of eternal security of the believer do not refer at
all to losing one's salvation but rather one's inheritance.**

1. You cannot lose salvation; you can lose your reward.

2. *You cannot be ejected from the Kingdom but you can come
short of what I called the 'second' level above, by:*

   a. Despising suffering when it comes.

   b. Not walking in the light.

CONCLUSION

The Kingdom of Heaven and the Kingdom of God are one and the same. God's kingdom is near to each believer but is invisible. Entrance to the kingdom is by the new birth. No-one who is not born again will enter the Kingdom of God. The monarch is Jesus.

Christ's kingdom is presently in two places, earth and heaven. He reigns over his visible church on earth and over the saints in glory. Being in the kingdom and not in the church is a contradiction in terms.

Believers experience God's kingdom in three stages: at conversion, as our inheritance (the earnest we have below and our reward in heaven), and in full glory at the Second Coming of Christ.

What about the connection between the Kingdom of God and miracles? When Jesus appeared there came with his power the authority over disease. To the extent we live in the realm of the ungrieved Spirit we should not be surprised to see signs and wonders. But never forget that the first two references to the Kingdom of Heaven were given in the context of repentance. Repentance leads to being saved, and salvation is more important than being healed.

29

BAPTISM

INTRODUCTION

A. This is not the most important subject in the Bible.
1. It has sadly divided the best of Christians.
2. *In my old denomination they wisely refused to major on two particular issues:*
   a. Eschatology (doctrine of 'last things') – i.e., the Second Coming of Christ.
   b. Baptism.
   c. Note: I have been influenced over the years by this approach.
3. I have nothing to 'prove' by doing this study!

B. Baptism (def.): an ordinance of the church by which one's profession of faith is sealed by water.
1. *For most Protestants there are two ordinances of the church.*
   a. Note: some Protestants shy away from the use of the word 'ordinance'.
   b. A sacrament usually implies that something automatically or necessarily happens, that is, grace is infused whether the subject has faith or not.
   c. Ordinance: a rule made by authority, or decree.
2. *Augustine is apparently the first to describe a sacrament as 'an outward expression of an inward work'.*
   a. For Protestants there are two sacraments, or ordinances of the church:
   (1) Baptism.
   (2) The Lord's Supper.
   b. For Roman Catholics there are seven:
   (1) Baptism.
   (2) Eucharist (the Lord's Supper).
   (3) Holy Orders (ordination).
   (4) Marriage.

(5) Confirmation.

(6) Extreme Unction (prayer for the sick, usually near death).

(7) Penance.

C. The main issues are, generally speaking, two-fold:

1. The subject of baptism (who can be baptised).

2. *The mode of baptism (whether by sprinkling or immersion).*

   a. Those who require a profession of faith before baptism and who usually immerse rather than sprinkle:

      (1) Baptists.

      (2) Most Pentecostals.

      (3) Some (but not all) Brethren.

   b. Those who baptise infants and usually by sprinkling are:

      (1) Roman Catholics.

      (2) Anglicans.

      (3) Most reformed churches, e.g., Presbyterians.

      (4) Lutherans.

   c. In Greek Orthodoxy there is infant baptism by immersion!

D. Why is this subject important?

1. *The Bible has a lot to say about it.*

   a. The verb *baptizo* is used 80 times.

   b. The noun *baptisma* is used 22 times.

2. We should know why baptism emerged in the first place.

3. We should know the purpose of baptism.

4. We should know the meaning of baptism.

5. We should know the reasons for the different points of view on baptism.

I. THE ORIGIN OF BAPTISM

A. Judaism

1. The antecedents of baptism are found in ancient Judaism.

2. It is not known precisely when it began.

3. But symbolic sprinkling with water as well as blood was used from ancient times. See Leviticus 8:6; 1 Kings 7:23; Jeremiah 52:17.

B. Proselyte baptism

1. Proselyte (def.): a convert to a religion.

2. *The Jews used water for the purpose of religious purification.*
  a. Proselyte baptism was possibly a specialised use of water in a ceremony by which converts were admitted to Judaism.
  b. There is however no reference to this in the Old Testament, the Apocrypha, Josephus or Philo.
  c. But there is no suggestion that John the Baptist was doing anything new when he baptised people.
  d. There is archaeological evidence for baptistries in the Qumran community, which was probably somewhat prior to John the Baptist.

C. John the Baptist

  1. *It may have been an extension of proselyte baptism when John began his ministry* (Luke 3).
    a. He was known as John the 'baptiser' or 'baptist'.
    b. He certainly popularised baptism. 'People went out to him from Jerusalem and all Judea and the whole region of the Jordan. Confessing their sins, they were baptised by him in the Jordan River' (Matt. 3:5-6).
  2. *However, John baptised Jesus* (Mark 1:9).
    a. His was a baptism regarding repentance.
      (1) Jews were still Jews but called to repent.
      (2) John called Pharisees and Sadducees to bear fruit that was in keeping with repentance (Matt. 3:8).
    b. His baptism was in preparation for the kingdom of God. 'In those days John the Baptist came, preaching in the Desert of Judea and saying, "Repent, for the kingdom of heaven is near"' (Matt. 3:1-2).
  3. He contrasted his baptism with one who would follow him but who would baptise with the Holy Spirit. '"I baptise you with water for repentance. But after me will come one who is more powerful than I, whose sandals I am not fit to carry. He will baptise you with the Holy Spirit and with fire' (Matt. 3:11).

D. The baptism of Jesus

  1. *John's most famous 'convert' was Jesus.*
    a. John must have recognised Jesus as someone who did not need to be baptised. 'But John tried to deter him, saying, "I need to be baptised by you, and do you come to me?"' (Matt. 3:14).

    b. But Jesus insisted. 'Jesus replied, "Let it be so now; it is proper for us to do this to fulfil all righteousness." Then John consented' (Matt. 3:15).

      (1) Since Jesus did not need to repent or confess sins (Heb. 4:15), why did he ask for baptism?

      (2) He fulfilled righteousness, that is, he was baptised for us!

2. *The seal of God was on Jesus as soon as he was baptised.*

    a. 'As soon as Jesus was baptised, he went up out of the water. At that moment heaven was opened, and he saw the Spirit of God descending like a dove and lighting on him' (Matt. 3:16).

    b. This is probably when John saw for sure who Jesus was. 'I would not have known him, except that the one who sent me to baptise with water told me, "The man on whom you see the Spirit come down and remain is he who will baptise with the Holy Spirit"' (John 1:33).

    c. It is probably then that Jesus was most fully conscious of his own divine origin and mission. 'And a voice from heaven said, "This is my Son, whom I love; with him I am well pleased"' (Matt. 3:17).

E. Etymology of the word

1. *Baptizo* means to 'immerse in water' or 'plunge into water'.

2. *Technically it is redundant to say 'baptise by immersion' since baptism already means that.*

    a. John the Baptist immersed people in the River Jordan.

    b. John Calvin, who sprinkled infants, acknowledges that the ancient mode was only immersion.

    c. Paintings of John the Baptist (c.300 AD) pouring water on Jesus were probably drawn to justify the emergence of a different mode, since immersion was not always convenient.

    d. The *Didache* (c.150 AD) calls for baptism in 'running water' (presumably in a river) but allows for pouring of water if the former were not available.

    e. The first reference to infant baptism in the early church was by Tertullian (c.200 AD), and he was against it.

      (1) Proponents of infant baptism none the less use this to prove it was in existence at that time.

      (2) There must have been a reason why infants were being
         baptised in 200 AD.

      (3) The suggestion is that it is a continuation from an earlier
         practice.

3. *The baptism of the Holy Spirit may be seen in two ways:*
    a. It could refer to being immersed in the Spirit, or 'drenched'.
    b. It could refer to pouring, since the Spirit would come with
       'power from on high' (Luke 24:49).
      (1) The Holy Spirit is said to 'fall' on the disciples; or 'come
         upon' them (Acts 8:16).
      (2) Indeed, Joel said that God would 'pour out his Spirit'
         (Acts 2:17).
    c. Ezekiel said, 'I will sprinkle clean water on you, and you will
       be clean; I will cleanse you from all your impurities and
       from all your idols' (Ezek. 36:25).
    d. Blood was 'sprinkled' on the people (Ex. 24:8). This is seen
       by some as a very good precedent indeed for doing the
       same with water and calling it baptism.

II. Other New Testament references to baptism

A. Among Jesus' last words before his ascension were these:
'Therefore go and make disciples of all nations, baptising them in
the name of the Father and of the Son and of the Holy Spirit'
(Matt. 28:19).
    1. *This was possibly the first reference of Jesus to baptism in water.*
      a. He referred to baptism but probably with reference to
        suffering. '"You don't know what you are asking," Jesus
        said. "Can you drink the cup I drink or be baptised with the
        baptism I am baptised with?"' (Mark 10:38).
      b. Some think he meant water baptism in John 3:5: 'Jesus
        answered, "I tell you the truth, no one can enter the kingdom
        of God unless he is born of water and the Spirit."'
    2. *This is the only reference to the Trinitarian formula, which*
    the church has traditionally carried out.
      a. The Trinitarian formula is not explicitly mentioned in the book
        of Acts, e.g.:
      (1) 'So he ordered that they be baptised in the name of Jesus
         Christ' (Acts 10:48a).

(2) 'On hearing this, they were baptised into the name of the Lord Jesus' (Acts 19:5).

   b. Some make an issue of this, following only the examples in Acts (cf. Acts 8:16).

   c. Our reply: being baptised in Jesus' name presupposed that they were baptised in the name of the Father, the Son and the Holy Spirit.

B. Baptism as entry into the church was preached from the day of Pentecost onward.

1. *After Peter's sermon, people asked, 'What shall we do?'* (Acts 2:37).

   a. 'Peter replied, "Repent and be baptised, every one of you, in the name of Jesus Christ for the forgiveness of your sins. And you will receive the gift of the Holy Spirit"' (Acts 2:38).

   b. 'Those who accepted his message were baptised, and about three thousand were added to their number that day. They devoted themselves to the apostles' teaching and to the fellow-ship, to the breaking of bread and to prayer' (Acts 2:41-42).

2. There was never a gender issue regarding baptism. 'But when they believed Philip as he preached the good news of the kingdom of God and the name of Jesus Christ, they were baptised, both men and women' (Acts 8:12).

3. Saul of Tarsus was baptised soon after his conversion. 'Immediately, something like scales fell from Saul's eyes, and he could see again. He got up and was baptised' (Acts 9:18).

4. Cornelius and those with him were baptised as soon as they were saved (Acts 10:47-48).

5. Philip baptised the Ethiopian eunuch as soon as he was converted (Acts 8:38).

6. Lydia was baptised as soon as the Lord 'opened her heart to repent' (Acts 16:14-15).

7. The Philippian jailer was baptised as soon as he believed (Acts 16:33).

8. The Corinthians not only believed but were baptised (Acts 18:8).

9. Even some who had been baptised by John the Baptist were baptised (Acts 19:5).

C. Pauline teaching

1. *Paul did not put a priority on baptism but on preaching.* 'For Christ did not send me to baptise, but to preach the gospel – not with words of human wisdom, lest the cross of Christ be emptied of its power' (1 Cor. 1:17).

   a. This of course did not mean he did not believe in it.

   b. It is a timely reminder that the message of the Gospel is more important (1 Cor. 1:21).

2. *The meaning of baptism.*

   a. 'Buried' with Christ in baptism (cf. Col. 2:9-13).

   b. Apart from the obvious implicit reference to the mode, it meant being identified with the person and work of Christ.

   (1) Identified with his death – and being dead to sin (Rom. 6:4,11).

   (2) Identified with his resurrection – and being raised to walk in 'a new life' (Rom. 6:4-8).

   c. In a word: baptism means a change of life. 'Therefore, if anyone is in Christ, he is a new creation; the old has gone, the new has come!' (2 Cor. 5:17).

3. *Paul says there is 'one baptism'* (Eph. 4:5).

   a. This does not mean there is not more than one use of the term.

   b. It means that once a person has been properly baptised, there is no more need to do it over again.

4. *Baptism is being 'clothed with Christ'* (Gal. 3:27).

   a. It symbolises what is true of those 'in Christ'.

   b. All that Jesus did for us is put to our credit by faith; baptism is a symbol of this truth.

5. *'Baptised into Moses'* (1 Cor. 10:2).

   a. This is a reference to being under the cloud and passing through the Red Sea. Moses is depicted as a type of Christ. 'For the law was given through Moses; grace and truth came through Jesus Christ' (John 1:17).

6. *Baptism for the dead.* 'Now if there is no resurrection, what will those do who are baptised for the dead? If the dead are not raised at all, why are people baptised for them?' (1 Cor. 15:29).

   a. This is not an easy verse to understand.

   b. Paul is not passing judgment on the practice but appealing to it for additional support for his argument about the resurrection of believers.

(1) Apparently some were worried about the state of their departed loved ones.

(2) Some asked for baptism on their behalf.

7. *Baptism being analogous to circumcision.* 'Having been buried with him in baptism and raised with him through your faith in the power of God, who raised him from the dead. When you were dead in your sins and in the uncircumcision of your sinful nature, God made you alive with Christ. He forgave us all our sins' (Col. 2:12-13).

   a. This strongly suggests that baptism replaces circumcision, a rite however that only related to male children.

   b. In any case, the link is there.

      (1) After the children of Israel crossed the Jordan River, they were commanded to be circumcised before they could gain their inheritance in Canaan.

      (2) If crossing the Jordan is a picture of conversion, it shows that circumcision, pre-figuring baptism, comes after conversion but prior to our inheritance.

D. The reference in 1 Peter 3:18-21: 'For Christ died for sins once for all, the righteous for the unrighteous, to bring you to God. He was put to death in the body but made alive by the Spirit, through whom also he went and preached to the spirits in prison who disobeyed long ago when God waited patiently in the days of Noah while the ark was being built. In it only a few people, eight in all, were saved through water, and this water symbolises baptism that now saves you also – not the removal of dirt from the body but the pledge of a good conscience toward God. It saves you by the resurrection of Jesus Christ.'

1. This is one of the most difficult passages n the New Testament.

2. *The meaning apparently is:*

   a. Christ's Spirit was in Noah.

   b. Those he preached to are 'now dead' (1 Pet. 4:6).

      (1) They weren't dead when Noah preached to them.

      (2) But they are dead today.

   c. Noah was saved by the water, i.e., by being in the ark (a symbol of Christ).

   d. The water symbolised baptism – 'a pledge' of a good conscience towards God.

E. A reference to Jesus baptising – and not baptising.

1. 'Now John also was baptising at Aenon near Salim, because there was plenty of water, and people were constantly coming to be baptised' (John 3:23).

2. 'The Pharisees heard that Jesus was gaining and baptising more disciples than John, although in fact it was not Jesus who baptised, but his disciples' (John 4:1-2).

3. This meant that Jesus' followers were baptised and approved of by him but he himself handed this over to the disciples.

III. SOME INFERENCES TO BE DRAWN

A. There was no waiting period between conversion and baptism.

1. As soon as people believed, they were baptised (cf. Acts 2:38-41).

2. *There is not a single case of a delay once a person believed.*
   a. Baptismal classes are not a bad thing.
   b. But strictly speaking, there is no biblical basis for them.

B. Every baptism followed believing the gospel.

1. *One was not baptised prior to conversion.*
   a. To claim that we are saved by baptism flies in the face of the Gospel: faith alone in Christ alone.
   b. The thief on the cross had no opportunity to be baptised but Jesus affirmed his salvation (Luke 23:42-43).
   c. In any case, Jesus was baptised for all of us; strictly speaking, no-one must be baptised, and in any case it is not necessary in order to be saved.

2. *There is no evidence of infants being baptised.*
   a. To assume that there would be infants in the cases of household baptisms is speculation.
   b. Paul's words, 'Believe in the Lord Jesus, and you will be saved – you and your household' (Acts 16:31) means:
      (1) The promise of salvation is to the household.
      (2) If they believe, they too can be baptised.
   c. To take Acts 16:31 literally without any conditions must otherwise mean that all children who are baptised are regenerated by baptism.

3. *The Ethiopian eunuch asked for baptism; it should be given only to those who request it.*

  a. Some manuscripts say that Philip replied, 'If you believe with all your heart, you may.'

  b. In any case, it was given because of the eunuch's personal faith.

C. Baptism was the way one publicly confessed faith in Christ.

  1. *The Ethiopian eunuch did this in front of the people around him.*

  a. He was a wealthy man and would have had a caravan of servants trailing behind.

  b. When he asked for baptism, he was nailing his colours to the mast.

  2. *The baptisms on the day of Pentecost were public.*

  a. It sent a signal to the Sanhedrin and every Jew in Jerusalem.

  b. It that showed one was not ashamed.

D. All baptisms were by immersion.

  1. *No-one travelled the desert without water.*

  a. The Ethiopian eunuch could therefore have been sprinkled.

  b. They waited until they came to an oasis. 'As they travelled along the road, they came to some water and the eunuch said, "Look, here is water. Why shouldn't I be baptised?"' (Acts 8:36).

  2. *This is borne out by John 3:23:* 'Now John also was baptising at Aenon near Salim, because there was plenty of water, and people were constantly coming to be baptised.'

  a. After being baptised, Jesus 'went up out of the water' (Matt. 3:16).

  b. Philip and the Ethiopian 'came up out of the water' (Acts 8:39).

CONCLUSION

There is a strong suggestion that baptism replaced the Old Testament rite of circumcision. The first Scriptural record of baptism is the work of John the Baptist whose baptism was administered on repentance of sins. John baptised Jesus who, having no sins of his own and no need to be baptised, bore our sins. Before his ascension Jesus commanded his followers to baptise and, from Pentecost onwards, baptism was practised in the early church. There are accounts of converts being baptised immediately on profession of faith, and of entire households being baptised.

The matter of baptism is not the most important issue in Christian theology. We should not seriously divide over our differences.

30

OFFICES IN THE CHURCH

A. The subject of this study touches on ecclesiology.
   1. *Ecclesiology (def.): doctrine of the church.*
      a. This comes from two Greek words:
         (1) *ekklesia*: The called out, translated 'church'.
         (2) *logos*: The word, sometimes meaning teaching or doctrine.
      b. This refers to the nature of the church rather than the politics
         of the church.
         (1) Ecclesiology refers to one's theology of the church.
         (2) Ecclesiastical refers, for example, to a clergyman's appoint-
            ment in a denomination; or to an ecclesiastical hierarchy.
   2. *Ecclesiology covers subjects such as:*
      a. One's view of baptism.
         (1) Is it for infants or believers only?
         (2) Is the mode by sprinkling or immersion?
      b. One's view of the Lord's Supper.
         (1) Is grace imparted when we partake?
         (2) Is it only a 'memorial'?
      c. Church government.
         (1) Is it episcopal (e.g. Church of England or Roman
            Catholic)?
         (2) Is it presbyterian (ruled by a presbytery)?
         (3) Is it congregational (when a congregation calls its own
            minister)?

B. Another aspect of ecclesiology is offices in the church.
   1. Is there a biblical basis for the papacy?
   2. What offices are described in the New Testament?
   3. Are there apostles today as well as in the earlier church?
   4. What is a bishop, or elder?
   5. What is a deacon?
   6. Are these titles or merely functions?

C. Definitions:

1. *Office: a position of authority or trust.*
   a. This would refer to a title.
   b. Thus apostle or deacon would be a person's title.
2. *Function: the special activity or purpose of a person.*
   a. This would refer to what he or she does.
   b. One could therefore function as an apostle without being called that.
3. Note: Other definitions will follow below.

D. Why is this an important lesson?

1. We should examine exactly what the New Testament has to say about each of these offices.
2. There are church leaders today who regard themselves as apostles; should we call them that?
3. Is there an office of prophet in the church?
4. Is there an office of evangelist in the church?
5. Can a woman be any of the above?
6. What is the difference between a bishop and a deacon?
7. What is the function of any of the above?

I. THE ASCENDED LORD AND OFFICES IN THE CHURCH

A. When Jesus ascended to the right hand of the Father he gave gifts and offices and functions to men.

1. *He gave gifts.* 'This is why it says: "When he ascended on high, he led captives in his train and gave gifts to men"' (Eph. 4:8).
   a. This may refer to several kinds of gift:
      (1) Motivational gifts (Rom. 12:3-8).
      (2) Gifts of the Spirit (1 Cor. 12:8-10).
      (3) Abilities in the body of Christ (1 Cor. 12:14-27).
   b. God sovereignly grants these:
      (1) 'He gives them to each one, just as he determines' (1 Cor. 12:11).
      (2) 'To one there is given through the Spirit the message of wisdom, to another the message of knowledge by means of the same Spirit' (1 Cor. 12:8).
      (3) 'God has combined the members of the body' (1 Cor. 12:24).

   2. *He gave offices.*
      a. In Ephesians 4:11 Paul lists five offices; it was Jesus who gave some to be:
        (1) Apostles.
        (2) Prophets.
        (3) Evangelists.
        (4) Pastors.
        (5) Teachers.
      b. In 1 Corinthians 12:28 Paul broadens the offices and overlaps them with various gifts:
        (1) 'First of all apostles.'
        (2) 'Second prophets.'
        (3) 'Third teachers.'
        (4) 'Then workers of miracles.'
        (5) 'Also those having gifts of healing.'
        (6) 'Those able to help others.'
        (7) 'Those with gifts of administration.'
        (8) 'And those speaking in different kinds of tongues.'
   3. *He gave various functions and abilities.*
      a. In Romans 12:6-8 Paul lists seven 'motivational' gifts (as some call them):
        (1) Prophesying.
        (2) Serving.
        (3) Teaching.
        (4) Encouraging.
        (5) Contributing to others' needs.
        (6) Leadership.
        (7) Showing mercy.
      b. In 1 Corinthians 12:14-27 Paul shows how various functions cohere with each other 'that there should be no division in the body.'

B. All the above happens as a result of our Lord's ascension.
   1. He began this immediately upon his taking his seat.
   2. He continues to intercede and bestow offices and functions to each generation of the church.
   3. Nothing is directly stated concerning bishops and deacons, but these would apply.

II. Offices in the church

A. Apostles

1. *Apostles are at the head of the list in both Ephesians 4:11 and 1 Corinthians 12:28.*

   a. God has appointed 'first of all apostles'.

   b. This implies that the office of an apostle was the highest office; in authority, power, profile and (probably) prestige.

2. Greek, *apostello*: 'to send'; a person sent.

   a. The word is of pre-Christian origin, but only in Christian literature does the idea come into its own.

   b. The order: they had priority in God's scheme; all the rest follow.

3. *There were levels of prominence.*

   a. The Eleven had priority of prominence.

   b. James the Lord's brother may have been more highly regarded than the Eleven.

      (1) 'I saw none of the other apostles – only James, the Lord's brother' (Gal. 1:19).

      (2) 'James, Peter and John, those reputed to be pillars, gave me and Barnabas the right hand of fellowship when they recognised the grace given to me. They agreed that we should go to the Gentiles, and they to the Jews' (Gal. 2:9).

      (3) 'Then he appeared to James, then to all the apostles' (1 Cor. 15:7).

      (4) 'When they finished, James spoke up: "Brothers, listen to me. . . . . It is my judgment, therefore, that we should not make it difficult for the Gentiles who are turning to God"' (Acts 15:13,19. cf. Acts 12:17; 21:18).

   c. There were further men referred to as apostles, with varying degrees of prominence:

      (1) Barnabas (Acts 14:14).

      (2) Andronicus and Junias (Rom. 16:7).

      (3) Possibly Silas (cf. 1 Thess. 1:6; 2:6).

      (4) The apostle Paul.

4. *Requirements of the original apostles.*

   a. To have seen the Lord (Acts 1:22; 1 Cor. 9:1).

   b. To found churches and oversee them (1 Cor. 9:1).

   c. To overrule when there was division (1 Cor. 14:37).

   d. To have supernatural gifts (2 Cor. 12:12).

5. *Title or function?*

    a. In New Testament times it was clearly a title.

        (1) Paul makes a big point of this (1 Cor. 9:1ff).

        (2) Wayne Grudem: apostles were the real successors of the Old Testament prophets.

    b. Many in the history of the church surely carried out the function of an apostle but did not call themselves that:

        (1) Athanasius.

        (2) John Calvin.

        (3) John Wesley.

        (4) Those who founded churches, some of which became denominations, functioned like apostles.

B. Prophets, who were ranked second (Eph. 4:11; 1 Cor. 12:28).

    1. *Note: If Wayne Grudem is correct, the New Testament apostles were the successors of the Old Testament prophets.*

    a. The Old Testament prophet had to speak infallibly.

        (1) 'But a prophet who presumes to speak in my name anything I have not commanded him to say, or a prophet who speaks in the name of other gods, must be put to death. You may say to yourselves, "How can we know when a message has not been spoken by the Lord?" If what a prophet proclaims in the name of the Lord does not take place or come true, that is a message the Lord has not spoken. That prophet has spoken presumptuously. Do not be afraid of him' (Deut. 18:20-22).

        (2) 'Then the prophet Jeremiah said to Hananiah the prophet, "Listen, Hananiah! The Lord has not sent you, yet you have persuaded this nation to trust in lies. Therefore, this is what the Lord says: 'I am about to remove you from the face of the earth. This very year you are going to die, because you have preached rebellion against the Lord.'" In the seventh month of that same year, Hananiah the prophet died' (Jer. 28:15-17).

    b. A New Testament apostle had to be absolutely right in his pronouncements.

        (1) 'They devoted themselves to the apostles' teaching' (Acts 2:42).

        (2) 'Built on the foundation of the apostles and prophets' (Eph. 2:20).

2. *Certain things were not necessarily required.*
  a. Infallibility.
     (1) 'Do not treat prophecies with contempt. Test everything. Hold on to the good' (1 Thess. 5:20-21). Obviously one might not always get it right.
     (2) If one prophesies he is admonished to do so according to the proportion of his faith (Rom. 12:6), which shows one might go beyond his faith and make mistakes.
     (3) Paul himself rejected New Testament prophecies given to him (Acts 21:10-13).
  b. Administrative gifts; there is no hint that a prophet, like Agabus, had this gift (Acts 11:28; 21:10-11).
  c. Teaching gift.
     (1) Some may have had this; Saul who became Paul was listed in Acts 13:1.
     (2) There is no indication that this gift was essential; what Agabus did did not require an acute theological mind.
3. *Purpose of a New Testament prophet.*
  a. Their rise paralleled the apostles, which is probably why they were listed second.
     (1) The first reference to the prophetic is in Acts 11:27, then Acts 13:1.
     (2) Several spoke prophetically (Acts 7), and received words like a prophet (Acts 8:26-29).
  b. Their ministry supplemented or complemented the work of apostles, filling a role teaching alone did not meet.
     (1) Apostles founded churches and laid doctrinal foundations.
     (2) Prophets gave direct words which confirmed God's will at a given moment.
  c. To warn (Acts 11:27-28).
  d. To encourage (1 Cor. 14:3).
  e. Note: there were varying degrees of prominence among the prophetic.
     (1) Some had profile, like Agabus.
     (2) Some were ordinary Christians, like those at Corinth who were encouraged to prophesy (1 Cor. 14:1ff).

C. Teachers

1. These are listed as 'third' in 1 Corinthians 12:28, but not so in Ephesians 4:11 where evangelists are listed third in order.
2. *If apostles were the successors of the Old Testament prophets, teachers were the successors to the apostles.*
   a. A prophet may not have a teaching gift.
   b. A teacher may not have had a prophetic gift.
   c. Signs and wonders may ebb and flow, but not teaching.
3. *Teaching, preaching and the evangelist.*
   a. When Paul listed the evangelist third in order (Eph. 4:11) he may have meant preaching.
      (1) Greek, *didasko*: teaching.
      (2) Greek, *evangelomai*: preaching – that is, the Gospel which was the work of the evangelist (Gr. *evangelistes*).
      (3) Preaching and teaching were often used interchangeably (Matt. 4:23; Acts 15:35).
   b. An evangelist is one who preaches the Gospel.
      (1) Philip is called an evangelist (Acts 21:8).
      (2) We are told he 'proclaimed' Christ (Acts 8:5).
      (3) Paul told Timothy to do the work of an evangelist (2 Tim. 4:5).
      (4) It is an aspect of teaching that largely centres on the gospel.
   c. There is obviously overlapping in many of the offices in the church.
      (1) The apostles had gifts in teaching and administration.
      (2) Philip the evangelist was also a deacon (Acts 6:5).
      (3) A teacher was also a preacher; Jesus was!
4. *Teaching, preaching and the pastor.*
   a. Paul linked 'pastors and teachers' (Eph. 4:11).
      (1) Is the pastor a separate office?
      (2) Or is the pastor also to be a teacher?
   b. The pastor's calling:
      (1) Shepherds of the flock (1 Pet. 5:2).
      (2) Be an 'overseer' (1 Pet. 5:2).
      (3) Paul gave this responsibility to the elders of the church at Ephesus (Acts 20:28).
   c. A person may be called to oversee a church and have a preponderant gift in one or the other.

(1) Some may have a pastoral heart but not be so strong on teaching.

(2) Some may have a teaching gift that is greater than his ability to care for people.

d. In the 'perfect world' one is all these in equal measure; as a teacher, preacher and pastor.

5. *Is there a difference between teaching and preaching?*

   a. As in all the above, functions overlap.

   b. A superficial distinction may be put this way:

   (1) A teacher sits (Matt. 5:1); a preacher stands (Acts 2:14).

   (2) Teaching is to the church; preaching is to the lost.

D. Elders and bishops and pastors

1. *These three terms are used interchangeably, and generally put on equal footing.*

   a. There are three Greek words.

   (1) *episkopoi*: bishop; literally overseer.

   (2) *presbuteroi*: elder; an older man.

   (3) *poimen*: pastor; a shepherd.

   b. All these are used interchangeably.

   (1) Paul told Titus to appoint 'elders' (Tit. 1:5).

   (2) He then called them elders, or bishops (Tit. 1:7).

   (3) The elders at Ephesus were to be overseers (Acts 20:28).

   (4) Peter told the shepherds to be overseers (1 Pet. 5:2).

2. *Bishops (elders) carried on the work of the apostles.*

   a. We saw above: teachers succeeded apostles; so too bishops.

   b. Paul taught Titus (a bishop) to appoint bishops who could 'encourage others by sound doctrine and refute those who oppose it' (Tit. 1:9).

   c. A bishop must be 'able to teach' (1 Tim. 3:2).

3. *Deacons*

   a. Greek, *diakonoi*: deacon; literally servant, deputy or attendant.

   b. Deacons were appointed by apostles (Acts 6:3-4).

   (1) They were however chosen by the people (Acts 6:5).

   (2) They were to make the work of the apostles easier. 'So the Twelve gathered all the disciples together and said, "It would not be right for us to neglect the ministry of the word of God in order to wait on tables. Brothers, choose seven men from among you who are known to

be full of the Spirit and wisdom. We will turn this responsibility over to them and will give our attention to prayer and the ministry of the word"' (Acts 6:2-4).

(3) The apostles were to devote themselves to prayer and the ministry of the Word.

(4) The deacons were to take care of the matters that arose that would divert the apostles from preaching and teaching.

c. They were not required to teach or preach (1 Tim. 3:8-14).

(1) Stephen was a powerful teacher however (Acts 6:9-11; Acts 7).

(2) Philip was an evangelist and powerful preacher (Acts 8:5,26-40).

d. Gr. *diakonon*: deaconess. 'I commend to you our sister Phoebe, a servant of the church in Cenchrea. I ask you to receive her in the Lord in a way worthy of the saints and to give her any help she may need from you, for she has been a great help to many people, including me' (Rom. 16:1-2).

(1) Some argue that this means a woman can be a deacon.

(2) The assumption elsewhere is that they would be men (Acts 6:3; 1 Tim. 3:8-13).

CONCLUSION

When Jesus ascended to the right hand of the Father he gave gifts, offices and functions to men. These were to ensure the proper government of the church on earth and the effectual spread of the gospel to those outside of the family of faith. Since his ascension Christ has continued to call men into service and to uphold them by his intercessory prayer ministry.

God appointed apostles, prophets, teachers, elders / bishops, pastors and deacons. He called men into service whom he fitted for the service they were called to do. While the offices have not ceased, at least in function, some of the names used have changed. Certain titles, however, could give rise to pride. I would not want to call myself a bishop, given today's conception of this term. If a person functions as an apostle or prophet, is there a need to call himself that?

The assumption in the New Testament is that leadership will be male. Women are given the gift of prophecy (Acts 2:17; 21:9). In my opinion a woman is allowed to evangelise (John 4:39). I am unhappy with a woman in pastoral authority (1 Cor. 11:3).

31

THE ROLE OF WOMEN
IN TODAY'S CHURCH

INTRODUCTION

A. 'Fools rush in where angels fear to tread' (Victor Hugo).

    1. *One of the most controversial subjects in the church today is the role of women.*

        a. This was not always the case.

        b. Until recent times, generally speaking, this issue has not been a problem in the church.

            (1) 'Women should remain silent in the churches. They are not allowed to speak, but must be in submission, as the Law says' (1 Cor. 14:34).

            (2) 'A woman should learn in quietness and full submission. I do not permit a woman to teach or to have authority over a man; she must be silent' (1 Tim. 2:11-12).

            (3) 'Your beauty should not come from outward adornment, such as braided hair and the wearing of gold jewellery and fine clothes. Instead, it should be that of your inner self, the unfading beauty of a gentle and quiet spirit, which is of great worth in God's sight. For this is the way the holy women of the past who put their hope in God used to make themselves beautiful. They were submissive to their own husbands, like Sarah, who obeyed Abraham and called him her master. You are her daughters if you do what is right and do not give way to fear' (1 Peter 3:3-6).

    2. *Things have changed; for various reasons, women have been assuming an ever-increasing role of leadership.*

        a. Some believe the above scriptures were products of their time; that they were written to a different culture and are not relevant today.

        b. Some believe these scriptures have been misinterpreted.

B. This lesson will address the role of women in the church in the light of the Bible.

1. At the end of the day, the Bible must decide.

2. *It is either God's infallible Word – or it isn't.*

    a. But is there a case to be made that cultures change and that the Bible itself takes this into account?

    b. Could it be that God inspired the writers to speak as they had to do, given the place of women in ancient times?

    c. Or are there loopholes that allow for women to do things that the Scriptures generally prohibit?

        (1) Loophole (def.): a way of evading a rule, especially through omission or inexact wording.

        (2) Would a loophole be an exception to the rule?

    d. Would the Holy Spirit speak today in a manner that goes against God's written Word?

        (1) Sometimes there is evidence that where the emphasis on the Spirit is the strongest, women seem to have the most prominent roles.

        (2) Does this mean that the Holy Spirit is revealing something different in the Bible from what has been traditionally assumed?

    e. Has the feminist movement spilled over into the church in a way that is pleasing to God?

        (1) The higher profile given to women in today's society has been very much paralleled in the church.

        (2) Is this a coincidence, or is it that the church has been directly influenced by feminism?

            (a) Feminism (def.): the belief that women should be given rights equal to those of men.

            (b) Christian or evangelical feminism is the belief that women should be given leadership roles in the church equal to those of men.

3. Is there a truly godly compromise whereby the standard of God's word is upheld and an equality of women's potential in the church is none the less honoured?

C. It will be granted that the Bible was written in ancient times in which patriarchalism prevailed.

1. Patriarchalism (def.): male headship or leadership.

2. *The proponents of the 'inclusive' biblical translations claim that it was 'often appropriate to mask the patriarchalism of the biblical writers.'*

    a. Behind this admitted bias is often a belief in the theory of evolution.

    b. Even theistic evolutionism (the belief that evolution was God's way of creating the world and all in it) tends to deny that the Fall occurred on a date in history at a place on the map.

    c. It follows that patriarchalism is a natural development, over which God had little or no control.

3. *Was this ancient situation one that was inherently displeasing to God at the time?*

    a. How did this patriarchalism get started?

    b. If it was displeasing to God, could not God who inspired the ancient prophets not also have led them to say things that would change this?

        (1) They spoke fearlessly against Baal worship.

        (2) They spoke fearlessly against the apostasy of the priesthood.

        (3) Why didn't they speak against patriarchalism?

    c. The reply often is: slavery was wrong and the Bible did not speak against slavery; therefore patriarchalism is to be condemned in much the same way. (However, modern slavery involves kidnapping which was punishable by death, according to the Bible.)

D. Why is this lesson important?

1. Sometimes the most controversial issues must be faced and answers given to people who sincerely want to know the truth.

2. The issue of biblical inspiration is at stake; is the Bible infallible and timeless – or not?

3. Many godly women are taking a higher role than ever; could such people be sincere but wrong?

4. Is there a case to be made for women preachers but not necessarily senior pastors or vicars?

5. Is woman the 'weaker' sex or partner; what does this mean?

I. THE CREATION OF WOMAN

A. The creation of woman was God's idea!
1. God created man first (Gen. 2:7; 1 Tim. 2:13).
2. *But the creation narrative in Genesis 1:27 views man and woman as equally created in the image of God.* 'So God created man in his own image, in the image of God he created him; male and female he created them.'
   a. Therefore men and women have equal values to God.
   b. Men and women have equal value to the church.
   c. This is because they have equal value as persons.
   d. It surely goes without saying: men and women have equal access to all the blessings of God's salvation.
3. *After the creation of Adam,* 'The Lord God said, "It is not good for the man to be alone. I will make a helper suitable for him"' (Gen. 2:18).
   a. No suitable helper was found from among the creation (Adam had named each living creature). 'So the Lord God caused the man to fall into a deep sleep; and while he was sleeping, he took one of the man's ribs and closed up the place with flesh' (Gen. 2:21).
   b. 'Then the Lord God made a woman from the rib he had taken out of the man, and he brought her to the man. The man said, "This is now bone of my bones and flesh of my flesh; she shall be called 'woman,' for she was taken out of man"' (Gen. 2:22-23).
4. This point became fundamental to Paul's treatment of women and their role in the church. 'For man did not come from woman, but woman from man' (1 Cor. 11:8).

B. Although God made male and female equal, the also made them different.
1. Because they are equal, there can be no question of the inferiority of either one to the other.
2. Because they are different, men and women must recognise their differences and not try to eliminate them or usurp one another's distinctions.
3. Matthew Henry put it like this: Eve was 'not made out of his head to top him, nor out of his feet to be trampled upon by

him, but out of his side to be equal with him, under his arm to
be protected, and near his heart to be beloved.'
4. Peter Lombard said: 'Eve was not taken from the feet of Adam
to be his slave, nor from his head to be his lord, but from his
side to be his partner.'

C. From what we have seen above it may be concluded:
1. Adam was created first, then Eve.
2. The purpose of the creation of woman was for the man.
3. *The way woman was created was from the man.*
   a. Note: These three principles are based on Genesis 2 (before
   the Fall) not on Genesis 3 (after the Fall).
   b. The primeval sexual equality was however distorted by the
   Fall: 'Your desire will be for your husband, and he will
   rule over you' (Gen. 3:16).

D. Peter's reference to the 'weaker sex'. 'Husbands, in the same
way be considerate as you live with your wives, and treat them
with respect as the weaker partner and as heirs with you of the
gracious gift of life, so that nothing will hinder your prayers' (1
Pet. 3:7).
1. Janet Richards (an ardent feminist) said: 'Presumably women
must in some sense tend to be weaker than men.'
2. Margaret Mead says: 'Still in every society men are by an large
bigger than women, and by an large stronger than women.'
3. *Peter may have meant more, possibly also referring to worries
as a result of the Fall.*
   a. This does not mean women are less intelligent, far from it!
   b. It refers to the way God made the two sexes.

II. THE NEW TESTAMENT AND THE ROLE OF WOMEN

A. Masculine 'headship'.
1. *In two places Paul writes that the husband is the head of the
   wife, and the head of the woman is man.*
   a. 'For the husband is the head of the wife as Christ is the head of
   the church, his body, of which he is the Saviour' (Eph. 5:23).
   b. 'Now I want you to realise that the head of every man is
   Christ, and the head of the woman is man, and the head of
   Christ is God' (1 Cor. 11:3).

2. *The relevant Greek word is* kephale: *head.*

    a. There are two schools of thought as to the meaning:

        (1) That it means 'authority'.

        (2) That is means 'source'.

    b. The evidence for *kephale* meaning 'authority'.

        (1) It never once means 'source' in the Septuagint.

        (2) How can a husband be the 'source' of his wife?

        (3) Paul uses *kephale* alongside 'authority' in Ephesians 1:21-22.

        (4) Christ is said to be 'the Head over every power and authority' (Col. 2:10), thus it must mean 'authority'.

    c. The evidence for *kephale* meaning 'source'.

        (1) Christ is the head of the body, the Church (Col. 1:18).

        (2) 'He has lost connection with the Head' (Col. 2:19).

    d. Wayne Grudem has made a scholarly search of 2,336 examples of *kephale* from a wide range of ancient Greek literature, which produced not one convincing example where *kephale* meant 'source'.

        (1) All the major lexicons that specialise in the New Testament period give the meaning 'authority over', whereas none give the meaning 'source'.

        (2) This strongly suggests that the meaning intended by the New Testament writers also was 'authority over' when they used the Greek word *kephale*. See Appendix I, 'The Meaning of Kephale', in *Recovering Biblical Manhood and Womanhood* (edited by John Piper and Wayne Grudem), Crossway, pp 425-268.

B. The husband-wife relationship.

    1. 'Now I want you to realise that the head of every man is Christ, and the head of the woman is man, and the head of Christ is God' (1 Cor. 11:3).

    2. *'For the husband is the head of the wife as Christ is the head of the church, his body, of which he is the Saviour'* (Eph. 5:23).

        a. 'Wives, submit to your husbands, as is fitting in the Lord. Husbands, love your wives and do not be harsh with them' (Col. 3:18-19).

        b. 'Wives, in the same way be submissive to your husbands so that, if any of them do not believe the word, they may be

won over without words by the behaviour of their wives,
when they see the purity and reverence of your lives... For
this is the way the holy women of the past who put their
hope in God used to make themselves beautiful. They were
submissive to their own husbands, like Sarah, who obeyed
Abraham and called him her master. You are her daughters
if you do what is right and do not give way to fear' (1 Pet.
3:1-2,5-6).
   c. 'Husbands, in the same way be considerate as you live with
      your wives, and treat them with respect as the weaker
      partner and as heirs with you of the gracious gift of life, so
      that nothing will hinder your prayers' (1 Pet. 3:7).
3. These verses speak for themselves; one however must never
   forget the responsibility of the husband to love this wife 'as
   Christ loved the church' (Eph. 5:25).

C. The role of women in the church; can they be church officers?
   1. *Not in the role of pastor or elder within a church.* 'A woman
      should learn in quietness and full submission. I do not permit a
      woman to teach or to have authority over a man; she must be
      silent. For Adam was formed first, then Eve. And Adam was
      not the one deceived; it was the woman who was deceived
      and became a sinner' (1 Tim. 2:11-14).
      a. The word 'head' is not used, but 'having authority over' is.
      b. This further suggests what *kephale* means.
      c. Authority is given to men.
   2. *Objections to this view:*
      a. This applies only to a specific situation which Paul is
         addressing.
         (1) It is alleged that women were teaching heretical doctrine
             within the church at Ephesus.
         (2) Reply to this objection:
             (a) There is no statement that women were actually
                 teaching false doctrine; only that they were gossiping
                 (I Tim. 5:13).
             (b) Paul's reason for this prohibition:
                 (i) Adam's creation before the Fall.
                 (ii) The way in which a change in male and female
                      roles occurred at the time of the Fall.

     b. Paul gave this prohibition because women were not well educated in the first century.
       (1) They were therefore not qualified for teaching or governing roles in the church.
       (2) Reply:
         (a) Paul does not give lack of education as his reason.
         (b) He points back to creation instead.
         (c) Note: it is precarious to base an argument on a reason Paul did not give instead of the reason he did give.

3. *The actual facts of the ancient church were these:*
     a. Formal training in Scripture was not required for leadership in the New Testament church (Acts 4:13).
     b. The skills of basic literacy and therefore the ability to read and study Scripture were available to men and women alike (cf. Acts 18:26; Rom. 16:1; 1 Tim. 2:11; Titus 2:3-4).
     c. There were many well-educated women in the ancient world, particularly in a cultural centre like Ephesus.
       (1) It was in this very church at Ephesus that Priscilla knew Scripture well enough to help instruct Apollos in 51 AD (Acts 18:26).
       (2) The reason: not lack of education but the order of creation which God established between men and women.

D. Can a woman speak publicly in a church?

     1. *Note 1 Corinthians 14:33b-36:* 'As in all the congregations of the saints, women should remain silent in the churches. They are not allowed to speak, but must be in submission, as the Law says. If they want to inquire about something, they should ask their own husbands at home; for it is disgraceful for a woman to speak in the church. Did the word of God originate with you? Or are you the only people it has reached?'
       a. Paul cannot be prohibiting all public speaking by women in the church.
         (1) He allowed them to pray and prophesy (1 Cor. 11:5).
         (2) The 'silence' therefore needs clarification in the light of their freedom to prophesy.
       b. The 'silence' in the context of 1 Corinthians 14 refers to evaluating and judging prophecies in the congregation.
         (1) 'Two or three prophets should speak, and the others should weigh carefully what is said' (1 Cor. 14:29).

    (2) Whereas women could speak and give prophecies, Paul
    does not allow them to speak up and give evaluation or
    critiques of the prophecies that have been given. It is
    noteworthy that no woman wrote a single book in the
    Bible; books do however bear their names.

      (a) This would be a ruling or governing function with
      respect to the whole church.

      (b) Therefore Paul is consistent in his view of the role
      of women in the church.

      (c) He is concerned to preserve male leadership in the
      teaching and governing of the church.

2. *A woman can prophesy but not govern.*

  a. Leadership is male.

    (1) 'Here is a trustworthy saying: If anyone sets his heart
    on being an overseer, he desires a noble task. Now the
    overseer must be above reproach, the husband of but
    one wife, temperate, self-controlled, respectable,
    hospitable, able to teach, not given to drunkenness, not
    violent but gentle, not quarrelsome, not a lover of money.
    He must manage his own family well and see that his
    children obey him with proper respect. (If anyone does
    not know how to manage his own family, how can he
    take care of God's church?) He must not be a recent
    convert, or he may become conceited and fall under the
    same judgment as the devil. He must also have a good
    reputation with outsiders, so that he will not fall into
    disgrace and into the devil's trap' (1 Tim. 3:1-7).

    (2) 'The reason I left you in Crete was that you might
    straighten out what was left unfinished and appoint elders
    in every town, as I directed you. An elder must be
    blameless, the husband of but one wife, a man whose
    children believe and are not open to the charge of being
    wild and disobedient. Since an overseer is entrusted with
    God's work, he must be blameless – not overbearing,
    not quick-tempered, not given to drunkenness, not violent,
    not pursuing dishonest gain. Rather he must be hospitable,
    one who loves what is good, who is self-controlled,
    upright, holy and disciplined. He must hold firmly to the
    trustworthy message as it has been taught, so that he

can encourage others by sound doctrine and refute those who oppose it' (Tit. 1:5-9).

b. These passages assume that pastors, elders or bishops are going to be men.

c. Joel prophesied that 'sons and daughters' would prophesy (Joel 2:28-29. cf. Acts 2:17-18).

d. The woman of Samaria was an effective evangelist (John 4:28-30,39): 'Then, leaving her water jar, the woman went back to the town and said to the people, "Come, see a man who told me everything I ever did. Could this be the Christ?" They came out of the town and made their way toward him. . . Many of the Samaritans from that town believed in him because of the woman's testimony, "He told me everything I ever did."'

3. *There are situations in which it is entirely proper for women to teach, and to teach men, provided that in doing so they are not usurping an improper authority over them.*

a. Content: the Scripture.

(1) Jesus appointed apostles as infallible teachers.

(2) They were all men.

(3) The canon of Scripture is completed.

(4) Women can now teach the Scriptures.

b. Context: women as part of a team at a local church.

(1) The pastor or vicar would be male.

(2) Women could serve as part of a team, not unlike Priscilla.

c. Style: humility.

(1) Deborah was a self-effacing prophet who urged Barak to come forward and respected his male ego! Judges 4.

(2) Women must be subservient to the authority of Scripture and to the church leader who is male.

4. *Referring to the Anglican situation John Stott writes:* 'I still do not think it biblically appropriate for a woman to become a Rector or Bishop.' But he suggests:

a. The church must recognise God's gift and calling in women.

b. The church must make appropriate spheres of service available to women.

c. The church should commission or authorise women to exercise their God-given ministries – in team situations.

5. I myself would come short of calling this 'ordination'.

CONCLUSION

This is a relatively 'new' issue. Until recently there was no question of women looking to hold office in church. Increasingly thinking is 'inclusive' and it is politically incorrect to suggest that God requires men only to serve in church office. It is often suggested that Scripture was written for the culture of the day and that we should change its teaching on this subject to fit our current cultural thinking. However, if the Bible is infallible it follows that it is unchangeable and that what it says applied to the early church is equally applicable to the church today. This is borne out by Scriptural teaching on masculine headship and the husband-wife relationship. However, there are many ministries which women can perform without breaching Biblical guidelines.

The danger of any concession in the direction of ordination – even at a 'team' level – is that it could open 'Pandora's box' and lead beyond what is suggested above. As long as a woman recognises the creation ordinance and is prepared to affirm the relevant passages above she may prove to be an exception, like Deborah.

I would recommend the following books for further study:

Wayne Grudem, *Systematic Theology*, pp 937-945.
John Stott, *Issues facing Christians Today*, pp 234-257.
John Piper and Wayne Grudem (editors), *Recovering Biblical Manhood and Womanhood*, as referred to already in the chapter..

32

PUBLIC AND PRIVATE WORSHIP

INTRODUCTION

A. **I want to begin by making an open, honest confession: I had not taken worship truly seriously until recently.**
   1. This is said despite the fact that I have written the book *Worshipping God* (Hodder & Stoughton), called *Before the Throne* in the USA (Broadman Press).
      (1) This is a book of thirty studies which have their origin in Philippians 3:3 ('we who worship by the Spirit of God').
      (2) The book got good reviews and I stand by every word of it.
   2. *It shows how one can say many good things but they come from the head more than the heart.*
      a. I doubt I would change a single word of any of the above.
      b. And yet I could probably re-read these studies and enjoy them more than I did at the time they were completed.

B. **I have previously defined worship, at least public worship, as the response to, or preparation for, preaching.**
   1. *I see nothing wrong with this definition. It emphasises:*
      a. The centrality of preaching (1 Cor. 1:21; Tit. 1:2-3).
      b. The need for preaching to inspire worship.
      c. The need for worship to made preaching better and easier to receive.

   2. *But this still camouflages my own bias and lack of appreciation for worship.*
      a. My anointing (as I understand it) is mainly preaching.
      b. Our church has a reputation (rightly or wrongly) for being a 'preaching centre'.
      c. Following Dr Lloyd-Jones, we have sought to made it *both*; a church which none the less centres on preaching.

3. *My problem was: I merely tolerated the worship.*

　　a. Many people who came here were the same; they only came for the preaching, and could generally have largely dispensed with much of what preceded the preaching.

　　b. Many felt this even more strongly as we began to sing more contemporary songs.

　　c. It was a sermon by Dr. Paul Cain that made me see there were other aspects to worship.

C. Greek words translated 'worship'.

1. Proskuneo *(used 60 times) means 'to adore', 'to give reverence to'.*

　　a. This word refers to the condition of the heart.

　　b. It is used by Jesus to the woman of Samaria: 'God is a spirit, and his worshippers must worship in spirit and in truth' (John 4:24).

2. Latreuontes *(used as a noun or verb 26 times) means 'service'.*

　　a. This is the word which is used to refer to public worship.

　　b. It is used by Paul in Philippians 3:3: '....who worship by the Spirit of God' (cf. Rom. 12:1): 'Therefore, I urge you, brothers, in view of God's mercy, to offer your bodies as living sacrifices, holy and pleasing to God – this is your spiritual act of worship.'

E. Why is this lesson important?

1. It shows how important worship is to God.

2. It shows how important worship should be to us.

3. It shows what worship does for God.

4. It shows what worship does for us.

5. It should inspire us to worship more fervently than ever – to do more of it publicly and privately.

I. THE RIGHT PERCEPTION OF WORSHIP

A. It is both the means and the end; it is what leads to blessing (the means) and becomes the blessing in itself (the end).

1. *Like so much that is taught regarding obedience, we first need to be motivated.*

　　a. We can be motivated by warning: 'Do not be deceived: God cannot be mocked. A man reaps what he sows. The one who sows to please his sinful nature, from that nature will reap destruction' (Gal. 6:7-8).

  b. We can be motivated by the promise of blessing 'Do not be deceived: God cannot be mocked. A man reaps what he sows. The one who sows to please his sinful nature, from that nature will reap destruction; the one who sows to please the Spirit, from the Spirit will reap eternal life' (Gal. 6:7-8).

  c. Then Paul adds: 'Let us not become weary in doing good, for at the proper time we will reap a harvest if we do not give up' (Gal. 6:9).

2. *Take tithing; most of us need some motivation that is both positive and negative – to get us moving in the right direction.*

  a. The negative side: the tithe is the Lord's already (Lev. 27:30).

  (1) He puts us on our honour to turn that one tenth over to him.

  (2) Not to do so is robbing God – a serious thing to do. '"Will a man rob God? Yet you rob me. But you ask, 'How do we rob you?' In tithes and offerings. You are under a curse – the whole nation of you – because you are robbing me"' (Mal. 3:8-9).

  b. The positive side: you cannot out-give the Lord.

  (1) He promises blessing to the tither: '"Bring the whole tithe into the storehouse, that there may be food in my house. Test me in this," says the LORD Almighty, "and see if I will not throw open the floodgates of heaven and pour out so much blessing that you will not have room enough for it"' (Mal. 3:10).

  (2) 'Remember this: Whoever sows sparingly will also reap sparingly, and whoever sows generously will also reap generously' (2 Cor. 9:6).

3. *But when we mature as we should, our obedience generally (including tithing) is not carried out by positive or negative motivation; we reach the place where obedience is sheer privilege.*

  a. Love is its own reward (1 Cor. 13).

  b. Obedience is its own reward.

  (1) At first it was the means to the end (namely, blessing).

  (2) Eventually obedience is *the* blessing.

B. So with worship

1. *I myself have gone through two stages.*

   a. At first I was motivated to worship by realising that worship brings down blessing.

      (1) This is borne out by Psalm 67:

         (a) 'May the peoples praise you, O God; may all the peoples praise you' (Ps. 67:5).

         (b) '*Then* the land will yield its harvest, and God, our God, will bless us' (Ps. 67:6).

      (2) The same thing is found in Psalm 68.

         (a) 'Praise God in the great congregation; praise the LORD in the assembly of Israel' (Ps. 68:26).

         (b) 'Summon your power, O God; show us your strength, O God, as you have done before' (Ps. 68:28).

         (c) 'Sing to God, O kingdoms of the earth, sing praise to the Lord' (Ps. 68:32).

         (d) 'You are awesome, O God, in your sanctuary; the God of Israel gives power and strength to his people' (Ps. 68:35).

   b. I then reached the stage that worshipping God was the blessing in itself; what a privilege to worship God.

      (1) 'Sing to the LORD a new song; sing to the LORD, all the earth. Sing to the LORD, praise his name; proclaim his salvation day after day' (Ps. 96:1-2).

      (2) 'Shout for joy to the LORD, all the earth, burst into jubilant song with music' (Ps. 98:4).

      (3) 'Exalt the LORD our God and worship at his footstool; he is holy' (Ps. 99:5).

      (4) 'Enter his gates with thanksgiving and his courts with praise; give thanks to him and praise his name' (Ps. 100:4).

      (5) 'I will sing of your love and justice; to you, O LORD, I will sing praise' (Ps. 101:1).

      (6) 'So the name of the LORD will be declared in Zion and his praise in Jerusalem when the peoples and the kingdoms assemble to worship the LORD' (Ps. 102:21-22).

      (7) 'Praise the LORD, O my soul; all my inmost being, praise his holy name. Praise the LORD, O my soul, and forget not all his benefits' (Ps. 103:1-2).

2. *After Paul Cain's sermon I was convicted and so ashamed that I determined I would make up for lost time.*

    a. I have sought to read Psalms and sing hymns and choruses that expressed sheer praise, if possible without asking for a single thing from the Lord.

    b. I became amazed how the subject of praise governed God's people when they were right with him and pleasing him.

II. Public worship

A. We must not underestimate what public worship means to God and does for him.

    1. *In worship God must be the centre of attraction.*

        a. When all focus on him simultaneously this honours him and exalts his name.

        b. 'When the builders laid the foundation of the temple of the LORD, the priests in their vestments and with trumpets, and the Levites (the sons of Asaph) with cymbals, took their places to praise the LORD, as prescribed by David king of Israel. With praise and thanksgiving they sang to the LORD: "He is good; his love to Israel endures for ever." And all the people gave a great shout of praise to the LORD, because the foundation of the house of the LORD was laid' (Ezra 3:10-11).

    2. *Had David succeeded the first time in his attempt to bring the Ark to Jerusalem (2 Sam. 6:1-9), the worship would have been minimal in comparison to what it became when he succeeded.*

        a. When David realised what he had done wrong (by not having the Ark carried according to God's Word (1 Chron. 15:13), he had time to make extra preparation for the worship.

        (1) 'David told the leaders of the Levites to appoint their brothers as singers to sing joyful songs, accompanied by musical instruments: lyres, harps and cymbals' (1 Chron. 15:16).

        (2) The Levites got on with the task and got the very best, for example, 'Kenaniah the head Levite was in charge of the singing; that was his responsibility *because he was skilful at it*' (1 Chron. 15:22).

      (3) This suggests that God wants the very best in quality of
          music and singing – leading public worship.
  b. There is good reason to believe God loves loud, noisy worship.
      (1) 'Praise him with the sounding of the trumpet, praise him
          with the harp and lyre, praise him with tambourine and
          dancing, praise him with the strings and flute, praise him
          with the clash of cymbals, praise him with resounding
          cymbals' (Ps. 150:3-5).
      (2) 'So all Israel brought up the ark of the covenant of the
          LORD with shouts, with the sounding of rams' horns and
          trumpets, and of cymbals, and the playing of lyres and
          harps' (1 Chron. 15:28).
      (3) 'No-one could distinguish the sound of the shouts of joy
          from the sound of weeping, because the people made so
          much noise. And the sound was heard far away' (Ezra
          3:13).
  c. One might therefore infer that David's first failure to bring
    the Ark to Jerusalem carried with it two things:
    (1) His failure to bring the Ark according to the Word.
    (2) His failure to make sufficient preparation for worship –
       which was carried out when he succeeded with the Ark.

**B. When we are worshipping publicly we must be careful to
remember to focus on God alone.**
  1. *There is no doubt that the quality of those leading worship
    makes a difference.*
    a. A good worship leader will not draw attention to himself or
      herself.
      (1) He or she should be good at what he or she does.
      (2) But the task of a worship leader is to get the people to
         worship – to adore and praise – God.
    b. A good worship group will not draw attention to itself.
      (1) One hopes for the highest quality of musicianship and
         singing – it does make a considerable difference.
      (2) The better they are, the more the people will want to
         praise God in singing.
      (3) The same is true of any instrumentalist; for example, the
         organist should not draw attention to his skill but play in
         a manner that precipitates warm, heart-felt worship.

2. *Each person present – whether in the worship group or the congregation – should sing to God as though no-one else were present.*

   a. The angels are watching; perhaps they will enter into our worship with us if we are truly caught up in the spirit of praise and adoration.

   b. What if all heaven were looking at just *you*; what would they see?

   (1) A person looking at his watch?

   (2) A person looking around to see who is there?

   (3) A person restless and waiting for this all to end?

   (4) Or a person caught up in sheer praise and worship?

C. **All this is done properly on one condition: it is carried out 'by the Spirit of God' (Phil. 3:3).**

   1. *When we worship by the Spirit we will please the Lord, not ourselves.*

   a. Caution: do not be carried along by what pleases *you*, but what honours God.

   (1) Some only want familiar tunes and words that were written ages ago – which is doing more for the one singing than for God.

   (2) Isaac Watts objected to boring worship

   (a) He began writing his own hymns.

   (b) But later people were stuck in to Isaac Watt's hymns only!

   b. Repeatedly the psalmist stressed singing unto the Lord a 'new' song!

   (1) Every movement of God has been characterised by an outbreak of singing contemporary with its age.

   (2) When new lively (provided they are biblical) hymns and songs are being written it is good evidence that the true God is at work and is pleased.

   c. Note also: repetitive singing of simple lines may seem trite to some but is both biblical and what is needed to focus on God's name.

   (1) Handel's Hallelujah Chorus is very repetitive!

   (2) We should equally never tire of singing:

Praise the Lord, Praise the Lord,
Praise the Lord, Hallelujah!
Praise the Lord, Praise the Lord,
Praise the Lord, Hallelujah!
King of kings and Lord of lords,
Praise his name forever!
Praise the Lord, Praise the Lord,
Praise the Lord, Hallelujah!

2. *Worship by the Spirit is in contrast to the flesh.*
  a. We will not aim to please ourselves.
  b. We will not allow our minds to wander.
  c. We will know this is God's time and we should honour every single minute of public worship.

III. PRIVATE WORSHIP

A. Not all worship that is toward the God of the Bible is singing of course.
  1. Reading the scriptures in the Spirit is true worship (1 Tim. 4:13).
  2. Listening to preaching in the Spirit is true worship (Luke 4:32).
  3. Praying in the Spirit is true worship (Eph. 6:18).
  4. We worship by our lives, twenty-four hours a day. See the chapter 'Lifestyle Worship' in *Worshipping God*.
  5. We are praising God when we thank him (Phil. 4:6).
  6. *Praise therefore may be done without singing.*
    a. Some cannot sing very well anyway; they do well to make a 'joyful noise'.
    b. But any act or attempt at praising God is pleasing to him.
    c. Merely raising your hands to God is pleasing to him. The Hebrew word for praise comes from a root word that means 'to lift up the hands'!

B. The chief thing about praise in private worship is that it is often a sacrifice.
'Through Jesus, therefore, let us continually offer to God a sacrifice of praise – the fruit of lips that confess his name' (Heb. 13:15).
  1. This of course can be true in public worship.
  2. *It is called 'sacrifice' because it isn't always easy; you must make an effort.*

     a. You sacrifice time.

     b. You sacrifice feelings – praising God when you don't feel like it.

     c. You sacrifice even asking God for things; you discipline yourself to do nothing bur praise him.

        (1) Read the Psalms.

        (2) Read from the hymnal or modern chorus books.

  3. *In this matter there are two kinds of worship.*

     a. Spontaneous praise – when God is pleasing us.

        (1) This is when it takes no effort – it just wells up from within (John 7:38).

        (2) Either you slept well, received good news – or the Lord just came down!

     b. Sacrificial praise – when we please God!

        (1) We don't feel like praising God; we do it anyway; God likes that. 'Though he slay me, yet will I hope in him' (Job 13:15).

        (2) We literally force ourselves to praise him, whether we are tired, ill, have received bad news.

     c. I truly believe that when we praise God as a sacrifice:

        (1) The angels are watching carefully; our praise then truly magnifies the Lord.

        (2) God is most pleased with us. Remember this if you forget all the above.

C. Recently I was gripped by the idea of being a 'complete worshipper'.

  1. *What is the complete worshipper?*

     a. One who lives to worship God.

     b. One who prefers the worship of God to having all his requests granted.

        (1) God knows what you want.

        (2) Have you asked him, 'What do *you* want?'

CONCLUSION

Worship is the expression of the Christian's relationship with God, not merely the forerunner to the preaching in the church service. It is to the glory of God and the blessing of the worshipper. In both public and private worship it is imperative to focus on God alone. True worship is a sacrifice: of time, feelings and self. Worship includes reading the Word, listening to it preached, and praying as well as praising.

We may have some severe regrets when we stand before God at the Judgement Seat of Christ (2 Cor. 5:10). For example, we will regret the wrong use of time and the wrong use of money. But we will not regret a single moment spent in worship to God when we stand before him at the Judgement Seat. There will be worship in heaven. We can get ready now to do what we will be doing there.

33

JUDGMENT AT THE LORD'S TABLE

INTRODUCTION

A. **This is not the first time we have looked at the Lord's Table. See Understanding Theology, Volume 1, chapter 29.**
1. In that lesson we introduced the subject generally.
2. We looked at various views of the Supper from church history.

B. **Our focus this time is mainly the two verses from Paul:**
1. 'Therefore, whoever eats the bread or drinks the cup of the Lord in an unworthy manner will be guilty of sinning against the body and blood of the Lord' (1 Cor. 11:27).
2. 'For anyone who eats and drinks without recognising the body of the Lord eats and drinks judgment on himself' (1 Cor. 11:29).

C. **This is a forgotten aspect of the Lord's Supper.**
1. *The Lord's Supper (sometimes called the Eucharist from the Greek* eucharisteo *'give thanks') is observed in varying frequency.*
   a. We in Westminster Chapel observe it twice a month.
   b. Some churches do it once a year.
   c. Some churches do it every Sunday (based on Acts 20:7).
   d. Some go to Mass every day.
2. *There is no clear mandate in Scripture how often it should be observed.*
   a. Acts 20:7 ('On the first day of the week we came together to break bread') does not say this was done regularly then or universally.
   b. Jesus simply said, 'Do this in remembrance of me' (Luke 22:19).
   c. Paul said, 'For whenever you eat this bread and drink this cup, you proclaim the Lord's death until he comes' (1 Cor. 11:26).

D. The main thing is not the frequency but the 'manner' in which it is done.

   1. *The word 'manner' (def.: the way a thing is done) is the NIV's understanding of the Greek* anaxios *('unworthily')*

   a. This Greek word is not found anywhere else in the New Testament.

   b. It is apparently not found in ancient Hellenistic literature.

   c. This makes it somewhat difficult to understand or translate.

   2. *But this much is obvious: it is no ordinary supper we are talking about.*

   a. One does not worry about the manner or one's 'worthiness' when it comes to ordinary food and drink.

   b. But the Lord's Supper is different.

   (1) To partake 'unworthily' is most serious.

   (2) The result of doing so may be judgment.

E. Judgment came at the Lord's Table in ancient Corinth.

   1. *Paul listed three melancholy results of their partaking unworthily* (1 Cor. 11:30).

   a. Weakness. Gr. *asthenes* (cf. Acts 4:9; Rom. 5:6; 1 Cor. 9:22).

   (1) Probably this refers to a weakened physical state.

   (2) It could refer to a poor spiritual state.

   b. Sickness. Gr. *arrostes* (cf. Matt. 14:14; Mark 16:18).

   (1) Some kind of illness had broken out in Corinth.

   (2) They would have known exactly what Paul was talking about.

   c. Death. 'A number of you have fallen asleep.'

   (1) This was a euphemism for death (John 11:13).

   (2) It meant a needlessly premature death.

   2. *This is a very serious matter; all because these people partook 'unworthily' at the Lord's Table.*

   a. Apparently they felt nothing at the time.

   b. Paul does not say they were struck immediately while partaking.

   c. It was an eventual result, possibly within a year or so.

   (1) All knew of the weakness, illness and of a number who had died.

   (2) Paul gives the explanation for this: divine judgment.

F. Why is this an important lesson?

1. Many of us take the Lord's Supper for granted; this lesson will remind us of what it is and why it is serious.
2. Many of us worry about the word 'worthy' when it comes to the Lord's Table. After all, who among us is worthy?
3. We will look at the background to what was apparently going on at Corinth, which helps explain what happened and why.
4. We will see the degrees of judgment that unfold in this study.
5. It helps us to appreciate the difference between earthly condemnation and eternal condemnation.

I. THE BACKGROUND IN CORINTH

A. The problem emerged largely because there were snobs in the church, sadly 'Christian snobs'.

1. *Snob (def.): A person who has an exaggerated respect for social position or wealth or for certain attainments or tastes and who despises people whom he or she considers inferior.*
   a. It is one thing for snobs to exist in secular society.
   b. It is unthinkable for this to exist in the church of God.
2. *It did in Corinth.*
   a. The situation was so grave that Paul said their meetings do 'more harm than good' (1 Cor. 11:17).
   b. It is pretty awful when some come to be with God's people and feel worse for doing so.
      (1)Meeting with God's people ought to make people feel uplifted.
      (2)Not here; only a privileged few – the snobs, as it turned out – felt like that.
   c. The snobs ruined the atmosphere and turned the Lord's Supper into something else. 'When you come together, it is not the Lord's Supper you eat' (1 Cor. 11:20).

B. The Lord's Supper in Corinth was apparently carried out in what has since been called *agape* or *koinonia* feasts. Cf. Jude 12.

1. Christians loved each other.
2. *It is not unlike when Christians come together for fellowship but also eat together.*

    a. They ate together.

    b. They ended with what was supposed to be the Lord's Supper.

  3. *There were two meals.*

    a. The common meal: ordinary physical food.

    b. The spiritual meal: bread and wine.

C. This seems to have taken place mid-week and in evenings; probably in the home of a well-to-do Christian: a house church.

  1. Those who were well off brought more food.

  2. *Many were poor and brought little or nothing.*

    a. Some apparently were slaves.

    b. The slaves often arrived later than the others since they could not get away from work till late.

  3. *They would eat each other's food; then they partook of the Lord's Supper.*

    a. The poor, probably the larger group, ate outside in the garden.

    b. The rich had the better food and the best wine.

      (1) The poor were left to themselves.

      (2) They often went away hungry.

    c. It is likely that all the poor received was only the bread and wine.

      (1) Paul says to the well off Christians: if it is only food you are coming for, stay at home.

      (2) Wait for each other before you eat (1 Cor. 11:33).

      (3) Conclusion: 'If anyone is hungry, he should eat at home, so that when you meet together it may not result in judgment' (1 Cor. 11:34).

    d. This helps to explain 1 Corinthians 11:20-22: 'When you come together, it is not the Lord's Supper you eat, for as you eat, each of you goes ahead without waiting for anybody else. One remains hungry, another gets drunk. Don't you have homes to eat and drink in? Or do you despise the church of God and humiliate those who have nothing? What shall I say to you? Shall I praise you for this? Certainly not!'

D. This situation brought God's anger.

  1. *He was highly displeased with this distinction that was made among the people of God.*

  a. The common people heard Jesus gladly.
  b. James said, 'Listen, my dear brothers: Has not God chosen those who are poor in the eyes of the world to be rich in faith and to inherit the kingdom he promised those who love him?' (Jas. 2:5).
2. *God has always been for the underdog and comes to their rescue.*
  a. God noticed, the angels watched, while this practice went on.
  b. The big mistake at Corinth: calling what they did the Lord's Supper.
    (1) Apparently the poor did not even observe the Supper with the rest.
    (2) Such discrimination and contempt for the poor reached God's eyes and ears, not unlike what James described. 'The cries of the harvesters have reached the ears of the Lord Almighty' (Jas. 5:4b).

II. WORTHINESS AND UNWORTHINESS AT THE LORD'S TABLE

A. **The AV 'unworthily' in 1 Corinthians 11:27 has possibly done incalculable damage**: 'Whosoever shall eat this bread, and drink this cup of the Lord unworthily, shall be guilty of the body and blood of the Lord.'
  1. *This translation has possibly had the following results:*
    a. Some avoid the Lord's Supper altogether, since they never feel 'worthy', that is, good enough.
    b. Some who do partake feel self-righteous, that is, 'worthy', since they feel they are good enough.
    c. Some are kept from the Lord's Supper (by pastor and/or elders) as they are judged not worthy enough.
      (1) This has been called 'fencing' the Table, building a fence around it so that only the worthy get inside.
      (2) But Paul said, 'A man ought to examine himself before he eats of the bread and drinks of the cup' (1 Cor. 11:28).
        (a) Others are not to judge whether I can partake of the Supper.
        (b) I am required to judge myself. 'But if we judged ourselves, we would not come under judgment' (1 Cor. 11:31).

2. *The NIV says 'unworthy manner', which helps little more.*
   a. Phillips: 'without proper reverence' comes closer to what Paul is after.
   b. Today's English Version: 'in a way that dishonours him'.
3. *The context shows why God sent judgment.*
   a. The snobs had marginalised the poor and observed the Supper.
   b. Their doing this was partaking in an 'unworthy manner' because:
      (1) They divided the body of Christ.
      (2) They showed no regard for the poor.
      (3) They saw the Supper as part of their 'own' time.
      (4) They showed no proper reverence for the body of Christ (the church) or Christ's person.
      (5) They therefore dishonoured Christ in the way they observed the Supper.

B. This implies moreover that our conduct and character as Christians relates to our being fit to partake of the Supper.
   1. *We are required to affirm the Lord's body.* 'For anyone who eats and drinks without recognising the body of the Lord eats and drinks judgment on himself' (1 Cor. 11:29).
      a. This I believe contains an intentional ambiguity:
         (1) The body of Christ, meaning the church.
         (2) The body of Christ, meaning his person or presence.
      b. To recognise Christ's body in either sense requires that our lives are fit and worthy.
         (1) I therefore must affirm every person at the Table, that is, showing love and respect.
         (2) I therefore must affirm Christ's presence in the Supper, that is, I believe he is there as he promised. 'I tell you, I will not drink of this fruit of the vine from now on until that day when I drink it anew with you in my Father's kingdom' (Matt. 26:29).
   2. *Therefore to do these two things invariably requires that we are right with God:*
      a. We affirm all present.
      b. We recognise our Lord.
   3. *But this is a far cry from the 'worthiness' that some people suppose.*

    a. They fear if they are not perfect, they cannot partake.

    b. Those who do partake, thinking it means being good enough, border on self-righteousness.

C. At the end of the day the worthiness is knowing you are unworthy.

  1. *Paradoxical as it seems, this is true.*

    a. Who deserves heaven?

    b. Who deserves the blood of Christ to cover his or her sins?

  2. *When we affirm Christ's body (recalling the intentional ambiguity above) we feel most unworthy indeed:*

    a. That we are being affirmed by others around us.

    b. That Christ would affirm us – which is exactly what the Supper is doing. 'This cup is the new covenant in my blood, which is poured out for you' (Luke 22:20).

    c. In a word: when you feel unworthy you are worthy.

      (1) The snobs felt worthy.

      (2) The truth was, they were unworthy – unfit – to participate in the Lord's Supper by the way they marginalised certain people.

III. THE JUDGMENT AND HOW TO AVOID IT

A. God was angry and stepped in. 'When we are judged by the Lord, we are being disciplined so that we will not be condemned with the world' (1 Cor. 11:32).

  1. *It was a temporal judgment.*

    a. This means it happens here and now as opposed to eternal condemnation.

    b. Far better that God judges us now than in the manner reserved for the unsaved.

  2. *It was a gracious judgment.* 'Why should any living man complain when punished for his sins?' (Lam. 3:39).

    a. It is not God's ultimate mode of punishment.

    b. To be 'condemned with the world' is to be punished eternally.

      (1) Those who were judged at the Supper were saved people, not lost.

      (2) God only steps in like this when true Christians misbehave; he postpones his wrath for those not saved.

3. It included the ultimate kind of chastening, or disciplining. 'We are being disciplined' (cf. Heb. 12:6): 'Because the Lord disciplines those he loves, and he punishes everyone he accepts as a son.'

    a. There are three kinds of chastening, or disciplining:

      (1)Internal, when God applies the Word to our hearts by the Holy Spirit; the best way to have God deal with you – Plan A!

      (2)External chastening, when God comes from without – e.g. sending the wind and a fish to swallow up as with Jonah; when he gets our attention by illness, financial reverse or something fairly drastic – Plan B.

        (a) This is what happened in Corinth.

        (b) 'That is why many among you are weak and sick' (1 Cor. 11:30).

      (3)Terminal chastening, when God says, 'Your time is up.'

        (a) John calls it the sin that leads to death (1 John 5:16).

        (b) It is what happened to Ananias and Sapphira (Acts 5:1-11).

        (c) At Corinth: 'fallen asleep' (1 Cor. 11:30).

B. Avoiding this judgment; which is done in two ways:

    1. *Examining ourselves.* 'A man ought to examine himself before he eats of the bread and drinks of the cup' (1 Cor. 11:28).

      a. Making sure we affirm those around us who partake at the Lord's Table.

      (1)No one is isolated.

      (2)All are affirmed by us.

      b. Making sure we recognise (AV: discern) the Lord's body; both the church and Christ's own presence: 'For anyone who eats and drinks without recognising the body of the Lord eats and drinks judgment on himself' (1 Cor. 11:29).

      (1)We must be prayerful, worshipful and conscious of the reason we are observing the Lord's Supper in the first place. 'For whenever you eat this bread and drink this cup, you proclaim the Lord's death until he comes' (1 Cor. 11:26).

      (2)We will be conscious of the Lord's presence – for he promised to be there, knowing he is the honoured guest.

2. *Judging ourselves.* 'But if we judged ourselves, we would not come under judgment' (1 Cor. 11:31).

   a. This prevents the need for the Lord to do it.

      (1) If we don't do it, he will.

      (2) This ought to sober us.

   b. Judging ourselves consists of three things:

      (1) That our trust is not in ourselves but in Christ's blood.

      (2) That we have put things right with those around us.

      (3) That we confess any known sin which the Holy Spirit brings to our attention (1 John 1:7-9).

CONCLUSION

There is no Scriptural teaching on how often the Lord's Supper is to be observed but there is about conduct at the ordinance. The teaching given was in response to problems in the Corinthian church but it also applies to the church today. Communion should not be taken lightly, thoughtlessly and without due preparation.

Scripture warns of judgment for any who take the Lord's Supper unworthily. Our worthiness is based on the worthiness of Christ. Only those whose knowledge of their own unworthiness has led them to seek refuge in Christ's worthiness can come to the Table expecting blessing rather than judgment. We need to examine ourselves before partaking of the Lord's Supper every time we take it, confessing our sins to God and ensuring we are right with our fellow men and women.

It does not follow that partaking of the Supper has to be a quiet, grave, stilted and sombre meeting. There is every reason to rejoice. After all, it is a celebration! All should be grateful and happy. The joy of the Lord should be manifest.

34

FELLOWSHIP

A. This subject is one of the most thrilling but also one of the most threatening we have dealt with.

  1. Thrilling: the possibility of fellowship with God and one another is what makes life worth living.

  2. *Threatening: the fear of intimacy.*

  a. Some fear intimacy with God.

  b. Some fear openness and being vulnerable with people.

B. This subject necessarily is in two parts:

  1. Vertical relationship: fellowship with God.

  2. Horizontal relationship: fellowship with one another.

C. Fellowship (def.): a reciprocal relationship of trust.

  1. *Objectively, there must be two or more parties involved.*

  a. One does not have true fellowship with himself alone.

  b. It involves at least one other person.

  2. *Subjectively, there must be a feeling of trust.*

  a. If there is no mutual trust, there is no fellowship.

  b. Fellowship must be felt both ways.

  3. *Note: fellowship is more than friendship.*

  a. The Oxford dictionary defines fellowship as a 'friendly association with others, companionship.' Or 'a number of people associated together, a society, membership of this.'

  b. But true fellowship is more than that.

  (1) The worldly person may have a friendly association with others.

  (2) The Communist Party will refer to its members as 'comrades' (def.: a companion who shares others' activities).

4. *Fellowship means trust that is felt by one another.*

    a. Greek, *koinonia*: 'communion' or 'sharing in'; the root *koine* means 'common'.

        (1) It is used twenty times in the New Testament.

        (2) *Koinoneo* (verb) means 'distributing' or 'sharing'; used eight times.

        (3) *Koinonos* (noun) means 'partaker' or 'one who shares in'; used ten times.

    b. Greek, *metochos*: 'partaking' or 'sharing in'; used six times (five times in Hebrews).

    c. Greek, *meteko* (verb): 'to share or partake'; used eight times.

5. *It will be seen that true fellowship is knowable only by a right relationship with God and therefore with one another.*

    a. This is begun by Atonement (Rom. 3:26; 2 Cor. 5:17-19).

    b. It is fulfilled by walking in the light (1 John 1:7).

D. Why is this study important?

1. *It focuses primarily on God.*

    a. What we *feel* may well be the result.

    b. But the cause is a right relationship with God.

2. It has ecclesiological implications, showing our role with the *ecclesia* – the 'called out', or people of God.

3. It shows our responsibility to God, the church and one another.

4. It highlights the distinction between the converted and those outside the faith (Cf. Acts 5:13).

5. It has special reference to the Lord's Supper.

I. THE VERTICAL RELATIONSHIP: FELLOWSHIP WITH GOD

A. The Old Testament

1. *Before the Fall there was unbroken fellowship with God, although it carried with it a grave responsibility.* 'The LORD God took the man and put him in the Garden of Eden to work it and take care of it. And the LORD God commanded the man, "You are free to eat from any tree in the garden; but you must not eat from the tree of the knowledge of good and evil, for when you eat of it you will surely die"' (Gen. 2:15-17).

    a. One can only imagine or speculate what this was like.

        (1) It is difficult to imagine what fellowship with God was like without any sin.

(2) The blood of Christ of course puts us back into a right
relationship; but we are still sinful creatures and must
live by faith.

b. A hint of what it was like is in the conversation between
Adam and God after the Fall – and the behaviour of Adam
and Eve.

(1) As soon as they sinned: 'Then the eyes of both of them
were opened, and they realised that they were naked; so
they sewed fig leaves together and made coverings for
themselves' (Gen. 3:7).

(2) 'Then the man and his wife heard the sound of the LORD
God as he was walking in the garden in the cool of the
day, and they hid from the LORD God among the trees of
the garden. But the LORD God called to the man, "Where
are you?"' (Gen. 3:8-9).

c. Things were never the same again.

(1) Then came the self-justification of both Adam and Eve
(Gen. 3:10-13).

(2) Then came God's curse but also the promise of
redemption (Gen. 3:14-19).

d. The first demonstration of redemption (besides the first
promise – Gen. 3:15) was in the Garden of Eden. 'The LORD
God made garments of skin for Adam and his wife and
clothed them' (Gen. 3:21).

(1) This involved the shedding of blood and the clothes of
righteousness, symbolising what Christ's death does for
us.

(2) This also shows God's love and care for a fallen people
and his desire for continued fellowship.

2. *After the Fall God began reaching out to men for fellowship.*

a. The basis of fellowship began with the need for a substitute.

(1) Abel brought forth 'fat portions from some of the
firstborn of his flock' (Gen. 4:4).

(2) Cain brought forth some of the 'fruits of the soil' as an
offering to the Lord (Gen. 4:3).

(3) 'The LORD looked with favour on Abel and his offering,
but on Cain and his offering he did not look with favour'
(Gen. 4:4-5).

      (4) This is a clear indication that any fellowship with the true God must begin with a 'go-between' – the sacrifice of blood.

b. There were those in the Old Testament who obviously developed an intimacy with God.

      (1) Enoch 'walked with God' (Gen. 5:24).

      (2) Noah 'walked with God' (Gen. 6:9).

      (3) Abraham became known as 'God's friend' (Jas. 2:23).

      (4) Moses developed such closeness to God that 'the Lord would speak to Moses face to face, as a man speaks with his friend' (Ex. 33:11).

c. Moses gave God's instructions to Israel as to how to know God – through the Law.

      (1) The Moral Law – the Ten Commandments.

      (2) The Civil Law – instructions how the people of God would live peaceably with one another.

      (3) The Ceremonial Law – how to worship God, which included the instructions as to offerings; the most important being on the Day of Atonement when the high priest went behind the curtain to sprinkle blood on the Mercy Seat.

d. David, perhaps like no other, aspired to intimacy with God.

      (1) He yearned for fellowship with God.

          (a) 'In the morning, O Lord, you hear my voice; in the morning I lay my requests before you and wait in expectation' (Ps. 5:3).

          (b) 'How long, O Lord? Will you forget me for ever? How long will you hide your face from me?' (Ps. 13:1).

          (c) 'May the words of my mouth and the meditation of my heart be pleasing in your sight, O Lord, my Rock and my Redeemer' (Ps. 19:14).

          (d) 'One thing I ask of the Lord, this is what I seek: that I may dwell in the house of the Lord all the days of my life, to gaze upon the beauty of the Lord and to seek him in his temple' (Ps. 27:4).

          (e) 'Do not cast me from your presence or take your Holy Spirit from me' (Ps. 51:11).

B. The New Testament

1. *Jesus and the Father*

a. His prayer life

(1) 'Very early in the morning, while it was still dark, Jesus got up, left the house and went off to a solitary place, where he prayed' (Mark 1:35).

(2) 'After he had dismissed them, he went up on a mountainside by himself to pray. When evening came, he was there alone' (Matt. 14:23).

(3) 'One of those days Jesus went out to a mountainside to pray, and spent the night praying to God' (Luke 6:12).

b. His dependence

(1) 'Jesus gave them this answer: "I tell you the truth, the Son can do nothing by himself; he can do only what he sees his Father doing, because whatever the Father does the Son also does' (John 5:19).

(2) 'By myself I can do nothing; I judge only as I hear, and my judgment is just, for I seek not to please myself but him who sent me' (John 5:30).

(3) 'Father, if you are willing, take this cup from me; yet not my will, but yours be done' (Luke 22:42).

2. *The Atonement*

a. Jesus had unbroken fellowship with the Father until the Cross. 'About the ninth hour Jesus cried out in a loud voice, "*Eloi, Eloi, lama sabachthani?*" – which means, "My God, my God, why have you forsaken me?"' (Matt. 27:46).

b. That was the precise moment when our sins were transferred to the Son of God. 'God made him who had no sin to be sin for us, so that in him we might become the righteousness of God' (2 Cor. 5:21).

(1) The curtain of the temple was torn in two from top to bottom (Matt. 27:51).

(2) Jesus has entered the presence of God 'on our behalf', making intimacy with the Father possible (Heb. 6:20).

3. *The apostle Paul*

a. We have been called into 'fellowship with his Son' (1 Cor. 1:9).

b. We may be encouraged by 'fellowship with the Spirit' (Phil. 2:1).

c. We may share in his sufferings (Phil. 3:10).

d. We have 'the fellowship of the Holy Spirit' (2 Cor. 13:14).

4. The apostle Peter. 'You may participate (*koinonos*) in the divine nature and escape the corruption in the world caused by evil desires' (2 Pet. 1:4).

5. The apostle John. 'Our fellowship is with the Father and with his Son, Jesus Christ' (1 John 1:3).

    a. A hard test whether or not we are in this relationship is 1 John 1:6: 'If we claim to have fellowship with him yet walk in the darkness, we lie and do not live by the truth.'

    b. But the remedy is immediately given: 'But if we walk in the light, as he is in the light, we have fellowship with one another, and the blood of Jesus, his Son, purifies us from all sin' (1 John 1:7).

II. THE HORIZONTAL RELATIONSHIP – FELLOWSHIP WITH EACH OTHER

A. The Old Testament

1. *Before the Fall God recognised that fellowship between Adam and God alone was not enough.*

    a. Man was still regarded as being 'alone'. 'The LORD God said, "It is not good for the man to be alone. I will make a helper suitable for him"' (Gen. 2:18).

    b. God therefore instituted marriage and the family.

        (1) He made Eve for Adam (1 Cor. 11:9).

        (2) 'For this reason a man will leave his father and mother and be united to his wife, and they will become one flesh' (Gen. 2:24).

    c. Wider fellowship was envisaged when God had said, 'Be fruitful and increase in number; fill the earth and subdue it' (Gen. 1:28).

    d. Note: This is a fairly strong hint to all of us that the vertical dimension of fellowship alone is not enough.

        (1) Many want fellowship with God 'alone' as it were.

        (2) God himself recognised man's loneliness even with God at hand – *before the Fall!*

        (3) Therefore it must be seen that the concept of fellowship was born in the Garden of Eden – which would embrace both fellowship with God and with one another.

2. *The Fellowship Offering* (Lev. 3; 7:11-21)

    a. The fellowship (or peace) offering was for fellowship with God but with particular reference to fellowship with people.

        (1) The fat of an animal (which the Israelites considered the best portion) was burned on the altar.

        (2) The meat was shared by the worshipper and his family.

    b. The fellowship offering was the horizontal side-effect of the atonement.

        (1) It may be seen as going out and having a party!

        (2) In the ancient system if one was not able (could not afford) to take a lamb he could bring two doves or two pigeons – so that the poor too could participate (cf. Lev. 5:7,11). Note: this factor has implications for the Lord's Supper (see below).

3. Laws pertaining to one's neighbour.

    a. Do not steal, lie or deceive one another (Lev. 19:11).

    b. Do not defraud or rob your neighbours (Lev. 19:13).

    c. Do not curse the deaf or put a stumbling-block in front of the blind (Lev. 19:14).

    d. Do not show partiality or favouritism to the poor or great (Lev. 19:15).

    e. Do not spread slander among the people. (Lev. 19:16).

    f. Do not seek revenge or bear a grudge, but love your neighbour as yourself (Lev. 19:18).

    g. Rise in the presence of the aged, show respect for the elderly (Lev. 19:32).

B. The New Testament

1. *One of the immediate consequences of Pentecostal power on the church was fellowship.* 'They devoted themselves to the apostles' teaching and to the fellowship, to the breaking of bread and to prayer' (Acts 2:42).

    a. According to this it was the second most important thing.

    b. This, then, is the result of the Spirit's power; we must ask, what priority do *we* give to fellowship?

2. *Sometimes fellowship is literally spelled out M–O–N–E–Y.* 'For Macedonia and Achaia were pleased to make a contribution for the poor among the saints in Jerusalem' (Rom. 15:26).

    a. Contribution is the translation of *koinonia*.

b. The expression 'Put your money where your mouth is' comes to mind; true fellowship will touch our wallets when circumstances of the needy call for it.

c. This is seen twice in 2 Corinthians.

   (1) 'They urgently pleaded with us for the privilege of sharing in this service to the saints' (2 Cor. 8:4).

   (2) 'Because of the service by which you have proved yourselves, men will praise God for the obedience that accompanies your confession of the gospel of Christ, and for your generosity in sharing with them and with everyone else' (2 Cor. 9:13).

d. This is the point in Hebrews 13:16.

3. *Fellowship is sometimes affirmed by official acceptance of one another; it is called 'the right hand of fellowship'* (Gal. 2:9).

   a. When Paul and Barnabas felt like 'nobodies' it was a wonderful moment for them to be accepted by the 'pillars of the church'.

   b. This is partly what church membership means.

   (1) The church is affirmed when one asks for membership.

   (2) The person is affirmed when one is accepted for membership.

   (3) This is officially carried out by the 'right hand of fellowship' – shaking hands and doing so not in a perfunctory but heart-felt manner.

4. *All converts become partners with those in the ministry.* 'Because of your partnership in the gospel from the first day until now' (Phil. 1:5).

   a. Not all are called to have public profile in their ministry.

   b. But all share in this ministry and can feel affirmed by knowing that ministers are their partners.

   (1) In business there is sometimes what is called the 'silent partner'.

   (2) In the church every converted person can know that he or she is a silent partner (in terms of public profile) who intercedes and encourages.

5. *Fellowship is even extended to the non-Christian by our very witness to the Christian faith.* 'I pray that you may be active in sharing your faith, so that you will have a full understanding of every good thing we have in Christ' (Phile. 6).

    a. It is done by sharing (*koinonia*) our faith.

    b. Note the unusual fringe benefit to the one who does this!

6. *This fellowship can only be truly enjoyed by finding at least one other person who has already experienced a vertical relationship.* 'We proclaim to you what we have seen and heard, so that you also may have fellowship with us. And our fellowship is with the Father and with his Son, Jesus Christ' (1 John 1:3).

    a. The 'downside' of this is that there is sometimes great loneliness when one has experienced the vertical relationship and cannot find another who has experienced the same thing.

    b. But when one finds those who know this fellowship with the Father the result is wonderful and thrilling.

    c. The 'fellowship' referred to in 1 John 1:7 may be an intentional ambiguity:

        (1) It most certainly means fellowship with the Father: 'with one another'.

        (2) It almost certainly assumes the horizontal relationship as well: 'with one another'.

        (3) The use in Ephesians 3:9 is puzzling where *koinonia* is translated 'administration'; it too may be intentional ambiguity.

7. *The Lord's Supper* (1 Cor. 10 and 11).

    a. Paul speaks of 'participation' (*koinonia*) in the blood of Christ and the body of Christ (1 Cor. 10:16).

        (1) The AV translates this 'communion'.

        (2) This is why we sometimes refer to the partaking of the Lord's Supper as 'eucharist' or 'communion'.

    b. The point is, there is genuine fellowship at the Lord's table.

        (1) One should feast on the bread and wine with faith so that one *feels* the Lord's presence.

        (2) Indeed, he promises to communicate with us at this time.

    c. Paul uses *metecho* interchangeably with *koinonia* translated 'partaking' (1 Cor. 10:17. cf. vv 21,30).

    d. Some Corinthians were ill and weak, some died owing to their abuse of the Lord's table. Why?

        (1) They did not affirm one another (1 Cor. 11:20ff, 33).

        (2) They did not discern the Lord's body (1 Cor. 11:29).

    e. 'The body of the Lord' may be an intentional ambiguity, referring to:

      (1) The person of Jesus.

      (2) The body of Christ, i.e., the church.

    f. The sweetest fellowship of all may well emerge at the time of sharing at the Lord's table.

CONCLUSION

Fellowship is experienced in two directions, upwardly with God and outwardly with fellow Christians. In the beginning God and man had unbroken fellowship. After the Fall and throughout the Old Testament record, individuals lived in fellowship with God. Jesus exemplified a life of fellowship with his Father, a fellowship only broken when Christ, on the cross, became sin for us. Through that act of atonement, Christians once again can enter into fellowship with their Maker.

One of the first effects of Pentecost was that the believers lived in fellowship: they accepted one another, held things in common, and were partners together in the ministry of the gospel. The Lord's Supper is a time of fellowship both with God and with those who are with us at the Table.

Fellowship is the reciprocal relationship of trust. This is what is happening with God and us. It is a covenant relationship. If we walk in darkness we forfeit this fellowship. It is the same between believers. There must be mutual trust, a two-way trust. When one walks in darkness, the fellowship disappears.

When this fellowship is powerful the world outside takes notice and respects it. 'No-one else dared join them, even though they were highly regarded by the people' (Acts 5:13).

35

DOCTRINE VERSUS EXPERIENCE

INTRODUCTION

A. An ancient theological problem has been the tension between doctrine and experience.

  1. *There are those who sincerely believe that the most important thing for the church is the upholding of sound doctrine, or objective truth (defined below).*

    a. By sound doctrine one usually refers to what is cerebral, or intellectual.

    b. This takes its form in things such as:

      (1) Creeds, e.g., the Apostles' Creed.

      (2) Confessions of faith, e.g., the Westminster Confession.

      (3) Catechisms, e.g., The Westminster Catechism.

    c. It is argued that if we lose our grasp of solid teaching the church will become weak, anaemic, woolly and eventually worthless.

  2. *There are those who equally believe that the most important thing for the church is a personal experience with God, what is subjective (defined below).*

    a. Such people would argue that the Word of God, however important, will be eventually worthless unless God himself is communicated, and experienced.

    b. This takes its shape in an emphasis on things such as:

      (1) Prayer and intimacy with God.

      (2) Gifts of the Spirit.

      (3) Seeing signs, wonders and miracles.

    c. It is argued that if we don't know God in our hearts, the church will become lifeless, dry, irrelevant and useless: 'Perfectly orthodox, perfectly useless.'

B. This problem is somewhat heightened by non-theological ingredients.

   1. *Culture or background*

      a. Our culture is often inherited.

      b. Those brought up in a church that has been largely 'confessional' tend to assume this is the most important thing. E.g.,

         (1) Presbyterians tend to emphasise doctrine.

         (2) Calvinists tend to emphasise doctrine.

      c. Those brought up in a church that has been raised up out of real experience with God assume this is surely the most important thing. E.g.:

         (1) Pentecostals and those in the Holiness Movement tend to emphasise experience.

         (2) Charismatics tend to emphasise experience.

      d. Somewhere in between are those who, despite a history of being confessional, aren't the slightest bit bothered by this sort of thing. E.g.:

         (1) The Church of England is seldom concerned about their Thirty-nine articles.

         (2) Many 'historic' denominations develop into a 'folk religion'.

   2. *Education and temperament*

      a. Education sometimes plays a part in whether one is more interested in doctrine or experience. E.g.:

         (1) Sometimes the more education someone has, the more interested he or she is in doctrine.

         (2) The less educated someone is sometimes inclines to an emphasis on experience.

         (3) There are of course exceptions to both of the above.

      b. Temperament, a person's nature as it controls the way he or she behaves and feels and thinks, sometimes plays a part in this issue. E.g.:

         (1) The more cerebral or intellectual a person is, the more he or she may tend to think that doctrine is more important.

         (2) The less cerebral or intellectual person may feel that experience is what should be emphasised.

   3. *Note: it should be stated that sound doctrine will automatically combine both confessional and experiential theology.*

  a. And this is absolutely true; our view in this lesson is precisely
  that – if there are not both, it is not sound teaching in the
  first place!
  b. But we must begin with where most people are (sadly), that
  there tends to be a separation.
  c. The purpose of this study is to address the problem and seek
  a biblical balance.
   (1) A silent divorce between these two has sadly taken place.
   (2) We pray for a remarriage, which this lesson hopes to
   shed some light on.

C. Why is this study important?

  1. *We must agree that there has been a silent divorce between the*
  objective and the subjective (defined below), and surely want
  to see the remarriage of the two.
  a. There are 'Word' churches, which stress:
   (1) We must get back to the Scriptures.
   (2) We must contend for the faith 'once delivered to the saints'.
   (3) We must know what we believe.
   (4) We need to know our church history, our theological roots.
   (5) We must emphasise those doctrines our fathers fought for:
    (a) The deity of Christ.
    (b) Justification by faith.
    (c) The sovereignty of God.
  b. There are 'Spirit' churches, which cry out:
   (1) We must have a personal experience with the Holy Spirit.
   (2) We must feel things in our hearts.
   (3) We must not be content with a Christianity that is devoid
   of the lively witness of the Holy Spirit.
   (4) We must recognise those high water marks of the church
   when God came down in power.
   (5) We must emphasise what was characteristic of the
   church when God came down:
    (a) Extraordinary conversions.
    (b) Intimacy with God.
    (c) Intercessory prayer.
    (d) Seeing God do things.
  2. *We need to call a spade a spade and admit that there is this*
  cleavage in the church today.

    a. The problem often is this:
        (1) Those who stress doctrine will claim they have all the experience that is needed.
        (2) Those who stress experience assume they already have sufficient teaching.
    b. Until it is granted there is a problem here, the impasse (deadlock) will probably stay where it is.
  3. *Were we to have the two together, the following would almost certainly be true:*
    a. We would have a biblical Christianity.
    b. We would be seeing far more conversions.
    c. The simultaneous combination would mean spontaneous combustion.
    d. In a word: Revival would be here.

D. Definitions:

  1. *Objective: what it true, whether we feel it or not.*
    a. It is what has real existence outside a person's mind.
        (1) Jesus is the eternal Son of God, whether we feel it or not.
        (2) The Holy Spirit is real, whether we feel him or not.
    b. It refers to what is true, regardless of our feelings or personal interest. Joni Eareckson Tada: 'I am a Christian not because of what Christianity does for me but because it is true.'
  2. *Subjective: what we feel, whether it is based on objective reality or not.*
    a. It is what exists in a person's mind and not necessarily produced by things outside it.
        (1) 'I feel the presence of God,' may be because of the immediate power of the Spirit; it may also be what one feels because of being in a good mood!
        (2) 'I feel led to worship the Virgin Mary,' may be a real feeling but it goes contrary to Scripture; therefore it has no objective basis in reality.
    b. It refers to what you think is true, what you feel is true, what you believe is true – even if it is not true. It is often said, 'If there were no heaven or hell, I would still be a Christian.'
        (1) I know what people mean by that.
        (2) But Paul cold not say that for a moment! 'If only for this life we have hope in Christ, we are to be pitied more than all men' (1 Cor. 15:19).

    c. If the Spirit is objectively present in a believer:

        (1) He or she may not necessarily feel this. Moses was 'not aware his face was radiant' (Ex. 34:29).

        (2) One may at times subjectively feel the Spirit's objective power. 'We are witnesses of these things, and so is the Holy Spirit, whom God has given to those who obey him' (Acts 5:32).

  3. Doctrine: objective teaching of Scripture.

  4. Experience: subjective feeling of the Spirit.

I. THE BIBLICAL IDEAL

A. Book of Acts

  1. *The coming of the Holy Spirit at Pentecost* (Acts 2:1-13).

    a. The objective presence of the Spirit.

        (1) The sound of a blowing, violent wind.

        (2) The Spirit filled the house.

        (3) They saw what seemed to be tongues of fire that separated and came to rest on each of them.

    b. The subjective experience of the Spirit.

        (1) They were filled with the Holy Spirit.

        (2) They spoke in other languages as they were enabled to do this.

        (3) Their behaviour led to the charge, 'They have had too much wine.'

  2. *The objective truth that lay behind Pentecost.*

    a. Certain things were already true about Jesus Christ.

        (1) Jesus had died on the Cross.

        (2) He rose bodily from the dead.

        (3) He appeared to the disciples, once up to five hundred, during the forty days after he rose.

        (4) He ascended to heaven.

    b. The objective Spirit entered the 120 who had tarried for ten days.

        (1) They felt his presence.

        (2) They also knew why Jesus died and where he was.

        (3) Jesus was as real to them at the level of the Spirit as he had been at the natural level (John 16:16).

        (4) Though in heaven, Jesus was so real that Peter quoted

Psalm 16:8 to support his experience: 'I have set the
LORD always before me. Because he is at my right hand,
I shall not be shaken.'

3. *Peter's preaching*
  a. Objectively he preached to describe what was true: Jesus
  was alive.
    (1) He quoted three passages: Joel 2:28-32, Psalm 16:8-11,
    Psalm 110:1.
    (2) He did this with the same power that had enabled the
    120 to speak in tongues! Acts 2:4 'enabled' and Acts
    2:14 'addressed' are the same word in the Greek.
  b. The subjective response was spontaneous:
    (1) 'When the people heard this, they were cut to the heart
    and said to Peter and the other apostles, "Brothers, what
    shall we do?"' (Acts 2:37).
    (2) 'Those who accepted his message were baptised, and
    about three thousand were added to their number that
    day' (Acts 2:41).

4. *Peter's defence later on:*
  a. 'We are witnesses of these things, and so is the Holy Spirit,
  whom God has given to those who obey him' (Acts 5:32).
  b. It is at this stage one can see how a separation between
  doctrine and experience could emerge.
    (1) Peter could never forget what he knew was objectively
    true – 'We are witnesses of these things.'
    (2) But would one always have the current immediate
    witness of the Spirit whereby he could also say: 'And
    so also is the Holy Spirit'?
  c. Church history and experience have shown that there can be
  a diminishing of power. E.g.:
    (1) When the Welsh Revival was over, it was over.
    (2) But one could never forget what it was like when the
    Spirit was present at the full tide of the Revival in late
    1904 and early 1905!

5. The balance was seen immediately after Pentecost. 'They
devoted themselves to the apostles' teaching and to the
fellowship, to the breaking of bread and to prayer' (Acts 2:42).

B. Paul's teaching and experience

1. *'My message and my preaching were not with wise and persuasive words, but with a demonstration of the Spirit's power'* (1 Cor. 2:4).

   a. This was the way it was with Paul.

   b. But by saying it as he did he showed the possibility of preaching with wise and persuasive words but without the Spirit.

2. *'Because our gospel came to you not simply with words, but also with power, with the Holy Spirit and with deep conviction. You know how we lived among you for your sake'* (1 Thess. 1:5).

   a. When he said that his gospel came not 'in word only' (AV), he implied the possibility that it might have.

   b. It was fortunately not that way with Paul (at least then), but how many of us who are preachers today have to admit (I am one of them) to preaching largely in word only?

3. *The objective and subjective are seen in Paul's farewell address to the Ephesians.*

   a. Subjective: 'I served the Lord with great humility and with tears' (Acts 20:19a).

   b. Objective: 'For I have not hesitated to proclaim to you the whole will of God' (Acts 20:27).

II. THE DIFFERENCE BETWEEN OBJECTIVE DOCTRINE AND SUBJECTIVE EXPERIENCE

A. Objective doctrine remains unchanging

1. *The truth about the Triune God*

   a. The Father's attributes remain the same. 'I the LORD do not change' (Mal. 3:6).

   (1) His omnipotence, omnipresence, omniscience.

   (2) His holiness and sovereignty.

   b. The Son's personhood. 'Jesus Christ is the same yesterday and today and for ever' (Heb. 13:8).

   (1) He is the eternal God-man.

   (2) He looks the same as he did when he was here (cf. John 20:27; Acts 1:11).

   c. The Holy Spirit is eternal (Heb. 9:14).

   (1) His deity is equal to that of the Father and the Son.

   (2) His personality remains the same.

2. *The truth about salvation*

    a. What God did for us in Christ was prefect and complete.

        (1) Christ's work on the cross was a finished work (John 19:30).

        (2) The resurrection of Christ vindicated the Father's plan (Acts 2:22-36).

    b. What faith achieves is final.

        (1) Our sins are forgiven (Rom. 3:25-26).

        (2) Christ's righteousness is imputed to us (Rom. 9:1-12).

    c. The Holy Spirit comes to dwell in the believer.

        (1) His abode is permanent. (John 14:16-17).

        (2) The Spirit seals our eternal redemption (Eph. 4:30).

3. *The gifts and calling of God.*

    a. They are sovereignly given (1 Cor. 12:11).

    b. They are irrevocable (Rom. 11:29. cf. 1 Sam. 19:23).

B. Our subjective experience can change

1. *Our doctrine may need correcting.*

    a. This is what happened to the Galatians (Gal. 3:3).

    b. Poor teaching is usually the reason for this (Gal. 3:1).

2. *We may remain immature.*

    a. The Corinthians were still carnal, worldly (1 Cor. 3:3).

    b. The Hebrew Christians needed someone to teach them! (Heb. 5:12).

3. We may cease walking in the light (1 John 1:7).

4. We may allow bitterness to creep in (Eph. 4:30-32).

    a. The result: the Holy Spirit is grieved.

    b. This means we lose clear thinking, presence of mind.

        (1) Such people cease to hear God.

        (2) Such people often lose assurance that they are saved.

        (3) In a word: they fall from experiencing God's grace.

    c. This sort of thing happened in the Book of Acts.

        (1) Ananias and Sapphira obviously lost something; they lied to the Holy Spirit (Acts 5:1-11).

        (2) Either Paul or Barnabas (or both) was wrong; when they abruptly parted company (Acts 15:39).

        (3) Paul retorted to the high priest, 'God will strike you, you whitewashed wall!' (Acts 23:3). (It was not Paul's finest hour.)

C. There is a danger of emphasising either doctrine or experience, to the neglect of the other.

    1. *Those who do this often do not realise that they are doing it.*

        a. Those who emphasise doctrine are convinced this is right.

            (1) They feel that the truth matters most.

            (2) They often have no sensitivity to the person of the Holy Spirit.

        b. Those who emphasise experience are convinced they are right.

            (1) They feel that experiencing God matters most.

            (2) They often have little grasp of sound doctrine.

    2. *We can concentrate on one aspect of biblical teaching and lose the other.*

        a. We can focus on objective truth and forget about such things as:

            (1) Intercessory prayer, communion and intimacy with God.

            (2) Witnessing to the lost, a burden for souls.

            (3) Grieving the Spirit; quenching the Spirit.

            (4) Openness to the person of the Spirit.

        b. We can focus on experience and forget:

            (1) The importance of sound Christology.

            (2) The imputed righteousness of Christ.

            (3) Our eternal standing in Christ.

            (4) The sovereignty of God.

    3. The result: we see in Scripture only what we are familiar with!

        a. Some see only the sovereignty of God when they read the book of Acts, concentrating on, e.g.:

            (1) 'This man was handed over to you by God's set purpose and foreknowledge; and you, with the help of wicked men, put him to death by nailing him to the cross' (Acts 2:23).

            (2) 'When the Gentiles heard this, they were glad and honoured the word of the Lord; and all who were appointed for eternal life believed' (Acts 13:48).

        b. Some see only the power of the Spirit, e.g.:

            (1) 'Taking him by the right hand, he helped him up, and instantly the man's feet and ankles became strong. He jumped to his feet and began to walk. Then he went with them into the temple courts, walking and leaping, and praising God. When all the people saw him walking and praising God, they recognised him as the same man who used to sit begging at the temple gate called Beautiful, and they were filled with wonder and amazement at what had happened to him' (Acts 3:7-11).

(2)'As a result, people brought the sick into the streets and laid them on beds and mats so that at least Peter's shadow might fall on some of them as he passed by. Crowds gathered also from the towns around Jerusalem, bringing their sick and those tormented by evil spirits, and all of them were healed' (Acts 5:15-16).

CONCLUSION

The chief way we grieve the Holy Spirit is by bitterness (Eph. 4:30-32). We may, generally speaking, hang on to sound objective doctrine at the intellectual level, but subjectively the Holy Spirit can be grieved, the result being loss of intimacy with God and presence of mind (clear thinking).

Some Christians believe that sound doctrine is paramount and others that personal experience is of greatest importance. Doctrine without experience is sterile and experience not based on sound doctrine leads to error. We should learn to recognise in which direction we lean and work to maintain a balance. And we must ensure that such differences are not allowed to fragment our congregations.

I do not know when exactly the silent divorce between the Word and the Spirit took place. It has no doubt happened many times in church history. Yet it did not seem to take place in the Book of Acts, despite obvious weaknesses in some, so it must have happened later. It was present in the churches, judging by the epistles, although it did not happen at the highest levels of leadership.

Today there is an obvious separation between the emphasis on the Word and emphasis on the Spirit. I am not arguing which 'side' is more wrong or more right, I am only calling the need to our attention. I long for the day when we have sound doctrine and experience of the Spirit in equal measure:

36

THE DIVINE TEASE

INTRODUCTION

A. For a number of years a recurring theme has surfaced in my own theological development which I want to explain.

1. *There may well be a better way to express it.*

2. *I have been calling it the 'divine tease'.*

    a. To tease (def.): to try to provoke in a playful or unkind way by jokes or questions or petty annoyances.

    b. This definition (Oxford dictionary) however does not fully capture the meaning I have in mind.

        (1) The divine tease is not designed to make us laugh, or to make us the butt of a joke.

        (2) It is not unkind and yet it is a no joking matter.

    c. It is God's veiled way of revealing his mind:

        (1) It is sometimes appearing to do the opposite of what he intends or wants.

        (2) It is done in order to discover exactly what our true motives and feelings are.

    d. It is one of God's ways of uncovering our purest motives.

        (1) He appears to mean the opposite of what he really feels.

        (2) Its purpose: to reveal what we really feel.

    e. 'God offends the mind to reveal the heart' (Paul Cain).

3. *Here are two examples:*

    a. 'When evening came, the boat was in the middle of the lake, and he was alone on land. He saw the disciples straining at the oars, because the wind was against them. About the fourth watch of the night he went out to them, walking on the lake. He was about to pass by them, but when they saw him walking on the lake, they thought he was a ghost. They cried out' (Mark 6:47-49).

        (1) It appeared that Jesus was not going to help them, that he did not even notice them!

(2) And yet he was obviously there for them – and no other reason.

(3) He did not speak, or get into the boat with them, until they cried out.

    (a) He was teasing them.

    (b) But he wasn't joking!

  b. 'As they approached the village to which they were going, Jesus acted as if he were going further. But they urged him strongly, "Stay with us, for it is nearly evening; the day is almost over." So he went in to stay with them' (Luke 24:28-29).

    (1) At that stage the two people on the road to Emmaus did not know it was Jesus.

    (2) And yet it was his explicit purpose to stay with them a while longer.

      (a) He was teasing them.

      (b) It was a test to see if they wanted more information about himself!

B. The divine tease (def.): God's set-up test by which he sometimes disguises his presence and purpose at first in order to reveal our real feelings.

1. *It is a divine set-up.*

  a. Jesus set up both of the above events.

    (1) He who controls all storms did not turn up until the fourth watch of the night – and still waited before he came to their rescue; they later realised he was at the bottom of it all!

    (2) He turned up on the road to Emmaus, 'but they were kept from recognising him' (Luke 24:16) until 'their eyes were opened and they recognised him, and he disappeared from their sight' (Luke 24:31); the whole thing was God's set-up.

  b. God has a way of setting us up!

    (1) Spy organisations like MI5 or the CIA are past masters at setting people up to get caught; they put people in vulnerable positions.

    (2) God does this so that our real motives and feelings can be found out.

   c. It is always a test to reveal what we are.

      (1) He is not learning anything new about us of course.

      (2) It is to let us see for ourselves – sometimes to let others see – what we really are.

2. *God disguises his presence and purpose.*

   a. His presence.

      (1) When Jesus walked on the sea his disciples thought he was a ghost (Mark 6:49).

      (2) Jesus himself walked with the two people on the road to Emmaus but 'they were kept from recognising him' (Luke 24:16).

   b. His purpose.

      (1) His purpose was to wait until the appointed time to unveil himself.

      (2) His purpose was also to see what their reaction would be:

         (a) If they would be 'willing to take him into the boat,' which they did (John 6:21).

         (b) If they would urge him 'to stay with them' (Luke 24:29).

3. *At first:*

   a. The point of the divine tease is to withhold the Lord's presence and purpose at first.

      (1) Had the disciples – either at sea or on the road to Emmaus – immediately recognised Jesus there would be no testing.

      (2) The essential purpose of the divine tease is to test us.

   b. Therefore at first there is no hint that:

      (1) It is really the Lord.

      (2) God is up to something.

4. *In order to show our real feelings.*

   a. In the words of the old spiritual:

> 'He knows what you do, he hears what you say;
> My Lord is writing all the time.'

      (1) The Lord watched the disciples 'straining at the oars' (Mark 6:48).

      (2) He listened to the two people as they lamented the events over the previous days (Luke 24:19ff).

    b. The real feelings of the disciples became evident in the end:

        (1) They became willing to receive Jesus into the boat and begged him to stay.

        (2) It emerged that their hearts were yearning to confess what was true about him:

           (a) 'Truly you are the Son of God' (Matt. 14:33).

           (b) 'They asked each other, "Were not our hearts burning within us while he talked with us on the road and opened the Scriptures to us?"' (Luke 24:32).

5. *In a word: the disciples passed the test in the aforementioned accounts.*

    a. They did not know how they were being tested at first.

    b. The divine tease is always a disguised test.

C. Why is this an important lesson?

1. *The Bible is full of illustrations of the divine tease.*

    a. The two aforementioned examples are perhaps more obvious.

    b. Once we grasp the nature of the divine tease we will see how much a part of God's nature is to test us in this manner.

2. *We must develop a sensitivity to the divine tease.*

    a. We must hope and pray to recognise it for what it is as soon as possible.

    b. 'They have not known my ways,' said God of Israel (Heb. 3:10); we must learn to know this aspect of God's ways.

3. We are all being tested in this manner from time to time, more often than we may have realised!

4. The divine tease is a most sobering matter; to fail the test is to be most impoverished.

5. *Spirituality can be defined partly by how long it takes to recognise the divine tease – not to mention whether we 'pass'!*

    a. Simon Peter soon realised that it was none other than Jesus himself who had told the disciples to throw their nets on the other side of the boat (John 21:6-7).

    b. He realised they had been graciously set up to be told, 'Feed my lambs' (John 21:15).

I. The divine tease is designed to let those 'off the hook' whose hearts are not right anyway

A. **It is not that they are set free from the responsibility of their own unbelief.**
   1. Not at all; that unbelief will later come to haunt them.
   2. But God gives immediate 'relief' to some.
      a. They are those whose minds are already made up.
      b. They are just looking for an excuse, 'waiting to catch him in something he might say' (Luke 11:54).

B. **Examples of being let 'off the hook' for a while:**
   1. *Israel in the desert.*
      a. All but two of the spies returned from Canaan with their minds made up.
         (1) 'And they spread among the Israelites a bad report about the land they had explored. They said, "The land we explored devours those living in it. All the people we saw there are of great size. We saw the Nephilim there (the descendants of Anak come from the Nephilim). We seemed like grasshoppers in our own eyes, and we looked the same to them"' (Num. 13:32-33).
         (2) Caleb and Joshua thought otherwise. 'Then Caleb silenced the people before Moses and said, "We should go up and take possession of the land, for we can certainly do it"' (Num. 13:30).
      b. The majority ruled; Israel failed the test.
         (1) 'So I declared on oath in my anger, "They shall never enter my rest"' (Heb 3:11).
         (2) 'And to whom did God swear that they would never enter his rest if not to those who disobeyed? So we see that they were not able to enter, because of their unbelief' (Heb. 3:18-19).
      c. It was a set-up.
         (1) God knew what was in their hearts.
         (2) Their unbelief and cowardice were unveiled.
      d. They were off the hook – they need not press on.
         (1) Indeed, they could not after then even if they tried!
         (2) They did try afterwards, and failed (Num. 14:39-45).

2. *Those who hated Jesus' words.*

   a. When Jesus said, 'I am the bread that came down from heaven,' the Jews were enraged.

   b. They needed an excuse not to believe such language and found it: 'They said, "Is this not Jesus, the son of Joseph, whose father and mother we know? How can he now say, 'I came down from heaven'?"' (John 6:42). This was a thinly veiled reference to Jesus' having been the illegitimate child of Joseph and Mary.

   c. They knew this all along, but didn't seem to mind as long as he fed the people miraculously with loaves and fish (John 6:10-13). They even wanted to make him king! (John 6:14-15). But Jesus knew what was in man (John 2:24-25).

   d. They hated the message not the miracles.

      (1) They wanted off the hook.

      (2) God set them up and let them off the hook. 'From this time many of his disciples turned back and no longer followed him' (John 6:66).

C. When God lets people off the hook they may carry on as though nothing happened.

  1. They feel absolutely right in their decision – at first.

  2. *Sooner or later they realise their folly.*

   a. With the Children of Israel they realised it sooner.

   b. With the nation of Israel it was a case of being blind – to this day, generally speaking.

  3. Note: Can you think of a modern example of how people get themselves off the hook by their dismissing the current move of the Spirit?

II. THE DIVINE TEASE IS DESIGNED TO CONFIRM THE FAITH OF THOSE WHO STAND THE TEST AGAINST THE ODDS

A. Jesus being like 'a root out of dry ground' was the divine set-up.

  1. *Israel had preconceived ideas – based on layers of tradition not Scripture – what Messiah would look like.*

   a. Any leading Pharisee or scribe would say, 'If Messiah turns up, I'll know him.'

   b. God said, 'Really?'

2. *Isaiah had that sinking feeling that the people of Israel would not be prepared for their Messiah.*
   a. 'Who has believed our message and to whom has the arm of the LORD been revealed?' (Isa. 53:1).
   b. Isaiah even saw how Israel would rationalise their rejection of Messiah:
      (1) 'We considered him stricken by God, smitten by him, and afflicted' (Isa. 53:4).
      (2) Indeed, when he appeared, 'All the people answered, "Let his blood be on us and on our children!"' (Matt. 27:25).

3. *Israel failed the test.*
   a. 'O Jerusalem, Jerusalem, you who kill the prophets and stone those sent to you, how often I have longed to gather your children together, as a hen gathers her chicks under her wings, but you were not willing' (Matt. 23:37).
   b. 'As he approached Jerusalem and saw the city, he wept over it and said, "If you, even you, had only known on this day what would bring you peace – but now it is hidden from your eyes. . . . Because you did not recognise the time of God's coming to you"' (Luke 19:41-42, 44).

B. The disciples – except for Judas Iscariot – passed.

1. After the hard sayings of Jesus (John 6:25-60), most of the people 'turned back and no longer followed him' – following the 'odds' that he was not worth following.

2. *Jesus then turned to the Twelve, '"You do not want to leave too, do you?" Jesus asked the Twelve'* (John 6:67).
   a. 'Simon Peter answered him, "Lord, to whom shall we go? You have the words of eternal life. We believe and know that you are the Holy One of God"' (John 6:68-69).
   b. The hard sayings of Jesus were a divine set-up.
      (1) The Twelve (save Judas) passed.
      (2) Most did not.

C. The life and times of Jesus are full of disguised testings. Note: testings.

1. *Mary and Martha*
   a. Jesus allowed Martha to feel fully justified in her indignation that she did the hard work while Mary sat at his feet.

(1) 'But Martha was distracted by all the preparations that had to be made. She came to him and asked, "Lord, don't you care that my sister has left me to do the work by myself? Tell her to help me!"' (Luke 10:40).

(2) Many of us feel justified in our being so busy regarding legitimate things – never having time to spend much time alone with the Lord.

b. But Jesus affirmed Mary.

(1) '"Martha, Martha," the Lord answered, "you are worried and upset about many things, but only one thing is needed. Mary has chosen what is better, and it will not be taken away from her"' (Luke 10:41-42).

(2) That encourages one not to feel guilty over spending a lot of time alone with the Lord.

2. *Surprise at the Judgement*

a. Those who are affirmed are surprised. 'Then the righteous will answer him, "Lord, when did we see you hungry and feed you, or thirsty and give you something to drink? When did we see you a stranger and invite you in, or needing clothes and clothe you? When did we see you sick or in prison and go to visit you?" The King will reply, "I tell you the truth, whatever you did for one of the least of these brothers of mine, you did for me"' (Matt. 25:37-40).

b. Those who are rejected gave the exact same rationale for not recognising Jesus when they saw the stranger (Matt. 25:41-46).

c. The poor, the stranger, the unemployed, the one rejected because of colour, culture, job, education or status – all are a part of the divine tease.

(1) 'Religion that God our Father accepts as pure and faultless is this: to look after orphans and widows in their distress and to keep oneself from being polluted by the world' (Jas. 1:27).

III. THE DIVINE TEASE IS MIRRORED IN THOSE WE COULD SO EASILY DISMISS AS BEING UNAUTHENTIC FOR OUR TASTES

A. Paul's enemies seized on the fact that he worked with his hands to support himself (Acts 18:3. cf. 1 Cor. 11:7-8).

   1. *No free Roman citizen would dare do manual labour.*
   2. *Philosophers and orators worth their salt commanded large fees.*
      a. Paul waived his rights to be paid by the Corinthians (2 Cor. 9:12-15).
      b. Sophisticated Greeks would see Paul as a nobody – not unlike that root out of dry ground! (cf. Luke 9:58).
      c. We too must be careful not to dismiss God's sovereign vessel because he doesn't suit our tastes!

B. The angel unawares, as the AV puts it.
   1. 'Do not forget to entertain strangers, for by so doing some people have entertained angels without knowing it' (Heb. 13:2. cf. Gen. 18:1ff; Judg. 13:3ff).
   2. The person near you may be a set-up by God to get your reaction to God's own enterprise.

C. Simon Peter's prejudices were smashed by his strange vision and consequent witnessing of God's power (Acts 10).
   1. He argued with the Lord (Acts 10:14).
   2. But he obeyed the Spirit and saw God's new movement of the Spirit to the Gentiles (Acts 10:19-22, 34ff).

CONCLUSION

The list is endless as to how we are being set up by God, to let us see what we are like. One example, had Joseph succumbed to the sexual temptation offered him (Gen. 39), he would never have become Prime Minister of Egypt. Another example: God suggested to Moses that his rebellious people be destroyed – and that he start all over with Moses. Moses said No! He pleaded that God would forgive them. It is what God really wanted Moses to do. Moses' real feelings were exposed; he himself did not hold a grudge against those who rebelled. This showed Moses' true greatness (Num. 14:11-19). A third example is *unanswered prayer and our reaction to it.* God may be testing us to see how earnest we are, whether we will persevere until the breakthrough comes.

37

HEARING GOD

A. One of the greatest possibilities presented to Christians is the possibility of hearing God.

1. We refer to hearing his voice – hearing him speak.

2. *John said,* 'This is the confidence we have in approaching God: that if we ask anything according to his will, he hears us. And if we know that he hears us – whatever we ask – we know that we have what we asked of him' (1 John 5:14-15).

   a. Notice the words, 'If we *know* that he hears us.'

   b. Knowing this means that we have heard *him.*

      (1) Otherwise, we could not know he has heard *us.*

      (2) That is a big 'if'; but it shows the possibility of hearing God.

   c. The greater questions is, how do we know that he has heard us?

B. 'Hearing God' is to be understood in the Hebraic sense.

1. *Shamar* (Heb.): to hear, to obey.

2. *Every ancient Jew knew 'the Shama'*: 'Hear, O Israel, the LORD our God, the LORD is one' (Deut. 6:4).

   a. *Shamar* means simultaneously 'to hear' and 'to obey'; there was no separation between the two.

   b. If one heard, he obeyed.

C. One of the essential attributes (characteristics) of the true God, that separates him from false gods, is that he hears and speaks.

1. False gods 'have mouths, but cannot speak, eyes, but they cannot see; they have ears, but cannot hear' (Ps. 115:5-6).

2. The prophets of Baal cried out, 'O Baal, answer us!' But 'there was no response' (1 Kgs. 18:26).

3. *The God of the Bible says to us,* 'Call to me and I will answer you and tell you great and unsearchable things you do not know' (Jer. 33:3).

   a. 'I love the LORD, for he has heard my voice; he heard my cry for mercy. Because he turned his ear to me, I will call on him as long as I live' (Ps. 116:1-2).

   b. 'The LORD has heard my cry for mercy; the LORD accepts my prayer' (Ps. 6:9).

   c. 'I sought the LORD, and he answered me; he delivered me from all my fears' (Ps. 34:4).

D. **The other side of the coin is, not only does God hear us but we can hear him.**

   1. In the unfallen state, Adam and Eve heard the sound (AV 'voice') of the LORD God as he was walking in the cool of the day... 'Where are you?' (Gen. 3:9).

   2. *In man's fallen state God spoke as well.* 'Then the LORD said to Cain, "Why are you angry? Why is your face downcast?"' (Gen. 4:6).

      a. God spoke to Noah (Gen. 6:13-21).

      b. The word of the Lord came to Abraham in a vision (Gen. 15:1).

   3. Generally speaking, God spoke in ancient times 'through the prophets at many times and in various ways' (Heb. 1:1).

E. **Hearing God (def.):**

   1. *When he hears us so that he obeys our request.*

      a. He always 'listens' but does not always 'hear' in the Hebraic sense referred to above.

      b. It is when our request is in his will (1 John 5:14-15; Rom. 8:26-27).

   2. *When we hear him: we 'know that we know' we have heard him, or have heard from him.*

      a. It may be immediate; a direct voice or vision; it is when no other person was the instrument in conveying God's will.

      b. It may be mediate; an indirect word, as a prophetic word, or word of knowledge that is so spot-on that you know 'only God' could have said that.

F. Why is this study important?

1. *God desires to have intimacy with his people.*
    a. God spoke to Moses 'face to face, as a man speaks with his friend' (Ex. 33:11).
    b. This study is designed to show that this kind of relationship is available to all of us. 'The LORD confides in those who fear him; he makes his covenant known to them' (Ps. 25:14).
2. Some wrongly assume that such intimacy was only possible in ancient or apostolic times; the truth is, what people experienced in biblical times can be ours too.
3. *We need to understand that God speaks in more than one way.*
    a. He may choose a mode of communication peculiar to you – and him.
    b. One must not lean on second-hand experiences or assume that the way God has spoken to another is the only way he will speak to you.
4. We need to see how God speaks today.
5. We need to refine our sense of two-way communication with God so that we know we are truly hearing from the true God – the God of the Bible – and are not being deceived.

G. We will from this point proceed from the general to the particular.

1. We begin with the Bible and the gospel.
2. We will then consider the role of the Spirit and the ways God sovereignly uses with us.

I. THE WORD OF GOD

A. We saw above that God generally spoke in ancient time through prophets and in various ways: '. . . . but in these last days he has spoken to us by his Son, whom he appointed heir of all things, and through whom he made the universe' (Heb. 1:2).

1. *The Word is to be understood in four ways:*
    a. The Word of God in Person. 'In the beginning was the Word, and the Word was with God, and the Word was God' (John 1:1).
    b. The Word of God in power. 'And we also thank God continually because, when you received the word of God,

which you heard from us, you accepted it not as the word of men, but as it actually is, the word of God, which is at work in you who believe' (1 Thess. 2:13). In a word, the gospel.

    c. The Word of God in print: the Bible.

        (1) 'All Scripture is God-breathed and is useful for teaching, rebuking, correcting and training in righteousness' (2 Tim. 3:16).

        (2) 'Above all, you must understand that no prophecy of Scripture came about by the prophet's own interpretation. For prophecy never had its origin in the will of man, but men spoke from God as they were carried along by the Holy Spirit' (2 Pet. 1:20-21).

    d. The Word of God by the Paraclete (the Holy Spirit).

        (1) 'The Spirit told Philip, "Go to that chariot and stay near it"' (Acts 8:29).

        (2) When they came to the border of Mysia, they tried to enter Bithynia, but the Spirit of Jesus would not allow them to' (Acts 16:7).

2. *The divine strategy was that the second person of the Godhead be known as 'the Word'.*

    a. Gr. *logos*, 'word', 'faculty of communication or thought'.

    b. This meant that *hearing* would be essential to knowing the Son.

        (1) He became flesh and lived among us (John 1:14).

        (2) But he would only be accepted by *hearing*.

    c. Even those who saw Jesus either believed or disbelieved by whether or not they believed his word.

        (1) Many believed for a while because of what they *saw* (John 6:1-15).

        (2) But they left Jesus because they eventually rejected what they *heard* (John 6:60ff).

B. The gospel is God's voice

1. *This is why Paul said 'faith comes from hearing'* (Rom. 10:17).

    a. God chose preaching as the instrument by which his good news is communicated (1 Cor. 1:21; Titus 1:3).

    b. Therefore if one receives the gospel it is because he or she *heard God*.

2. *If you are a Christian you have already heard God.*
    a. It was not by vision or a voice.
    b. You heard the word – and believed it. Why?
        (1) The Holy Spirit gripped you, convicting you of sin and righteousness and judgement (John 16:7ff).
        (2) The same Holy Spirit pointed you to Christ who died on a cross; you embraced his saving work and that is why you can call yourself a Christian.

C. Having heard the gospel (so that you believed and obeyed), you are qualified to hear God speak further.
    1. A divine network was set up in your mind and heart the moment you believed.
    2. This means the potential is there – from then on – to hear God speak.
    3. *Caution: any communication that purports (pretends, or seems) to be from God will be verified or nullified by whether or not it coheres with Scripture.*
        a. God will not say anything to you that is at variance with his Word.
        b. If what you 'heard' contradicts the Word of God in print, no matter how clear it was to you, you must have the humility and integrity to say that it was not truly God after all.
            (1) This is where the difficulty often comes.
            (2) In our pride and vanity we hate to admit that, just maybe, we got it wrong.
        c. This is a delicate but important subject; for that reason holy Scripture must reign supreme.

II. THE VOICE OF GOD AFTER OUR CONVERSION

A. Saul of Tarsus actually heard God's audible voice when he was converted. 'He fell to the ground and heard a voice say to him, "Saul, Saul, why do you persecute me?"' (Acts 9:4).
    1. *This however is unusual; his conversion was in many ways extraordinary.*
        a. Whereas it was 'normal' in the sense that God reached him through the gospel; he heard Stephen preach.
        b. Paul himself later said he was 'an example for those who

would believe on [Christ] and receive eternal life' (1 Tim. 1:16).

2. Most of us cannot testify to such an audible voice or to the fact of seeing Jesus.

B. Not far away Ananias was given both a vision and a hearing of God's audible voice. 'In Damascus there was a disciple named Ananias. The Lord called to him in a vision, "Ananias!" "Yes, Lord," he answered' (Acts 9:10).

  1. *This was clearly God's immediate communication after conversion.*

    a. There appears to have been no prophet coming to him.

    b. It was clear, immediate and direct.

  2. *This too may have been unusual, but subsequent events in Acts show that this sort of thing happened from time to time.*

    a. We too should not underestimate this – or its equivalent – in our lives.

    b. The remainder of this lesson will focus on this aspect of hearing God.

C. Intimacy with God

  1. *Note: no degree of closeness to God will unveil truth which the Bible has not already revealed.*

    a. For example, the problem of evil.

      (1) Do not expect to get a 'word' on this.

      (2) That will be revealed in heaven.

    b. Or, the date of Christ's coming (Mark 13:32).

      (1) No 'expert' in eschatology can tell you when Christ will come without lying to you.

      (2) Only God the Father knows this.

  2. *Intimacy with God can lead to the following:*

    a. The nearness of his presence (Ex. 33:11).

      (1) 'Come near to God and he will come near to you' (Jas. 4:8).

      (2) 'You can have as much of God as you want' (A W Tozer).

      (3) 'I have set the LORD always before me. Because he is at my right hand, I shall not be shaken . . . . . . You will fill me with joy in your presence, with eternal pleasures at your right hand' (Ps. 16:8,11).

b. A definite word in time of need. 'Last night an angel of the God whose I am and whom I serve stood beside me and said, "Do not be afraid, Paul. You must stand trial before Caesar; and God has graciously given you the lives of all who sail with you"' (Acts 27:23-24).

(1)God may reserve the unusual word for the unusual trial.

(2)Don't get in to the bondage of needing a word every time you go to the shops!

c. Power, spilling over into your life and usefulness.

Deposit Account	Current Account
(1)Building up treasure in heaven.	Needs supplied below.
(2)Dignifying persecution.	Anointing below.
(3)Walking in the light.	Fellowship below.
(4)Postponing vindication.	Peace below.
(5)Turning the cheek.	Christ-likeness below.
(6)Quiet suffering.	Power below.
(7)Honour of God only.	Joy below.

Note: When the Deposit Account is concentrated on your personal life being aimed toward God's glory, some dividends are transferred to your current account – giving you power now! (2 Tim. 2:21).

d. Extraordinary communication.

(1)Voice – sometimes so clear it is as though audible – word for word.

(2)Vision – sometimes prophetic (which will be fulfilled) or which shows you the present situation.

(3)Reading the Bible with unusual power.

(4)Understanding a particular verse or doctrine.

D. Why hear from God? Why is this such a wonderful thing?

1. *To know his will.*

a. Revealed will is always available – the Bible.

(1)Know the Bible so well that you will safely know what God would want you to do.

(2)There are no short cuts to this.

b. Secret will, which the Holy Spirit may sovereignly reveal.

(1)Intimacy with God leads to this more and more.

(2)But intimacy must be prized above all other ambitions.

2. *Fellowship.* 'But if we walk in the light, as he is in the light, we have fellowship with one another, and the blood of Jesus, his Son, purifies us from all sin ' (1 John 1:7).

    a. This comes by walking in the light.

    b. The result: two-way communication.

        (1) The Lord shows you things. He *may* even confide in you (if you will keep quiet about it) (Ps. 25:14).

3. *To find out what he is doing.* 'Therefore do not be foolish, but understand what the Lord's will is' (Eph. 5:17).

    a. If you want to know what is going on around you, find out! God may tell you.

    b. He may let confusion overtake you in order to get your attention – so you will seek him.

4. *Intimacy with him.* 'One thing I ask of the LORD, this is what I seek: that I may dwell in the house of the LORD all the days of my life' (Ps. 27:4).

    a. This comes by seeking his face, not his hand.

    b. 'Face' means his presence; 'hand' means what he might do for you.

E. What is 'hearing God'?

1. Communication from him so real and definite that you know you are not being deceived.

2. *Caution: learn to know the purpose of his presence.*

    a. He can be real and you can still make mistakes by wanting or concluding what he never intended. Illustration: Peter at the transfiguration.

    b. His presence may not convey all to you that you may want to know.

        (1) Be content with his presence.

        (2) No good thing will he withhold from you (Ps. 84:11).

3. *Sometimes this communication is peace, or a definite 'check' not to proceed* (Acts 16:6-7).

    a. 'Peace' may be a green light to carry on.

    b. A feeling of unease may equally be the Spirit's warning.

F. When, or where, do we hear from God?

1. *Any time, anywhere.*

    a. It may be in a time of solitude.

    b. It may be at church, or riding on a bus!

2. Chances are, the more time you spend alone with God – and reading his Word – the more likely he will turn up spontaneously and unexpectedly.

G. How do we hear from God?

1. *By being absolutely open and neutral.*
   a. If your mind is made up, don't even expect anything more.
   b. Be equally prepared for 'yes' or 'no' or any manner in which he chooses to reveal himself.
2. By being obedient; walking in the light.
3. By listening when you read his Word.
4. By expectancy that he will speak (as long as you are neutral and not biased).
5. By being faithful in the least thing (Luke 16:10).
6. By not trying to manipulate him to come down 'on your side' (Josh. 5:13-14).
7. By spending a lot of time doing nothing but praising him (Heb. 13:15; Eph. 5:19).
8. *By not taking yourself too seriously when he does speak.*
   a. Don't claim to have 'arrived' (Phil. 3:13ff).
   b. Be overly willing to keep quiet about what he tells you.
9. By being utterly devoid of grudges, hurt feelings and self-pity (Eph. 4:30ff).
10. By regarding the knowledge of his Word an achievement beyond any gift, sign or wonder.

CONCLUSION

God is not cut off from his creation but fully involved in it, even to the extent of speaking and listening to men and women. He hears his people's prayers and he speaks, most clearly through his Word. God relates to his children and is in two way communication with them.

38

SEEING GOD

A. We have previously noted the 'silent divorce' between the Word and the Spirit in today's church, speaking generally.

   1. When there is a divorce some children stay with the mother, some stay with the father.

   2. *In the silent divorce between the Word and the Spirit:*

      a. Some are on the Word side – and wish to stay there.

         (1) When people come to such churches they don't expect to see anything, they only expect to hear.

         (2) 'Thank you for the word'; 'That was a good word', the people will sometimes say to the minister.

         (3) The hearing was what they came for, that is what they got.

      b. Some are on the Spirit side – and wish to remain there.

         (1) When people come to such churches they don't much expect to hear anything, they have mainly come to see.

         (2) They have come to see God work, and they are often not disappointed.

         (3) To see is why they mainly come, that is what they get.

      c. Question: what is wrong with either emphasis? Answer: nothing.

         (1) Both are exactly right.

         (2) But surely that is not enough! Why not both together?

   3. *I envisage a day when there is coalescence between the Word and the Spirit, the Scriptures and the power of God.*

      a. That simultaneous combination will mean spontaneous combustion.

      b. Then those who come to see will hear, and those who come to hear will see.

B. This study deals with the question: can we see God?

   1. *One of God's attributes is his invisibility.*

      a. Invisibility (def.): unable to be seen.

      b. Attributes (def.): characteristics, e.g., God is:

         (1) Omnipotent (all-powerful).

         (2) Omniscient (knows everything).

         (3) Omnipresent (is everywhere).

  2. *God is actually referred to as invisible.*

      a. 'He is the image of the invisible God, the firstborn over all creation' (Col. 1:15).

      b. 'Now to the King eternal, immortal, invisible, the only God, be honour and glory for ever and ever. Amen' (1 Tim. 1:17).

      c. 'Who alone is immortal and who lives in unapproachable light, whom no-one has seen or can see. To him be honour and might for ever. Amen' (1 Tim. 6:16. cf. Heb. 11:27).

  3. Jesus said, 'God is spirit, and his worshippers must worship in spirit and truth' (John 4:24).

C. Why deal with this question since God is invisible?

  1. *Because of the claims of some to have seen him:*

      a. 'In the year that King Uzziah died, I saw the Lord seated on a throne, high and exalted, and the train of his robe filled the temple' (Isa. 6:1).

      b. '"We are doomed to die!" he said to his wife. "We have seen God!"' (Judg. 13:22).

  2. *Because of the promises of seeing God.*

      a. 'Blessed are the pure in heart, for they will see God' (Matt. 5:8).

      b. 'Make every effort to live in peace with all men and to be holy; without holiness no-one will see the Lord' (Heb. 12:14).

D. Why is this subject important?

  1. It makes us face the problem often raised, that the Bible seems to contradict itself.

  2. It forces us to see if there is a distinction between the promise of seeing God now and seeing him in heaven.

  3. It gives us a look at hermeneutics (def.): the science or art of biblical interpretation.

  4. It shows how God accommodates us by using a figure of speech rather than what is literal.

5. *It should inspire us to want to see God:*
    a. See him work – now.
    b. See his glory – as much as is possible.
    c. See him literally – in heaven.

I. FACING THE CONTRADICTIONS

A. A number of scriptures attest to the impossibility of seeing God.
    1. Because he is invisible in the first place (see above).
    2. *Because we could not stand to see God, that is, we could not cope with seeing him and yet live.*
        a. This was implied in Judges 13:22: 'We are doomed to die.... We have seen God.'
        b. God said to Moses, 'You cannot see my face, for no-one may see me and live' (Ex. 33:20).
        c. The awesomeness of his glory is the apparent explanation for the inability to see God (as well as his being invisible): 'Who lives in unapproachable light, whom no-one has seen or can see' (1 Tim. 6:16).
    3. *John's writings state this repeatedly:*
        a. 'No-one has ever seen God, but God the One and Only, who is at the Father's side; has made him known' (John 1:18).
        b. 'And the Father who sent me has himself testified concerning me. You have never heard his voice nor seen his form' (John 5:37).
        c. 'No-one has seen the Father except the one who is from God; only he has seen the Father' (John 6:46).
        d. 'No-one has ever seen God; but if we love one another, God lives in us and his love is made complete in us' (1 John 4:12).

B. At the same time there are those claims to have seen God.
    1. *Intimacy with God:*
        a. 'The LORD would speak to Moses face to face, as a man speaks with his friend' (Ex. 33:11a).
        b. 'Then the LORD came down in a pillar of cloud; he stood at the entrance to the Tent and summoned Aaron and Miriam. When both of them stepped forward, he said, "Listen to my words: When a prophet of the LORD is among you, I reveal myself to him in visions, I speak to him in dreams.

But this is not true of my servant Moses; he is faithful in all my house. With him I speak face to face, clearly and not in riddles; he sees the form of the LORD. Why then were you not afraid to speak against my servant Moses?"' (Num. 12:5-8).

2. *Prophetic visions:*
   a. 'Micaiah continued, "Therefore hear the word of the LORD: I saw the LORD sitting on his throne with all the host of heaven standing round him on his right and on his left"' (1 Kings 22:19).
   b. 'In the year that King Uzziah died, I saw the Lord seated on a throne, high and exalted, and the train of his robe filled the temple' (Isa. 6:1).
   c. 'In the thirtieth year, in the fourth month on the fifth day, while I was among the exiles by the Kebar River, the heavens were opened and I saw visions of God' (Ezek. 1:1).

C. The explanation for these apparent contradictions.

1. *No unglorified human being can directly look at the face of God the Father.*
   a. Jesus is God – as fully God in deity as the Father; yet people saw Jesus.
   b. We must understand that Scripture does refer to seeing the face of God the Father before we get to heaven.
   c. Some angels apparently could look at the Father, some could not.
      (1)'See that you do not look down on one of these little ones. For I tell you that their angels in heaven always see the face of my Father in heaven' (Matt. 18:10).
      (2)Isaiah's vision suggests that the seraphim did not look on God (with their wings they 'covered their faces') (Isa. 6:2).

2. *The references to seeing God have further explanations.*
   a. Language of accommodation
      (1) God frequently does this, as when God said to Abraham, 'Now I know that you fear God' (Gen. 22:12). God did not learn from Abraham but accommodated Abraham's understanding of himself.
      (2)When God spoke to Moses face to face (Ex. 33:11; Num. 12:5-8), it was language of accommodation, showing their intimacy.

(3) This is the only explanation since in the very same chapter God said, '"You cannot see my face, for no-one may see me and live." Then the LORD said, "There is a place near me where you may stand on a rock. When my glory passes by, I will put you in a cleft in the rock and cover you with my hand until I have passed by. Then I will remove my hand and you will see my back; but my face must not be seen"' (Ex. 33:20-23).

    b. It was an angel that they actually saw but it was like seeing God.

        (1) This is what happened with Gideon even though at times it says the Lord did the talking (Judg. 6:16. cf. 6:11-23).

        (2) This is what happened with Samson's parents (Judg. 13:6-23).

II. PROMISES THAT WE WILL SEE GOD

A. Eschatological promises.

    1. Eschatology (def.): doctrine of last things.

    2. *We will see Jesus, the God-man, at his Second Coming.*

        a. Peter spoke twice of Jesus Christ being revealed (1 Pet. 1:7,13).

            (1) We are in the category of those who have not seen him but love him (1 Pet. 1:8).

            (2) Only a handful saw Jesus after the resurrection.

        b. Seeing Jesus face to face will result in our glorification.

            (1) 'And those he predestined, he also called; those he called, be also justified; those he justified, he also glorified' (Rom. 8:30).

            (2) 'Dear friends, now we are children of God, and what we will be has not yet been made known. But we know that when he appears, we shall be like him, for we shall see him as he is' (1 John 3:2. cf. 1 Cor. 13:12).

        c. There will be a seeing of the God-man that will not result in glorification.

            (1) 'Look, he is coming with the clouds, and every eye will see him, even those who pierced him; and all the peoples of the earth will mourn because of him. So shall it be! Amen' (Rev. 1:7).

       (2) This will result in all having to bend the knee to the Son of God but not because they love him (Rom. 14:10; Phil. 2:8-10).

3. *Will we see God the Father?*

    a. Matthew 5:8 suggests this, the pure in heart 'will see God'.

    b. Hebrews 12:14 suggests this too but this could refer to seeing Jesus: 'Without holiness no-one will see the Lord.'

    c. Revelation 22:4 is ambiguous: 'They will see his face, and his name will be on their foreheads.'

        (1) Revelation 22:3 refers to the throne of God and of the Lamb (Jesus).

        (2) It could refer to God's face or Jesus' face.

    d. A good case can be made however that we will see the Father's face (even if 'face' is a metaphor).

        (1) John 1:18 says no-one has seen God – only Jesus. 'No-one has ever seen God, but God the One and Only, who is at the Father's right side, has made him known.'

        (2) If our glorification is the result of seeing him face to face, perhaps we too will see the Father.

B. Seeing the glory of God (before we get to heaven).

  1. *There are degrees, or stages, of seeing God's glory (the order may vary below).*

    a. Conversion (2 Cor. 3:10-4:6)

        (1) Blindness is taken away.

        (2) We are enabled to see the glory of Jesus Christ:

           (a) Who he is (the God-man).

           (b) What he did (died for our sins, rose from the dead, ascended to God's right hand).

    b. Growth in grace and knowledge (2 Pet. 1:5-8; 3:18)

        (1) This comes through prayer and Bible reading.

        (2) This comes through worship and teaching/preaching.

    c. Experiencing answered prayer (Acts 12:5-17)

        (1) Nothing encourages or increases one's faith like an undoubted answer to prayer.

        (2) When this happens it is like seeing God!

    d. The immediate and direct witness of the Holy Spirit: the miraculous within.

        (1) The baptism (or sealing) of the Holy Spirit.

        (2) Inexpressible joy and peace.

        (3) Gifts of the Spirit.

    e. Seeing the outwardly miraculous (Luke 5:17-26). 'We have seen remarkable things today' (v.26).

        (1) Healings, signs, wonders, miracles.

        (2) Supernatural guidance (Ex. 40:38).

        (3) Fulfilled visions.

        (4) Fulfilled prophecies.

    f. Utter intimacy with God (1 John 1:7; Ps. 25:14).

        (1) When communion is like seeing him (Ex. 33:11; Ps. 27:4).

        (2) When endurance in tribulation is like seeing him (Heb. 11:27; Acts 14:22).

    g. Discerning the Lord at his table (1 Cor. 11:23-32).

        (1) This will be known in varying degrees.

        (2) We are required to recognise or discern his presence.

2. *There are limits to what we can see and grasp.*

    a. Moses' lesson when he saw the burning bush (Ex. 3:1-6).

        (1) He wondered why the bush didn't burn up.

        (2) God said, 'Stop!' – we can only get so close!

    b. Moses also had to wait before he saw the fuller expression of the miraculous (cf. Luke 16:10).

        (1) Moses saw God work as a token, when his staff turned into a snake and then turned back into a staff (Ex. 4:1-5).

        (2) The plagues upon Egypt emerged generally in ever-increasing measure of extraordinary phenomena.

        (3) The two greatest events of the Old Testament – the Passover and the crossing of the Red Sea on dry land – were the culmination of signs and wonders in Egypt.

    c. God leads us by faith, step by step, so that what comes next is not so hard to accept. E.g.:

        (1) God did not take Moses immediately from the miracle of the staff to the Red Sea!

        (2) God doesn't lead us from A to Z but from A to B, B to C, etc..

    d. Moses asked to see God's glory (Ex. 33:18).

        (1) This followed a time of precious intimacy with God, when the Lord spoke to him 'face to face, as a man speaks with his friend' (Ex. 33:11).

        (2) There followed one of the profoundest revelations God

ever gave about himself. 'And the LORD said, "I will cause all my goodness to pass in front of you, and I will proclaim my name, the LORD, in your presence. I will have mercy on whom I will have mercy, and I will have compassion on whom I will have compassion"' (Ex. 33:19).

    (a) This helped Paul's own concept of election (Rom. 9:11-16).

    (b) The glory of God and the sovereignty of God have an inseparable and intimate connection.

(3) But God drew the line. '"But," he said, "you cannot see my face, for no-one may see me and live"' (Ex. 33:20).

    (a) This is because our mortal bodies and unglorified minds could not cope with God's full glory directly.

    (b) This fact about God became so known in Israel that Samson's father exclaimed, 'We are doomed to die! We have seen God!' But in fact it was only an angel that was seen (Judg. 13:16-22).

(4) A compromise followed with Moses and his request. 'Then the LORD said, "There is a place near me where you may stand on a rock. When my glory passes by, I will put you in a cleft in the rock and cover you with my hand until I have passed by"' (Ex. 33:21-22).

    (a) All Moses saw was God's 'back'.

    (b) What this was and what it was like is something we will never know for sure until we get to heaven.

    (c) It is possible that this was the nearest any human being came to seeing the glory of God directly.

3. *The glory of God in the Law and the gospel.*

  a. Paul said that the Law came with glory (2 Cor. 3:7).

    (1) The Israelites could not even look at Moses' face because of its radiance (Ex. 34:29-35).

    (2) There is a sense then in which the Israelites saw God's glory in this event.

  b. When we turn to the Lord (which is first done at conversion) a process of being changed from glory to glory emerges (2 Cor. 3:18).

    (1) This comes as we reflect on or contemplate his glory.

    (2) It is therefore seeing God in a sense – in our hearts. 'For God, who said, "Let light shine out of darkness," made

his light shine in our hearts to give us the light of the
knowledge of the glory of God in the face of Christ' (2
Cor. 4:6).

III. HOLINESS AND SEEING GOD

A. There are two explicit promises regarding seeing God.
  1. *Both refer to our godly character*
      a. 'Blessed are the pure in heart, for they will see God' (Matt.
         5:8).
         (1) Purity of heart may refer to conversion (Acts 15:9).
         (2) Purity of heart may refer to walking in the light (1 John
             1:7).
      b. 'Make every effort to live in peace with all men and to be
         holy; without holiness no-one will see the Lord' (Heb. 12:14).
         (1) Two things presuppose seeing the Lord:
             (a) Living in peace with all men.
             (b) Holiness.
         (2) The Greek indicates that both are prerequisites, not just
             'holiness'.
  2. *These two passages show clearly that purity of heart and a
     godly life are essential to seeing God.*
      a. If they are referring to seeing God absolutely and
         immediately and not just God's 'back', they must be
         eschatological.
      b. This means that only the pure in heart and those who have
         followed holiness and peace will see God.
      c. This leads to obvious questions:
         (1) Will not all who are saved see God?
         (2) What about those 'saved by fire' (1 Cor. 3:15), which
             suggests they were not as holy as others?
         (3) Who can be sure that he or she is sufficiently 'pure' or
             at 'peace with all men' and has enough 'holiness' that
             one knows one is qualified to see God?

B. I answer:
  1. *Matthew 5:8 and Hebrews 12:14 do not primarily refer to
     eschatology but to seeing God here below.*
      a. The pure in heart hunger for more of God and are blessed
         with seeing him as outlined above.

b. The same is true with walking in love ('peace with all men') and holiness: one sees God work in power.

(1) The epistle to the Hebrews encourages us to experience God's 'oath', which is like seeing the Lord. (See 'The Promise and the Oath' – Lesson 3; summer term 1993.)

(2) Hebrews 12:14 is motivating us to please the Lord that we might experience this.

2. *If these verses refer to seeing God in heaven:*

a. It is because Christ is our sanctification (1 Cor. 1:2).

b. Any lack of holiness will be burned by fire at the Judgement Seat of Christ (1 Cor. 3:15) to prepare us for the sight of his glory.

CONCLUSION

God told Moses, 'You cannot see my face, for no-one may see me and live' (Ex. 33:22). However, there are Scriptural instances of people seeing God, Moses, Isaiah and Ezekiel among them. Because no unglorified person can see God, these references must relate to experiences other that actually looking on the Holy One.

As Christians we have the assurance that we will see God. On earth we see something of the glory of God in the Law, the gospel and in the experience of Jesus Christ. The more holy our lives the clearer will be our vision of God. In heaven we will see him face to face, never again to have anything come between us.

39

FINDING GOD

A. We have said repeatedly that our theological studies must combine doctrine with experience.

   1. *There is nothing more disappointing than arid, heavy theology that is largely intellectual and cerebral.*

   a. It may appeal to the academic and there may be a place for this.

   b. But that is not what we are interested in here.

   2. *There is a theology of knowing about God but far more important is a theology that enables us to know God himself.*

   a. Facts about God, ever pertinent and biblical, are important.

   b. At the end of the day we must ask: Do we know this God?

   (1) The God of the Bible is 'knowable'.

   (2) Pharaoh told the truth when he said, 'I do not know the LORD' (Ex. 5:2).

   3. Before we can know him we must find him.

B. There are a number of relevant scriptures on this.

   1. 'Seek the LORD while he may be found; call on him while he is near' (Isa. 55:6).

   2. Job said, 'If only I knew where to find him; if only I could go to his dwelling!' (Job 23:3).

   3. David said, 'Therefore let everyone who is godly pray to you while you may be found; surely when the mighty waters rise, they will not reach him' (Ps. 32:6).

C. The greatest discovery that can be made in life is finding God.

   1. To those who had not believed there was a God at all, then discover that he is there, the experience is almost overwhelming.

   2. *And yet people generally are not the slightest bit bothered about finding God.*

a. Most don't want to know.

b. They certainly hope he doesn't exist since they feel a freedom to live as they please in their blissful ignorance.

D. Finding God (def.): discovering that he is there and that he is very real indeed. 'And without faith it is impossible to please God, because anyone who comes to him must believe that he exists and that he rewards those who earnestly seek him' (Heb. 11:6).

  1. To find (def.): to discover by search, effort, inquiry or by choice. (Oxford Dictionary).

  2. *Generally speaking, then, finding is the result of seeking.*

  a. Those who find God were seeking him.

  b. The exceptions (and thank God for them – it happens in a sense to all): when God found us even though we were not seeking him.

E. There are two levels of finding God.

  1. *Conversion: when God found us.*

  a. We may have been seeking him in some sense.

  (1) Pascal: There is a God-shaped blank in every person.

  (2) Augustine: Thou hast made us for Thyself; our hearts are restless until they find their repose in Thee.'

  b. We may not have been seeking him at all (at least consciously).

  (1) This is when he steps in and intervenes.

  (2) When we weren't thinking of him he was thinking of us. 'I revealed myself to those who did not ask for me; I was found by those who did not seek me' (Isa. 65:1).

  I sought the Lord and afterward I knew
  He moved my heart to seek Him, seeking me;
  It was not I that found, O Saviour true
  No, I was found of Thee.

  2. *The quest for intimacy with God after conversion.*

  a. When we are saved we begin a relationship with God.

  b. Conversion is not the end but the beginning of knowing God.

  (1) There is a sense in which we want to find him.

  (2) This therefore means discovering how real God is.

F. Why is this lesson important?
   1. It shows the importance of seeking God.
   2. It shows how our seeking God is because God is seeking us.
   3. It shows the work of the Spirit – the motivation for seeking God.
   4. It shows how we can find God.
   5. It shows how we can discover how real God is.

I. SEEKING GOD

A. God asks us to seek him.
   1. *God created us so that we would seek him.*
      a. The care he went to in making us, determining when and where we would be born and where we should live was with the very purpose of our seeking God.
      b. 'From one man he made every nation of men, that they should inhabit the whole earth; and he determined the times set for them and the exact places where they should live. God did this so that men would seek him and perhaps reach out for him and find him, though he is not far from each one of us' (Acts 17:26-27).
   2. *God made us for fellowship with him.*
      a. Adam had a beautiful fellowship with God before his sin in the Garden of Eden.
      b. This fellowship was disrupted after Adam and Eve sinned. 'Then the man and his wife heard the sound of the LORD God as he was walking in the garden in the cool of the day, and they hid from the LORD God among the trees of the garden. But the LORD God called to the man, "Where are you?"' (Gen. 3:8-9).
         (1) It was an awful moment for Adam.
         (2) One senses the feelings of God in missing this fellowship with Adam when he called out, 'Where are you?'
   3. *The whole purpose of redemption was that people would seek God.*
      a. This is because by nature we would not actively seek him.
         (1) 'No-one seeks God' (Rom. 3:11).
         (2) 'The LORD looks down from heaven on the sons of men to see if there are any who understand, any who seek God. All have turned aside, they have together become

corrupt; there is no-one who does good, not even one'
(Ps. 14:2-3. cf. Ps. 53:1-3).

b. This is because we are born in a post-fallen state.

　　(1) We are born dead – spiritually. 'As for you, you were
　　dead in your transgressions and sins' (Eph. 2:1).

　　(2) We none the less have a conscience; which renders us
　　'without excuse' (Rom. 1:20).

B. God warns us not to take this seeking for granted.

1. *We may not find him whenever we suddenly decide to look for him.*

　　a. Jonathan Edwards preached a sermon called 'Will you
　　always call upon God?'

　　b. We may take for granted that we can snap our fingers at
　　God, expecting him to jump.

2. *For this reason, Isaiah warned:* 'Seek the LORD while he
may be found; call on him while he is near' (Isa. 55:6).

　　a. 'While he may be found' means:

　　　　(1) There is a time when he may be found.

　　　　(2) It is only then that he may be found.

　　　　(3) He may not be found at just any time.

　　b. This means:

　　　　(1) While we are still alive.

　　　　　　(a) People will be seeking God in hell.

　　　　　　(b) 'So he called to him, "Father Abraham, have pity on
　　　　　　me and send Lazarus to dip the tip of his finger in
　　　　　　water and cool my tongue, because I am in agony in
　　　　　　this fire"' (Luke 16:24).

　　　　(2) When his Spirit is at work.

　　　　　　(a) 'The wind blows wherever it pleases. You hear its
　　　　　　sound, but you cannot tell where it comes from or
　　　　　　where it is going. So it is with everyone born of the
　　　　　　Spirit' (John 3:8).

　　　　　　(b) One should take full advantage of the Spirit's presence.

　　　　　　(c) The old expression 'Strike while the iron is hot' is
　　　　　　relevant here.

　　　　　　(d) God can be powerfully present in a service today –
　　　　　　but not necessarily tomorrow.

　　　　(3) If we refuse God will not accommodate us in the end
　　　　but reject us:

         (a) 'Since you rejected me when I called and no-one
               gave heed when I stretched out my hand. . . I in turn
               will laugh at your disaster; I will mock when calamity
               overtakes you' (Prov. 1:24,26).
         (b) 'Then they will call to me but I will not answer;
               they will look for me but will not find me. Since
               they hated knowledge and did not choose to fear the
               LORD' (Prov. 1:28-29).
     c. Isaiah repeats this when he says, 'Call on him while he is near'.
       (1) There are times when God is 'near'.
         (a) He is everywhere at all times of course.
         (b) This is what is meant by the omnipresence of God
               (Ps. 139:7-12).
       (2) This means when God is near by:
         (a) A clear teaching of his Word.
         (b) A manifest sense of his presence.

II. THE PROMISE OF FINDING GOD

A. This promise is contained initially in the gospel.
    1. *There is the appeal to those who know their state.*
      a. That they are sinners (Rom. 5:8).
      b. They know they are lost (Luke 19:10).
    2. *There is the appeal to those who have been further prepared:*
      a. They are broken. 'Come to me, all you who are weary and
         burdened, and I will give you rest' (Matt. 11:28).
      b. They are thirsty. 'The Spirit and the bride say, "Come!"
         And let him who hears say, "Come!" Whoever is thirsty,
         let him come; and whoever wishes, let him take the free
         gift of the water of life' (Rev. 22:17).
    3. *There is the appeal to those who do not realise their perilous state.*
      a. 'With many other words he warned them; and he pleaded
         with them, "Save yourselves from this corrupt generation"'
         (Acts 2:40).
      b. 'You disowned the Holy and Righteous One and asked that a
         murderer be released to you. . . Now, brothers, I know that
         you acted in ignorance, as did your leaders. . . Repent, then,
         and turn to God, so that your sins may be wiped out, that
         times of refreshing may come from the Lord' (Acts 3:14,17,19).

4. *Note: the gospel has a self-contained intent that motivates people into seeking and finding God.*

  a. The Lord Jesus comes seeking.

    (1) 'For the Son of Man came to seek and to save what was lost' (Luke 19:10).

    (2) 'On hearing this, Jesus said, "It is not the healthy who need a doctor, but the sick. But go and learn what this means: 'I desire mercy, not sacrifice.' For I have not come to call the righteous, but sinners"' (Matt. 9:12-13).

  b. The Holy Spirit applies the gospel to those who up to then may not have been consciously seeking God.

    (1) Saul of Tarsus was not consciously seeking God – he thought he knew God already.

    (2) But God was working in Saul. 'We all fell to the ground, and I heard a voice saying to me in Aramaic, "Saul, Saul, why do you persecute me? It is hard for you to kick against the goads"' (Acts 26:14).

B. God puts his integrity on the line with those who truly want to find him.

  1. *'But if from there you seek the LORD your God, you will find him if you look for him with all your heart and with all your soul'* (Deut. 4:29).

    a. God puts obstacles in our way to test how sincere and earnest we are.

    b. This is why he says: 'If you look for him with all your heart and with all your soul.'

      (1) He will not be manipulated by us who think we are doing him a favour in calling to him.

      (2) He rewards those who 'earnestly' (AV 'diligently') seek him (Heb. 11:6).

  2. *Jeremiah says the same thing:* 'You will seek me and find me when you seek me with all your heart' (Jer. 29:13).

    a. This is a wonderful promise.

      (1) He had just said, '"For I know the plans I have for you," declares the LORD, "plans to prosper you and not to harm you, plans to give you hope and a future"' (Jer. 29:11).

      (2) God knows all about each of us.

   (a) Augustine: God loves every person as though there
   were no-one else to love.
   (b) He has a plan for each of us – to bless us.
b. But if we do not seek him with all our hearts we will forfeit
   what was rightfully ours.
   (1) 'I love those who love me, and those who seek me will
      find me' (Prov. 8:17, AV): 'Those who seek me early
      shall find me.'
   (2) Jesus sought his Father very early in the day. 'Very early
      in the morning, while it was still dark, Jesus got up, left
      the house and went off to a solitary place, where he
      prayed' (Mark 1:35).
3. *God promised Solomon: 'If you seek him, he will be found by*
   you' (1 Chron. 28:9. cf. 2 Chron. 15:2).
   a. King Josiah, while he was still young, began to seek God (2
      Chron. 34:3).
   b. The result: the Book of the Law was found, reform was
      begun, and Passover was celebrated with the greatest
      worship that could be remembered (2 Chron. 35:18).
4. David made a vow, narrowing all his desires to one: 'One thing
   I ask of the LORD, this is what I seek: that I may dwell in the
   house of the LORD all the days of my life, to gaze upon the
   beauty of the LORD and to seek him in his temple' (Ps. 27:4).

C. Jesus put his seal on all the above:
   1. 'So I say to you: Ask and it will be given to you; seek and you
      will find; knock and the door will be opened to you. For
      everyone who asks receives; he who seeks finds; and to him
      who knocks, the door will be opened' (Luke 11:9-10).
   2. There is a benefit in seeking God's kingdom first before anything
      else: we will always have enough food, shelter and clothing.
      'But seek first his kingdom and his righteousness, and all these
      things will be given to you as well' (Matt. 6:33).

III. HOW DO WE SEEK GOD?

A. In the gospel
   1. *We must always begin here, never taking this for granted.*
      a. Do you know for sure that, were you to die today, you would
         go to heaven?

b. If you were to stand before God and he were to say to you, 'Why should I let you into my heaven?' what would you say?

2. *Transfer your trust from your good works to Christ's death on the cross.*

    a. As long as your hope (under a lie detector) is in yourself in the slightest way, you are trusting not Christ but your works.

    b. Be sure 'all of your eggs are in one basket': the blood of Jesus.

        (1) This is where you find God – in his Son.

        (2) This paves the way to knowing and finding God for yourself in greater degrees of intimacy with him.

B. In his Word

1. *The Bible is God's integrity on the line.*

    a. 'All Scripture is God-breathed and is useful for teaching, rebuking, correcting and training in righteousness' (2 Tim. 3:16).

    b. 'Above all, you must understand that no prophecy of Scripture came about by the prophet's own interpretation. For prophecy never had its origin in the will of man, but men spoke from God as they were carried along by the Holy Spirit' (2 Pet. 1:20-21).

2. *Have a Bible reading plan. I recommend Robert Murray M'Cheyne.*

    a. Be sure that you seek God in his Word every day.

    b. This affirms his integrity and your sincerity and earnestness in wanting to find him.

        (1) It is not a sign of great maturity to seek the prophetic word from another, no matter how gifted or godly that person may be.

        (2) Seek God directly – in his Word; get to know his Word so well that you know his 'ways' (cf. Heb. 3:10).

C. In private prayer

1. *I recommend thirty minutes a day (minimum) alone with God.*

    a. We show how important a person is to us by how much time we give to them.

    b. How much time have you been giving to God?

2. *I further recommend:*

    a. A prayer list:

        (1) Personal needs and desires.

        (2) Intercession for others.

b. Pausing just to worship.

    (1) Talk to God, tell him you love him.

    (2) Praise him, thank him for everything.

3. *Learn to listen to him – to know his voice.*

    a. Don't do all the talking.

    b. Wait before him, seek to hear him with all your heart and soul.

D. Commitment to obedience

1. Walking in the light in your own life (1 John 1:7).

2. Resisting temptation (Jas. 1:3ff).

3. Resisting the devil (1 Pet. 5:8).

4. *Service to the church.*

    a. Membership.

    b. Involvement.

5. Witnessing to others.

6. Helping others in need (Jas. 1:27).

    a. Caring for the poor.

    b. Getting your hands dirty with valid projects.

IV. WHAT EXACTLY DO WE FIND WHEN SEEKING GOD?

A. The primary discovery:

1. *That God is so real*

    a. It is when faith almost becomes sight. 'By faith he left Egypt, not fearing the king's anger; he persevered because he saw him who is invisible' (Heb. 11:27).

    b. You discern – God is literally there, he shows himself to you in a manner 'you know that you know'.

        (1) You may not be able to convey this to another person.

        (2) But is was just for you after all.

2. *Joy*

    a. God wants you to experience the fruits of the Spirit (Gal. 5:22ff).

    b. God will be so real to you that you see the meaning of these words: 'For the kingdom of God is not a matter of eating and drinking, but of righteousness, peace and joy in the Holy Spirit' (Rom. 14:17).

3. *Intimacy with him.* 'We proclaim to you what we have seen and heard, so that you also may have fellowship with us. And our fellowship is with the Father and with his Son, Jesus Christ' (1 John 1:3).

    a. It is pure fellowship with the Father.

    b. You discover that Moses' experience is yours as well; you speak to God face to face as one talks with his or her friend (Ex. 33:11. cf. Ps. 25:14).

B. Secondary discoveries:

    1. *Answers to prayer* (Heb. 11:6).

        a. You begin to see things happen.

        b. God loves to answer prayer.

    2. Vindication. 'He will receive blessing from the LORD and vindication from God his Saviour. Such is the generation of those who seek him, who seek your face, O God of Jacob' (Ps. 24:5-6).

    3. Life and favour. 'For whoever finds me finds life and receives favour from the LORD' (Prov. 8:35).

    4. Rest of soul (Matt. 11:29-30).

C. A W Tozer: We can have as much of God as we want.

    1. Joseph Tson: 'How far are you prepared to go in your commitment to God?'

    2. To those who seek with all their hearts – they find the above.

CONCLUSION

The greatest discovery that can be made is finding God. God invites us to seek him, promising that those who seek will find. He can be found in the gospel, in his Word, through prayer and in commitment to obedience. There are two levels at which we find God. The first is at conversion and the second in our post conversion quest for intimacy with him.

40

LIVING BY FAITH NOT WORKS

INTRODUCTION

A. The purpose of theology is to change lives.

1. *There are two potential audiences for doing theology:*
   a. the theologians.
   b. the people.
   (1) I used to want to write theology for theologians and academics.
   (2) Since 1982 my goals have changed, I'd rather reach the people. 'The common people heard him gladly' (Mark 12:37, AV).

2. *For our lives to be changed by theology two things must follow.*
   a. That we are sure we are getting the truth, not one's private opinions.
   b. That we are prepared to apply that theology to our everyday lives.
   (1) We must be convinced and convicted.
   (2) We prove this by application (bringing into action).

B. This lesson provides a theological basis for the way we live.

1. It begins by looking at how we are saved.
2. It continues by seeing its relevance for our daily Christian living.

C. There are two assumptions that will govern this study – but which we shall prove by Scripture.

1. We are justified by faith, not works.
2. *What is good enough to save us is good enough to live by.*
   a. 'So then, just as you received Christ Jesus as Lord, continue to live in him' (Col. 2:6).
   b. 'I have been crucified with Christ and I no longer live, but Christ lives in me. The life I live in the body, I live by faith in the Son of God, who loved me and gave himself for me' (Gal. 2:20).
   (1) Sadly, the NIV does not translate the Greek literally.

(2) The AV says, 'I live by the faith of the Son of God'; the Greek literally translates, 'I live by faith, viz. that of the Son of God.'

(3) We will be able to see the relevance of this below.

D. The purpose of this lesson is to show how the doctrine of justification by faith is broader than its reference to conversion.

1. It is to show us how to live as well as how to be saved.

2. *It is to show that we are assured of being saved by the same way we are actually saved.*

    a. What is good enough to justify us is good enough to assure us.

    b. What is good enough to assure us is good enough to live by.

3. *This will show that there is no dichotomy between the way we are converted and the way we are assured (and, as a consequence of that assurance, live the Christian life).*

    a. Dichotomy (def.): a division into two parts or kinds.

    b. Some hold that you are saved one way, assured another way, e.g.:

        (1) We are saved by grace, we are assured by works.

        (2) We are saved by grace, we must stay saved (or stay assured of being saved) by good works (or sanctification).

E. Why is this lesson important?

1. It is a reminder of the most important issue in theology: how we are saved, viz., by faith alone.

2. It is a good introduction to a doctrine of assurance of salvation (that is, how do you know you are saved?).

3. It is an emancipating teaching, setting free from guilt and fear.

4. Many Christians live with guilt and the fear they are not saved – largely because they have a faulty theology.

5. *It will show the place of good works, or sanctification, in the Christian life, namely:*

    a. How we are saved and kept.

    b. Why we must be careful to show good works.

I. Basic assumption: justification by faith alone

A. To justify means to make righteous.

1. *The question: how? By works? By faith?*

    a. Justification by works: producing the righteousness God requires by what we do.

b. Justification by faith: receiving the righteousness God requires by believing.

2. *If we are to be justified by works it means:*

    a. We must produce the righteousness of the law:

        (1) Keeping the Ten Commandments: moral law.

        (2) Keeping the civil (how a nation is to be governed) and ceremonial (how to worship) laws.

        (3) Keeping the minutiae (small details) of the law, including dietary laws and dress codes. E.g., Leviticus 19:19,26-27; Exodus 23:18-19.

    b. We are not allowed to be selective, that is, keep the parts that may be easier than others; we must take it all.

        (1) '"Cursed is the man who does not uphold the words of this law by carrying them out." Then all the people shall say, "Amen!"' (Deut. 27:26).

        (2) 'For whoever keeps the whole law and yet stumbles at just one point is guilty of breaking all of it' (Jas. 2:10).

    c. Two things follow:

        (1) We are unable to keep the law (Acts 15:10).

        (2) We can never be sure if we are sufficiently righteous to claim we are now justified.

3. *If we are saved by faith it means:*

    a. Receiving instead of doing.

        (1) It is receiving a person. 'Yet to all who received him, to those who believed in his name, he gave the right to become children of God – children born not of natural descent, nor of human decision or a husband's will, but born of God' (John 1:12-13).

        (2) It is receiving a righteousness, a righteousness that 'comes from God' (Rom. 10:3).

    b. This receiving is by faith.

        (1) Faith (def.): believing God, i.e., believing his Word.

        (2) 'But the righteousness that is by faith says: "Do not say in your heart, 'Who will ascend into heaven?'" (that is, to bring Christ down) "or 'Who will descend into the deep?'" (that is, to bring Christ up from the dead). But what does it say? "The word is near you; it is in your mouth and in your heart," that is, the word of faith we are proclaiming: That if you confess with your mouth,

"Jesus is Lord," and believe in your heart that God raised him from the dead, you will be saved. For it is with your heart that you believe and are justified, and it is with your mouth that you confess and are saved' (Rom. 10:6-10).

c. Faith counts for righteousness.

(1) Righteousness is 'imputed' (def.: put to our credit) by faith alone.

(2) 'Now when a man works, his wages are not credited to him as a gift, but as an obligation. However, to the man who does not work but trusts God who justifies the wicked, his faith is credited as righteousness' (Rom. 4:4-5).

B. Behind this privilege of being justified by faith are two things:

1. *Christ's perfect life and faith*

a. Jesus never sinned.

(1) 'For we do not have a high priest who is unable to sympathise with our weaknesses, but we have one who has been tempted in every way, just as we are – yet was without sin' (Heb. 4:15).

(2) 'He committed no sin, and no deceit was found in his mouth' (1 Pet. 2:22).

b. Jesus did all that is required of us.

(1) He was baptised for us. 'Jesus replied, "Let it be so now; it is proper for us to do this to fulfil all righteousness." Then John consented' (Matt. 3:15).

(2) He believed for us. 'And again, "I will put my trust in him." And again he says, "Here am I, and the children God has given me"' (Heb. 2:13).

(3) He fulfilled the law for us. 'Do not think that I have come to abolish the Law or the Prophets; I have not come to abolish them but to fulfil them' (Matt. 5:17).

2. *Christ's sacrificial death*

a. He fulfilled the law as outline in the Levitical sacrificial system.

(1) The sacrifices of the law did not satisfy. 'The law is only a shadow of the good things that are coming – not the realities themselves. For this reason it can never, by the same sacrifices repeated endlessly year after year, make perfect those who draw near to worship' (Heb. 10:1).

(2) Christ's death did satisfy. 'But when this priest had offered for all time one sacrifice for sins, he sat down at the right hand of God' (Heb. 10:12).

b. God provided Jesus in our place. 'We all, like sheep, have gone astray, each of us has turned to his own way; and the Lord has laid on him the iniquity of us all' (Isa. 53:6).

(1) He was our substitute.

(2) He was out satisfaction.

C. All the above is summed up by Paul's teaching of the faith of Jesus Christ.

1. *Jesus believed perfectly for us because he had the Spirit without any limit.* 'For the one whom God has sent speaks the words of God, for God gives the Spirit without limit' (John 3:34).

a. We believe, all of us, in proportion to our faith (Rom. 12:3).

b. Therefore our own faith is mixed with doubting.

c. But Jesus never doubted, therefore his very faith saved us – as long as it is joined by our faith.

2. *Paul said that the righteousness of God is revealed 'from faith to faith'* (Rom. 1:17 margin).

a. Why the two references to faith – faith to faith? Answer:

(1) The first reference to faith is the faith of Jesus.

(2) The second reference to faith is our own faith.

b. This is borne out by two passages:

(1) 'Even the righteousness of God which is by faith of Jesus Christ unto all and upon all them that believe' (Rom. 3:22 AV).

(2) 'Knowing that a man is not justified by the works of the law, but by the faith of Jesus Christ, even we have believed in Jesus Christ, that we might be justified by the faith of Christ' (Gal. 2:16 AV).

3. *John Calvin refers to three causes of justification:*

a. The meritorious cause: the work of Christ.

b. The effectual cause: the Holy Spirit.

c. The instrumental cause: our faith.

(1) We are saved by Christ in whom we have faith.

(2) Our faith is God's gift. 'For it is by grace you have been saved, through faith – and this not from yourselves, it is the gift of God' (Eph. 2:8).

(3) In a word: we are saved by faith alone in Christ alone.

II. Assurance of being justified

A. Assurance (def.): confidence, or knowing, that you are saved.
1. Does faith alone assure?
2. Or does faith plus something else (e.g. works) provide assurance that we are saved?

B. Paul has already established that we are saved, or justified, by faith alone.
1. Works allow for boasting. 'If, in fact, Abraham was justified by works, he had something to boast about – but not before God' (Rom. 4:2).
2. Does God allow boasting? No, 'it is excluded' (Rom. 3:27).
3. Paul summed it up; it is by grace. 'Not by works, so that no one can boast' (Eph. 2:9).

C. If, then, one is assured by good works it follows that one could boast on the basis of assurance.
1. Some say: we are justified by faith but assured by works.
2. *I answer: this means we have something of which to boast.*
   a. It equally follows that what saves (faith) is insufficient to assure (faith).
   b. This puts a dichotomy in the doctrine of assurance which the Scriptures do not allow.

D. How can we be sure we are assured by faith alone?
1. *Faith is assurance.* 'Now faith is being sure of what we hope for and certain of what we do not see' (Heb. 11:1).
   a. The object of faith is Christ and all he did for us.
   b. We know in our heart of hearts whether our trust is in Christ – or not.
      (1) If it is in Christ, we are saved.
      (2) If it is in works, we are not saved.
2. *To say you are saved by Christ but assured by works is to put your trust in that which cannot save.*
   a. Why ever would anyone want to be assured by what cannot save?
   b. If works cannot save it is fatal to turn around and trust works for assurance.

3. *If we are saved by faith but assured by works, how will we ever know if we have sufficient works by which to be assured?*
   a. We would always be unsure.
   b. If we were – given that premise – we would be self-righteous.
   c. There would always be some doubt whether or not we are truly saved.

E. In a word: it is not great faith that saves but faith in a great Saviour!

> My hope is built on nothing less
> Than Jesus' blood and righteousness.
> I dare not trust the sweetest frame
> But wholly lean on Jesus' name.
> On Christ, the solid Rock, I stand,
> All other ground is sinking sand.
>
> Edward Mote

III. LIVING BY FAITH

A. Three times in the New Testament there is to be found a reference to Habakkuk 2:4: 'The righteous will live by his faith (margin: faithfulness).'
   1. Romans 1:17: 'The righteous will live by faith.'
   2. Galatians 3:11: 'The righteous will live by faith.'
   3. Hebrews 10:38: 'But my righteous one will live by faith.'

B. In Habakkuk 2:4 the Hebrew word is in fact: faithfulness.
   1. If one lives by his own faithfulness it smacks of self-trust, the opposite of the teaching of Scripture.
   2. *The 'faithfulness' of Habakkuk 2:4 refers to the faithfulness of God.*
      a. This is borne out by the context: 'For the revelation awaits an appointed time; it speaks of the end and will not prove false. Though it linger, wait for it; it will certainly come and will not delay' (Hab. 2:3).
      b. This is the way the commentary found in the Dead Sea Scrolls reads (showing how the ancient authorities understood the Hebrew), namely: the righteous will live by the faithfulness of God.

    c. This is further demonstrated by the context of Hebrews 10:38, namely (Heb. 10:37): 'For in just a very little while, "He who is coming will come and will not delay."'

        (1) One lives by knowing that God is faithful.

        (2) 'He who promised is faithful' (Heb. 10:23).

        (3) Abraham 'considered him faithful who made the promise' (Heb. 11:11).

    d. In a word: our faith is in the faithfulness of God

        (1) This is consistent with the way we are saved: 'from faith to faith'; Christ's faith is ratified (put into effect) by our faith.

        (2) We live therefore by trusting that God is faithful.

C. All the above is mirrored by Paul's statement in Galatians 2:20:

    1. *'I live by the faith of the Son of God,' that is, (Greek) 'I live by faith, viz., that of the Son of God.'*

        a. Paul isn't leaning on his own faith.

        b. He is leaning on Christ's faith.

            (1) This is the way we are saved.

            (2) This is the way we live – living by faith not works.

    2. *Now the question follows: of what does Christ's faith consist?*

        a. His obedience when on earth.

            (1) His faith was a perfect faith.

            (2) His perfect faith resulted in a perfect obedience; indeed, an obedience sufficient to make us righteous. 'For just as through the disobedience of the one man the many were made sinners, so also through the obedience of the one man the many will be made righteous' (Rom. 5:19).

            (3) This is why Paul could say, 'For if, when we were God's enemies, we were reconciled to him through the death of his Son, how much more, having been reconciled, shall we be saved through his life!' (Rom. 5:10).

        b. His intercession at God's right hand.

            (1) He prayed with a perfect faith on earth. 'I always do what pleases him' (John 8:29; cf. John 5:19,30).

            (2) Those for whom he prayed would be saved. 'I pray for them. I am not praying for the world, but for those you have given me, for they are yours' (John 17:9).

(3) This would include those who crucified him (Luke 23:34).
(4) He intercedes for us at God's right hand.
  (a) 'Who is he that condemns? Christ Jesus, who died –
      more than that, who was raised to life – is at the right
      hand of God and is also interceding for us' (Rom.
      8:34).
  (b) 'Therefore he is able to save completely those who
      come to God through him, because he always lives to
      intercede for them' (Heb. 7:25).

3. *In a word: Paul lives by Christ's faith.*
  a. He is saved by Christ's faith when he was on earth.
  b. He continues to live by the faith of Christ who prays at
     God's right hand.

IV. THE PLACE OF GOOD WORKS IN THE CHRISTIAN LIFE

A. **Good works, or sanctification, spring from gratitude** (see
   Chapter 41, The Doctrine of Gratitude).
   1. We do not show good works to be saved.
   2. Because we are saved we show good works.
   3. Sanctification is the doctrine of gratitude.

B. **Because God puts us on our honour, Paul warned that we
   must be 'careful' to show good works (Tit. 3:8). Why?**
   1. Gratitude must be taught and learned.
   2. Gratitude glorifies God.
   3. Gratitude is a testimony to the world that leaves it without excuse.

C. **Works neither save nor assure but nonetheless please God
   and bring his blessing.**
   1. 'God is not unjust; he will not forget your work and the love you
      have shown him as you have helped his people and continue to
      help them' (Heb. 6:10).
   2. *They become the basis of two things:*
      a. Our inheritance – leading to a greater anointing.
      b. Our reward in heaven – so we will not be saved by fire (1
         Cor. 3:15).

D. The absence of good works brings about God's displeasure.
  1. *Being disciplined:*
      a. Internal chastening: by the Word.
      b. External chastening: when God steps in from without.
      c. Terminal chastening: when God steps in by premature death.
  2. *Any lack of holiness is displeasing to God.*
      a. He does not discipline those who are not his (Lam. 3:39).
      b. He disciplines only those who are his (Heb. 12:5-11).

CONCLUSION
Justification is through faith and by grace. Works play no part in justification otherwise man would be contributing something to his own salvation. Following conversion Christians live by faith: the faith of Jesus Christ through whom their salvation was secured, God's faithfulness to his commitment to his children, and the gift of faith imparted to them by the Holy Spirit. While good works are not instrumental in justification they are an evidence of the gratitude the believer feels to his Saviour. Scripture indicates that good works should be part of every Christian life, as they bring glory to God. But we do not look to them for assurance of being saved. Our works are the basis of our reward in heaven.

41

THE DOCTRINE OF GRATITUDE

INTRODUCTION

A. Is gratitude actually a doctrine? Yes.
1. The word 'doctrine' means 'teaching'.
2. Gratitude is something which must be taught.

B. In reformed theology the doctrine of sanctification (the holy life) is called the 'doctrine of gratitude'.
1. Why? Because a holy life is partly our way of saying 'thank you' to God for saving us.
2. *We are not saved by being sanctified.*
   a. If sanctification were either the cause or the precondition of salvation, salvation would ultimately be by works not by grace.
   b. But if we are saved by grace not works, where does sanctification come in? Answer:
   (1) It is like a PS at the end of a letter.
   (2) Sanctification is our way of saying:

   'Thank you, Lord, for saving my soul,
   Thank you, Lord, for making me whole;
   Thank you, Lord, for giving to me
   Thy great salvation so rich and free.'

C. Definitions:
1. *Gratitude: Showing that one values the kindness of God in saving us.*
   a. It is a feeling, but it is more than a feeling.
   b. Gratitude is what we *do*; it may be a sacrifice in that we don't have an overwhelming feeling.
   (1) Sometimes we *feel* grateful, sometimes we do not.
   (2) But we must always *be* grateful, whether or not we feel it.

c. Gratitude shows that we set a value on God's kindness.

(1)'In order that in the coming ages he might show the incomparable riches of his grace, expressed in his kindness to us in Christ Jesus' (Eph. 2:7).

(2)'But when the kindness and love of God our Saviour appeared, he saved us, not because of righteous things we had done, but because of his mercy. He saved us through the washing of rebirth and renewal by the Holy Spirit, whom he poured out on us generously through Jesus Christ our Saviour, so that, having been justified by his grace, we might become heirs having the hope of eternal life' (Tit. 3:4-7).

2. *Sanctification: the process by which we are made holy.*

a. It is a process not a crisis experience.

(1)There is a sense in which sanctification is something that happens to every Christian: 'To open their eyes and turn them from darkness to light, and from the power of Satan to God, so that they may receive forgiveness of sins and a place among those who are sanctified by faith in me' (Acts 26:18).

(2)We are all sanctified in Christ. 'It is because of him that you are in Christ Jesus, who has become for us wisdom from God – that is, our righteousness, holiness and redemption' (1 Cor. 1:30).

b. It is progressive and is never completed until we are glorified.

(1)'Therefore, I urge you, brothers, in view of God's mercy, to offer your bodies as living sacrifices, holy and pleasing to God – this is your spiritual act of worship. Do not conform any longer to the pattern of this world, but be transformed by the renewing of your mind. Then you will be able to test and approve what God's will is – his good, pleasing and perfect will' (Rom. 12:1-2).

(2)'Not that I have already obtained all this, or have already been made perfect, but I press on to take hold of that for which Christ Jesus took hold of me. Brothers, I do not consider myself yet to have taken hold of it. But one thing I do: Forgetting what is behind and straining towards what is ahead, I press on towards the goal to win the prize for which God has called me heavenwards in Christ Jesus' (Phil. 3:12-14).

c. Sanctification is a life sentence.

   (1) If we 'got it' completely along the way, we could forget about it from then on!

   (2) But only glorification will mark the end of this life sentence. 'And those he predestined, he also called; those he called, he also justified; those he justified, he also glorified' (Rom. 8:30).

D. Why is this theological study important?

1. Gratitude must be taught; we must never assume that it comes automatically.

2. Sanctification must be preached; that is why all Paul's epistles urge its acceptance and practice.

3. Many Christians are confused as to the place of sanctification in the Christian life; this lesson will put it in a sound theological and biblical framework.

4. It is sobering to realize how much God hates ingratitude; the warning may well be timely for many of us.

5. It is encouraging to know how much God loves our gratitude; this should spur us on to be more thankful than ever.

I. SANCTIFICATION DOES NOT PRECEDE BUT FOLLOWS REGENERATION

A. Regeneration (def.): being born again.

1. *Regeneration is an unconscious work of the Holy Spirit.*

   a. It is what produces faith (1 Thess. 2:13).

      (1) Faith does not produce regeneration.

      (2) Faith shows that life was already there, or one could not have faith.

   b. Many people can tell you the 'day and the hour' when they were born again.

      (1) This is probably not always quite true, although one knows what such people mean by this.

      (2) What is more likely true is that some people can tell you the day and hour when they were *conscious* of being saved; in other words, when they came to assurance of salvation.

2. *Regeneration is the life of God in the soul of man* (1 John 5:11-12).

a. It is what awakened him or her from being 'dead' (Eph. 2:1).

   (1) Until one was given life there was no way one could believe.

   (2) Life came first; faith followed (Eph. 2:4-5).

b. It is called a 'new creation.' 'Therefore, if anyone is in Christ, he is a new creation; the old has gone, the new has come!' (2 Cor. 5:17).

   (1) It is what God does and is as supernatural as when God initially said, 'Let there be light' and light came (Gen. 1:3).

   (2) God's new creation is done by a Sovereign Redeemer. (Eph. 1:7).

B. As faith follows regeneration, so too sanctification.

   1. *We cannot enter into the process of being made holy until life, made possible by the Spirit, is there to make this possible.*

   a. It is like making the horse follow the cart by making a person holy before he has faith.

   b. It is asking a person to manifest good works when he really needs to know he is saved by Christ's work.

   2. *We are saved by faith alone in Christ alone.*

   a. God's righteousness is given 'through faith in Jesus Christ' (Rom. 3:22).

   b. The object of that faith is Christ's blood (Rom. 3:25).

C. The gospel of Christ is the good news that we are saved without works.

   1. *It is not given to the man who works for it but to the one who does not work for it.*

   a. 'However, to the man who does not work but trusts God who justifies the wicked, his faith is credited as righteousness' (Rom. 4:5).

   b. Where is boasting then? 'It is excluded' (Rom. 3:27).

   2. It is absolutely free – upon the condition of faith. 'For it is by grace you have been saved, through faith – and this not from yourselves, it is the gift of God – not by works, so that no-one can boast' (Eph. 2:8-9).

D. If we have understood the nature of the gospel (that we are saved unconditionally) we are going to ask, 'What shall we say, then? Shall we go on sinning, so that grace may increase?' (Rom. 6:1).

    1. If we don't ask that question, chances are, we haven't understood the gospel!

    2. *And yet if we think that we must go on sinning it shows we still haven't understood it!*

        a. This is the reason for Romans 6, which shows that the old self 'was crucified' (Rom. 6:6).

        b. Not that we are unable to sin but because we are able not to sin! Augustine's four stages of man:

            (1) Able to sin (before the Fall).

            (2) Not able not to sin (after the Fall).

            (3) Able not to sin (after regeneration).

            (4) Not able to sin (glorification).

        c. Paul therefore says to the regenerated person, 'Count yourselves dead to sin but alive to God in Christ Jesus' (Rom. 6:11).

            (1) 'Therefore do not let sin reign in your mortal body so that you obey its evil desires' (Rom. 6:12).

            (2) 'It is God's will that you should be sanctified: that you should avoid sexual immorality' (1 Thess. 4:3).

E. Sanctification must be preached and taught; this is why we have the epistles of Paul (1 Cor. 6:9-11).

    1. Sanctification is not a condition of salvation; otherwise we would look to our sanctification to be sure we are saved, which would be a gospel of works (Gal. 1:6ff).

    2. *Sanctification is obedience to God as evidence of our gratitude to him for graciously saving us* (2 Pet. 1:10).

        a. It is obedience, but obedience that must be taught.

        b. It is gratitude, gratitude that must be taught. 'This is a trustworthy saying. And I want you to stress these things, so that those who have trusted in God may be careful to devote themselves to doing what is good. These things are excellent and profitable for everyone' (Tit. 3:8).

II. GOD HATES INGRATITUDE AND LOVES OUR BEING THANKFUL

A. In Romans 1 Paul demonstrates the justice of God's wrath on men.

1. They suppress the truth by their wickedness (Rom. 1:18).
2. What is known about God is made plain to them so that they are without excuse (Rom. 1:19-20).
3. Such people 'neither glorified him as God *nor gave thanks to him*' (Rom. 1:21).

B. Paul lists conditions of wickedness in the last days. 'People will be lovers of themselves, lovers of money, boastful, proud, abusive, disobedient to their parents, *ungrateful*, unholy' (2 Tim. 3:2).

1. In a generation that did as they 'saw fit' (Jud. 21:25), their backsliding was rooted in ingratitude. 'The Israelites did evil in the eyes of the LORD; they forgot the LORD their God and served the Baals and the Asherahs' (Jud. 3:7).
2. *'But they forgot the LORD their God; so he sold them into the hands of Sisera, the commander of the army of Hazor, and into the hands of the Philistines and the king of Moab, who fought against them'* (1 Sam. 12:9).
   a. 'They forgot what he had done, the wonders he had shown them' (Ps. 78:11).
   b. 'But they soon forgot what he had done and did not wait for his counsel' (Ps. 106:13).
3. Ingratitude is so serious that Moses warned: 'If you ever forget the LORD your God and follow other gods, and worship and bow down to them, I testify against you today that you will surely be destroyed. Like the nations the LORD destroyed before you, so you will be destroyed for not obeying the LORD your God' (Deut. 8:19-20. cf. Lev. 26).

C. Jesus healed ten lepers, but only one came back to thank him.

1. The one who expressed gratitude 'threw himself at Jesus' feet and thanked him' (Luke 17:15-16).
2. 'Jesus asked, "Were not all ten cleansed? Where are the other nine?"' (Luke 17:17).

D. God has made it abundantly clear how he appreciates gratitude.

1. 'I will praise God's name in song and glorify him with thanksgiving' (Ps. 69:30).

2. 'Let us come before him with thanksgiving and extol him with music and song' (Ps. 95:2).

3. 'Enter his gates with thanksgiving and his courts with praise; give thanks to him and praise his name' (Ps. 100:4).

4. 'Sing to the LORD with thanksgiving; make music to our God on the harp' (Ps. 147:7).

5. 'Do not be anxious about anything, but in everything, by prayer and petition, with thanksgiving, present your requests to God' (Phil. 4:6).

6. 'Devote yourselves to prayer, being watchful and thankful' (Col. 4:2).

E. One reason that Jesus instituted the Lord's Supper is that we would never forget. 'And he took bread, gave thanks and broke it, and gave it to them, saying, "This is my body given for you; do this in remembrance of me"' (Luke 22:19).

1. An essential ingredient in gratitude is *remembering* what God has done.

2. We are put on our honour to remember to be thankful.

III. HOW DO WE SHOW OUR GRATITUDE?

A. By a holy life

1. We are not saved by being holy; we are holy because we have been saved.

2. *But because we are still sinners – 'prone to wander, Lord, I feel it' – we easily forget and become careless.*

   a. Sanctification is not only possible but inevitable if we are saved.

   b. But the depth of our holiness is determined by how grateful we are.

B. By our worship. 'Through Jesus, therefore, let us continually offer to God a sacrifice of praise – the fruit of lips that confess his name' (Heb. 13:15).

1. *This does not merely refer to our public worship – singing hymns and choruses etc. – though this is important.*
   a. The public worship encouraged by King David centred on instrumental music and singing.
      (1) 'David told the leaders of the Levites to appoint their brothers as singers to sing joyful songs, accompanied by musical instruments: lyres, harps and cymbals' (1 Chron. 15:16).
      (2) On the day the Ark was brought to Jerusalem David committed to Asaph and his associates a 'psalm of thanks to the LORD: Give thanks to the LORD, call on his name; make known among the nations what he has done' (1 Chron. 16:7ff. cf. Ps. 105).
   b. Public worship to God honours him; he inhabits our praises.
      (1) Like the mist that rises to the heavens and forms clouds that make rain, so our praise brings down blessing.
      (2) 'May the peoples praise you, O God; may all the peoples praise you. Then the land will yield its harvest, and God, our God, will bless us' (Ps. 67:5-6).
2. *This is done by each of us individually in our time alone with God.*
   a. 'Let the word of Christ dwell in you richly as you teach and admonish one another with all wisdom, and as you sing psalms, hymns and spiritual songs with gratitude in your hearts to God' (Col. 3:16).
   b. We can learn to praise God and sing *just to him* when we are alone.

C. By giving him one tenth of our income.

1. *Tithing was made legal under the Law* (Lev. 27:30).
   a. This means it was required.
   b. Under Abraham it emerged as a principle when Abraham, and Jacob after him, gave one tenth voluntarily (Gen. 14:20. cf. Gen. 28:22).
2. *We are not under Law but under grace.*
   a. We are not required to tithe as a condition of salvation.
   b. But God promises to bless those who do (he didn't have to): '"Bring the whole tithe into the storehouse, that there may be food in my house. Test me in this," says the LORD Almighty, "and see if I will not throw open the floodgates of heaven

and pour out so much blessing that you will not have room
enough for it"' (Mal. 3:10).

    (1) This principle continues in the New Testament (1 Cor.
16:2).

    (2) The principle of receiving is also continued: 'Remember
this: Whoever sows sparing will also reap sparingly, and
whoever sows generously will also reap generously' (2
Cor. 9:6).

D. By sharing our faith. 'As the Father has sent me, I am sending
you' (John 20:21).

1. We show our gratitude to God for saving us by our sharing our
faith with others.

2. What if our gratitude to God were summed up entirely by our
witnessing to others – what gratitude to God would *you* have
manifested until now?

3. There is a glorious benefit in sharing our faith: 'I pray that you
may be active in sharing your faith, so that you will have a full
understanding of every good thing we have in Christ' (Phile 6).

E. By the amount of time we spend alone with God.

1. We reveal how important another person is to us by the actual
amount of time we give to them.

2. *How much time do you give solely to God by being utterly*
alone with him and talking only to him?

    a. There will be no praying like this in heaven.

    b. Are you happy about your personal prayer life? If not, do
something about it now – starting today!

F. By discovering what pleases the Lord.

1. *This comes by experiencing two things:*

    a. Walking in the light (1 John 1:7).

    b. Becoming acquainted with the ungrieved Spirit of God (Eph.
4:30).

2. When we discern what pleases him we know better how to
please him!

G. By disciplined church attendance.

1. It is no small insult to God's name when his people are not
found regularly meeting together.

2. 'Let us not give up meeting together, as some are in the habit of doing, but let us encourage one another – and all the more as you see the Day approaching' (Heb. 10:25).

H. By respecting those God has put over you.
1. 'Hold them in the highest regard in love because of their work. Live in peace with each other' (1 Thess. 5:13).
2. 'Remember your leaders, who spoke the word of God to you. Consider the outcome of their way of life and imitate their faith' (Heb. 13:7).

I. By doing good works such as helping when it is needed.
1. The AV refers to the gift of 'helps' ('those able to help others' – NIV) (1 Cor. 12:28).
2. *This can include:*
   a. Visiting the sick, the widow, the helpless (Jas. 1:27).
   b. Feeding the poor (Jas. 2:6,14ff).
   c. Giving someone a ride to church.
   d. Doing things in your church that nobody wants to do: cleaning up, help with flowers, or whatever needs to be done.
   e. Whatever makes your pastors's job easier so that 10% of the people won't be doing nearly all the work.

IV. FOR WHAT ARE YOU GRATEFUL?
A. Salvation: God sending his Son to die on a cross.
B. That he gave you faith.
C. Your church – that person who had a hand in leading you to Christ.
D. Your Minister whose preaching and pastoring feeds your soul.
E. Your job – your income.
F. Your health.
G. The Bible.
H. What God did for you yesterday.

CONCLUSION
There is no end to the list by which we can demonstrate our gratitude to God. The highest level of gratitude is not expecting thanks from God who has enabled you to obey. 'So you also, when you have done everything you were told to do, should say, "We are unworthy servants; we have only done our duty"' (Luke 17:10).

42

IF GOD KNOWS THE FUTURE, WHY PRAY?

<small>INTRODUCTION</small>

A. In this chapter, we are plunging into the 'deep end'.

    1. We are in over our heads, so we must swim.

    2. *This subject is as profound as we can imagine.*

        a. It is complicated; we open up the question of the sovereignty and omniscience of God.

            (1) Sovereignty of God (def.): God's own right to do as he pleases.

            (2) Omniscience of God (def.): God's perfect wisdom and knowledge.

        b. Yet it need not be complicated, if we can be like children – who trust a loving Father. 'I tell you the truth, anyone who will not receive the kingdom of God like a little child will never enter it' (Mark 10:15).

            (1) If we are overly intellectual or cerebral we will be in difficulty.

            (2) If we are like children – who take God's Word simply, we will proceed with great freedom and trust.

B. This lesson begins with the assumption: God knows the future.

    1. *This assumption has been under attack in recent years.*

        a. The consensus of Christians generally has been to accept uncritically the belief that God knows the future.

        b. The historic concept regarding God's attributes takes this for granted, for example:

            (1) God is omnipotent: he is able to do anything. 'I am the LORD, the God of all mankind. Is anything too hard for me?' (Jer. 32:27). 'For nothing is impossible with God' (Luke 1:37).

            (2) God is omnipresent: he is everywhere. 'Where can I go from your Spirit? Where can I flee from your presence?

> If I go up to the heavens, you are there; if I make my
> bed in the depths, you are there. If I rise on the wings of
> the dawn, if I settle on the far side of the sea, even there
> your hand will guide me, your right hand will hold me
> fast' (Ps. 139:7-10).

(3) God is omniscient: he knows everything. 'O LORD, you
have searched me and you know me. You know when I
sit and when I rise; you perceive my thoughts from afar.
You discern my going out and my lying down; you are
familiar with all my ways. Before a word is on my tongue
you know it completely, O LORD' (Ps. 139:1-4).

c. In Protestantism two points of view have emerged:

(1) Reformed view (Calvinism): centring on predestination
and the sovereignty of God.

(2) Arminianism: modifying Calvin's doctrine of
predestination and affirming the free will of man.

d. This view has not however divided Arminians and Calvinists.

(1) Whatever differences they had with each other, both
agreed that God knows the future – and knows perfectly
well how it will work out.

(2) The difference: Calvinists say that God chose who would
be saved; Arminians say that God knew who would be
saved and chose them.

(3) This is a theological quarrel within the Protestant family;
both John Calvin and John Wesley (an Arminian) will be
in heaven.

e. We therefore are not opening up the quarrel between
Calvinists and Arminians since both are agreed that God
knows the future.

2. *We need not spend very long in providing evidence that
God knows the future.*

a. Here is a sample of biblical evidence:

(1) 'Your eyes saw my unformed body. All the days ordained
for me were written in your book before one of them
came to be' (Ps. 139:16).

(2) 'I make known the end from the beginning, from ancient
times, what is still to come. I say: My purpose will stand,
and I will do all that I please' (Isa. 46:10).

(3) 'Then the LORD said to him, "Know for certain that your

descendants will be strangers in a country not their own,
and they will be enslaved and mistreated four hundred
years"' (Gen. 15:13).

(4) 'Therefore I told you these things long ago; before they
happened I announced them to you so that you could not
say, "My idols did them; my wooden image and metal
god ordained them"' (Isa. 48:5).

(5) 'You have made known to me the paths of life; you will
fill me with joy in your presence' (Acts 2:28).

b. One may wish to say that these writers were misinformed:

(1) That they were expressing their personal views.

(2) What is certain: the people God chose to use to write the
Bible believed God knows the future.

C. But there is a reasonable question that comes out of the assumption that God knows the future: Why pray?

1. Why bother to pray if the future is already known to the God
we pray to?

2. Since the future is known it is also fixed and unchangeable;
what good do our prayers do?

3. Since the future is unchangeable, our prayers cannot change
God; therefore what is the use in talking to him?

4. It would seem that our praying is a waste of time and energy.

D. Why is this lesson important?

1. The question 'Why pray since God knows the future?', this is a
reasonable question to ask.

2. We need to inquire as to whether there is a good answer to the
question: Why pray if God knows the future?

3. If the answer is Yes – we should pray even though God knows
the future, we want to know why that answer is yes.

4. God has told us to pray; therefore every lesson on prayer is in
line with God's desire for us.

5. God has told us that he knows the future; therefore we need to
see if there is any harmony, or logical connection, in praying
even though we know God knows the future.

6. Any subject that has to do with the nature of God is edifying to
us – and glorifying to him.

7. We all need to be reminded to pray – the more, the better.

I. THE EXAMPLE OF JESUS

A. Jesus affirmed the God of the Old Testament as his Father (never forget this).

1. *He knew that his Father knew the future and yet he was a man of prayer.*
   a. 'Very early in the morning, while it was still dark, Jesus got up, left the house and went off to a solitary place, where he prayed' (Mark 1:35).
   b. 'After he had dismissed them, he went up on a mountainside by himself to pray. When evening came, he was there alone' (Matt. 14:23).
   c. 'One of those days Jesus went out to a mountainside to pray, and spent the night praying to God' (Luke 6:12).
2. Not that Jesus himself knew that future perfectly. 'No one knows about that day or hour, not even the angels in heaven, nor the Son, but only the Father' (Mark 13:32).

B. Jesus knew that the elect (chosen) would, sooner or later, come to him. 'All that the Father gives to me will come to me' (John 6:37).

1. He wasn't merely speaking of the Twelve; they had already come to him.
2. He was speaking of those who hadn't yet believed, that they, sooner or later, would come to him.
3. *And yet he prayed none the less that they would believe!*
   a. 'My prayer is not for them alone. I pray also for those who will believe in me through their message' (John 17:20).
   b. As for the Twelve, they had come to him already (John 17:6-12).

C. Jesus knew that those who came to him would be kept and therefore would never be lost.

1. 'Whoever come to me I will never drive away' (John 6:37, AV): 'I will in no wise cast out.'
2. 'No one can come to me unless the Father who sent me draws him, and I will raise him up at the last day' (John 6:44).
3. 'My sheep listen to my voice; I know them, and they follow me. I give them eternal life, and they shall never perish; no one can snatch them out of my hand' (John 10:27-28).

4. *And yet at the same time Jesus prayed that they would be kept!* 'Protect them by the power of your name' (John 17:11,15).

  a. The only exception: Judas. 'While I was with them, I protected them and kept them safe by that name you gave me. None has been lost except the one doomed to destruction so that Scripture would be fulfilled' (John 17:12).

  b. Jesus knew from the beginning who would betray him. 'He meant Judas, the son of Simon Iscariot, who, though one of the Twelve, was later to betray him' (John 6:71).

D. Jesus knew that Simon Peter would betray him, yet he prayed for him.

  1. 'Jesus answered, "I tell you, Peter, before the rooster crows today, you will deny three times that you know me"' (Luke 22:34).

  2. 'Simon, Simon, Satan has asked to sift you as wheat. But I have prayed for you, Simon, that your faith may not fail. And when you have turned back, strengthen your brothers' (Luke 22:31-32).

E. Jesus knew he came to the world to die on a cross.

  1. Jesus knew he would be crucified and raised from the dead (Matt. 17:22ff).

  2. Yet he prayed in the Garden of Gethsemane, 'Father, if you are willing, take this cup from me; yet not my will, but yours be done' (Luke 22:42).

F. The first way we answer the question, 'If God knows the future, why pray?' is: Because Jesus did.

  1. We are not better than Jesus!

  2. *He, more than any of us, knew that God knows everything – past, present, future – but he prayed. It did not stop him.*

  a. As for the present, he even shared with the Father what the Father already knew. 'I have revealed you to those whom you gave me out of the world. They were yours; you gave them to me and they have obeyed your word' (John 17:6).

  b. We could ask, if God knows the present, why tell him? Answer: because Jesus did.

3. *God invites us to enter into the life of Jesus, to follow him as he did and to pray as he did.*
   a. To share our hearts – what we feel; this is intimacy.
   b. To ask him to act; this is intercession.

II. MAKING SENSE OF PRAYER IN THE LIGHT OF GOD'S OMNISCIENCE AND SOVEREIGNTY

A. The danger of being controlled by logic alone, or only part of Scripture.
   1. *If we carry logic too far, here is what we might wrongly conclude:*
      a. God is the author of sin.
         (1)He had the power to stop Satan's revolt and Adam's fall.
         (2)But he didn't; therefore he is the cause of it by allowing it.
      b. God is the architect of all evil and suffering.
         (1)He could stop it at any moment.
         (2)He appears not to do so; therefore he is to be blamed.
      c. God is responsible for the lost going to hell.
         (1)He chose who would be saved before the creation of the world (Eph. 1:4).
         (2)He obviously did not write the names of some in the book of life (Rev. 17:8).
         (3)Therefore he is the architect of damnation.
      d. God is brutal by creating people he knew would be lost.
         (1)He knows who will be saved.
         (2)Why doesn't he stop people from being born?
   2. *We must be controlled by faith and obedience, not by logic.*
     "'For my thoughts are not your thoughts, neither are your ways my ways," declares the LORD. "As the heavens are higher than the earth, so are my ways higher than your ways and my thoughts than your thoughts'" (Isa. 55:8-9).
      a. Faith is believing God, taking him at his word.
      b. Obedience is carried out because we take God's Word seriously.
      c. Logic will drive us to doing nothing, if not to despair.
         (1)There are some things that are unknowable.
         (2)Moses was prohibited from coming too close to the burning bush (Ex. 3:5).
         (3)Moses was not allowed to see the face of God, only a fleeting glimpse of his back (Ex. 33:21-23).

B. The antinomy and prayer.

1. Antinomy (def.): parallel principles that are irreconcilable but equally true. J I Packer: they only appear to be irreconcilable.
2. *We accept the antinomy with regard to the basic teachings:*
   a. The person of Christ.
      (1) Jesus is not fifty percent man and fifty percent God.
      (2) Jesus is one hundred percent man and one hundred percent God.
   b. Evangelism and the sovereignty of God.
      (1) God has chosen his elect (Rom. 8:30; 2 Tim. 1:9).
      (2) He has equally chosen to use preaching to save the elect – to be carried out to all nations (Matt. 28:19; Acts 17:30).
3. *This applies to prayer.*
   a. The same God who knows the future (because he is God) has chosen to work through prayer. 'Ask of me, and I will make the nations your inheritance, the ends of the earth your possession' (Ps. 2:8).
   b. Isaac need not have worried about having a son.
      (1) He had God's oath to Abraham going for him (Gen. 22:15-18).
      (2) But when his wife Rebekah was barren, he prayed, and the Lord answered his prayer (Gen. 25:21).
   c. Jesus said we should 'always pray, and not give up' (Luke 18:1).
   d. God knew that the Holy Spirit would descend on the Day of Pentecost, yet Jesus told the disciples to pray until the Spirit came.
      (1) God knew the future but the disciples didn't.
      (2) Therefore 'they all joined together constantly in prayer' (Acts 1:14).

C. Obedience pleases God more than sound head knowledge.

1. *Those who are the most articulate theologically sadly are sometimes the least zealous.*
   a. Sound theology sometimes breeds self-righteousness.
      (1) Some feel smug because they uphold 'the truth'.
      (2) They do not realise that they dishonour God's name. They honour the Lord with their lips but 'their hearts are far from me' (Isa. 29:13).

    b. God uses obedient men and women not those who are 'sound' only.

        (1) Cerebral theology often allows people to feel justified by what they hate when in fact they lose their first love.

        (2) The church at Ephesus hated the practices of the Nicolaitans but forsook their first love (Rev. 2:4-6).

        (3) God removes the lampstand from its place, which means he will reject some from being used and find those who will be obedient.

2. *Those who are most articulate theologically sadly are sometimes the quickest to betray unbelief when they fall into a crisis.*

    a. They uphold the sovereignty of God in their hearts.

    b. They panic when trouble comes to them.

    c. This is the danger of believing with the head and not the heart.

3. *If one says, 'God knows how it will turn out,' but opts not to pray:*

    a. They will be in disobedience.

    b. They will not enjoy seeing answered prayer.

    c. They will grieve the Holy Spirit.

4. *Note: obedience without sound knowledge may not please God either.*

    a. After all, the Pharisee could be obedient (Luke 18:11-12).

    b. Paul lamented that the Jews had zeal without knowledge (Rom. 10:2).

D. If one is motivated to pray only if he or she thinks God doesn't know the future, it follows:

1. *Some only pray to God so long as God pleases them.*

    a. Some don't like a God who knows everything.

    b. They need to feel God doesn't know all in order to pray.

    c. The like the God who fits with our concept of what God should be like.

2. *Some people only pray to God if they think God isn't all powerful.*

    a. This puts the person praying in a position of power.

    b. Instead of God being sovereign and powerful they are equal partners with him.

    c. Note: those who don't believe God knows the future almost invariably deny his omnipotence (being all-powerful).

  3. *They pray to a God who may or may not be up to our requests,* that is, able to answer even if he wants to.

  4. *God is no more knowledgeable than the devil.*

    a. If God knows only the past and present perfectly, this is true of the devil as well.

    b. Sadly some want a God who takes his cue from us before he decides what to do.

E. Maintaining the equal balance honours and pleases God most.

  1. *He who knows the end from the beginning gave us the privilege of prayer.*

    a. He is honoured and pleased when we affirm his attributes.

    b. He is honoured and pleased when we take prayer equally seriously.

  2. Those who don't believe in his infinite knowledge cannot be sure of his power to answer; therefore they pray with little or no assurance.

  3. Those who believe in his infinite knowledge often tend to pray perfunctorily and without earnest zeal.

  4. *Those who have the balance will be those who pray:*

    a. Knowing that God already knows everything (Matt. 6:8).

    b. Knowing our prayer makes a difference. 'You do not have, because you do not ask God' (Jas. 4:2).

    c. Spurgeon: When I don't pray, all I know is, coincidences don't happen; when I pray, coincidences happen.

    d. This is because God has ordained that some things will not happen apart from prayer.

    e. John Wesley: God does nothing but in answer to prayer.

F. God uses suffering to drive us to pray. 'He said: "In my distress I called to the Lord, and he answered me. From the depths of the grave I called for help, and you listened to my cry"' (Jon. 2:2).

  1. When Jonah was in the belly of the fish, 'Then Jonah prayed' (Jon. 2:1, AV).

  2. *At the most despairing moment of David's life, he prayed.*

    a. He believed in the sovereignty of God. 'If I find favour in the Lord's eyes, he will bring me back [to Jerusalem]' (2 Sam. 15:25).

b. Soon afterwards, when he heard that his wisest advisor had sided with Absalom, David prayed, 'O LORD, turn Ahithophel's counsel into foolishness' (2 Sam. 15:31). God answered (2 Sam. 17:14).

3. *The greatest demonstrations of corporate prayer came in the midst of trial:*

    a. When the church was persecuted (Acts 4:23-31).

    b. When Peter was imprisoned they prayed 'earnestly' (Acts 12:5).

G. God knows the future but remembers that we are in the present.

1. We pray not because we know the outcome, we pray because we don't.

2. Jesus knew he would raise Lazarus from the dead but wept with Mary and Martha (John 11:35).

3. God sometimes steps into the present to motivate us to pray. 'Call to me and I will answer you and tell you great and unsearchable things you do not know' (Jer. 33:3).

H. Praying gives us the privilege of changing things.

1. Answered prayer gives us the feeling of God's approval.

2. Answered prayer means we had a hand in averting disaster.

3. God brings us to agony that we will pray in agony to see him work.

I. The promises and command of God regarding prayer.

1. Perhaps the greatest motivation of all is the promise of God to answer prayer.

2. *We have a warrant to hold God to his promise.*

    a. If Jesus commanded that we should always pray and not give up, we are in disobedience not to pray (Luke 18:1).

    b. What is more, Jesus said, 'And will not God bring about justice for his chosen ones, who cry out to him day and night? Will he keep putting them off? I tell you, he will see that they get justice, and quickly. However, when the Son of Man comes, will he find faith on the earth?' (Luke 18:7-8).

3. *In a word: two things ultimately should motivate us to pray:*

    a. The command to pray.

    b. God's promise to answer.

CONCLUSION

God is omniscient, he knows everything. He is sovereign, ordaining all that happens. Jesus, accepting the omniscience and sovereignty of God, had a full prayer life on earth and continues in intercessory prayer in heaven. He is our example. We pray, not because we understand how prayer 'works' but because we are commanded to do so and because God promises to hear and answer us.

43

VARIOUS KINDS OF PRAYER

A. We have sought to deal with the question, 'If God knows the future, why pray?'
  1. We gave several reasons why we should pray even though God knows the future (hence the outcome).
  2. *In a word: we should pray because we are commanded to pray.*
    a. In much the same manner, God knows who will be saved.
    b. We are none the less commanded to preach the Gospel to every creature – and therefore witness to every person.
    (1) As though their destiny depends on us.
    (2) As though their destiny depends on them.

B. There are many types of prayer in the Bible, and this lesson seeks to investigate what they are and how they apply to us.
  1. *Church history reveals various kinds of prayer, and these have been repeated many times. For example:*
    a. The Book of Common Prayer in the Church of England.
    (1) Many of the prayers were written by some of the English Reformers, especially Thomas Cranmer.
    (2) They are timeless and are used by many to this day.
    b. The same is said of some Roman Catholic saints, e.g. the famous prayer of St Francis of Assisi:

Lord, make me an instrument of thy peace
Where there is hatred, let me sow love
Where there is injury, pardon
Where there is doubt, faith
Where there is despair, hope
Where there is darkness, light
And where there is sadness, joy.
Grant that I might not so much seek to be consoled as to console,

To be understood as to understand
To be loved as to love.
For it is in giving that we receive
It is in pardoning that we are pardoned
And it is in dying that we are born to eternal life.

2. *The Bible includes prayers of the saints, not to mention the Lord's Prayer, and these are often used in public worship.*
   a. The Psalms.
   b. The prayer of the corporate early church (Acts 4:24-30).
   c. Prayers of the apostle Paul (Eph. 1:17ff; 3:14-21; Phil. 1:9-11; Col. 1 9-12).
3. No study of this brevity could deal with every kind of prayer, within church history or the Bible, but we will focus on those we feel are important at this time.

C. Why is this lesson important?
   1. Prayer is God's idea and we can never say enough about it.
   2. We all need encouragement and motivation to pray, and this lesson hopes to do this.
   3. It is easy to forget that there are various kinds of prayer; this lesson could help us to get out of any rut we might be in and widen our perspective regarding prayer.
   4. It should encourage us to pray for others, not just for ourselves.
   5. We can never be reminded too often: God answers prayer.

I. PRAYER OF CONVERSION (HOW TO BECOME A CHRISTIAN)

A. Jesus summarised this by referring to the prayer of the tax collector in the Temple:
   1. *'Two men went up to the temple to pray, one a Pharisee and the other a tax collector. The Pharisee stood up and prayed about himself: "God, I thank you that I am not like other men – robbers, evildoers, adulterers – or even like this tax collector. I fast twice a week and give a tenth of all I get"'* (Luke 18:10-12).
      a. Jesus did not approve of this prayer.
      b. The reason: the man was self-righteous, full of himself and felt no need before God (Luke 18:11).

2. *'But the tax collector stood at a distance. He would not even look up to heaven, but beat his breast and said, "God, have mercy on me, a sinner"'* (Luke 18:13).

    a. Jesus said this man 'went home justified before God' (Luke 18:14).

    b. The reason: he was devoid of self-righteousness.

        (1) God hates self-righteousness (Isa. 64:6).

        (2) This is why Jesus said, 'It is not the healthy who need a doctor, but the sick. I have not come to call the righteous, but sinners' (Mark 2:17).

B. Note three aspects of the prayer for conversion:

1. He was sorry. 'He would not even look up to heaven, but beat his breast.'

2. *He asked for mercy.*

    a. Mercy – to be mercy – means it can be given or withheld and justice be done either way.

    b. Instead of demanding that God do something, this man just pleaded for mercy.

        (1) Note: the Greek literally means 'Be propitiated' – the same word used for the ancient mercy seat where the blood of the sacrifices was applied on the Day of Atonement.

        (2) It therefore is an implicit prayer for the blood of Jesus to be applied.

3. He acknowledged freely that he was a sinner.

II. Prayer of a discouraged Christian

'Let us then approach the throne of grace with confidence, so that we may receive mercy and find grace to help us in our time of need' (Heb. 4:16).

A. The Hebrew Christians were discouraged.

1. Otherwise, there was no need to say, 'So do not throw away your confidence; it will be richly rewarded. You need to persevere so that when you have done the will of God, you will receive what he has promised' (Heb 10:35-36. cf. Heb. 12:5ff).

2. *Why were they discouraged?*
  a. The signs, wonders and miracles which they had previously experienced appeared to be absent (Heb. 2:4).
  b. Vindication had been withheld (the temple was still standing).
  c. Old friends had left (Heb. 10:25).

B. Note four aspects of this prayer:
  1. *They were to come with confidence.*
    a. This confidence was based not on their performance, for they were on the verge of giving up!
    b. It was to be based upon what was later called 'a new and living way,' namely, the blood of Jesus (Heb. 10:19-20).
  2. *God's throne is a throne of grace.*
    a. It will reveal itself as a throne of judgment later (Heb. 9:27; Rev. 20:11).
    b. But not now; God wants to show favour (Heb. 12:18-24).
  3. *We ask for mercy.*
    a. This is how we were converted!
    b. This is a timely reminder: we never outgrow the need of mercy!
  4. *Grace will come in our time of need.*
    a. God knows what the need is and when we need it.
    b. He is never too late, never too early, but always just on time.

III. PRAYER OF CONSECRATION

'Father, if you are willing, take this cup from me; yet not my will, but yours be done' (Luke 22:42).

A. The prayer Jesus prayed in the Garden of Gethsemane is perhaps the best way we can pray when we renew our consecration.
  1. Consecration (def.): dedicating ourselves to God's service and worship.
  2. *When we face an unhappy ordeal, there is no better prayer.*
    a. Note: Jesus wasn't asking to know what God's will was.
      (1) This is often misused by some people, especially when they are in unbelief.

(2) Jesus knew exactly what he had to do.

b. It is one thing to ask for clarification – is there any other way?

c. At the end of the day, when we know in our heart of hearts what we must do, we bow to God's sovereign will.

B. Note three aspects of this prayer:

1. Asking for God's change of mind, should he be willing.
2. Asking to be made exempt from the awful ordeal, if God is willing.
3. Submitting to God's will if it cannot be changed.

IV. THE PRAYER OF COMMITMENT

'Cast all your anxiety on him because he cares for you' (1 Pet. 5:7).

A. One might say the prayer of commitment is the same as above (the prayer of consecration).

1. *This is true in a sense, because one submits to God's will – which certainly is commitment.*
   a. Commitment (def.): a conscious irrevocable decision.
   (1) It is in the mind – conscious.
   (2) It is in the heart – no turning back.
   (3) It is in the will – you carry it out.
   b. 'Commit your way to the LORD; trust in him' (Ps. 37:5).
2. *But the prayer of commitment that involves trust takes the prayer of dedication a step further: giving God your care.*
   a. AV: 'Casting all your care upon him.'
   b. This means turning over to God all that gets you down.
   (1) Jesus called it, 'Take my yoke upon you. . . . My yoke is easy and my burden is light' (Matt. 11:29-30).
   (2) When the yoke (def.: oppression) is overwhelming, Jesus says, 'Give it to me – my yoke is easy.'

B. Note three aspects of this prayer:

1. *We are to cast (def.: throw away or shed yourself of) your anxiety.*
   a. This means you take it off – throw it away.
   b. You literally say, 'The burden is now yours' – and you walk away.

2. *We give all our care to God. Note the word 'all': whatever gets you down.*

    a. The same God who forgives sin is the God to whom we give our care.

    b. God is bearing our burdens all the time, so why not give them to him indeed? 'Praise be to the Lord, to God our Saviour, who daily bears our burdens' (Ps. 68:19).

3. *God wants our care because he cares for us.*

    a. He is more concerned about us than we are about ourselves.

    b. He loves us more than we love ourselves.

    c. He loves it when we trust him enough to bear our burdens for us – without our doing it!

V. THE PRAYER OF FORGIVING OTHERS

'Jesus said, "Father, forgive them, for they do not know what they are doing"' (Luke 23:34).

A. It is difficult to know which is harder to do: casting all your anxiety on God or forgiving others.

    1. *Either of these shows great progress in God's grace.*

        a. The prayer of commitment shows great trust in God.

        b. The prayer of forgiveness shows great love.

    2. *Jesus' prayer on the cross is our example.*

        a. He had already told us to forgive others.

            (1) 'For if you forgive men when they sin against you, your heavenly Father will also forgive you. But if you do not forgive men their sins, your Father will not forgive your sins' (Matt. 6:14-15).

            (2) 'And when you stand praying, if you hold anything against anyone, forgive him, so that your Father in heaven may forgive you your sins' (Mark 11:25).

        b. But this prayer is that God will forgive them.

            (1) To forgive is one thing.

            (2) To ask God to forgive them is another.

B. Note three aspects of Jesus' prayer:

    1. *You are asking the Father to forgive them.*

        a. If you really mean that, it shows you have forgiven them.

        b. Jesus said, 'Pray for those who ill-treat you' (Luke 6:28).

2. *You are asking the Father to guarantee that they will be blessed and not punished.*

    a. You are saying, 'Yes, Lord, let them get away with what they did.'

    b. You may sense God saying to you: 'Do you really mean that?'

        (1) If you do, pray it – and pray hoping he will answer you.

        (2) Otherwise, don't play games with yourself – or God; don't pray it at all until you hope God hears you.

        (3) However, a case can be made that we should pray for our enemies even if we don't feel like it.

3. *The people you pray for don't know what they have done.*

    a. Ninety percent of those we have to forgive sincerely don't believe (even under a lie detector) that they have done anything wrong.

    b. You don't wait for them to say, 'I'm sorry.' Jesus didn't.

VI. THE PRAYER OF FAITH

A. There are two instances of this kind of prayer.

1. *By the elders of the church praying for the sick, anointing them with oil.* 'And the prayer offered in faith ['prayer of faith' – AV] will make the sick person well; the Lord will raise him up. If he has sinned, he will be forgiven' (Jas. 5:15).

    a. This is when one's faith has touched God.

    b. This is when one's prayer was in God's will. 'This is the confidence we have in approaching God: that if we ask anything according to his will, he hears us' (1 John 5:14).

2. *By anybody.* '"Have faith in God," Jesus answered. "I tell you the truth, if anyone says to this mountain, 'Go, throw yourself into the sea,' and does not doubt in his heart but believes that what he says will happen, it will be done for him. Therefore I tell you, whatever you ask for in prayer, believe that you have received it, and it will be yours"' (Mark 11:22-24).

    a. The 'faith of God' is literally what the Greek says in Mark 11:22.

    b. The result is knowing you've been heard, even as you prayed, as in 1 John 5:15: 'And if we know that he hears us – whatever we ask – we know that we have what we asked of him.'

B. Note three aspects of this prayer:
  1. *It accomplishes most extraordinary things.*
    a. Moving mountains, which only God can do (which is why it is surely the 'faith of God').
    b. Healing the sick, which only God can do.
  2. *It may or may not always be a conscious prayer of faith.*
    a. Mark 11:23-24 implies that the one praying this prayer knows in himself that he has sufficient faith indeed.
    b. The prayer of James 5:14 is done by two or more elders, so the person who is healed will not know who prayed in faith.
    c. Note: I have prayed the prayer of faith at times but didn't know for sure until later – when the person claimed to be healed.
      (1) This is why I wouldn't push too far the point of being conscious of praying the prayer of faith.
      (2) What is more, those who may think they've prayed this kind of prayer must be careful not to blame anyone who is not healed for their lack of faith.
  3. *Often forgotten: Mark 11:25, which immediately followed the above:* 'And when you stand praying, if you hold anything against anyone, forgive him, so that your Father in heaven may forgive you your sins.'
    a. This is a fairly strong hint that there is a connection between the prayer of faith and forgiving others.
    b. If this is true of Mark 11:22-25, it must be true of James 5:15 as well. All those who wish to pray the prayer of faith be warned!

VII. COVENANT PRAYING

'Again, I tell you that if two of you on earth agree about anything you ask for, it will be done for you by my Father in heaven' (Matt. 18:19).

A. This is something we in Westminster Chapel have been doing in recent years.
  1. *Covenant (def.): an agreement between two parties, possibly based upon a condition.*
    a. Two or more people agree to pray:
      (1) A particular request or requests.

        (2) To keep up this covenant by praying regularly (e.g. daily).

        (3) To keep up this praying for a period of time – or until you believe the prayer has been answered.

    b. You claim two promises:

        (1) Matthew 18:19 (above).

        (2) The word of Jesus that introduced the Parable of the Importunate Widow. 'Then Jesus told his disciples a parable to show them that they should always pray and not give up' (Luke 18:1).

2. *One makes a covenant in order to keep this up – no matter what.*

    a. You have promised each other.

    b. You have promised God.

    c. In ancient times a covenant was joined by a sacrifice; therefore you pray this covenant in the name of Jesus who died and shed his precious blood.

B. Note three things about this prayer:

    1. *It is not necessarily prayed in full assurance of faith.*

        a. This means you don't really know if God will hear you.

        b. But you have Jesus' words to fall back on; obviously what Jesus hinted at in Luke 18:1-8 is not the faith in our prayer but our faithfulness (keeping it up).

    2. *The people involved must be agreed on the validity of the request.*

        a. This need not be done only by the whole church.

        b. Any two people – husband and wife, friends – may do this any time.

    3. *God promises to answer.*

        a. We aren't required to have a perfect faith.

        b. God obligates himself by virtue of these biblical conditions.

VIII. PRAYER OF INTERCESSION

'So Peter was kept in prison, but the church was earnestly praying to God for him' (Acts 12:5).

A. Intercessory prayer is pleading on behalf of someone else.

    1. To intercede (def.): to intervene on behalf of another.

    2. *Moses was one of the world's greatest intercessors.*

        a. He didn't 'farm out' the ministry of intercession but did it himself.

(1) 'So he said he would destroy them – had not Moses, his chosen one, stood in the breach before him to keep his wrath from destroying them' (Ps. 106:23).

(2) 'In accordance with your great love, forgive the sin of these people, just as you have pardoned them from the time they left Egypt until now' (Num. 14:19).

b. Intercessory prayer is unselfish and hard work. 'I looked for a man among them who would build up the wall and stand before me in the gap on behalf of the land so I would not have to destroy it, but I found none' (Ezek. 22:30).

B. Note three things:
1. A great need arose: Peter was in prison.
2. There was corporate intercession: the church prayed.
3. *They prayed with a burden: 'earnestly'.*
  a. This is a key to intercessory prayer.
  b. It is done with considerable burden, feeling and pain.
  c. This characterised the church's intercession in the face of persecution.
    (1) They 'raised their voices together in prayer' (Acts 4:24).
    (2) If that isn't praying out loud together, you could have fooled me!

IX. PRAYING IN THE SPIRIT

'But you, dear friends, build yourselves up in your most holy faith and pray in the Holy Spirit' (Jude 20).

A. I believe this is either of the following, if not both:
1. *Praying in tongues.*
  a. 'So it is with you. Since you are eager to have spiritual gifts, try to excel in gifts that build up the church' (1 Cor. 14:12).
  b. This may be what Paul means in Romans 8:26: 'In the same way, the Spirit helps us in our weakness. We do not know what we ought to pray for, but the Spirit himself intercedes for us with groans that words cannot express.'
2. Consciously praying in the will of God (1 John 5:14-15; Mark 11:24).

B. This kind of praying is:
1. Self-edifying.
2. Intercession.
3. Worship.

X. WORSHIP

'We who worship by the Spirit of God' (Phil. 3:3).

A. This is essentially praise and adoration and is pleasing to God when done 'by the Spirit.'

B. This is a taste of the kind of praying we will do in heaven.

CONCLUSION

Prayer is a many faceted privilege. In Scripture we find prayers uttered for mercy, in discouragement, at times of consecration and commitment, and prayers of forgiveness, of faith and intercession. Covenant praying (where two or three covenant to pray for a particular request over a specific period) is a useful practice. The phrase 'praying in the Spirit' (Jude 20) may refer either to praying in tongues or to praying consciously in the will of God. Worship is adoration and adoration is prayer.

Prayer will not be a feature of our lives in heaven as God's purposes will be fully and finally carried out. Only one aspect of prayer, worship, will continue in heaven.

44

THE CHRISTIAN'S PRIVATE PRAYER LIFE

INTRODUCTION

A. Some time ago I spoke to a hundred London church leaders on the subject of 'The Minister's Private Prayer Life'.

1. *The original purpose of deacons was to give the apostles time to pray and preach.* 'Brothers, choose seven men from among you who are known to be full of the Spirit and wisdom. We will turn this responsibility over to them and will give our attention to prayer and the ministry of the word' (Acts 6:3-4).

2. *The average clergyman (according to a survey) spends an average of four minutes a day in his own quiet time. And we wonder why the church is powerless!*

   a. Listen to these words from Martin Luther's journal: 'I have a very busy day today. Must spend not two, but three hours, in prayer.'

   b. John Wesley arose every morning at 4 a.m. to spend two hours in prayer – alone with God.

3. *It is my view that every minister should spend an average of at least one hour a day alone with the Lord.*

   a. 'Not many of you should presume to be teachers, my brothers, because you know that we who teach will be judged more strictly' (Jas. 3:1).

   b. This is not because we should merely set an example; the work to which we are called demands it.

   (1) I discerned when I was young that the ministers, preachers and evangelists I happened to admire the most also happened to pray the most.

   (2) This left a profound effect on me, an impact which remains with me.

B. The present study however is for every Christian.

1. If there are those Christians who have time to give an hour a day, they should certainly do this.

  2. *But I will come right to the point: it is my belief that every Christian should spend no fewer than thirty minutes a day alone with God.*

    a. I got this from my father (a layman), who as a daily practice spent thirty minutes on his knees before he left for work.

    b. I presume his pastor had urged this; otherwise I do not know where he got it.

      (1) That pastor was Gene Phillips (now with the Lord).

      (2) Gene Phillips preached with more power than any man I ever heard; he was probably the most formative influence in my life.

C. Why is this lesson important?

  1. *Theology which is not born out of and bathed in prayer is worthless.*

    a. There is nothing worse than arid, sterile theology.

    b. Theology that is set on fire is what is needed today; such is not possible apart from much prayer.

  2. *We must also examine the theology of prayer.*

    a. Prayer surely has a theological basis.

    b. We need to see what kind of theology lies behind prayer.

  3. No Christian worth his or her salt dare not have a rich prayer life. Why?

  4. Many Christians do not have strong prayer lives because they haven't been taught. This study will hopefully make a contribution in this case.

  5. Some Christians literally do not know how to pray.

  6. Many Christians have not discerned the value of a private prayer life.

  7. If all Christians in Britain would take this study seriously and put it into practice, it would have a profound impact on the church and nation as a whole – I guarantee it!

I. WHY PRAY?

A. Prayer is to be understood in at least five ways:

  1. *Intimacy with God.* 'The LORD confides in those who fear him; he makes his covenant known to them' (Ps. 25:14).

    a. Can you think of anything more wonderful than for God to confide in you?

        (1) Why do we confide in another? Because we trust them.

        (2) If God confides in us it is because he trusts us.

  b. The key to intimacy is secrecy. 'The secret of the LORD is with them that fear him; and he will shew them his covenant' (Ps. 25:14, AV).

        (1) When God shows his covenant he reveals what is special.

        (2) He may have plans for his relationship with me that he does not want you to know about; I therefore must be willing to be shown things I never reveal to another.

2. *Worship.* 'One thing I ask of the LORD, this is what I seek: that I may dwell in the house of the LORD all the days of my life, to gaze upon the beauty of the LORD and to seek him in his temple' (Ps. 27:4).

  a. This is a matter of the heart.

        (1) It is when we feel God's love and feel our love for him.

        (2) This comes by spending sufficient time with him.

  b. It comes from a prior commitment: 'One thing I ask of the LORD, this is what I seek.'

        (1) It is following through with what you desire.

        (2) You prove your worship of God by doing it: 'to gaze upon the beauty of the Lord.'

3. *Seeking God.* 'My heart says of you, "Seek his face!" Your face, LORD, I will seek' (Ps. 27:8).

  a. Sometimes God hides his face. 'Truly you are a God who hides himself, O God and Saviour of Israel' (Isa. 45:15).

        (1) It is our job to seek his face.

        (2) When he is revealing his face, prayer is no duty!

  b. Much of prayer is wrestling with God (Gen. 32:24).

        (1) This means it can be a struggle, and you do not know at first what the outcome will be!

        (2) But the result is worth waiting for. 'Then the man said, "Your name will no longer be Jacob, but Israel, because you have struggled with God and with men and have overcome."' (Gen. 32:28).

4. *Intercession: asking God to act.* 'It is time for you to act, O LORD' (Ps. 119:126).

  a. It is pleading with God to step down from heaven and intervene.

        (1) It may be at a time when we are desperate. 'Now, Lord, consider their threats and enable your servants to speak your word with great boldness. Stretch out your hand to

heal and perform miraculous signs and wonders through
the name of your holy servant Jesus' (Acts 4:29-30).

(2) It may be a daily procedure when you repeat the same
request to God (Luke 18:1-8).

   b. This intercession may be with regard to a personal need or
   praying on behalf of others.

   (1) Hannah's intercession was personal (1 Sam. 1:9-20).

   (2) The church interceded for Peter's safety (Acts 12:5).

5. *Praying in the Spirit.* 'But you, dear friends, build yourselves
up in your most holy faith and pray in the Holy Spirit' (Jude 20).

   a. This kind of praying may be:

   (1) Knowing you are praying in God's will (Mark 11:24; 1
   John 5:14-15).

   (2) Not knowing how to pray (Rom. 8:26-27).

   b. The latter of the above (for those who have the gift) may be
   praying in tongues (1 Cor. 12:10).

   (1) Such people do not know what they are praying for. 'For
   anyone who speaks in a tongue does not speak to men
   but to God. Indeed, no-one understands him; he utters
   mysteries with his spirit' (1 Cor. 14:2).

   (2) But such prayer is edifying to the one who does it.

**B. There are basically two Greek words for prayer in the New
Testament.**

   1. *Proseuche* (used 37 times as a noun, 57 times as a verb).

   a. It is a general term for prayer; it means 'to ask' or 'to beseech'.

   b. It is used in Acts 1:14; 2:42; 3:1: 6:4; 10:4, 31; 12:5.

   2. *Deosis* (used only as a noun 19 times; the verb *deomai* is used
   22 times).

   a. It basically means 'petition'; it also means 'seeking'.

   b. It is used of Zechariah's prayer in Luke 1:13; also in Luke
   2:37; 5:33; Romans 10:1.

C. The reasons for praying therefore are:

   1. *We are commanded to pray.*

   a. 'Then Jesus told his disciples a parable to show them that
   they should always pray and not give up' (Luke 18:1).

   b. 'I urge, then, first of all, that requests, prayers, intercession
   and thanksgiving be made for everyone' (1 Tim. 2:1).

    c. 'I want men everywhere to lift up holy hands in prayer, without anger or disputing' (1 Tim. 2:8).

2. *God answers prayer.*

    a. Jonah said 'In my distress I called to the LORD, and he answered me. From the depths of the grave I called for help, and you listened to my cry' (Jon. 2:2).

    b. 'The LORD has heard my cry for mercy, the LORD accepts my prayer' (Ps. 6:9).

    c. 'I sought the LORD, and he answered me; he delivered me from all my fears' (Ps. 34:4).

    d. Note: *shamar* (Heb.) means 'to hear so as to obey'; if God 'hears' us it means he 'obeys' our request.

3. *God often answers prayer when we were not aware we had actually prayed in God's will.*

    a. There is a difference between praying in God's will and knowing that we have been heard.

        (1) If we pray in God's will, he hears us (1 John 5:14).

        (2) We may or may not 'know' we have been 'heard' (1 John 5:15).

    b. Zechariah prayed in God's will but didn't know it until many years later! (Luke 1:13).

        (1) Any prayer prayed in God's will will be answered.

        (2) But the shape answered prayer takes is determined by our readiness at the time (Luke 1:20).

4. *God rewards us.*

    a. 'Then your Father, who sees what is done in secret, will reward you' (Matt. 6:6).

        (1) It may be a reward given when we get to heaven.

        (2) It may be a reward given to us here below.

    b. Do not be afraid to see answered prayer as a reward; Jesus is the one who put it that way!

        (1) Prayer is sometimes sheer work – and a good work at that.

        (2) 'But as for you, be strong and do not give up, for your work will be rewarded' (2 Chron. 15:7. cf. Jer. 31:16).

5. *It affirms how important you think God is in your life.*

    a. We show how important another is to us by how much time we grant to them.

    b. How much time do you give to God?

II. WHY PRAY ALONE?

A. One must not take lightly praying with others.

1. *It is important to pray with one other person, when possible.*
   - **a.** Husband and wife should pray daily together.
   - **b.** You should, if possible, take another person as a prayer partner (Matt. 18:19).
   - **c.** Prayer meetings when several (the more the better) pray together are vital for the life of every church (Acts 1:14; 2:42; 3:1; 4:24-31; 12:5).
2. *There are two extremes to be avoided:*
   - **a.** Some want only to pray alone, and avoid any contact with groups of people who come together and pray.
   - **b.** Some pray only when they are with others, and never do any serious praying alone.

B. What then are the reasons to pray alone?

1. *Jesus did*
   - **a.** When the Son of God had a need to get away from the multitudes just to be with his Father, surely we too need this (Matt. 14:23; Mark 6:46).
   - **b.** When did Jesus pray alone?
     - **(1)** In the evening. 'After he had dismissed them, he went up on a mountainside by himself to pray. When evening came, he was there alone' (Matt. 14:23).
     - **(2)** In the mornings. 'Very early in the morning, while it was still dark, Jesus got up, left the house and went off to a solitary place, where he prayed' (Mark 1:35).
     - **(3)** All night. 'One of those days Jesus went out to a mountainside to pray, and spent the night praying to God' (Luke 6:12).
   - **c.** We therefore have biblical examples to pray any time!
2. *Great men of God did*
   - **a.** Jacob: Genesis 32:9, 24-30; 35:1; 46:2.
   - **b.** Moses: Exodus 19:3; 32:1; 33:11.
   - **c.** Gideon: Judges 6:36,39.
   - **d.** David: 2 Samuel 7:18; the Psalms *passim.*
   - **e.** Elijah: 1 Kings 18:42; 19:3ff.
   - **f.** Hezekiah: 2 Kings 20:2ff.
   - **g.** Isaiah: 2 Kings 20:11.

   h. Ezra: Ezra 9:5ff.
   i. Nehemiah: Nehemiah 2:4.
   j. Jeremiah: Jeremiah 32:16.
   k. Daniel: Daniel 6:10; 9:3.
   l. Peter: Acts 10:9.
   m. Paul: Ephesians 3:14; 2 Timothy 1:3.
3. *Jesus told us to do this.* 'But when you pray, go into your
   room, close the door and pray to your Father, who is unseen.
   Then your Father, who sees what is done in secret, will reward
   you' (Matt. 6:6).
   a. This is an explicit command to be alone.
   b. We shut the door – God sees us in secret.
4. *We develop intimacy with the Lord.*
   a. This is not likely to happen when praying with others.
      (1) And yet the more you pray alone, the more prayer will
         mean to you when you do pray with others.
      (2) You develop a pattern and a confidence, if not a healthy,
         uncontrived familiarity with God so that praying with
         others is easier.
   b. One must be alone to develop this intimacy.
      (1) The world must be shut out.
      (2) The TV is off, the radio if off, friends are elsewhere.
5. *We generate internal power.*
   a. The more we are alone with God, the more we feel him with
      us all day long, wherever we are.
   b. We develop confidence, a sense of his presence that is unlikely
      to be real when we have not had time alone with him.
   c. We have presence of mind wherever we are, so that a verse
      like Matthew 10:20 means more: 'For it will not be you
      speaking, but the Spirit of your Father speaking through you.'
6. *It paves the way for insight into God's Word.*
   a. This is the Lord confiding in us; sharing his secrets.
   b. The Word becomes more precious generally, understanding
      more a reality particularly.
7. *The quantity of time for the rest of the day is greater.*
   a. Illustration: tithing; give God 10% and the 90% we keep
      goes as far if not further.
   b. When we give God, say, thirty minutes a day, we get far
      more time the rest of the day (Luther's comment on p. 446).

III. PRACTICAL HELPS

A. Let the pattern of the Lord's Prayer set the stage for your own private prayer life. See Matthew 6:9-13.
1. You begin with praise: focusing on God.
2. You bring in your petitions: focusing on your needs.
3. You end with praise: focusing on God.

B. Pick the time of day that best suits you.
1. *If you are not a 'morning' person, wait a while – or even pray in the evening.*
   a. Ideally, morning is best; we begin the day with God and we may well feel his presence all day long.
   b. But don't be in a bondage; pick a time when your intimacy with God will be most edifying.
2. *But consider thirty minutes with God as important as you would regard your job.*
   a. You get up and go to work, whether you feel like it or not, don't you?
   b. Give that thirty minutes time priority as you would to your lunch of coffee break!

C. Develop a prayer list.
1. *Write on a card (or cards) the things you sincerely want.*
   a. Don't be afraid to be a bit selfish; the widow Jesus referred to had a rather selfish request: 'Grant me justice against my adversary' (Luke 18:3).
   b. Ask yourself: what do I really want – if God really would hear me? Write it down – go for it!
2. *As a suggestion, put categories on each card; e.g.:*
   a. Praying for others: names and the thing you want God to do.
   b. Praying for yourself:
      (1) Spiritual needs.
      (2) Physical needs.
   c. Wider requests: the nation; the church; missionaries and evangelists; your pastor and family; church leaders, etc..
   d. Your enemies. (I'm serious – Matt. 5:44.)
3. Refine it and update it from time to time.

D. Remember to be thankful (Phil. 4:6).
   1. Think of what God has done over the years.
   2. Thank him for the gift of his Son; the Holy Spirit; the Bible.
   3. Thank him for what he did yesterday.

E. Posture: sitting or kneeling.
   1. There are a lot of biblical examples for kneeling.
   2. But David 'sat' before the Lord – not a bad example!

F. Remember that Jesus is at your right hand (Ps. 16:8).
   1. 'Set' him before you; David did.
   2. You do this because he is there anyway; it enables you to focus
      on him so your mind won't wander so much.

CONCLUSION

Jesus prayed alone. His private prayer life is our example. The practice of private prayer develops our intimacy with God, opens us as channels of his power, prepares us to receive insights into his Word, and enables us for whatever service we can offer. Prayer should begin by focusing on God, only then to focus on our needs, and end by refocusing on God.

The use of a prayer list helps in the development of a disciplined prayer life.

How much time we are prepared to spend in private with God is an indication of how much he means to us. And God hears and answers prayer!

You will not regret the time you spent in prayer when you get to heaven.

45

THE DEVIL'S ROLE IN GOD'S SCHEME

INTRODUCTION

A. **This study will focus on Christ's chief enemy in the light of God's greater purposes.**
   1. Christ's chief enemy is the devil, or Satan.
   2. The devil exists to fight God and his Son.

B. **The question is: why did God create the devil?**
   1. Does it make sense that God would create his own enemy?
   2. Is not God greater than the devil?
   3. How does Satan fit into God's whole plan?

C. **When the church is revived, so is the devil too, said Jonathan Edwards.**
   1. *Not that the devil was asleep when the church was asleep.*
      a. The church's being asleep is the work of Satan.
      b. He wants chiefly to keep the church asleep; this way his own interests are not threatened.
      c. Three things are true when we are asleep:
         (1) We don't know we are asleep until we wake up.
         (2) We do things in our dreams we would not do if we were awake.
         (3) We hate the sound of an alarm.
   2. *But when the church is revived, the devil is threatened.*
      a. The church's being awakened is a serious set-back for Satan.
      b. It is no small victory for the church and the honour of God's Name when we are awakened and revived.
      c. It means we have overcome many obstacles.
   3. *When the church is revived, Satan must counter-attack.*
      a. He will try to imitate what God has done (Ex. 7:11).
      b. He will find weak spots in the fellowship to create dissension and murmuring (Acts 6:1).

    c. He will challenge the leadership God has ordained (Num. 16:1-7).

    d. He will persecute (Acts 4:1-7. Cf. Rev. 12:4).

    e. He will divide close friends (Acts 15:39).

D. Names, or nicknames, for the devil:

  1. *Satan: adversary or accuser* (Job 1:6-12)

    a. 'Then he showed me Joshua the high priest standing before the angel of the LORD, and Satan standing at his right side to accuse him. The LORD said to Satan, "The LORD rebuke you, Satan! The LORD, who has chosen Jerusalem, rebuke you! Is not this man a burning stick snatched from the fire?"' (Zech. 3:1-2).

    b. 'Appoint an evil man to oppose him; let an accuser stand at his right hand' (Ps. 109:6). Note: 'accuser' is the translation of 'Satan'.

    c. 'Satan rose up against Israel and incited David to take a census of Israel' (1 Chron. 21:1).

    d. 'Again, the devil took him to a very high mountain and showed him all the kingdoms of the world and their splendour. "All this I will give you," he said, "if you will bow down and worship me." Jesus said to him, "Away from me, Satan! For it is written: 'Worship the Lord your God, and serve him only.'" Then the devil left him, and angels came and attended him' (Matt. 4:8-11).

  2. *Abaddon, or Apollyon* (destroyer). 'They had as king over them the angel of the Abyss, whose name in Hebrew is Abaddon, and in Greek, Apollyon' (Rev. 9:11).

  3. *Belial (very wicked person)*

    a. It is used parallel to the word 'death' in Psalm 18:4: 'The cords of death entangled me; the torrents of destruction overwhelmed me.'

    b. 'What harmony is there between Christ and Belial? What does a believer have in common with an unbeliever?' (2 Cor. 6:15).

  4. *Tempter*

    a. 'For this reason, when I could stand it no longer, I sent to find out about your faith. I was afraid that in some way the tempter might have tempted you and our efforts might have been useless' (1 Thess. 3:5).

    b. 'The tempter came to him and said, "If you are the Son of God, tell these stones to become bread"' (Matt. 4:3).

5. *Beelzebub (lord of flies), the god of Ekron, whom Ahaziah wished to consult, but was prevented by Elijah's interruption* (2 Kings 1:1-6,16).

    a. Called 'the prince of demons' (Matt. 12:24).

    b. 'If Satan drives out Satan, he is divided against himself. How then can his kingdom stand? And if I drive out demons by Beelzebub, by whom do your people drive them out? So then, they will be your judges. But if I drive out demons by the Spirit of God, then the kingdom of God has come upon you' (Matt. 12:26-28).

6. Accuser of the brothers. 'Then I heard a loud voice in heaven say: "Now have come the salvation and the power and the kingdom of our God, and the authority of his Christ. For the accuser of our brothers, who accuses them before our God day and night, has been hurled down. They overcame him by the blood of the Lamb and by the word of their testimony; they did not love their lives so much as to shrink from death' (Rev. 12:10-11).

7. The god of this age. 'The god of this age has blinded the minds of unbelievers, so that they cannot see the light of the gospel of the glory of Christ, who is the image of God' (2 Cor. 4:4).

8. Ruler of the kingdom of the air, a spirit. 'In which you used to live when you followed the ways of this world and of the ruler of the kingdom of the air, the spirit who is now at work in those who are disobedient' (Eph. 2:2).

9. Serpent. (Gen. 3:1. cf. 2 Cor. 11:3).

10. The prince of this world (John 14:30).

11. A liar and the father of lies (John 8:44).

E. Why is this subject important?

    1. *It is a reminder that there is a very real enemy – the devil.*

        a. We are told to be aware of his possible attack at any moment. 'Be self-controlled and alert. Your enemy the devil prowls around like a roaring lion looking for someone to devour. Resist him, standing firm in the faith, because you know that your brothers throughout the world are undergoing the same kind of sufferings' (1 Pet. 5:8-9).

    b. There are two opposite extremes regarding attention given to the devil, and he is happy with either:

        (1) To be preoccupied with him; e.g.:

            (a) Worrying about him all the time.

            (b) Being too interested in things pertaining to the occult, even if we are against it.

            (c) Trying to diagnose every ill as a case of demon possession.

        (2) To forget him, or deny his existence.

            (a) Unbelief in the devil is the devil's work (2 Cor. 4:4).

            (b) Dismissing his efforts to attack.

            (c) Neglecting what the Bible says about him.

2. *It is a reminder that our Lord's chief foe is Satan* (Rev. 12).

    a. Satan wants to defeat Christ's purposes.

        (1) He wanted to kill Jesus (Matt. 4:6. cf. Luke 4:28ff).

        (2) His final effort was through Judas Iscariot (John 13:2).

    b. Satan immediately knew who Jesus was.

        (1) That he was God's Son (Matt. 4:3).

        (2) That he was the Holy One of God (Mark 1:23-24).

3. *It is a reminder that God has an eternal purpose* (Eph. 1:11).

    a. God is in control of history generally (Isa. 46:9-10).

    b. He has a plan for each of us particularly (Eph. 5:17).

4. *It enables us to put all things in perspective: that God is sovereign, and that he is bigger than the devil.*

    a. Some Christians seem to have a greater fear of the devil than they have of God.

    b. At the end of the day we have nothing to fear in this regard. 'You, dear children, are from God and have overcome them, because the one who is in you is greater than the one who is in the world' (1 John 4:4).

5. *We must never forget that we have been given a preview of Satan's final downfall* (Rev. 20:10).

    a. We've read the last page of God's history!

    b. 'When Satan reminds you of your past, remind him of his future' (Stephen Gaukroger).

I. THE DEVIL IS A PART OF GOD'S FALLEN CREATION

A. The devil is a creature, that is, he has been created.

    1. This means he is not eternal by nature.

    2. *There was a time when he did not exist.*

    a. Only God and the persons of the Godhead have no creation. 'In the beginning was the Word, and the Word was with God, and the Word was God. He was with God in the beginning' (John 1:1-2).

    b. There was a time when there was literally nothing but God – the Father, the Word (the Son), the Spirit. This means:

      (1) A time there were no stars, no sun, no moon, no animals, no planet earth.

      (2) A time when there was no devil.

3. *Therefore the fact of the devil's existence is owing to God creating him; indeed Jesus Christ created him:*

    a. 'Through him all things were made; without him nothing was made that has been made' (John 1:3).

    b. 'For by him all things were created: things in heaven and on earth, visible and invisible, whether thrones or powers or rulers or authorities; all things were created by him and for him' (Col. 1:16).

B. It does not follow however that God created the devil as he now exists.

    1. *The devil is personal wickedness to an extreme degree*; God is purest holiness (1 John 1:5).

    2. *The devil we have to deal with is what he became not what he once was.*

      a. How he was before he became like he is, is based on a bit of speculation; we take our case from Isaiah 14:12: 'How you have fallen from heaven, O morning star, son of the dawn! You have been cast down to the earth, you who once laid low the nations!'

      b. This is the nearest we come (that I know of) to discerning what went on in the heavens. 'You said in your heart, "I will ascend to heaven; I will raise my throne above the stars of God; I will sit enthroned on the mount of assembly, on the utmost heights of the sacred mountain. I will ascend above the tops of the clouds; I will make myself like the Most High." But you are brought down to the grave, to the depths of the pit' (Isa. 14:13-15).

    3. *It would seem that the devil tried to recruit every angel in God's created realms to enter into a rebellion against God.*

a. 'For if God did not spare angels when they sinned, but sent them to hell, putting them into gloomy dungeons to be held for judgment' (2 Pet. 2:4).

b. 'And the angels who did not keep their positions of authority but abandoned their own home – these he has kept in darkness, bound with everlasting chains for judgment on the great Day' (Jude 6).

4. *At what point this apparent revolt took place in God's time is not clear, but it would seem that:*

   a. It was before God created man; for the serpent was already the 'father of lies' when he approached Eve (Gen. 3:1ff).

   b. It was obviously after God created the heavens and the earth. 'In the beginning God created the heavens and the earth' (Gen. 1:1).

   c. Perhaps the angels were created before God created the earth; 'the heavens' is listed first.

   d. The angels were probably a part of the 'heavens', the invisible realm of God's creation.

   e. It could be that the revolt of Satan took place, then, after God created the heavens but before he created the earth.

C. How evil entered into Satan's heart when God is utterly holy will always remain a mystery to us as long as we are on earth.

   1. No-one will solve the problem of evil.

   2. The most we can say is, God permitted it. Why? Nobody knows.

II. GOD GAVE THE DEVIL CERTAIN POWERS AND AUTHORITY, BUT THEY ARE LIMITED

A. He is therefore called the 'ruler of the kingdom of the air' (Eph. 2:2).

   1. *One does not know what precisely is meant by 'air'.*

   a. Does this mean Satan has been given a measure of power regarding the weather?

   b. Is he behind the trend toward pollution of the air?

   2. *Since 'air' is invisible is it rather a metaphor to refer to the spiritual realm?*

   a. He is therefore the chief ruler of the fallen spiritual world.

   b. He therefore operates as a 'spirit' in all unregenerate men.

   3. Jesus called him 'the prince of this world' (John 14:30).

B. Satan holds the power of death (Heb. 2:14).

　　1. *Apparently God gave him this authority.*

　　　　a. It was the devil who tempted Eve in the light of God's warning to Adam that if he ate of the tree of the knowledge of good and evil, he would surely die (Gen. 2:17).

　　　　b. Since he succeeded in tempting Eve, who persuaded Adam to do the same (Gen. 3:6), he was given the power of death.

　　2. *We may be sure that all sickness and disease came as a result of the Fall.*

　　　　a. It does not follow that all illness is the immediate result of Satan entering in, but rather the ultimate explanation people get sick and die.

　　　　b. Neither does it follow that Satan determines when people die.

C. Whatever power Satan has, it is limited.

　　1. God never surrendered to the devil his supreme power.

　　2. *Satan was given a limited scope in which to operate.*

　　Some think he has been given charge over certain areas of the world. They believe this is the reason certain areas of the world are more evil and threatening than others, e.g., there is a high-ranking demon over South America, or India, or China, etc. They would base this on Daniel 10:13, or Revelation 2:13.

III. God is greater than the devil in every way

A. Some of us are more ready to fear the devil than to trust God.

　　1. *This is a spirit of fear* (2 Tim. 1:7, NIV 'timidity').

　　　　a. A spirit of fear may have one of two sources:

　　　　　　(1) The flesh – those who are naturally negative.

　　　　　　(2) The devil, who plays into our natural fears.

　　　　b. A spirit of fear may be an angel of light (2 Cor. 11:14).

　　　　　　(1) An angel of light poses as God's instrument.

　　　　　　(2) One therefore thinks he is listening to God when it is Satan.

　　2. *This may also be the result of theology or experience.*

　　　　a. Theologically, some assume that God does not work in power today – only in apostolic times.

　　　　　　(1) There is no biblical support for this.

　　　　　　(2) It comes from an assumption that, since nothing extra-ordinary seems to happen, it must be God's eternal plan.

b. Experimentally, some have never seen God work in power.

　　(1) Therefore if they see any kind of power, they assume it must be the devil.

　　(2) This may be true with healing, prophecies, word of knowledge or any spiritual gift.

B. God uses the devil to advance his purposes.

1. *The Fall of man did not take God by surprise, for Christ was the Lamb chosen before the creation of the world* (1 Pet. 1:20).

　　a. God was ready with a word for the devil immediately after the Fall: 'And I will put enmity between you and the woman, and between your offspring and hers; he will crush your head, and you will strike his heel' (Gen. 3:15).

　　b. In that moment God's eternal purpose in redeeming man was in operation.

2. *The entire scenario of the children of Israel in Egypt was part of God's scheme; years before God had prophesied,* 'Know for certain that your descendants will be strangers in a country not their own and they will be enslaved and ill-treated four hundred years' (Gen. 15:13).

　　a. Pharaoh's rebellion against Moses was a part of God's plan. 'For the Scripture says to Pharaoh: "I raised you up for this very purpose, that I might display my power in you and that my name might be proclaimed in all the earth"' (Rom. 9:17. cf. Ex. 9:16).

　　b. Note: we shall see any enemy of Christ as a part of God's overall plan.

　　　　(1) 'God uses my enemies to advance his purpose' (Josif Tson).

　　　　(2) Man's wrath even brings God praise (Ps. 76:10).

3. *The king of Babylon was God's instrument to humble Israel.*

　　a. Jeremiah warned that Babylon would occupy Jerusalem, but no-one believed him.

　　b. But it happened; it was part of God's scheme to teach Israel a lesson (Jer. 39).

　　c. Note: God can use our enemies as his instrument to humble us and discipline us.

4. *The enemies' conspiracy during the time of the Babylonian captivity backfired and resulted in exalting the very people they wanted to destroy; and God got more glory than ever!*

a. The three Hebrews. Daniel 3.

    (1) When they were delivered from the fiery furnace, 'Then Nebuchadnezzar said, "Praise be to the God of Shadrach, Meshach and Abednego, who has sent his angel and rescued his servants! They trusted in him and defied the king's command and were willing to give up their lives rather than serve or worship any god except their own God. Therefore I decree that the people of any nation or language who say anything against the God of Shadrach, Meshach and Abednego be cut into pieces and their houses be turned into piles of rubble, for no other god can save in this way"' (Dan. 3:28-29).

    (2) They were given a promotion (Dan. 3:30).

b. Daniel, who kept on praying.

    (1) He was delivered from the lions' mouths (Dan. 6:22).

    (2) The king vindicated 'the God of Daniel' (Dan. 6:26).

5. *The chief example: the death of Jesus.*

    a. It was a conspiracy of Satan (John 13:2).

        (1) God used the jealousy of the Jews (Matt. 27:18) as he had previously used the jealousy of Joseph's brothers (Acts 7:9).

        (2) God always uses jealousy to advance his purpose if we will not raise a finger to defend ourselves!

    b. When Jesus breathed his last breath on the cross, Satan thought he'd won.

        (1) Satan probably said, 'He is finished'; Jesus said, 'It is finished' (John 19:30).

        (2) The bottom line: 'None of the rulers of this age understood it, for if they had, they would not have crucified the Lord of glory' (1 Cor. 2:8).

C. Minor squabbles, or major ones – when it concerns God's work – are usually caused by Satan, who plays into people's fears, pride, greed and hurt feelings.

    1. *The murmuring of certain widows threatened to divert the apostles from their main calling* (Acts 6:1).

        a. The result: Deacons were chosen to attend to affairs other than preaching the gospel (Acts 6:2-6).

        b. The result: 'So the word of God spread. The number of disciples in Jerusalem increased rapidly, and a large number of priests became obedient to the faith' (Acts 6:7).

   (1) Stephen turned out to be a preacher as well! (Acts 6:8-15).

   (2) The bottom line: Satan's efforts backfired.

2. *The devil filled the hearts of Ananias and Sapphira when the church had become so detached from material things* (Acts 4:32; Acts 5:3).

   a. Ananias and Sapphira were struck dead by the Spirit (Acts 5:5,10).

   b. This might have been so upsetting that the devil would close down the church!

      (1) No; great fear seized the whole church and everybody else (Acts 5:11).

      (2) 'Nevertheless, more and more men and women believed in the Lord and were added to their number' (Acts 5:14).

3. The obsession of Saul of Tarsus resulted in his conversion (Acts 9:1-8).

4. The bickering of the Jews against Peter resulted in a Council that led to unity (Acts 15:1-35).

5. The disagreement between Paul and Barnabas resulted in greater usefulness (Acts 15:36-41).

CONCLUSION

God did not create the devil as he now is. Satan is part of God's fallen creation. Although he has certain powers and authority, the devil is strictly limited in what he can do. Ultimate power is securely in the hands of the sovereign God. Despite Satan's opposition, the Lord uses him to work out his will in the world and to further the cause of his kingdom.

Satan does all he does by God's permission (this includes every temptation and trial). This is one of the chief lessons of the book of Job.

One of Satan's strategies is to persuade people that he does not exist. Christians should remember this and be aware of his activity. Cultivate a healthy respect for the devil. But don't be too afraid of him – he would love that.

46

RECOGNISING STRONGHOLDS

INTRODUCTION

A. This chapter is taking this idea of spiritual warfare a step further. See *Understanding Theology*, Volume 1, chapter 35.
  1. We saw that spiritual warfare is essentially defensive.
  2. *We are not ordered to 'pick a fight' with the devil.*
    a. We wait for his attack.
    b. Then we 'stand'. See Ephesians 6:10-20.

B. The word 'stronghold' comes from 2 Corinthians 10:4-5: 'The weapons we fight with are not the weapons of the world. On the contrary, they have divine power to demolish strongholds. We demolish arguments and every pretension that sets itself up against the knowledge of God, and we take captive every thought to make it obedient to Christ.'
  1. Greek, *ochuroma*, used only here in the New Testament.
  2. *In ancient military times the stronghold was often a fortified place inside a walled city.*
    a. It was an impregnable fortress.
      (1) Soldiers would defend from within the stronghold.
      (2) But once the stronghold was taken the battle was over.
    b. Paul however uses this word not in a military but a spiritual sense.
      (1) The strongholds we have to subdue belong to the spiritual order.
      (2) They must be fought with spiritual not worldly strategy.
    c. The context of 2 Corinthians 10:4-5 shows that this spiritual warfare is none the less defensive.
      (1) Paul had been attacked from within a stronghold by those who claimed to speak for God.
      (2) These people had undermined Paul's credibility and had influence among certain Christians in Corinth; the

weaponry used against Paul were not weapons of the
Holy Spirit – which was why he knew victory was in his
hands!

C. We are taking two lessons to deal with this important subject:
  1. How to recognise strongholds.
  2. How to bring down strongholds.

D. Why is this lesson important?
  1. *We are facing strongholds of varying degrees all the time.*
     a. We may not have used this word to describe them, but that is
        what they are!
     b. We will probably incorporate this word into our vocabularies
        from now on!
  2. Once we have understood what a stronghold is (defined below),
     we need to learn how to recognise them and identify them.
  3. How we cope with a stronghold reveals how spiritual we are;
     therefore this matter touches the heart of our lives.
  4. The devil does not want us to recognise them – which is all the
     more reason we must learn what they are!
  5. We need to refine our sense of spiritual discernment and
     recognise our own spiritual weaponry to deal with strongholds.

I. THE STRONGHOLD IS CHIEFLY IN OUR OWN MINDS

A. This does not mean there is no enemy outside of us – hardly!
  1. *The devil is very real.*
     a. He does not want you to believe he is there.
     b. Unbelief in the devil is the devil's work (2 Cor. 4:4).
        (1) He blinds the minds of the unregenerate (those not born
            again) from seeing the glory of Christ.
        (2) He likewise blinds people from seeing him.
  2. *Those the devil uses are very real.*
     a. Paul had real enemies.
        (1) In the case of 2 Corinthians 10:4-5 they were Jews who
            professed faith in Christ but who hated Paul's gospel;
            they are commonly called Judaizers.
        (2) They wanted the Mosaic Law (the law of Moses) to
            replace the Holy Spirit in Christian living.
     b. They fished only in the Christian pond.

(1) They were not interested in the lost going to hell.

(2) They followed Paul and seized on his converts, in order to undermine the gospel.

B. But the battle is in the mind.

1. *If we let the devil convince us there is no hope he has already won!*

   a. Goliath the giant was a stronghold (1 Sam. 17).

   (1) He caused all Israel to fear (1 Sam. 17:11).

   (2) There was a feeling of hopelessness among the Israelites.

   b. David however saw Goliath as a mere uncircumcised Philistine who had defied God (1 Sam. 17:26).

   (1) To David's brothers he was a giant nobody could defeat.

   (2) To David Goliath was already finished! 'David said to the Philistine, "You come against me with sword and spear and javelin, but I come against you in the name of the LORD Almighty, the God of the armies of Israel, whom you have defied. This day the LORD will hand you over to me, and I'll strike you down and cut off your head. Today I will give the carcasses of the Philistine army to the birds of the air and the beasts of the earth, and the whole world will know that there is a God in Israel. All those gathered here will know that it is not by sword or spear that the LORD saves; for the battle is the LORD's, and he will give all of you into our hands"' (1 Sam. 17:45-47).

2. *The stronghold therefore, though real outside of us, is chiefly in our perception.*

   a. If we let the stronghold intimidate us we have already lost the battle.

   b. If we see that the battle is the Lord's and we are without fear, then victory is assured.

C. Stronghold (def.): when the mind is convinced that the situation is unchangeable and hopeless.

1. This is a summary taken from Ed Silvoso's most comprehensive and brilliant definition: 'A spiritual stronghold is a mindset impregnated with hopelessness which causes us to accept as unchangeable situations we know are contrary to the will of God.'

2. *To the Israelites Goliath was a stronghold; to David the stronghold hardly existed!*

   a. To the Israelites there was no hope.

   b. To David Goliath didn't have a chance!

3. *This is why we say that the stronghold is chiefly in the mind; it is a mindset.*

   a. Mindset (def.): when the mind is locked into but one way of seeing something.

   b. If the devil erects a mindset in us we are virtually defeated.

4. *This is why Paul says* 'We demolish arguments and every pretension that sets itself up against the knowledge of God' (2 Cor. 10:5).

   a. AV: 'Casting down imaginations, and every high thing that exalteth itself against the knowledge of God, and bringing into captivity every thought to the obedience of Christ.'

   b. There are two operative words:

      (1) Arguments. Gr. *logismos*: 'thoughts'. He does not mean a petty squabble when people are arguing with each other; he means powerful reasoning.

      (2) Pretension. Gr. *hupsoma*: 'height'. This refers to the pompous reasoning of the devil, as when Goliath said 'This day I defy the ranks of Israel' (1 Sam. 17:10).

II. IDENTIFYING A STRONGHOLD; GENERAL EXAMPLES:

A. A highly negative situation

1. *When we find ourselves in a highly negative situation which is so intimidating that we tend to see it as insurmountable, it is a stronghold.*

   a. But it is in our minds; the reason Paul uses two words:

      (1) Arguments, powerful reasoning that you do not feel you can contradict or refute.

      (2) Pretension, an arrogant claim that makes you feel defeated before you start. 'Then the commander stood and called out in Hebrew, "Hear the words of the great king, the king of Assyria! This is what the king says: Do not let Hezekiah deceive you. He cannot deliver you. Do not let Hezekiah persuade you to trust in the LORD when he says, 'The LORD will surely deliver us; this city

will not be given into the hand of the king of Assyria""'
(Isa. 36:13-15).

    b. It is satanic thinking that causes us to see the negative situation
as insurmountable.

  2. *Negative thinking is the work of the devil.*

    a. It poses so often as being godly when it is a spirit of fear.
'For God did not give us a spirit of timidity, but a spirit of
power, of love and of self-discipline' (2 Tim. 1:7).

    b. The essence of negative thinking: there is nothing you can
do – so give in, give up.

B. An intimidating situation

  1. *Intimidating (def.): being influenced by fright or threats.*

    a. It is when the devil says, 'You can't make it through,' 'You
can't possibly succeed,' 'Give up.'

    b. We have seen the examples of Goliath and Sennacharib.

  2. *Whenever you feel intimidated know at that moment this
feeling is not from God* (2 Tim. 1:7).

    a. God does not intimidate, he gives confidence and hope.

    b. The devil always intimidates.

      (1) Caleb and Joshua were outnumbered by the majority of
the spies who said, 'We can't attack those people; they
are stronger than we are' (Num. 13:31).

      (2) Gideon was at first intimidated. 'The LORD answered, "I
will be with you, and you will strike down all the
Midianites together"' (Judg. 6:16).

      (3) Even Elijah was intimidated, threatened by Jezebel. 'Elijah
was afraid and ran for his life. When he came to
Beersheba in Judah, he left his servant there, while he
himself went a day's journey into the desert. He came
to a broom tree, sat down under it and prayed that he
might die. "I have had enough, LORD," he said. "Take
my life; I am no better than my ancestors"' (1 Kgs.
19:3-4).

C. Temptation

  1. *The devil causes us to rationalise, having made God look
unreasonable.*

    a. 'Now the serpent was more crafty than any of the wild
animals the LORD God had made. He said to the woman,

"Did God really say, 'You must not eat fruit from the any tree in the garden'?'" (Gen. 3:1).

b. "'You will not surely die," the serpent said to the woman. "For God knows that when you eat of it your eyes will be opened, and you will be like God, knowing good and evil"'" (Gen. 3:4-5).

c. 'When the woman saw that the fruit of the tree was good for food and pleasing to the eye, and also desirable for gaining wisdom, she took some and ate it. She also gave some to her husband, who was with her, and he ate it' (Gen. 3:6).

2. *Temptation is almost always 'providential'; that is, it looks like a set-up by God and therefore it is right to give in.*

a. Jonah ran from the Lord, wanted to go to Tarshish – there was a boat ready to sail for Tarshish! (Jonah 1:3).

b. David saw a beautiful woman bathing, and her husband happened to be away (2 Sam. 11:2-3).

c. 'When tempted, no-one should say, "God is tempting me." For God cannot be tempted by evil, nor does he tempt anyone; but each one is tempted when, by his own evil desire, he is dragged away and enticed. Then, after desire has conceived, it gives birth to sin; and sin, when it is full-grown, gives birth to death' (Jas 1:13-15).

3. *Temptation always poses as too great to resist.*

a. This is a stronghold – a set-up of Satan.

b. God's Word tells us that any temptation is resistible. 'No temptation has seized you except what is common to man. And God is faithful; he will not let you be tempted beyond what you can bear. But when you are tempted, he will also provide a way out so that you can stand up under it' (1 Cor. 10:13).

D. Intellectual arguments against God and the Bible

1. *Intellectual temptation is much like sexual temptation; you never know how strong you will be.*

a. Some people fancy themselves 'great intellects' and have no fear considering intellectual pursuits that are anti-God.

b. Many a young person has entered university or seminary with every intention of preaching the gospel one day; then come out an unbeliever.

2. *But when intellectual temptation is thrust upon you, know there is a way out!*
   a. Satan will put up arguments that imply:
      (1) God does not exist.
      (2) The Bible cannot be trusted.
   b. Intellectual argument is but a stronghold – in the mind.
      (1) 'And without faith it is impossible to please God, because anyone who comes to him must believe that he exists and that he rewards those who earnestly seek him' (Heb. 11:6).
      (2) 'All Scripture is God-breathed and is useful for teaching, rebuking, correcting and training in righteousness' (2 Tim. 3:16).
3. Every intellectual argument of Satan can be smashed.

III. How strongholds are erected

A. Satan is the architect and builder of all strongholds.
   1. *He is at work day and night, looking for any opportunity to move in where we are vulnerable and exploit it the situation.*
      a. Paul said he was not ignorant of Satan's schemes (2 Cor. 2:11).
      b. We must also be aware of the way Satan works and how he develops strategy.
         (1) Jonathan Edwards reminds us that the devil (before his revolt) was trained in the 'heaven of heavens'.
         (2) He therefore knows God's ways to a great extent and has an advantage over us in this way.
   2. *He works when we are sleeping!* (Matt. 13:25,39).
      a. He constantly looks for ways to take people 'captive to do his will' (2 Tim. 2:26).
      b. His aim: to erect strongholds.

B. Satan erects strongholds by exploiting situations where we are most vulnerable.
   1. *Damaged emotions (we all have them)*
      a. This refers largely to childhood experiences.
         (1) We are probably more impressionable when we are very young.

  (2) Negative experiences leave scars, making us vulnerable in certain areas.
  b. Influences generally include the impact made on us by:
   (1) Parents or relatives.
   (2) Authority figures – school teachers, church leaders.
   (3) Other children, who can be so cruel.
  c. Some examples of damaged emotions (all leading to personality weaknesses):
   (1) Too little or too much gratification; the result may be an arrested development at a certain age, leaving us emotionally immature.
   (2) An overly dominant parent; the result may be that we never feel we achieve or come up to standard, making us perfectionists.
   (3) Sexual abuse; the result may be that we struggle with our sexuality and lack confidence in forming healthy relationships.
   (4) Lack of sufficient attention from the parent of the same sex; the result may be homosexual tendencies whereby we try to make good a relationship we never had as we grew up.
   (5) An absent parent; the result may be an insecurity in forming normal relationships, especially with authority figures.
  d. Note: Satan often exploits these weaknesses in us.
   (1) A stronghold is erected.
   (2) We tend to think the stronghold is unchangeable and never consider that it may be brought down.
2. *An unforgiving spirit*
  a. Some may have more difficulty at this point than others; however, we all struggle here.
  b. The refusal to forgive those who have hurt us is virtually an invitation to Satan to walk all over us! And he will!
  c. Here are some common results of not totally forgiving others:
   (1) Self-righteousness, or a judgemental spirit.
   (2) Fear.
   (3) Anger, irritability.
   (4) Any weakness – whatever the cause – which Satan exploits, resulting in physical and emotional problems.

3. *Jealousy*
   a. This is one of those traits easiest to see in others, but hardest to see in ourselves.
   b. It is frequently an unconscious motivation that lies behind so much of what we say and stand for:
      (1) It is what often makes us critical of others, especially those we don't like.
      (2) It is what makes us gossip – and like to do it.
      (3) It is what makes us vindictive.
4. *Unrealistic expectations*
   a. This may come from the following:
      (1) Ambition that exceeds ability.
      (2) A prophetic word that was not from God.
      (3) Assuming that your spouse will compensate for the lack of fulfilment from childhood experiences.
      (4) Believing that material things – or money – will buy joy.
      (5) Placing too much confidence in people, even the best of people.
   b. The result: a tendency to live in a dream world, which becomes a stronghold.
5. *Inability to handle money*
   a. Not living within income.
   b. Often the result of robbing God (Mal. 3:8-10).
6. *Unanswered prayer*
   a. If God has not answered prayer the reason must be:
      (1) We did not ask in God's will (1 John 5:14-15).
      (2) God will still answer – in his time (Luke 1:5-20).
   b. Satan moves in on unanswered prayer, to accuse God.
7. *Unbelieving community*
   a. The area around your church.
   b. Unsaved friends or relatives.
   c. Institutions generally:
      (1) Government.
      (2) Educational system.
      (3) Royal family.
      (4) An apostate church.
      (5) Entertainment industry.

C. Any of the above can lead to the erection of strongholds, e.g.:
  1. Broken marriages; dysfunctional families.
  2. Disunity in the church; cliques.
  3. Personality problems; insecure people.
  4. Debt.

CONCLUSION

When a situation seems hopeless the devil has produced just the mindset he intended. He does this particularly by intimidating us, tempting us, exploiting our vulnerabilities and confronting us with intellectual arguments against gospel truths. We need to recognise that God does not intimidate, tempt, exploit or argue against himself. When we meet the hopeless feelings that such situations provoke, Satan is at work. Learn to recognise such strongholds. Know their architect and builder is the devil.

47

BRINGING DOWN STRONGHOLDS

A. In the previous chapter we have provided some details with regard to recognising strongholds.

1. The architect and builder of strongholds in the Christian life is the devil.

2. *The devil erects strongholds to defend his interests.*

   a. He wants to threaten and reverse the progress made by the gospel.

   b. He does this by giving us a feeling of hopelessness and despair so we will completely give up.

B. When we recognise a stronghold we have two choices:

1. To consider the situation hopeless and remain defeated, the position of most of the Israelites when they were threatened by Goliath (1 Sam. 17:11).

2. *To see past the stronghold and recognise the power of God, the position of David* (1 Sam. 17:45ff).

   a. We will recall that in ancient times a stronghold was a fortified place inside a walled city.

   b. If the stronghold was taken, victory was assured.

      (1) Paul uses the word (2 Cor. 10:4 – its only use in the New Testament) not in a military but a spiritual sense.

      (2) The stronghold must be defended with spiritual weapons.

   c. A stronghold (def.): when the mind is convinced that the situation is unchangeable and hopeless.

      (1) 'A spiritual stronghold is a mindset impregnated with hopelessness which causes us to accept as unchangeable situations we know are contrary to the will of God' (Ed Silvoso).

      (2) The key: it is in the mind – our perception.

         (a) Not that there is no Goliath out there.

         (b) But whether or not in our perception the situation is hopeless.

C. It is one thing however to recognise a stronghold; it is another to bring down a stronghold.

    1. *It is very important to recognise a stronghold – the first step.*

        a. We must call a spade a spade.

        b. There must be no pretending or sweeping under the carpet what is obvious – any stronghold we face:

            (1) The inability to forgive.

            (2) The need for reconciliation.

            (3) The marriage on the rocks.

            (4) The difficult person or situation we live with.

            (5) The unsaved.

    2. *But Paul could say, We 'demolish strongholds'* (2 Cor. 10:4).

        a. He saw them as reasonings which the devil made up.

        b. Paul was not threatened by them; 'we demolish strongholds'.

    3. *The question is: can we?*

        a. Was this an anointing reserved only for apostles?

        b. Or can we too bring them down?

D. It should be fairly obvious why this lesson is important:

    1. *We all face strongholds of many kinds.*

        a. There will be more than one in every life.

        b. These strongholds will have varying degrees of hold over us.

    2. We must realise that no trial or temptation is unique; it is 'common to man. And God is faithful; he will not let you be tempted beyond what you can bear. But when you are tempted, he will also provide a way out so that you can stand up under it' (1 Cor. 10:13).

    3. There is therefore a way forward; this lesson will show what we can do.

    4. This will help us help others who face strongholds.

    5. Learning how to bring down strongholds will be life-changing – the real purpose of theology!

I. THE EXTERNAL AND THE INTERNAL STRONGHOLD

A. The external is 'Goliath'.

    1. The enemy, the devil, will always see to it that there is a Goliath out there who will threaten and seek to demoralise us.

    2. Even if Goliath falls or walks away, another Goliath will appear.

B. The internal stronghold is the way we perceive Goliath.

1. If we are like the Israelites in 1 Samuel 17, we will remain hopeless and in perpetual despair.

2. *If we are like David we will see Goliath for what he is and God's power for what it is.*

   a. Golaith's threats were against God's will.

      (1) He was but an uncircumcised Philistine.

      (2) He defied the armies of the living God.

   b. David saw Goliath as fallen before he fell! 'This day the LORD will hand you over to me, and I'll strike you down and cut off your head. Today I will give the carcasses of the Philistine army to the birds of the air and the beasts of the earth, and the whole world will know that there is a God in Israel' (1 Sam. 17:46).

      (1) In David's *mind* Goliath was already defeated.

      (2) Internally, then, the stronghold was brought down.

C. You may want to say: I will have the internal victory (when my mind is convinced) once there is an objective external victory.

1. *But that is 'putting the cart before the horse'.*

   a. For the Israelites and David's cynical brothers, there was no real victory.

      (1) They rejoiced, yes.

      (2) They shared in Goliath's fall.

   b. But they got no *spiritual* victory.

      (1) The real victory must be internal.

      (2) We are called to be 'Davids' – not those weak Israelites!

2. *If you wait for the problem to be solved externally before you experience the internal power of the Holy Spirit, you will have no real victory.*

   a. For example, if you can only rejoice when:

      (1) The other person apologises to you –

      (2) The 'problem' person or situation is removed –

      (3) Things get better externally –

      You are like the Israelites and David's brothers.

      That is not bringing down a stronghold.

   b. Bringing down a stronghold is not what 'they' do or what someone else does for you. Rather:

    (1) When you have the victory inside before the answer is externally given to you (in other words, the problem is still there).

    (2) When you have totally forgiven, whether or not the other person apologised.

    (3) When you have the victory (inside) before the situation external to you is resolved.

3. *The stronghold is in your mind – it is you!*

    a. Not that David wasn't thrilled – or even relieved – when he cut off Goliath's head (1 Sam. 17:50-54).

    b. But David got the victory internally first.

        (1) This is the order God wants for all of us.

        (2) That is what is meant by bringing down strongholds.

II. How the internal victory is achieved

A. Know that the battle is the Lord's.

    1. *This was the key to David's triumph.* 'All those gathered here will know that it is not by sword or spear that the LORD saves; for the battle is the LORD's, and he will give all of you into our hands' (1 Sam. 17:47).

    2. *When King Jehoshaphat faced his greatest crisis:*

        a. He proclaimed a fast (2 Chron. 20:3).

        b. He led the people in public prayer (2 Chron. 20:5-12).

            (1) He was scared! 'We do not know what to do, but our eyes are upon you' (2 Chron. 20:12).

            (2) We too feel this way when facing a stronghold, in this case the Moabites and Ammonites came to make war on Jehoshaphat (2 Chron. 20:1).

        c. The Lord spoke: 'The battle is not yours, but God's' (2 Chron. 20:15). 'You will not have to fight this battle. Take up your positions; stand firm and see the deliverance the LORD will give you, O Judah and Jerusalem. Do not be afraid; do not be discouraged. Go out to face them tomorrow, and the LORD will be with you' (2 Chron. 20:17).

B. Know what weapons to use. 'We do not wage war as the world does. The weapons we fight with are not the weapons of the world' (2 Cor. 10:3-4).

1. *When you are up against a spiritual stronghold, take a look at the weapons the enemy uses.*

   a. The enemy will *always* wage war according to the flesh – 'the standards of this world' (2 Cor. 10:2).

   b. Here is how the enemy operates; he uses:

      (1) Fear: his chief weapon; to threaten or intimidate.

         (a) Goliath used fear (1 Sam. 17:10,44).

         (b) Sennacharib's method: fear (Isa. 37:9-13).

         (c) This is the reason a lion *roars* before attacking his prey. 'Be self-controlled and alert. Your enemy the devil prowls around like a roaring lion looking for someone to devour' (1 Pet. 5:8).

         (d) Note: when the enemy tries to intimidate this is your dead giveaway that he is using warfare according to the flesh.

      (2) Lies, as seen with Goliath and Sennacharib.

         (a) '"You will not surely die," the serpent said to the woman, "For God knows that when you eat of it your eyes will be opened, and you will be like God, knowing good and evil"' (Gen. 3:4).

         (b) The devil is a liar and is the father of lies (John 8:44).

         (c) The enemy will lie to you, propagate lies and try to get you to believe what is not true.

      (3) Deceit or flattery: buttering you up to get a favour.

         (a) They 'flatter others for their own advantage' (Jude 16).

         (b) 'A flattering mouth works ruin' (Prov. 26:28. cf. Prov. 28:23; 29:5).

         (c) Many of us are gullible and vulnerable at this point; Satan knows this and will use it to the hilt!

      (4) Deceit by outward appearance.

         (a) The actual stronghold Paul faced was the Judaizers who bolstered their own stature by an aura of prestige.

         (b) When your enemy claims that the people are against you and the majority on their side, it is clear that he (or they) are waging warfare according to the flesh.

         (c) 'For everything in the world – the cravings of sinful man, the lust of his eyes and the boasting of what he has and does – comes not from the Father but from the world' (1 John 2:16).

(5) Divisiveness, or stirring up dissent.
   (a) Satan fears unity in the body of Christ.
   (b) Warfare according to the flesh: when the enemy finds something wrong and uses it to breed discord.
   (c) 'The LORD hates...a man who stirs up dissension among brothers' (Prov. 6:16,19).
e. Note: when you discern or detect that the enemy is waging warfare according to the flesh, be encouraged; it is the easiest battle of all to fight!

2. *Be absolutely sure your weapons are spiritual:*
   a. Never, never, never threaten.
      (1) It is the enemy who uses fear as a tactic.
      (2) Once you use fear you are in that moment disqualified to wage war in the Spirit; no stronghold will be demolished.
      (3) 'There is no fear in love. But perfect love drives out fear, because fear has to do with punishment. The one who fears is not made perfect in love' (1 John 4:18).
   b. Maintain transparent integrity. 'To thine own self be true.' Shakespeare.
      (1) When you are on the side of truth, live by it.
      (2) 'You know how we lived among you for your sake' (1 Thess. 1:5).
      (3) 'Speaking the truth in love' (Eph. 4:15).
   c. Avoid feigned affection or admiration.
      (1) There is a place for encouraging others, of course.
      (2) But the need to pour on a lot of compliments and accolades often springs from:
         (a) Insecure people.
         (b) Insincere people.
      (3) Paul: 'We never used flattery' (1 Thess. 2:5).
   d. Don't try to impress by prestige or proving yourself.
      (1) 'It is mine to avenge' (Rom. 12:19. cf. Deut. 32:35).
      (2) 'When words are many, sin is not absent, but he who holds his tongue is wise' (Prov. 10:19).
      (3) 'Methinks the lady doth protest too much' (Shakespeare).
      (4) The greatest freedom is having nothing to prove. E.g.:
         (a) By education or culture.
         (b) By position or who you know.

    e. Be a peacemaker.

        (1) 'Blessed are the peacemakers, for they will be called sons of God' (Matt. 5:9).

        (2) 'Make every effort to keep the unity of the Spirit through the bond of peace' (Eph. 4:3).

        (3) You will often find yourself in a position to widen a gap or close it – this is a wonderful time to be gracious and to be a true healer between estranged people.

C. Be yourself and walk in the light (1 John 1:7).

    1. *David rejected Saul's armour* (1 Sam. 17:39).

        a. He knew he must live in the anointing God gave him.

        b. God never promotes us to the level of our incompetence.

    2. *By living within the anointing God gave him (not outside of it), David knew in his heart what he could do* (1 Sam. 17:34-37).

        a. We all have our gifts (1 Cor. 12:11).

        b. In the body of Christ we must not pretend to be the eye or the ear if we are the hand or small intestine (1 Cor. 12:12-27).

    3. *The light God gives will be known by inner peace* (Rom. 14:19).

        a. We will never be called by God to violate our peace.

        b. David had peace to proceed; he slew Goliath.

    4. *At the end of the day the stronghold comes down by what God does and what we do.*

        a. Paul stated an apparent contradiction.

            (1) 'They' – meaning spiritual weapons – what God does (2 Cor. 10:4).

            (2) 'We' – meaning what we are consequently able to do – viz. demolish strongholds (2 Cor. 10:5).

        b. Sometimes God will require us to act; when we have followed the principles above:

            (1) We will know when to act.

            (2) We will have total peace.

            (3) The strongholds will come down.

        c. Jehoshaphat appointed men to sing to the Lord! 'As they began to sing and praise, the LORD set ambushes against the men of Ammon and Moab and Mount Seir who were invading Judah, and they were defeated' (2 Chron. 20:22).

III. REPLACING STRONGHOLDS

A. This refers to what we do as a parallel responsibility in bringing the stronghold down: 'And we take captive every thought to make it obedient to Christ' (2 Cor. 10:5).
   1. This is not just follow-up to all the above.
   2. *This is done parallel to carrying out these principles.* And
      a. It is done simultaneously to:
         (1) Knowing the battle is the Lord's.
         (2) Knowing the right weaponry.
         (3) Being ourselves and walking in the light.
      b. Walking in the light consists in:
         (1) 'Casting down imaginations' (2 Cor. 10:5, AV).
         (2) 'Bringing into captivity every thought to the obedience of Christ' (2 Cor. 10:5, AV).
         (3) Note: 2 Corinthians 10:5 is so profound we almost need several translations to fathom the depth of it.

B. If this parallel responsibility does not emerge, the old stronghold will likely rebuild!
   1. *This means that what has been demolished must be replaced with something!*
      a. After the dentist drills the cavity, the tooth is filled.
      b. It was one thing for the Berlin Wall to fall, quite another to help those who lived on the other side of it.
   2. *We have therefore three steps before there is a total victory:*
      a. Recognising the stronghold.
      b. Bringing the stronghold down (internally).
      c. Replacing the stronghold.

C. Two things replace the stronghold:
   1. *We take captive every thought: sinful thinking, imaginary conversations, etc., so that strongholds won't creep back in.*
      a. We have been given authorization to make prisoners of war the very thoughts that rebel against the will of God.
      b. Paul does not mean he can 'out-debate his opponents and drive them shamefaced from the stage' (D. A. Carson).
      c. It means to reject thoughts Satan puts there:
         (1) Accusations of the devil.
         (2) Temptations of the flesh.

(3) Feelings of self-pity.

(4) The attempt to take vengeance into your own hands.

2. *We make every thought obedient to Christ.*

    a. Instead of making God conform to my wish, I acquiesce to what he wants – no matter how much it hurts.

      (1) It means climbing down from what I wanted.

      (2) It means affirming what he wants.

    b. This may mean:

      (1) Showing a submissive spirit to leadership (or to your husband).

      (2) Showing unselfish love for those near you (or to your wife).

    c. Obedience means that Christ gave a word that was to be obeyed. There are no exceptions: '*Every* thought.'

CONCLUSION

When we recognise a stronghold we can either be defeated or we can recognise the power of God to demolish it. The choice is ours. The battle is the Lord's and he has already won the victory. We will triumph over strongholds if we recognise them for what they are, devices of the devil, and if we attack them with spiritual rather than human weapons. Satan's weapons are lies, deceit etc. Ours are the weapons of prayer, integrity and godliness.

The stronghold may come down in varying degrees. Sometimes the external stronghold comes down in one go – like David slaying Goliath. At other times a stronghold is taken a little bit at a time. Even Jesus healed in two stages (Mark 8:22-25). An internal stronghold may be demolished in stages; e.g.: totally forgiving others often takes time; we may continue to struggle with having to reject weapons according to the flesh. The chief thing to realise is that the stronghold is a mindset. This means we must get the internal victory. If the enemy falls in our minds – because we are going to let the Lord fight our battle – the stronghold has come down.

And what if the external stronghold never comes down? 'Though the fig-tree does not bud and there are no grapes on the vines, though the olive crop fails and the fields produce no food, though there are no sheep in the pen and no cattle in the stalls, yet I will rejoice in the LORD, I will be joyful in God my Saviour' (Hab. 3:17-18).

48

TEMPTATION

INTRODUCTION

A. The first book I ever saw that was written by Dr R T Williams (the man I was named after) was *Temptation.*

   1. *The big difference between his theology and mine is this:*

      a. He believed that if you gave in to temptation you lost your salvation.

      b. I believe that if you give in to temptation:

         (1) You lose fellowship with God (1 John 1:7).

         (2) You lose the joy of your salvation (Ps. 51:12).

         (3) You lose your reward in heaven unless you repent in the meantime (1 Cor. 3:15).

   2. *But the impact of Dr Williams's book will hopefully be matched by my lesson: temptation is to be resisted.*

      a. We give in to it to our peril and regret.

      b. Even though 'all things work together for good to those who love God,' (Rom. 8:28, AV), it is better not to have sinned.

         (1) Jonah's big lesson was: it wasn't worth it (Jon. 2:8).

         (2) And the fact that something works together for good (and it will) doesn't mean it was right at the time.

B. Greek:

   1. *Peirazo*; used 39 times in the New Testament.

      a. Verb: 'to test someone' or 'to make an attempt'.

      b. E.g., Matthew 4:1; Acts 5:9; Hebrews 4:15; James 1:13.

   2. *Peirasmos*, used 21 times.

      a. 'Being put to the test'; 'making an effort'.

      b. E.g., Matthew 6:13; 26:41; 1 Corinthians 10:13; 1 Timothy 6:9.

   3. *The problem: 'trial' and 'temptation' come from the same word.*

      a. Only the context suggests which is meant.

         (1) James 1:2: 'trials'.

         (2) James 1:3: 'tempted'.

    b. Sometimes they are interchangeable, as in 1 Corinthians 10:13: 'No temptation has seized you except what is common to man. And God is faithful; he will not let you be tempted beyond what you can bear. But when you are tempted, he will also provide a way out so that you can stand up under it.'

C. Definition: the state of being attracted to say, do or feel what is wrong.

1. *We don't need a degree or further training in how to be tempted!*
   - **a.** We were born in sin (Ps. 51:5).
   - **b.** We came from our mother's womb speaking lies (Ps. 58:3).
2. *And yet even Eve in an unfallen state was tempted* (Gen. 3:6). *As Augustine put it:*
   - **a.** We were created 'able to sin.'
   - **b.** After the fall we were 'not able not to sin.'
   - **c.** After conversion we are 'able not to sin.'
   - **d.** When we are glorified we will be 'unable to sin.'
3. *Clarification of our definition:*
   - **a.** Being attracted to what is wrong.
     - (1) The wrong: sin.
     - (2) Temptation may sometimes apply to what is not necessarily sin, but for our purposes in this lesson we refer to temptation and sin.
   - **b.** To say, do or feel.
     - (1) We sin by our words.
     - (2) We sin by our deeds.
     - (3) We sin by our thoughts.

D. Why is this lesson important?

1. It touches the whole of our lives; nobody is exempt from temptation.
2. If we can learn about the origin of temptation, we can better understand ourselves and what is going on when we are tempted.
3. *We need to see that there are many kinds of temptation.*
   - **a.** To some, 'sex' is the first thing that enters people's minds when the word 'temptation' is used.
   - **b.** To others, pride or the love of money is what one thinks of.
4. We must see that resisting temptation is essential to Christian living.
5. We must remember that only Jesus perfectly resisted temptation and we shall examine some of his temptations.

I. GOD AND TEMPTATION

A. One of the hardest lines to draw is how to explain exactly the origin of temptation.

  1. *James 1:13-15 is explicit:* 'When tempted, no-one should say,"God is tempting me." For God cannot be tempted by evil, nor does he tempt anyone; but each one is tempted when, by his own evil desire, he is dragged away and enticed. Then, after desire has conceived, it gives birth to sin; and sin, when it is full-grown, gives birth to death.'

  a. This removes God from the responsibility for our being tempted.

  b. The easiest thing in the world to do is to conclude hastily 'God is tempting me.' Why?

  (1) Temptation is so natural; it comes passively.

  (2) Temptation is so 'providential' (Jon. 1:1-3).

  2. *And yet James also said:* 'Consider it pure joy, my brothers, whenever you face trials of many kinds, because you know that the testing of your faith develops perseverance.' (Jam. 1:2).

  a. It is the same Greek word but almost certainly 'trial' is correct.

  b. It is also implied that God is behind the trial.

  (1) This is why it is a difficult problem.

  (2) It is a hard line to draw.

  3. *Providences and temptation.*

  a. Genesis 22:1 clearly says that God 'tested' Abraham.

  (1) In the Septuagint it is the same Greek word; hence the AV says that God 'did tempt'.

  (2) 'Tested' is obviously the better word.

  b. Matthew 4:1 says, 'Then Jesus was led by the Spirit into the desert to be tempted by the devil.'

  (1) Jesus was to be tempted by Satan.

  (2) And yet he was led by the Holy Spirit to be tempted!

B. The only conclusion:

  1. *God is the architect of the situation that lies behind our being tempted.*

  a. He doesn't do the 'tempting'.

  b. But he tests us by letting us be tempted.

2. *In a word: he permits the temptation.*

    a. He creates a situation that lets us see how strong we are.

    b. He does not directly *tempt* us but the situation he brings about is his *test* for us.

        (1) Never forget 1 Corinthians 10:13 'No temptation has seized you except what is common to man. And God is faithful; he will not let you be tempted beyond what you can bear. But when you are tempted, he will also provide a way out so that you can stand up under it.'

        (2) And yet a petition in the Lord's Prayer is: 'And lead us not into temptation, but deliver us from the evil one' (Matt. 6:13).

    c. Every temptation must be seen as a 'test' from God – for us to see what we are. 'But when envoys were sent by the rulers of Babylon to ask him about the miraculous sign that had occurred in the land, God left him to test him and to know everything that was in his heart' (2 Chron. 32:31).

C. The reverse: our tempting God.

1. *This is one thing (you may be sure) God doesn't like!*

    a. 'Do not test the Lord your God as you did at Massah' (Deut. 6:16).

    b. Jesus quoted this back to Satan who had just said, 'If you are the Son of God ... throw yourself down. For it is written: "He will command his angels concerning you, and they will lift you up in their hands, so that you will not strike your foot against a stone."' 'Jesus answered him, "It is also written: 'Do not put the Lord your God to the test'"' (Matt. 4:6, 7).

2. *How might we tempt or test God?*

    a. By challenging him, as the devil tempted Jesus to do.

        (1) To challenge his power, since God can do anything.

        (2) To take advantage of his promise, as the devil did by quoting (above) Psalm 91:11-12.

    b. By presumption, assuming you will not get found out.

        (1) 'Peter said to her, "How could you agree to test the Spirit of the Lord? Look! The feet of the men who buried your husband are at the door, and they will carry you out also"' (Acts 5:9).

    (2) Ananias and Sapphira underestimated the power of the Spirit that was present.

  c. By sulking, thinking that your anger will move God to do something.

    (1) 'For the wrath of man worketh not the righteousness of God' (Jas. 1:20 AV).

    (2) We sometimes fancy that God will feel sorry for us when we sulk in his presence. Wrong.

  d. By deliberately walking into temptation.

    (1) 'Rather, clothe yourselves with the Lord Jesus Christ, and do not think about how to gratify the desires of the sinful nature' (Rom. 13:14).

    (2) We may fancy we will be strong enough; the truth is, most of us have a shrewd suspicion where temptation is likely to emerge.

3. The only exception: (Mal. 3:10-12).

II. TEMPTATION AND THE FLESH

A. The flesh is the sinful part of the soul.

  1. That is not the only way the word is used in the New Testament of course (cf. 1 Cor. 15:39).

  2. *But that is a prominent strain in Paul's letters.*

    a. 'So I say, live by the Spirit, and you will not gratify the desires of the sinful nature' (Gal. 5:16).

    b. 'The acts of the sinful nature are obvious: sexual immorality, impurity and debauchery; idolatry and witchcraft; hatred, discord, jealousy, fits of rage, selfish ambition, dissensions, factions and envy; drunkenness, orgies, and the like. I warn you, as I did before, that those who live like this will not inherit the kingdom of God' (Gal. 5:19-21).

  3. *The flesh therefore largely refers to fallen nature.*

    a. It is what we inherited from Adam's fall (Rom. 5:12).

    b. We are born with it and therefore have to reckon with it – even after our conversion.

  4. *The immediate origin of the temptation therefore is the flesh.* 'When tempted, no-one should say,"God is tempting me." For God cannot be tempted by evil, nor does he tempt anyone; but each one is tempted when, by his own evil desire, he is dragged away and enticed' (Jas. 1:13-14).

   a. James will not allow us to lay the responsibility for temptation in God's lap.

   b. We *can* resist it – 1 Corinthians 10:13!

(1) We therefore must reckon God would not allow it were we not able to resist it.

(2) We have only ourselves to blame if we give in.

B. Kinds of temptation

   1. *Sex*

   a. Sex is a God-given, biological desire.

   (1) Like hunger, we would not eat if there were no appetite.

   (2) God gave us hunger to keep us alive.

   b. If sex were not desirable there would be no motive to 'be fruitful and increase in number' (Gen. 1:28).

   (1) God made sex fun!

   (2) Sex was not born in Hollywood but at the Throne of Grace.

   c. But God decreed that sex be two things:

   (1) Monogamous – with one partner in marriage only.

   (2) Heterosexual – with the opposite sex only.

   d. Sex outside marriage is therefore sin.

   (1) It is adultery when one or both is already married.

   (2) It is fornication (immorality) if unmarried.

   2. *Pride, or self-esteem*

   a. Sex and pride are closely akin. Some are sexually tempted, or involved in tempting, when their self-esteem needs to be bolstered.

   b. Pride also manifests itself in:

   (1) Ambition: Ecclesiastes 4:4.

   (2) Jealousy: 1 Samuel 18:9.

   (3) Gossip: James 3.

   (4) Slander: Ephesians 4:31-32.

   (5) Unforgiving spirit: Matthew 18:23-35.

   (6) Need for prestige: 1 John 2:16.

   (7) Prejudice: (racial, cultural, educational) Acts 22:21-22.

   (8) Hatred: 1 John 2:9,11.

   (9) Not witnessing: James 4:17; Matthew 28:19-20.

   (10) Self-righteousness: Job 42:6.

   (11) Legalism: Galatians 3:4.

(12)Self-pity: 1 Kings 19:4.

(13)Anger: Jonah 4.

3. *Insecurity, resulting in:*

  a. Greed, or the love of money (1 Tim. 6:10).

  b. Controlling others, e.g.:

   (1) Taking power.

   (2) Manipulating people.

  c. Jealousy, slander, etc..

  d. Not tithing (Mal. 3:10).

  e. Fear (2 Tim. 1:7).

4. *Unbelief*

  a. The first temptation is often this:

   (1) To doubt God's Word (Gen. 3:1).

   (2) To doubt one's position or calling (Matt. 4:3).

  b. This of course is the opposite of faith.

   (1) It was Israel's downfall in the desert (Heb. 3:12).

   (2) It is subtle and possibly the most dangerous of all
       temptations (Heb. 4:11).

5. *Cares of this life.*

  a. This temptation seems so harmless at first (Matt. 6:25-34).

  b. Martha felt justified in such (Luke 10:40).

  c. The result: the temptation to let prayer, Bible reading,
     commitment to God's work, take less of a priority.

   (1) Our minds wandering in worship.

   (2) Not worshipping at all.

   (3) Not witnessing for the Lord.

III. TEMPTATION AND THE DEVIL

A. The devil basically tempts in two ways:

 1. *Directly, when he confronts you as though apart from the flesh.*

  a. He may come on to you with a spirit of fear.

  b. He may take those captive who have not been living close to
     God (2 Tim. 2:26).

 2. *Indirectly, his common procedure.*

  a. This is when he takes advantage of the flesh (see all the
     above).

  b. It is when he plays into our weaknesses, superimposing the
     force of his power on what is weak already, e.g.:temptation
     to sex or temptation to fear.

    c. He will use people (almost always) to get at you:
- **(1)** Through misunderstanding.
- **(2)** Hurting your feelings.
- **(3)** Through lies.
- **(4)** Accusation.

B. The devil's chief weapon: to accuse.

1. *He is called 'the accuser of the brothers'* (Rev. 12:10).
   - **a.** He will say, 'You cannot possibly be a Christian.'
   - **b.** He will say, 'God surely doesn't love you.'
   - **c.** He will throw up every skeleton in your cupboard (we all have them).
2. *He will use people who are intimidating:*
   - **a.** To make you feel guilty.
   - **b.** To make you feel you cannot succeed.

C. In a word: he works through our weaknesses.

But remember: the devil can proceed no further than God allows (Job 1). And never forget: (1 Cor. 10:13)!

IV. TEMPTATION AND JESUS

A. Jesus as a man knew temptation.

1. 'Because he himself suffered when he was tempted, he is able to help those who are being tempted' (Heb. 2:18).
2. 'For we do not have a high priest who is unable to sympathise with our weaknesses, but we have one who has been tempted in every way, just as we are – yet was without sin' (Heb. 4:15).

B. Jesus was tempted throughout the whole of his life, but we know of certain explicit examples.

1. *When he was tempted by the devil at the beginning of his ministry* (Matt. 4:1-11; Mark 1:12-13; Luke 4:1-13).
   - **a.** He was tempted to unbelief (Matt. 4:3).
   - **b.** He was tempted to give in because he was hungry (Matt. 4:3).
   - **c.** He was tempted to test God (Matt. 4:5-7).
   - **d.** He was tempted to pride and to worship Satan (Matt. 4:8-10).
   - **e.** Note: this account is by no means the whole of Jesus' temptation; Hebrews 4:15 makes that clear.

2. *During the whole of his ministry.*

    a. Knowing what Judas was like but never revealing it (John 2:25; 6:70ff).

    b. His relationship with his critics.

        (1) 'The Pharisees and Sadducees came to Jesus and tested him by asking him to show them a sign from heaven' (Matt. 16:1).

        (2) 'Then the Pharisees went out and laid plans to trap him in his words' (Matt. 22:15. cf. Matt. 22:18).

        (3) The same was true with the question and illustration put to him by the Sadducees (Matt. 22:23-33).

        (4) 'Hearing that Jesus had silenced the Sadducees, the Pharisees got together. One of them, an expert in the law, tested him with this question: "Teacher, which is the greatest commandment in the Law?"' (Matt. 22:34-36).

3. *His final hours.*

    a. Betrayal (John 13:27-30).

    b. Loneliness (Mark 14:37).

    c. Rejection (Matt. 26:56).

    d. Peter's denial (Matt. 26:69-74. Cf. Matt. 26:31-35).

    e. The 'trial'.

        (1) Before the Sanhedrin (Matt. 26:57-67).

        (2) Before Pilate (Matt. 27:11-26).

        (3) Before Herod (Luke 23:6-11).

        (4) Before Pilate (Luke 23:13-25; John 18:28-19:16).

    f. The crucifixion.

        (1) Refusing to retort (Luke 23:34).

        (2) Not explaining himself.

    g. Feeling deserted by the Father (Mark 15:34).

V. Resisting temptation

A. Any temptation can be resisted (1 Cor. 10:13).

1. *Satan will accuse God by saying,* '1 Corinthians 10:13 is not true.'

2. *In weakness we want to justify ourselves and claim, 'This is too great a temptation – I cannot but give in.'*

    a. All temptation appears 'providential'.

    b. We never know how strong we will be.

    c. Satan exploits our vulnerability.

B. The order by which temptation is to be resisted:
1. *'Watch and pray'* – *in that order* (Mark 14:38).
    a. If we pray, then watch, we tend to 'pass the buck' to God for not answering our prayer!
    b. Watching first – up to us – is to be our priority.
2. *Make no provision for the sinful nature* (Rom. 13:14).
    a. Be shrewd enough to know where temptation can be found – and avoid it.
    b. This may refer to people as well as places.
    c. Billy Sunday: 'The reason so many Christians fall into sin is that they treat temptation like strawberry shortcake instead of a rattlesnake.'
3. *Consider how awful you will feel if you give in.*
    a. Jonah concluded: 'It wasn't worth it' (Jon. 2:1ff).
    b. So will you; spare yourself the heartache and possibly years of regret.

CONCLUSION

No-one is exempt from temptation, nor will we be until the day we die. God in his sovereignty allows the situations in which we are tempted, but he does not tempt. However, he uses our temptations to test us. Satan exploits our weaknesses and, when we fall, he uses the situation to tempt us to doubt our standing with God.

Every temptation can be resisted. A strategy for resisting temptation: (1) watch and pray, (2) avoid situations in which we know we are likely to be tempted, (3) think how we will feel if we give in.

Jesus was tempted. He understands our struggles.

49

SOUL SLEEP

A. Our lesson brings us to the area of eschatology generally and the intermediate state particularly.
  1. *Eschatology (def.): the doctrine of 'last things'.*
     a. Prophecy and the Second Coming of Christ.
     b. The final judgment, the final destiny of men and women.
  2. *Intermediate state (def.): the time between death and the Final Resurrection.*
     a. Intermediate (def.): coming between two things in time or place or order.
     b. The intermediate state therefore is the time between our death and the time of Jesus' Second Coming.

B. The issue: what happens when we die?
  1. Do believers go to heaven immediately after they die?
  2. Do unbelievers go to hell immediately after they die?
  3. Are these people conscious from the moment they die or do they go into a state of unconsciousness?

C. Soul sleep (def.): when people die they go into a place of unconscious existence, and the next thing that they are conscious of will be when Christ returns and raises their bodies.
  1. The meaning is, the body is dead and the soul 'sleeps', that is, is unaware of anything.
  2. Those who are dead are unaware of anything.
     a. They are in no pain.
     b. They are in no bliss.
     c. When they die they know absolutely nothing.
        (1) Life goes on for the living of course.
        (2) Those who are dead have no sense of time (since they are unconscious).
        (3) They 'wake up' when Jesus comes.

(4) It is like a person who falls asleep as soon as his head hits the pillow and the next thing they remember is waking up the next morning.

3. *This teaching has not found wide acceptance in the church until recent times.*
   a. Some Anabaptists taught this during the Reformation.
   b. Many cultists have taught this.
   c. In recent years a number of evangelicals have taught this, especially those who espouse the doctrine of annihilation.
      (1) Annihilation (def.): that body and soul are totally destroyed, as though they never existed.
      (2) Some see eternal punishment as being annihilation.
   d. Many who believe in annihilation also believe in soul sleep.
   e. Many who believe in soul sleep also believe in annihilation.

D. Why is this subject important?

1. We all want to know what happens the moment after we die, for all of us will die sooner of later (unless Jesus comes first). 'Just as man is destined to die once, and after that to face judgment' (Heb. 9:27).
2. *We all want to know what happens to our loved ones and friends when they die.*
   a. Are they consciously in heaven?
   b. Are they consciously in a place of judgment?
3. The Bible does use the term 'sleep' at times when it comes to death; could this not mean that the people are asleep, that is, unaware of their existence or surroundings?
4. Why would the Bible use the term 'sleep' at times to refer to death if it is not literally that – being asleep?
5. Since a rising number of Christians are embracing this view, should we not know why?
6. We should earnestly seek to get to the bottom of this teaching and know if the Bible really teaches it.

I. SOME PRELIMINARY ASSUMPTIONS

A. All Christians die sooner or later.

1. *Death is not a punishment for Christians* (Rom. 8).
   a. The penalty for our sins has been paid.
   b. Even the 'premature' death of some Christians in Corinth

was seen as a disciplinary or chastening process – so they would not be condemned with the world (1 Cor. 11:30-32). Note: Not all who die young of course die as a result of judgment.

   c. Death is but the final outcome of living in a fallen world.

     (1) The wages of sin is death (Rom. 6:23).

     (2) Because we are born sinners, we will die – as Adam did.

2. *God uses the experience of death to bring about our glorification.*

   a. Between justification and glorification is the process of sanctification.

   b. But when we are glorified that process stops (Rom. 8:30).

B. Christians should not fear death.

1. Paul says he would rather be away from the body and be at home with the Lord (2 Cor. 5:8; Phil. 1:21).

2. We naturally feel sorrow when our loved ones die, even if we know they are saved (Acts 8:2; John 11:35).

C. We must not presume the final destiny of those who did not appear to be saved.

1. A person may call on the name of the Lord as they are dying without others knowing it.

2. Who knows what knowledge of the gospel or Scriptures they may have heard – and call on the Lord in their hearts?

D. The souls of believers go immediately to God's presence.

1. Death is a temporary cessation of bodily life and a separation of the soul from the body.

2. Paul said, 'We are confident, I say, and would prefer to be away from the body and at home with the Lord' (2 Cor. 5:8).

3. His desire was 'to depart and be with Christ, which is better by far' (Phil. 1:23).

4. Jesus said to the dying thief, 'Today you will be with me in paradise' (Luke 23:43).

5. We come even now to the presence of God where also are to be found 'the spirits of righteous men made perfect' (Heb. 12:23).

   a. Note: This shows also there is no such thing as purgatory.

(1) In Roman Catholic teaching, purgatory is the place where the souls of believers go to be further purified from sin until they are admitted to heaven.

(2) The sufferings of purgatory are given to God in substitution for the punishment for sins that the believers should have received in time.

b. In 1 Corinthians 3:15 Paul says that one's works (wood, hay or straw) will be burned up on the Day of Judgment.

(1) This does not speak of a person being burned up.

(2) It is one's work being tested by fire.

II. THE CASE FOR SOUL SLEEP

A. Old Testament passages that seem to teach that the dead do not have a conscious existence.

1. 'No one remembers you when he is dead. Who praises you from the grave?' (Ps. 6:5).

2. 'It is not the dead who praise the Lord, those who go down to silence' (Ps. 115:17).

3. 'Whatever your hand finds to do, do it with all your might, for in the grave, where you are going, there is neither working nor planning nor knowledge nor wisdom' (Ecc. 9:10).

4. 'For the grave cannot praise you, death cannot sing your praise; those who go down to the pit cannot hope for your faithfulness.' (Isa. 38:18).

5. 'Multitudes who sleep in the dust of the earth will awake: some to everlasting life, others to shame and everlasting contempt' (Dan. 12:2).

B. New Testament passages that speak of the state of death as 'sleep' or 'falling asleep'.

1. 'He said, "Go away. The girl is not dead but asleep." But they laughed at him' (Matt. 9:24).

2. 'The tombs broke open and the bodies of many holy people who had died [AV 'saints which slept'] were raised to life' (Matt. 27:52).

3. 'After he had said this, he went on to tell them, "Our friend Lazarus has fallen asleep; but I am going there to wake him up"' (John 11:11).

4. 'Then he fell on his knees and cried out, "Lord, do not hold this sin against them." When he had said this, he fell asleep' (Acts 7:60).

5. 'For when David had served God's purpose in his own generation, he fell asleep; he was buried with his fathers and his body decayed' (Acts 13:36).

6. *'After that, he appeared to more than five hundred of the brothers at the same time, most of whom are still living, though some have fallen asleep'* (1 Cor. 15:6).

   a. 'Then those also who have fallen asleep in Christ are lost' (1 Cor. 15:18).

   b. 'But Christ has indeed been raised from the dead, the firstfruits of those who have fallen asleep' (1 Cor. 15:20).

7. 'Listen, I tell you a mystery: We will not all sleep, but we will all be changed' (1 Cor. 15:51).

8. 'Brothers, we do not want you to be ignorant about those who fall asleep, or to grieve like the rest of men, who have no hope' (1 Thess. 4:13).

9. 'He died for us so that, whether we are awake or asleep, we may live together with him' (1 Thess. 5:10).

C. Everybody who has ever lived will be judged at the same time.

1. *To those who died hundreds of years ago, time will mean absolutely nothing, not even one second!*

   a. They will 'wake up' on the Final Day, as though they just died.

   b. When Jesus comes they will be raised, awakened.

2. *All – those who died and those alive at the time of the Second Coming of Christ – will simultaneously be brought to stand before God's Great White Throne.*

   a. There is no point in the suffering of the lost in the intermediate state; eternal punishment will still come.

   b. There is no point in the believers getting to be with the Lord in advance of others; they will enjoy heaven when the rest do.

3. *This is suggested by Daniel 12:2:* 'Multitudes who sleep in the dust of the earth will awake: some to everlasting life, others to shame and everlasting contempt.'

D. This teaching is said to provide comfort for those who are still alive and have had to say good-bye to friends and loved ones.

1. We need not worry about our loved ones who are unsaved, that they are at this moment suffering torment.

2. Those who are saved will enjoy the bliss of heaven when all the rest of God's people come together.

E. This teaching makes more sense of the Final Judgment.

1. If the saved go to be with the Lord when they die, it means they will go to heaven without being judged.

2. As for the lost, they too have been sent to punishment without judgment; what sense does it make for them to be brought out of hell to be judged – only to return there?

III. THE CASE AGAINST SOUL SLEEP

A. The Old Testament passages that indicate that the dead do not praise God:

1. They should be understood from the perspective of life in this world.

2. *From our perspective it appears that once people die, they do not engage in their activities any longer.*

   a. Psalm 115:17 says that it is not the dead who praise God.

   b. But Psalm 115:18 says that those who believe in God will bless the Lord forever: 'It is we who extol the Lord, both now and forevermore. Praise the Lord.'

B. There are Old Testament passages that indicate that the souls of believer go immediately into God's presence in heaven.

1. 'Enoch walked with God; then he was no more, because God took him away' (Gen. 5:24).

2. Elijah was taken immediately to heaven. 'As they were walking along and talking together, suddenly a chariot of fire and horses of fire appeared and separated the two of them, and Elijah went up to heaven in a whirlwind' (2 Kgs. 2:11).

3. David was confident that he would dwell in the house of the Lord forever (Ps. 23:6; 16:10-11).

4. David's own conviction about this is confirmed by the thought of being with his dead son again. 'But now that he is dead, why

should I fast? Can I bring him back again? I will go to him, but
he will not return to me' (2 Sam. 12:23).

C. **When Jesus answered the Sadducees, he reminded them
that God says, 'I am the God of Abraham, the God of Isaac,
and the God of Jacob' (Matt. 22:32).**
   1. This is one of the strongest verses against soul sleep.
   2. Abraham, Isaac and Jacob were living at that very moment,
      and God was their God.
   3. When Jesus was transfigured before the disciples 'there
      appeared before them Moses and Elijah' (Matt. 17:3).
   4. *In the story of the rich man and Lazarus, Jesus does not say
      that Lazarus is unconscious but reports Abraham as saying
      about Lazarus, 'Now he is comforted here'* (Luke 16:25).
      a. Some say that there was no conscious existence of the Old
         Testament saints until Jesus' death and the bodies of the
         saints arose (Matt. 27:53).
      b. But since the story of the rich man and Lazarus preceded
         Christ's resurrection, Lazarus was in the same situation as
         the Old Testament saints.

D. **'Sleep' is merely a metaphorical expression used to indicate that
death is only temporary for Christians, as sleep is temporary.**
   1. When Jesus said, 'Our friend Lazarus has fallen asleep,' he
      never said that the soul of Lazarus was sleeping.
   2. There is no passage that says that the soul of a person is sleeping
      or unconscious.
   3. For the doctrine of soul sleep to be proved, there must be a
      Scripture that mentions the soul with reference to sleep or
      unconsciousness; there is none at all.
   4. Jesus said, 'Lazarus is dead' (John 11:14).

E. **The New Testament makes it clear that we go immediately
into God's presence and enjoy fellowship with him there.**
   1. 'We are confident, I say, and would prefer to be away from the
      body and at home with the Lord' (2 Cor. 5:8).
   2. 'I am torn between the two: I desire to depart and be with Christ,
      which is better by far' (Phil. 1:23).
   3. 'Jesus answered him, "I tell you the truth, today you will be
      with me in paradise"' (Luke 23:43).

4. 'To the church of the firstborn, whose names are written in heaven. You have come to God, the judge of all men, to the spirits of righteous men made perfect' (Heb. 12:23).

    a. Note: it does not say 'spirits of righteous men who are sleeping in an unconscious state' but 'spirits of righteous men made perfect.'

        (1) This denies the teaching of purgatory.

        (2) This shows that we are perfected – without sin – and the reason Paul could say, 'Now we know that if the earthly tent we live in is destroyed, we have a building from God, an eternal house in heaven, not built by human hands' (2 Cor. 5:1).

    b. Hebrews 12:1 says, 'We are surrounded by such a great cloud of witnesses.'

        (1) This immediately followed a discussion of people of faith who had died.

        (2) It is the nearest the New Testament comes to hinting that those who have gone before even have the awareness of what is going on in the earth.

5. *Revelation 6:9-11 actually refers to souls who died and all in the intermediate state:* 'When he opened the fifth seal, I saw under the altar the souls of those who had been slain because of the word of God and the testimony they had maintained' (Rev. 6:9).

    a. These had obviously gone to heaven.

    b. Far from sleeping, or being unconscious, 'They called out in a loud voice, "How long, Sovereign Lord, holy and true, until you judge the inhabitants of the earth and avenge our blood?"' (Rev. 6:10).

    c. They are also seen 'standing before the throne and in front of the Lamb. They were wearing white robes and were holding palm branches in their hands. And they cried out in a loud voice: "Salvation belongs to our God, who sits on the throne, and to the Lamb"' (Rev. 7:9-10).

F. The souls of unbelievers go immediately to eternal punishment.

1. *In the story of the rich man and Lazarus, the rich man went immediately to Hades.*

    a. That in itself might have meant the end of the story.

    b. But the rich man was conscious and cried out, 'Father Abraham, have pity on me and send Lazarus to dip the tip of his finger in water and cool my tongue, because I am in agony in this fire' (Luke 16:24).

    c. This also shows there is no second chance to trust in Christ after death: 'And besides all this, between us and you a great chasm has been fixed, so that those who want to go from here to you cannot, nor can anyone cross over from there to us' (Luke 16:26).

2. *Hebrews 9:27 connects death with the consequence of judgment in close sequence:* 'Just as man is destined to die once, and after that to face judgment.'

    a. As for the believers or the unbelievers going immediately to heaven or hell without standing before the judgment:

        (1) 'The Lord knows those who are his' (2 Tim. 2:19).

        (2) Likewise the Lord knows who have not trusted his Son.

    b. Although unbelievers pass into a state of eternal punishment immediately upon death, their bodies will not be raised until the day of Final Judgment.

        (1) On that day their bodies will be raised and reunited with their souls. 'Then I saw a great white throne and him who was seated on it. Earth and sky fled from his presence, and there was no place for them. And I saw the dead, great and small, standing before the throne, and books were opened. Another book was opened, which is the book of life. The dead were judged according to what they had done as recorded in the books' (Rev. 20:11-12).

        (2) They will stand before God's throne for final judgment to be pronounced upon them in the body (Matt. 25:41-46; John 5:28-29; Acts 24:15).

G. When Jesus died his soul went immediately to the presence of the Father in heaven.

1. His body remained on earth and was buried.

2. His soul went to Paradise (Luke 23:43), which Paul calls 'third heaven' (2 Cor. 12:2-4).

3. *This is why he said,* 'Father, into your hands I commit my spirit' (Luke 23:46).

      a. His soul was not left in Hades (Acts 2:27).

      b. The body of Jesus did not experience decay.

  4. *In a word: Christ in his death experienced what believers experience when they die.*

      a. The body will remain in the grave until it is resurrected.

      b. The soul goes immediately to heaven until it is reunited with the body in resurrection.

CONCLUSION

Soul sleep is the concept of 'falling asleep' at death and remaining in an oblivious state until the Lord's Second Coming. If that is what happens those who have died in the Lord are not yet in his presence and those who died unsaved have not yet felt the pains of hell. Scripture argues against this. The thief on the cross was promised he would be in paradise that very day. And in Jesus' story of the rich man and Lazarus, the rich man was already in hell.

When we die our souls will go to their eternal home, whichever that is, to be reunited with our risen bodies at Jesus' coming in glory. The saved will then know the fullness of bliss and the unsaved the eternal wrath of the Lord.

50

HEAVEN – WHAT CAN WE KNOW ABOUT IT NOW?

INTRODUCTION

A. **We will all know a lot more about heaven five minutes after we are there than all the speculation made about it now.**
   1. Will there be literal gates of pearl? (Rev. 21:21).
   2. Will there be literal streets of gold? (Rev. 21:21).
   3. Will we see the Person of God the Father? (Rev. 22:3-4).
   4. Will we look like we did at the age we died – or when we were younger? What about babies who died? The unborn?
   5. Will we go fishing? Horseback riding? Sailing? Play football?
   6. Since there will be no procreation, will married couples still stay together? If so, what about those who were widowed and re-married?
   7. Will we eat in heaven?
   8. What will we do in heaven?
   9. Will we remember our failures on earth in heaven?
   10. How can we be happy if we know certain loved ones and friends are not there – and therefore in hell?

B. **One thing is for sure: all whose sins are covered by the blood of Jesus are going to heaven!**
   1. This is the main reason Jesus died on the cross.
   2. *The heart of the gospel is this: Christ died for our sins so that we will go to heaven and not to hell.*
      a. We must never forget this.
      b. Sadly some want to make the gospel almost entirely a 'here and now' experience with heaven thrown in.
      c. The truth is, the gospel means that we are going to heaven; any 'here and now' experience that is good is given according to God's will.
         (1)God may or may not give us health or prosperity.
         (2)But God will guarantee heaven!

C. Definition:
1. Heaven: our final and permanent home (Rev. 21 and 22).
2. Hell: the final and permanent place of the lost (Matt. 25:41).
3. *Intermediate state: where people are after death but prior to the second coming of Jesus.*
   a. The saved are with Christ (Luke 23:43; Phil. 1:23).
   b. The lost are in *hades*, or hell (Luke 16:23-31).
4. The second coming: Jesus' personal return to execute judgement and be glorified in his people (2 Thess. 1:10).
5. *The Judgement Seat of Christ: the Final Judgement Throne before which all will stand* (Rev. 20:11).
   a. Rewards will be given to the saved, although some Christians may not have a reward (1 Cor. 3:14-15).
   b. The lost will be sent to hell, being judged by their works rather than Christ's righteousness (Rev. 20:12ff).

D. Limitations of our study.
1. *It is not about the intermediate state.*
   a. There are some similarities between heaven and the state of the saved in the intermediate state, e.g., there is no more suffering (Rev. 7:16-17; 21:4).
   b. Those who are 'with Christ' now are rightly said to be in heaven; but that is not exactly what this study is about.
2. We will not deal with the chronology of the Second Coming and Judgement.
3. We will not deal with the details of the Final Judgement. For this, please read chapter 8. 'The Rewarding God.'
4. This study will centre on what we can know about our final home – once the Second Coming and Judgement are behind us.

E. Why is this study important?
1. It is a reminder of the main purpose of the gospel: to fit us for heaven (John 3:16).
2. It is a reminder that this world is not our home; our citizenship is in heaven (Phil. 3:20).
3. It is to give us an appetite for things eternal, for looking beyond, lest we become too attached to this life (1 John 2:15-17).
4. For those Christians who have felt 'cheated' in some way here below – having so little in terms of health, prosperity and

prestige, that our future home will more than make up for it (Rom. 8:18).

5. It focuses on certain things on which the Bible is very clear, so that we may know that the hope set before us is based upon the objective truth of God's Word.

I. WHAT WON'T BE IN HEAVEN

A. Satan (Rev. 20:10)

1. *Can you imagine life without Satan's interference?*
   a. It is hard to imagine.
   b. All our trouble here below can ultimately be traced to Satan.
2. *All that Satan now seeks to do will be totally and absolutely absent in heaven.*
   a. To accuse us (Rev. 12:10).
   b. To tempt us (1 Thess. 3:5).
   c. To prevent us from doing what we wanted to do (1 Thess. 2:18).
   d. To bring about death (Heb. 2:14).
   e. To oppress us (2 Tim. 2:26).
   f. To oppose us (Acts 16:16ff; Eph. 6:10-18).
   g. To cripple people (Luke 13:16).
   h. To intimidate us (1 Pet. 5:8).
   i. To masquerade as an angel of light (2 Cor. 11:14).

B. Sin

1. *There will be no sin in heaven; this means:*
   a. We will not have sin within ourselves to contend with (Jer. 17:9; 1 John 1:8).
   b. We will not have to contend with any wickedness around us, for there will be no sinning nor sinners in heaven (Rev. 21:8).
2. *Imagine a life that knows:*
   a. No temptation; to pride, sex, greed, selfish ambition.
   b. No warfare within (Gal. 5:17).
   c. No rival spirit or competition; no envy.
   d. No hurt feelings.
   e. No trouble controlling the tongue; no gossiping.
   f. No partiality or respecting persons; no racism.
   g. No fear of insecurity, worry about income or food.

h. No worry about where to live, what to wear.

i. No fear of being mugged or robbed.

j. No fear of sickness or accident.

C. Sorrow. 'He will wipe every tear from their eyes. There will be no more death or mourning or crying or pain, for the old order of things has passed away' (Rev. 21:4).

1. *Loss of a loved one. 'No more death.'*

　　a. The shortest verse in the Bible is, 'Jesus wept' (John 11:35).

　　　　(1) This was when Jesus wept with Mary and Martha in their grief over Lazarus' death.

　　　　(2) Even though Jesus knew he would shortly be raising Lazarus from the dead, he wept with them.

　　b. The sorrow of sorrows in this life is almost certainly the result of losing a husband, wife, parent, child, fiancé, friend.

　　　　(1) Death was the result of sin (Gen. 2:17; Rom. 6:23).

　　　　(2) But heaven means no more death.

2. *Fear of death. 'No more death'.*

　　a. The fear of death is very real to all of us, no matter how much we may try to repress it.

　　b. This fear may be due to:

　　　　(1) The fear of our own death; this is why we dread some horrible disease.

　　　　(2) The fear of another's death, when one is close to us.

3. *Pain. 'He will wipe every tear from their eyes.'*

　　a. Physical pain.

　　　　(1) We will not have any physical pain, for we will have perfect bodies (Phil. 3:21).

　　　　(2) Sin that is the cause of disease and pain will have been removed; there will be no illness, no disabled persons; no blind or deaf people.

　　b. Emotional pain. 'No more crying.'

　　　　(1) The pain of depression, anxiety; the fear of not getting it right.

　　　　(2) The pain of guilt – possibly the greatest pain in the world.

　　c. Pain from losing a job, or fear of not getting a job.

　　　　(1) Work became drudgery when God cursed us for sin. 'By the sweat of your brow you will eat your food until you return to the ground, since from it you were taken; for dust you are and to dust you will return' (Gen. 3:19).

(2) A job gives a person dignity, yet many people are not happy with their jobs; in heaven we will not have that worry at all! 'For the old order of things has passed away.'

4. *Question: what about our loved ones and friends not in heaven?*

    a. Martin Luther said: 'When I get to heave I expect to have three surprises: some will be there I didn't expect to see, some will be missing I thought would be there, but the greatest surprise of all is that I am there myself.'

    b. Will we have sorrow over loved ones not there? No.

        (1) It will be out of our minds, as though these people never existed; 'He will wipe every tear.'

        (2) It is hard for us to imagine this possibility; but God will not let such a thought come to mind. It may well come to mind now, but not then.

        (3) In any case, we will feel as God does toward all his enemies (Rev. 19:1ff.); we will not be sentimental as we are today.

D. Sacrifice

1. *There will be no evangelism in heaven.*

    a. All present will be converted.

    b. All who were ever converted will be there.

    c. Those not converted cannot be saved then (Luke 16:26).

        (1) This is a reminder that if any soul-winning is to be done, it must be done now!

        (2) We will have no regrets over any efforts we gave to soul-winning while on earth.

2. *Tithing.*

    a. Sadly for some there was no tithing on earth!

    b. Those who were faithful will be so thankful for all they gave here below.

3. *Trial of any kind.*

    a. There will be no need to dignify a trial in heaven.

    b. This is because sin and the devil will not be around.

E. Sea. 'There was no longer any sea' (Rev. 21:1).

1. I don't understand this; what is more lovely than the sea?

2. This will be part of God's idea of what will make heaven beautiful – we will leave it to him!

3. Perhaps it means there will be no geographical boundaries that cause separation which makes it difficult to reach another area – I don't know.

F. Sun. 'There will be no more night. They will not need the light of a lamp or the light of the sun, for the Lord God will give them light. And they will reign for ever and ever' (Rev. 22:5).
1. There will be no night, not even a shadow in heaven.
2. The brilliance of the glory of God will occupy every particle of space, removing the possibility of any shadow.

G. Note: all the above is true because 'No longer will there be any curse' (Rev. 22:3).
1. *God cursed the earth immediately after the sin of Adam and Eve, which included:*
   a. The pain of childbearing and the rule of the husband. 'To the woman he said, "I will greatly increase your pains in childbearing; with pain you will give birth to children. Your desire will be for your husband, and he will rule over you"' (Gen. 3:16).
   b. The curse on the ground (Gen. 3:17-18).
   c. The need to work hard (Gen. 3:19).
2. Man was banished from the Garden of Eden as a result of the Fall (Gen. 3:23-24).
3. With the curse being finally and forever removed, John said, 'And I heard a loud voice from the throne saying, "Now the dwelling of God is with men, and he will live with them. They will be his people, and God himself will be with them and be their God"' (Rev. 21:3).

II. WHAT WILL HEAVEN BE LIKE?

A. It is a place, not a mere state of mind.
1. *Some say they believe in hell – 'hell in the mind'.*
   a. There is some truth in this; God gives to the Christian a little bit of heaven to go to heaven in.
   b. God gives to the wicked a little bit of hell to go to hell in.
2. Heaven is a place. 'I saw the Holy City, the new Jerusalem, coming down out of heaven from God, prepared as a bride beautifully dressed for her husband' (Rev. 21:2).

a. This may not please all – especially those who don't like cities!

b. But perhaps the New Jerusalem is only part of the 'new heaven and new earth' (Rev. 21:1) and there will be ample countryside!

B. It is a place where God will dwell with us and we with God (Rev. 21:3).
1. The pure in heart will see God (Matt. 5:8).
2. *We shall see Jesus as he is* (1 John 3:2).
    a. 'Now we see but a poor reflection as in a mirror; then we shall see face to face. Now I know in part; then I shall know fully, even as I am fully known' (1 Cor. 13:12).
    b. What a sight for those who are blind: their first sight – the face of Jesus!
    c. For the deaf: their first sound – God's trumpet! (1 Thess. 4:16).
3. 'They will see his face, and his name will be on their foreheads' (Rev. 22:4).

C. It is a place where we will see those we have heard and read about.
1. 'There are countless people I'm waiting to see. Queen Esther, Daniel, Jonah, and, of course, Mary and Martha. What's amazing is that I'll immediately recognize these people and all the other redeemed whom I never met on earth. If the disciples were able to recognize Elijah and Moses standing next to Jesus on the Mount of Transfiguration – saints they had never laid eyes on – then the same is true for us. I can't wait to meet them all!' Joni Eareckson Tada in her book, *Heaven*.
2. I look forward to meeting Calvin, Luther, John Wesley, John Newton, Martyn Lloyd-Jones.
3. (Whether those who die meet all these immediately – or wait until the Second Coming, I am not so sure.)

D. It is a place where we will have new bodies and new minds (1 Cor. 15:52ff; Phil. 3:21).
1. Our bodies will be like that of Jesus – glorified.
2. Our minds will be without evil thoughts – no envy will be in heaven, no rival spirit.
3. I believe we will be ever learning and always able to grasp (as

opposed to 'always learning but never able to acknowledge the truth' – 2 Tim. 3:7).

4. "'Who will rescue me from this body of death? Thanks be to God – through Jesus Christ our Lord!" (Romans 7:24-25). One day Jesus will come back to complete the salvation He began when I first believed. One day He will release me from the presence and influence of evil. That's why the bad news of Romans chapter 7 is followed by the good news of Romans chapter 8: "We ourselves, who have the firstfruits of the Spirit, groan inwardly as we wait eagerly for our adoption as sons, the redemption of our bodies" (Romans 8:23).

'Right here is the highest and most exalted reason that "flesh and blood cannot inherit the kingdom of God" (1 Corinthians 15:50). Entrance to heaven requires a redeemed body. The body must be rid of the law of sin at work in its members. At this present time, the spirit is willing but the flesh is weak. The day is coming, however, when instead of being a hindrance to the spirit, the body will be the perfect vessel for the expression of my glorified mind, will, and emotions. Right now, we wear our souls on the inside. But one day we will be "clothed in righteousness" as we wear our souls on the outside, brilliant and glorious.

'I can't wait to be clothed in righteousness. Without a trace of sin. True, it will be wonderful to stand, stretch, and reach to the sky, but it will be more wonderful to offer praise that is pure. I won't be crippled by distractions. Disabled by insincerity. I won't be handicapped by a ho-hum halfheartedness. My heart will join with yours and bubble over with effervescent adoration. We will finally be able to fellowship fully with the Father and the Son.

'For me, this will be the best part of heaven' (Joni Eareckson Tada, *Heaven*).

E. It will be a place where we will understand 'why' (1 Cor. 13:12).

1. *Our questions will be answered:*
   a. Why did God let this or that happen?
   b. Why was I born at this time and place – with my particular parents?
   c. Did I please God in this or that incident?

2. *God will clear his name.*
   a. Some say, 'God has a lot to answer for.'
   b. I say: he has nothing to answer for and he will show why –
   then and there. And not before.

F. A place of beauty beyond imagination (Rev. 21:10-26).
   1. Streets of gold.
   2. Gates of pearl.
   3. Walls of jasper.

G. A place of perfect worship. 'The throne of God and of the Lamb will be in the city, and his servants will serve him' (Rev. 22:3).
   1. There is no temple in the city, because 'the Lord God Almighty and the Lamb are its temple' (Rev. 21:22).
   2. *This means the whole place will be filled with perfect worship.*
      a. Charles Wesley's wish 'O for a heart to praise my God, a heart from sin set free' will be perfectly fulfilled, realized and enjoyed.
      b. What will it be like? It is difficult to imagine!
         (1) Praise now is often a sacrifice (Heb. 13:15).
         (2) Then it will be sheer bliss.
      c. We will never tire of thanking God:
         (1) That we are there.
         (2) That Jesus died for us.

CONCLUSION
Heaven is a real place, the eternal home of every believer from every age and place. There we will meet the Lord face to face. Satan is barred from heaven as are all who have rejected the gospel. There will be no sin there and no sorrow, not even the sorrow of mourning for those who are unsaved. There will be perfection in everything: beauty, peace, worship etc. Nothing will enter heaven to spoil it or mar our eternal enjoyment. We cannot begin to conceive of heaven's glory.

Will there be rewards in heaven? Yes. They will be given at the Judgement Seat of Christ (2 Cor. 5:10).

I conclude with some inspiring words from Joni:

'What does a crown in heaven look like? Does it look like the Shah of Iran's with spotted ermine, studded with pearls and diamonds, or the kind Queen Victoria wore with a cross on top? Watch it, I have a sneaking suspicion we're edging close to earthly imagery again.

'Psalm 149:4 gives a hint as to what kind of crown God means, "For the Lord takes delight in his people; he crowns the humble with salvation." Aha! God probably doesn't mean a literal crown, because salvation isn't something you put on your head. Heavenly crowns must represent something He does, something He gives, as when He crowns us with salvation. Anyway, this is more resplendent and illustrious than any old hunk of platinum with sparkly things on it.

'There's also the *crown of life* in James 1:12, reserved for those who persevere under trials. This means God awards us with life eternal.

'There's the *crown of rejoicing* in 1 Thessalonians 2:19, given to believers who introduce others to Christ. This means God awards us with joy that lasts forever.

'The *incorruptible crown* in I Corinthians 9:25, presented to those who are found pure and blameless on the judgment day. Nothing God gives will ever perish, spoil, or fade.

'And in I Peter 5:2-4, there's the *crown of glory*, reserved for Christian leaders who have guided others. God awards us glory that will never diminish, but only increase.

'And my favourite, the *crown of righteousness* mentioned in 2 Timothy 4:8 for those who are itching to have Jesus come back. God will award us right-standing with Him that never changes.

'Get ready for crowns!' (Joni Eareckson Tada, *Heaven*).

51

THINGS WE WON'T BE
DOING IN HEAVEN

INTRODUCTION

A. Is there any knowledge greater than this: we will be going to heaven.

    1. *There is a sense in which the bottom line of the Christian faith is this: those who trust Christ's death on the cross are going to heaven and not to hell.*

        a. Martin Luther regarded John 3:16 as the 'Bible in a nutshell'. 'For God so loved the world that he gave his one and only Son, that whoever believes in him shall not perish but have eternal life.'

        b. This verse implies heaven and hell.

            (1) Those who believe in the Son will not perish, i.e., will not go to hell.

            (2) Those who believe in the Son will have everlasting life, i.e., will go to heaven.

    2. *Too often the Christian message becomes clouded with what in fact are but secondary benefits of the gospel, e.g.:*

        a. We are so much better off here below.

            (1) The change of our lives.

            (2) Feeling happier than before.

        b. Society is all the better when the Gospel has made an impact.

    3. *The main reason Jesus died on the cross was to make it possible for us to go to heaven when we die.*

        a. Christianity is essentially about our death.

            (1) The wages of sin is death.

            (2) Jesus came to reverse what Adam lost in the Garden of Eden.

        b. The gospel is essentially this.

            (1) Some say, 'If there were no heaven I'd still be a Christian.'

    (2)I know what people mean by this but it is contrary to the thinking of Paul. 'If only for this life we have hope in Christ, we are to be pitied more than all men' (1 Cor. 15:19).

B. We will know a lot more about heaven five minutes after we've been there than all the speculation this side of heaven.
    1. Will there be literal streets of gold?
    2. Will there be literal mansions in which we will live?
    3. How will we spend our time – i.e., if time exists in some way?
    4. In a word: what will we do in heaven?

C. In a sense it is easier to predict what we won't be doing in heaven than what we will be doing there.
    1. It is easy to see, according to Revelation 21:4, some things we most certainly won't be doing in heaven: 'He will wipe every tear from their eyes. There will be no more death or mourning or crying or pain, for the old order of things has passed away.'
        a. We won't see death.
        b. We won't do any crying.
        c. We won't be in any pain.
    2. That however is not what I have in mind for this study.

D. This lesson will focus on what we won't be doing in heaven but what we can be doing on earth – and will wish we did while here.
    1. Whether we will feel this way throughout eternity I don't know.
    2. I know it is the way we will feel at the Judgment Seat of Christ. 'For we must all appear before the Judgment Seat of Christ, that each one may receive what is due him for the things done while in the body, whether good or bad' (2 Cor. 5:10).
    3. *In a word: now is the time to do what we will not do in heaven.*
        a. This may be because we aren't able to do such then.
        b. This may be because it won't be required then.
        c. These days here on earth are precious days, far more precious than we may have imagined.
        d. It won't always be like it is now.
            (1) These days matter a lot to God.
            (2) They should matter a lot to us.

E. Why is this lesson important?
   1. It is a timely reminder that life at its longest is still short.
   2. It is a reminder that we will all stand before the Judgment Seat of Christ.
   3. *The Judgment Seat of Christ will reveal a number of things.*
      a. Who is saved and who is lost (1 Pet. 4:17-18).
      b. Who among the saved will receive a reward and who will be saved by fire (1 Cor. 3:15).
   4. There is time to make a difference; this lesson should motivate us to live in such a manner that will leave us with fewer regrets at the Judgment Seat of Christ.
   5. The purpose of doing theology is to change lives, which this lesson might do.

F. Note: I pass over the obvious things we won't be doing in heaven, e.g.:
   1. No working by the sweat of the brow (cf. Gen. 3:19).
   2. No procreation of the race – we will be like the angels (Matt. 22:30).
   3. There will be no sleeping in heaven – we will never be tired.
   4. There will be no temptation in heaven – we will be glorified and the tempter will have been dealt with (Rev. 20:10).

I. THERE WILL BE NO FAITH IN HEAVEN

A. Faith is described in Hebrews 11:1 'Now faith is being sure of what we hope for and certain of what we do not see.'
   1. *In order for faith to be faith it follows that one must trust God without evidence.*
      a. Faith (def.): believing God.
         (1) Not merely believing that there is a God.
         (2) The devil believes in God. 'You believe that there is one God. Good! Even the demons believe that – and shudder' (Jas. 2:19).
      b. Faith is believing God – relying on him – alone.
         (1) It is believing his word to be true.
         (2) It is proving this by trusting that word.
   2. *In heaven all the evidences of God and his Word will be before our eyes.*
      a. Faith will become sight!

b. At the cross the enemies of Jesus scoffed: 'Let this Christ, this King of Israel, come down now from the cross, that we may see and believe' (Mark 15:32).

    (1) 'Seeing is believing,' says the world.

    (2) But to God it is the other way around: believing is to see.

c. In heaven everybody will see everything clearly.

    (1) At the moment of the Second Coming nobody will need faith. 'Look, he is coming with the clouds, and every eye will see him, even those who pierced him; and all the peoples of the earth will mourn because of him. So shall it be! Amen' (Rev. 1:7).

    (2) The reason for the weeping: no faith is needed; all will 'believe' but such believing cannot be graced with the title 'faith'.

B. Since there will be no faith in heaven we have opportunity now to do what we can't do there: to please God by faith.

1. *Faith pleases God.* 'And without faith it is impossible to please God, because anyone who comes to him must believe that he exists and that he rewards those who earnestly seek him' (Heb. 11:6).

2. *We might ask: will we not please God in heaven?*

    a. Answer: yes. But it won't be pleasing him by faith!

        (1) This is something we can only do now.

        (2) We can never get these days back.

3. *I want to please God now – in a way I cannot please him then.*

    a. I can bring a measure of glory and pleasure to God now which I will be unable to do then.

    b. How? By trusting him more and more.

C. What ought we to do now?

1. *Pray for more faith.*

    a. 'The apostles said to the Lord, "Increase our faith!"' (Luke 17:5).

    b. 'Immediately the boy's father exclaimed, "I do believe; help me overcome my unbelief!"' (Mark 9:24).

2. *Trust God now in a way you will be glad you did then.*

    a. It is like the feeling we sometimes get at the end of a trial.

    b. When the trial is over (which we thought would never end) we sometimes blush over our unbelief.

3. We won't be trusting God in heaven; we will be seeing him; therefore we won't need faith.

II. THERE WILL BE NO SOUL-WINNING IN HEAVEN

A. 'He who wins souls is wise' (Prov. 11:30).
1. Have you ever won a soul for Christ?
2. How many of you have never led another person to Jesus Christ?

B. Everybody in heaven will have been saved.
1. *All of us will be in heaven because we were converted on earth.*
    a. We heard the gospel – and believed.
    b. In most cases our coming to Christ was because someone on earth led us to Christ or brought us to the place where we could hear the gospel.
2. *Those not in heaven, sadly, will be in hell.*
    a. Those in hell cannot be won.
        (1) We are only saved by faith.
        (2) In hell all will 'believe' – that is for sure (cf. Luke 16:24, 27).
    b. The sobering thought is that heaven and hell are both unending, and one cannot get from either place to the other. 'And besides all this, between us and you a great chasm has been fixed, so that those who want to go from here to you cannot, nor can anyone cross over from there to us' (Luke 16:26).

'Only one life – t'will soon be past.
Only what's done for Christ will last.'

C. How do you suppose you will feel at the Judgment Seat of Christ if you were not a soul-winner here below?
1. This is something you will not be doing in heaven but which you can do on earth and will be glad you did.
2. *There is still time!*
    a. The days are going quickly. 'As long as it is day, we must do the work of him who sent me. Night is coming, when no one can work' (John 9:4).
    b. 'The longer I live the faster time flies' (Billy Graham).

III. THERE WILL BE NO NEED OF DISCIPLINE IN HEAVEN

A. I refer not to what is called 'church discipline'.

1. This means turning a person out of the church for reasons that relate to the honour of Christ's name (cf. 1 Cor. 5:1-5).

2. This of course won't be done in heaven, but it might result in doing some an enormous favour – when necessary – here below. After all, the man in Corinth was awakened (cf. 2 Cor. 2:5-11).

B. By discipline, I mean self-discipline.

1. *Discipline (def.): training that produces self-control.*

   a. That training is provided in more than one way.

   (1) Some are taught it at home.

   (2) Some are taught it by watching others (getting inspired).

   b. I would like to think my teaching (if not my example) would encourage people to be self-disciplined.

2. *Examples of self-discipline:*

   a. Control of the tongue (Jas. 3). 'Do not let any unwholesome talk come out of your mouths, but only what is helpful for building others up according to their needs, that it may benefit those who listen' (Eph. 4:29).

   b. Resisting temptation (Matt. 26:41). 'When tempted, no one should say, "God is tempting me." For God cannot be tempted by evil, nor does he tempt anyone' (Jas. 1:13).

   c. Redeeming the time (Eph. 5:16).

   d. Dignifying the trial (Jas. 1:2).

   (1) 'For it has been granted to you on behalf of Christ not only to believe on him, but also to suffer for him' (Phil. 1:29).

   (2) Trials are actually predestined. 'So that no one would be unsettled by these trials. You know quite well that we were destined for them' (1 Thess. 3:3).

IV. THERE WILL BE NO PRAYING IN HEAVEN

A. Praising yes; praying no.

1. *In heaven we will worship God perfectly* (Rev. 7:9-12).

   a. We will have no temptation to divert us.

   b. We will have no wandering minds.

   c. There will be no Satan to defeat us.

2. *But we will not be praying.*
    a. Praying is asking God to act.
    b. Praying is intercession.
    c. In heaven we will not need to intercede or ask God to do this or that.

B. When we stand before God we will not regret one moment spent alone with him in prayer.
    1. What praying that is done must be done now.
        a. How much time do you spend in prayer?
        b. How often and how much do you read your Bible?

C. I am sure there will be growth and development in heaven.
    1. That growth will come as a result of our being glorified.
    2. Growth here below is the result of faith and discipline.
    3. *What if (which I happen to believe) our quality of growth and capacity to learn and develop in heaven is based upon our quality of growth here below?*
        a. Here below there are those who are ever learning but never able to come to the knowledge of the truth (2 Tim. 3:7).
        b. In heaven we will be ever learning but able to grasp truth.
        c. It is my own conviction that our reward in heaven will partly consist in having a certain ability to grow that was based on our personal development as Christians here on earth.

V. WE CANNOT ADD TO OUR REWARD AFTER WE ARE IN HEAVEN

A. Jesus said, 'Do not store up for yourselves treasures on earth, where moth and rust destroy, and where thieves break in and steal. But store up for yourselves treasures in heaven, where moth and rust do not destroy, and where thieves do not break in and steal' (Matt. 6:19-20).
    1. To deposit (def.): to store or entrust for safe keeping.
    2. God doesn't forget anything. 'Anyone who receives a prophet because he is a prophet will receive a prophet's reward, and anyone who receives a righteous man because he is a righteous man will receive a righteous man's reward. And if anyone gives even a cup of cold water to one of these little ones because he is my disciple, I tell you the truth, he will certainly not lose his reward' (Matt. 10:41-42).

3. He will hold on deposit for us treasure that will make the Judgment Seat of Christ a sweet event not a dreadful one.

B. How do we ensure there is a deposit in heaven?
   1. By totally forgiving those who have hurt us (Luke 6:37).
   2. By going beyond the call of duty (1 Cor. 9:18).
   3. *By tithing* (Mal. 3:10).
      a. There will be no tithing in heaven.
      b. For some there has been no tithing below.

CONCLUSION

There are activities we engage in on earth which we won't have the opportunity to do in heaven. There is no need of faith in heaven nor any opportunity to come to faith. Because souls will not be won in heaven, we should engage in evangelism as long as we are on earth. There will be no self-discipline there, for there we will be perfectly sanctified. No prayers will be uttered in heaven, apart from those of worship, as God's purposes will have been fully realised. Our opportunity to lay up treasure in heaven ceases when we get there. That must be done while we are on earth. There is much service we can render to the Lord while we are here, that will cease when we die. Thereafter our service will be wonderfully different. Only in glory will we know what it will involve.

I want to receive what Peter calls a 'rich welcome' into heaven (2 Pet. 1:11). This will come about in proportion to how we lived as Christians here below: by doing things now we cannot do there.

PERSONS INDEX

BIBLE CHARACTERS INDEX

SUBJECT INDEX

SCRIPTURE INDEX

Christian Focus Publications

Our mission statement –

STAYING FAITHFUL
In dependence upon God we seek to impact the world through literature faithful to His infallible Word, the Bible. Our aim is to ensure that the Lord Jesus Christ is presented as the only hope to obtain forgiveness of sin, live a useful life and look forward to heaven with Him.

Our books are published in four imprints:

CHRISTIAN FOCUS

Popular works including biographies, commentaries, basic doctrine and Christian living.

CHRISTIAN HERITAGE

Books representing some of the best material from the rich heritage of the church.

MENTOR

Books written at a level suitable for Bible College and seminary students, pastors, and other serious readers. The imprint includes commentaries, doctrinal studies, examination of current issues and church history.

CF4•K

Children's books for quality Bible teaching and for all age groups: Sunday school curriculum, puzzle and activity books; personal and family devotional titles, biographies and inspirational stories – because you are never too young to know Jesus!

Christian Focus Publications Ltd,
Geanies House, Fearn, Ross-shire,
IV20 1TW, Scotland, United Kingdom.
www.christianfocus.com